INDIANA

OFF THE BEATEN PATH®

OFF THE BEATEN PATH® SERIES

ELEVENTH EDITION

INDIANA

OFF THE BEATEN PATH®

DISCOVER YOUR FUN

BY PHYLLIS THOMAS

REVISED AND UPDATED
BY JACKIE SHECKLER FINCH

Globe
Pequot

Guilford, Connecticut

This book is dedicated to my family—Kelly Rose; Mike Peters; Sean Rose; Stefanie, Will, Trey, and Arianna Scott; and Logan Peters.

A special remembrance to my husband, Bill Finch, whose spirit goes with me every step of the way through life's journey.

All the information in this guidebook is subject to change. We recommend that you call ahead to obtain current information before traveling.

Globe
Pequot

An imprint of The Rowman & Littlefield Publishing Group, Inc.
4501 Forbes Blvd., Ste. 200
Lanham, MD 20706
www.rowman.com

Distributed by NATIONAL BOOK NETWORK

Maps by Melissa Baker

British Library Cataloguing in Publication Information available

Library of Congress Cataloging-in-Publication Data available

ISBN 978-1-4930-5355-1 (paper)
ISBN 978-1-4930-5356-8 (electronic)

About the Author

Jackie Sheckler Finch has written about a wide array of topics—from birth to death, with all the joy and sorrow in between. An award-winning journalist and photographer, Jackie has done more than a dozen travel guidebooks for Globe Pequot and is a member of the Society of American Travel Writers and the Midwest Travel Journalists Association. She has been named the Mark Twain Travel Writer of the Year a record five times, in 1998, 2001, 2003, 2007, and 2012. She became a Hoosier more than three decades ago when she moved from Massachusetts to become city reporter for *The Herald-Times* in Bloomington, Indiana. One of her greatest joys is taking to the road to find the fascinating people and places that wait over the hill and around the next bend.

NORTHWEST
INDIANA

NORTHEAST
INDIANA

CENTRAL
INDIANA

SOUTHEAST
INDIANA

SOUTHWEST
INDIANA

South Bend

Elkhart

Fort Wayne

Lafayette

Muncie

Indianapolis

Richmond

Terre Haute

Bloomington

Columbus

Evansville

Contents

Acknowledgments

If I were to personally thank each person who has contributed in some way to the writing of this book, the list would be longer than the contents of the book itself. I have talked to many people during my travels throughout Indiana. They were, without exception, warm, gracious, and kind. We met as strangers and parted as friends. I am grateful to each and every one of them.

Introduction

When you visit Indiana, it's best to leave preconceived notions behind. There's a lot more to the state than the Indianapolis 500 and cornfields. State highways and byways lead to some of the finest travel gems in the nation. There are natural wonders and man-made splendors, irreplaceable slices of Americana and futuristic marvels, places stately and sublime, others weird and wacky—a cornucopia of attractions, restaurants, and inns that for the most part lie off the well-trodden paths and are overlooked by major travel guides.

The most difficult part of writing this book was deciding not what to include but what, because of space limitations, to leave out. Therefore, what you will find within these pages is merely a sampling of all that Indiana has to offer. It is my sincere hope that this book will help awaken your sense of adventure and encourage you to seek out other such places on your own.

Indiana's geography is sometimes a bit puzzling to strangers. They are often surprised to learn that South Bend is one of the northernmost cities in the state, while North Vernon is not far from the Ohio River, which forms Indiana's southern boundary. Along the Ohio-Indiana border on the east lies West College Corner, while way down in the southwest corner, just across the Wabash River from Illinois, there's East Mt. Carmel. And the towns of Center, Center Square, and Centerville are about as off-center as you can get.

To further confuse the traveler, a look at the official state road map (available free from the **Indiana Department of Transportation,** 100 N. Senate Ave., Indianapolis 46204; 855-463-6848; in.gov/indot) reveals four Buena Vistas, three Fairviews, three Georgetowns, three Jamestowns, two Klondykes and one Klondike, three Mechanicsburgs, four Millersburgs, five Mt. Pleasants, three Needmores, and four Salems. Pairs of towns with the same name are too numerous to mention, but would you believe two Pumpkin Centers? No wonder the US Postal Service insists on zip codes!

But never mind—this book will at least put you in the right county. And if you do get lost, you're likely to meet such warm, friendly people along the way that you won't mind it a bit. Please note that state roads mentioned in this book are designated by SR and county roads are designated by CR.

If all else fails, you can call the Indiana tourism hotline for help. Dial (800) 677-9800 or (800) 289-6646 to request free printed materials that will help you plan your itinerary. The toll-free numbers are answered 24 hours a day and are accessible from anywhere in the contiguous United States. You can also visit their website at visitindiana.com or write to the **Indiana Office of Tourism**

Development, 1 N. Capitol St., Suite 600, Indianapolis 46204; (317) 232-8860 or (800) 677-9800.

We have noted which counties are in the Central Time Zone. All others are in the Eastern Time Zone.

Happy wandering!

Central Indiana

Indianapolis, at the hub of central Indiana, is crisscrossed by more interstate highways than any other metropolitan area in the country. I-65, I-69, I-70, and I-74 run through the heart of the city, and I-465 encircles it. More than 876,000 people live in Indianapolis (affectionately known to Hoosiers as Indy), making this the seventeenth largest city in the country.

Leave Indy behind and head in any direction, and in minutes you will find yourself in the heart of rural Indiana—open fields that seem to stretch forever, patches of scenic woodland, and charming small towns rich with local color.

Central Indiana offers a mix of the best Indiana has to offer—big-city excitement, pastoral serenity, and the friendly folks for which the Hoosier State is justly famous.

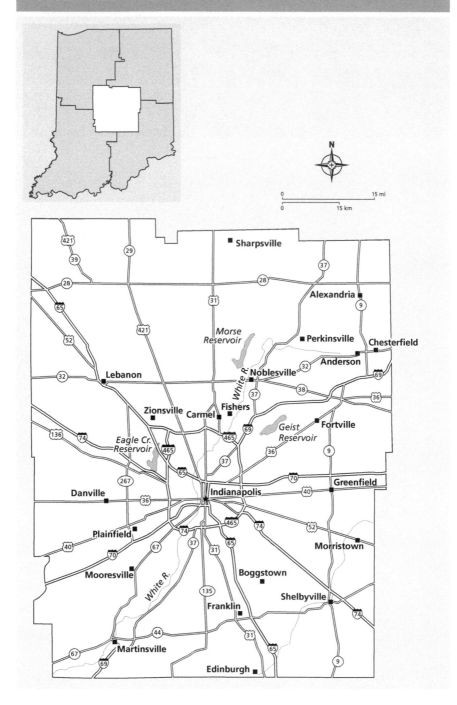

Boone County

The entire community has pitched in to help restore the glory of yesteryear to **Zionsville**'s downtown business district, and its citizens have succeeded admirably. Now known as the **Zionsville Colonial Village,** it's filled with interesting shops to explore. Brick-paved Main Street, in the heart of the village, is decorated with gas lamps and planters and is lined with many charming and interesting shops to explore.

Three vine-covered buildings filled with a variety of unusual items and nestled in an English garden setting at 315 N. Main St. are known collectively as **Brown's Antiques.** Founded in 1945, Brown's is the oldest antique shop in Indiana. Open 10 a.m. to 5 p.m. Monday through Saturday; call (317) 873-2284 or visit brownsantiques.com.

AUTHOR'S FAVORITE ATTRACTIONS/ EVENTS IN CENTRAL INDIANA

Camp Chesterfield
Chesterfield
(765) 378-0235
campchesterfield.net

Circle of Lights
Indianapolis; November
(017) 237-2222
downtownindy.org

Conner Prairie Interactive History Park
Fishers
(317) 776-6000 or (800) 966-1836
connerprairie.org

Eiteljorg Museum of American Indians and Western Art
Indianapolis
(317) 636-9378
eiteljorg.org

Eiteljorg Museum Indian Market
Indianapolis; June
(317) 636-9378
eiteljorg.org

Heartland Film Festival
Indianapolis; October

(317) 464-9405
heartlandfilm.org

Indiana Medical History Museum
Indianapolis
(317) 635-7329
imhm.org

Children's Museum of Indianapolis
Indianapolis
(317) 334-4000 or (800) 820-6214
childrensmuseum.org

Indianapolis Greek Festival
Carmel; September
(317) 733-3033
indygreekfest.org

Indianapolis Museum of Art
Indianapolis
(317) 923-1331
discovernewfields.org

Indy 500 Festival Parade
Indianapolis; May
(317) 927-3378
500festival.com/parade

Zionsville is also home to the **SullivanMunce Cultural Center,** a small gem dedicated to assembling and preserving local history. The museum is named for Boone County's first white settler, Patrick Henry Sullivan, whose great-granddaughter, the late Iva Etta Sullivan, set up a trust fund to establish a historical foundation in Zionsville in his memory. Ms. Sullivan, a former librarian, had the financial wherewithal to set up the trust in part because she accepted the investment advice of her onetime employer, the late film director Cecil B. DeMille.

The museum, patterned after early-nineteenth-century architecture, rotates exhibits that feature period furnishings, antique clothing, farm tools, artwork, and quilts. A genealogical library houses a growing collection of family histories, diaries, letters, family Bibles, property deeds, maps, photos, and newspapers. Ms. Sullivan and her great-grandfather would be pleased. Admission is free, but donations are appreciated. Hours are 10 a.m. to 4 p.m. Tuesday through Friday. Closed major holidays. Visitors will find the museum at 225 W. Hawthorne St.; call (317) 873-4900 or visit sullivanmunce.org.

At the **Antique Fan Museum** in Zionsville, you'll see some 450 desk and ceiling fans dating from the 1800s. Displays include fans powered by steam, water, batteries, alcohol, and electricity; wind-up, wall, desk, pedestal, rail car, and ceiling fans; and fans that don't even look like fans. Hundreds of hand-held fans (the wave-in-your-face kind) feature advertisements from politicians, movie stars, retailers, and manufacturers. The museum is housed in the headquarters building of Fanimation, a company that designs and manufactures modern-day fans. Museum hours are 10 a.m. to 4 p.m. Monday through Friday or by appointment; admission is free. It's located at 10983 Bennett Pkwy.; call (317) 733-4113 or visit fanimation.com/museum.

The **Boone County Courthouse** in **Lebanon,** built in the early 1900s, once drew sightseers from around the world. They came to marvel at the eight columns that adorn the north and south entrances, believed to be the largest one-piece limestone columns in the world. Each gigantic pillar—36 feet high, 4.5 feet in diameter, and weighing about 40 tons—is shaped from a single block of limestone. Inside, you can see the second-largest stained-glass dome in the state.

Lebanon is also the home of Indiana's answer to Willie Wonka's chocolate factory. Any dyed-in-the-wool chocoholic will love a tour of **Donaldson's Finer Chocolates.** Watch through glass doors as chocolates are cooked in copper kettles and fudge is kneaded on a marble slab. Donaldson's produces and sells seventy-five varieties of chocolates, including almond bark, chocolate-covered caramels, hand-dipped creams, and assorted nut clusters. Free guided tours are available by advance arrangement; by tour's end, just when you think you can't stand it another minute, you're given a free sample. The tours won't cost you a cent, and you're certainly under no obligation to buy, but if you don't, you have more willpower than most of us. You'll find Donaldson's at 600 S. SR 39, just south of where it intersects I-65 on the south side of Lebanon. The shop is open 9 a.m. to 6 p.m. Monday through Friday and 9 a.m. to 5 p.m. Saturday. For more information, call (800) 975-7236 or (765) 482-3334. You may also visit donaldsonschocolates.com.

Hamilton County

Conner Prairie, often ranked as one of the nation's top five "living museums," is Indiana's only Smithsonian Institution–affiliate museum. Within its 850-acre grounds, a restored pioneer village breathes life into history, permitting visitors to wander at their leisure through the homes, shops, school, and other buildings that might have made up a pioneer community in the early 1800s. "Residents" keep busy at tasks that must be performed to keep the settlement going; they also answer questions about the typical lifestyle of that era.

Ongoing meticulous research helps ensure the authenticity of the settlement. The orchard, for instance, was first planted in neat rows, but when it was learned that this was a twentieth-century method, fruit trees were scattered about at random. It was also discovered, much to everyone's surprise, that men did not wear beards in 1836, so all whiskers except muttonchops had to go. All lace trim had to be removed from the women's dresses—as it was not authentic either.

Also located on the 250-acre tract is a Federal-style mansion built in 1823 by Indiana statesman William Conner. Visitors can tour the main house and grounds, which feature a springhouse, a still, and a loom house where Conner Prairie staff members duplicate textiles used during the 1830s.

At Makesmith Workshop, trained craftspeople are on hand to assist visitors who want to learn pioneer skills firsthand. You can try your hand at such pastimes as weaving on an authentic loom, making candles, and whittling with period tools.

Nearby, a Lenape Indian camp and log trading post offer a glimpse of Indiana frontier life in 1816, the year in which Indiana became a state.

Weather permitting, visitors can float 350 feet above the park in a tethered hot-air balloon.

The 1863 Civil War Journey depicts an 1863 raid on Indiana by Confederate general John Hunt Morgan, the only Civil War battle that took place on Hoosier soil. The multimedia attraction is open April through October.

The Conner Prairie Store includes a shop that sells items handcrafted by Conner Prairie artisans, a restaurant that features a mix of modern and historical foods, and a bakery that offers nineteenth-century breads, pastries, and cookies. An Apple Store (no, not the computer kind) sells hand-dipped caramel apples, candy, cider, and other treats. Check the website for when the Apple Store is open.

Special events are also in keeping with the pioneer theme. Once a month the Methodist circuit rider arrives to preach his sermon. A presidential election is held in the fall, just as it was in 1836. Weddings, too, are authentic, and visitors are often surprised to learn that even in the mid-1800s women did not promise to "obey" their spouses. Brides agreed to "love, honor, and assist" their husbands, who in turn promised to "love, honor, and maintain" their wives.

On some weekends, a 90-minute program entitled "Follow the North Star" allows visitors to realistically experience what life was like for runaway slaves. The role-playing is so intense that many visitors must take time-outs along the way.

Conner Prairie is located in **Fishers,** 4 miles south of Noblesville. Open 11 a.m. to 3 p.m. on Wednesday; 10 a.m. to 3 p.m. on Thursday and Friday; and 10 a.m. to 5 p.m. on Saturday and Sunday. Hours vary so check the website. The outdoor and indoor exhibits are open from May through October; the indoor exhibits are also open in November and December, but hours vary; closed Monday except Labor Day. Special daytime and evening programs are presented throughout the year. Admission: adults $18; senior citizens $17; children (ages 2–12) $13. Contact Conner Prairie Interactive History Park, 13400 Allisonville Rd., Fishers 46038-4499; call (317) 776-6006 or (800) 966-1836; or visit online at connerprairie.org.

Carmel is home to the charming **Museum of Miniature Houses,** filled with Lilliputian works of art. Visitors will see an amazing array of wee things faithfully replicated. Kitchens contain tiny canned goods, eating utensils, cookie cutters, and rolling pins. Elsewhere, a cat lays claim to a chair, a dog snoozes on a hearth, and a minuscule Monopoly board stands at the ready. One room box depicts a museum, wherein suits of armor, dinosaurs, and Oriental works of art await the scrutiny of visitors. An antique dollhouse, documented by its English builder, dates from 1861. Special collections that range from cars and cannons to dolls and teddy bears are exhibited on a rotating basis. The nonprofit museum also offers traveling exhibits and seasonal displays. Visitors may purchase such items as handcrafted miniatures, books, and periodicals in the museum's gift shop (small in size, of course). Admission: adults $10; senior citizens $8; children (ages 3–9) $5. The museum is located at 111 E. Main St.; open 11 a.m. to 4 p.m. Friday and Saturday; 1–4 p.m. Sunday; closed major holidays and the first two school weeks of January. Special hours can be arranged in advance for large groups and out-of-town visitors; call (317) 575-9466 or go online at museumofminiatures.org.

The charming little building at 40 W. Main St. in Carmel bills itself as the **World's Smallest Children's Art Gallery,** and it really is. The *Guinness Book of World Records* says so. The single-story building measures 9 feet 5 inches by 15 feet 4 inches (about the size of an average bedroom). The artwork showcased within comes from the art classes of various Carmel schools on a rotating basis and from Carmel's sister city, Kawachinagano, Japan. Although all the artwork is done by children, the exhibits reveal some amazing talent. Visit the website carmelartscouncil.org. After you have visited, sit on a park bench nearby and enjoy the ambience of the city's Arts & Design District in which the gallery is located.

A popular attraction for visitors and locals alike is the artesian well in **Flowing Well Park.** Discovered by accident in 1902, the free-flowing fountain provides mineral water free of charge to anyone who has an empty jug. You'll find the park on the northeast corner at the intersection of Gray Road and E. 116th St. at 5100 E. 116th St. in Carmel. Don't be surprised if the well, housed in a small white gazebo, is surrounded by a thirsty crowd. The 18-acre park also features two hiking trails. For additional information, contact Carmel-Clay Parks and Recreation, 1235 Central Park Dr. E., Carmel 46032; (317) 848-7275; carmelclayparks.com.

indianatrivia

Carmel, population 93,510, is home to more roundabouts than any other US town. As of September 2020, more than 125 of the circular alternatives to stoplights had been built, and more are planned.

ANNUAL EVENTS IN CENTRAL INDIANA

Indiana Black Expo
Indianapolis; July
(317) 925-2702
indianablackexpo.com

Indy Greek Fest
Indianapolis; September
(317) 733-3033
indygreekfest.org

Indiana State Fair
Indianapolis; August
(317) 927-7500
indianastatefair.com

Indy Jazz Fest
Indianapolis; September
(317) 966-7854
indyjazzfest.net

Indy Irish Fest
Indianapolis; September
(317) 713-7117
indyirishfest.com

Morgan County Fall Foliage Festival
Martinsville; October
(765) 342-0332
morgancountyfallfoliagefestival.com

Children's Museum Haunted House
Indianapolis; October
(317) 334-3322
childrensmuseum.org

Red Gold Chili Cook-Off
Elwood; October
(765) 552-0180

Indy International Festival
Indianapolis; November
(317) 262-3000
visitindy.com

Heartland Apple Festival
Danville; October
(317) 745-4876
beasleys-orchard.com

Hancock County

Hancock County is James Whitcomb Riley country. He was born and raised and found the inspiration for many of his poems here, including such classics as "When the Frost Is on the Punkin," "Little Orphant Annie," "The Raggedy Man," and "The Old Swimmin' Hole."

Riley was born on October 7, 1849, in what is now the kitchen of a white frame house built by his father, who was an able carpenter as well as a lawyer noted for his oratory. Located at 250 W. Main St. (US 40) in *Greenfield,* this house was immortalized in Riley's poems. It contains the rafter room where "the gobble-uns'll git you ef you don't watch out," the dining room "where they et on Sundays," and the side porch where Mary Alice Smith, who worked for the Riley family and is believed to have been the real-life "Little Orphant Annie," would "shoo the chickens off the porch." The *James Whitcomb Riley Boyhood Home and Museum,* complete with a collection of Riley memorabilia, is open to the public from 11 a.m. to 4 p.m. Tuesday through Saturday, April through October. Admission: adults $4; senior citizens $3.50; children (ages 6–17) $1.50. Call (317) 462-8539 or visit greenfieldin.org.

Although Riley was a lifelong bachelor and never had children of his own, he dearly loved them, and they returned his love. The statue of the famous Hoosier poet, seen today on the lawn of the Hancock County Courthouse (110 S. State St., Greenfield), was purchased entirely with funds contributed by the schoolchildren of Indiana.

Not far east of the Riley home, at the northwest corner of the intersection of US 40 and Apple Street, you'll find *Riley Memorial Park.* A boulder, into which are carved the words "Riley's Old Swimmin' Hole," stands on the banks of Brandywine Creek within the 20-acre park and marks the exact spot where Riley and the friends of his youth once whiled away the hours on hot summer days. The youth of today frolic in a modern pool nearby. For additional information, contact the Hancock County Tourism and Visitor Center, 119 W. Main St., Greenfield 46140; (317) 477-8687; visithancock.org.

Although Riley eventually left Greenfield, he maintained his residence in Indiana until his death in 1916. You'll find his Indianapolis home and burial site described later in this section under Marion County.

Another place of interest in Riley Park is the two-story **Old Log Jail Museum.** Since log jails could hardly be called escape-proof, their builders resorted to various ingenious methods to keep prisoners incarcerated. This jail features an upstairs cell room and logs filled with nails to prevent prisoners from "sawing out." There's a nominal admission fee. For additional information, contact the Hancock County Historical Society, PO Box 375, Greenfield 46140; (317) 462-7780; hancockhistory.org.

If you happen to pass through **Fortville,** you might want to visit the town's unofficial ambassador—a **life-size pink elephant** wearing black eyeglasses and sipping from a martini glass, complete with olive, wrapped in his trunk. You'll find him standing in front of the Elite Beverages liquor store at 308 W. Broadway St., where he's been a fixture since the 1980s. For info, call (317) 485-6262.

Hendricks County

Rising from the cornfields of Hendricks County near **Plainfield,** the 124-acre complex of the **Islamic Society of North America** has served Muslims throughout the continent as a religious and educational center since 1982. The site, which is the national headquarters for several Islamic organizations, was selected for both its central location and its receptive environment. During the 1991 war with Iraq, the center's staff members were asked by the Pentagon to advise US military leaders of the religious needs of the several thousand Muslims who serve in the military. The center also answers questions from non-Muslims who are interested in learning more about Islam. One item of interest is the fact that the society elected its first female president in August 2006; she served in that capacity for four years. When former heavyweight boxing champion Mike Tyson was released from a nearby state correctional facility in 1995, after serving nearly four years on a rape conviction, this was the first place he came. Tyson converted to Islam while in prison. The public is welcome to tour the mosque, library, and teaching center; contact the center's public relations department at (317) 839-8157 to arrange a visit. You'll find the center, distinguished by its modern Middle Eastern design, approximately 3 miles south of Plainfield at 6555 S. CR 750 East. Visit isna.net for additional information.

Johnson County

The *Johnson County Museum of History* is well worth the attention of history buffs. Housed in a former Masonic Temple, the museum displays more than 20,000 items, including antiques, Indian artifacts, guns, tools, and an interesting collection of nineteenth-century dresses. Four of its rooms have been furnished to depict the period between the Civil War and the early 1900s.

On the lawn outside the museum is an authentic log cabin built in 1835. It was discovered when an old house elsewhere in the county was being demolished—the house had been built around the cabin.

The museum, located at 135 N. Main St. in *Franklin,* is open 9 a.m. to 4 p.m. Tuesday through Friday; 10 a.m. to 3 p.m. Saturday. Admission is free, but donations are appreciated; (317) 346-4500 or johnsoncountymuseum.org.

Avid golfers will want to visit the **Indiana Golf Hall of Fame** in Franklin. Housed within the Indiana Golf Office at 2625 Hurricane Rd., the hall includes a rare ballot box from St. Andrews, Scotland, home of the oldest golf course in the world. The box dates to the late 1800s and was used by members to accept or reject new members. Other memorabilia include a 1954 scorecard of Ben Hogan's, a putter used by Hoosier native Fuzzy Zoeller when he won the 1979 Masters Tournament, and mementos from Pete and Alice Dye. Pete, with the assistance of his wife and partner, Alice, designed more than 110 golf courses all over the country; Pete was the fifth golf course architect to be inducted into the World Golf Hall of Fame and is considered by many to be the rock star of golf course designers. Pete died on January 9, 2020, at the age of ninety-four. Alice Dye passed away on February 1, 2019, at the age of ninety-one. Biographies of members who have been elected to the Indiana Hall hang on the walls. The museum and a golf library are open free of charge from 8 a.m. to 5 p.m. Monday through Friday; (317) 738-9696, (800) 779-7271, or indianagolf.org.

The *grave of Nancy Kerlin Barnett* is a top contender for Indiana's most unusual burial site. Nancy, who died in 1831 at age thirty-nine, often expressed her wish to be buried at a favorite spot overlooking Sugar Creek. Through the years Nancy's grave was joined by others. A footpath through the small cemetery eventually became a road. Increased traffic made it necessary to widen the road, and the graves had to be relocated—all, that is, but Nancy's. It's reported that one of Nancy's relatives greeted the road-wideners with a shotgun and threatened to shoot anyone who disturbed her resting place. That same relative persuaded county officials to give Nancy a special dispensation, and her grave can still be seen today, skirted on both sides by CR 400 South (Camp Hill Road), near *Amity.* There's even a historical marker to honor Nancy's memory and, perhaps, to forestall questions from curious passersby. To see Nancy's grave, go to the intersection of US 31 and CR 400 South at the south end of Amity; then turn east onto CR 400 South and drive approximately 1.3 miles to the grave in the middle of the road.

If you like popcorn, you're sure to find a flavor to your liking at *Not Just Popcorn* in *Edinburgh.* And if you shouldn't see or smell anything that tantalizes your taste buds among the more than 250 flavors provided—though that's hard to imagine—the popcorn folks will try to create a flavor that does appeal to you. While munching on the treat of your taste, you can view the extensive display of Coca-Cola collectibles. Open 10 a.m. to 5 p.m. Monday through Thursday, 10 a.m. to 6 p.m. Friday, and 10 a.m. to 5 p.m. Saturday. Located at 101 E. Main Cross St.; (812) 526-8256, (800) 231-5689, or notjustpopcorn.com.

Since its founding in 1942, *Camp Atterbury* near Edinburgh has hosted thousands of US soldiers as they have passed through here on their way to every one of our country's wars since World War II. Visitors can learn about its proud history, from its inception as a World War II troop training center in 1942 to its present-day role as a mobilization center for troops heading overseas and a training center for those fighting today's war on terrorism, at the Camp Atterbury Museum. The indoor museum features such exhibits as model airplanes, medals, news clippings, uniforms on life-size mannequins, and documents depicting the role of Blacks in the military. In an outdoor museum nearby, you'll see an old mobile rocket launcher affectionately known as "Honest John," an 8-inch howitzer, a Humvee, and a silver streamliner train car. The museum, located in Building 427 on Egglestone St. near the main entrance, is open Monday through Friday from 9 a.m. to 4 p.m. and Saturday from 10 a.m. to 2 p.m. No admission charge, but you'll need to pick up a pass at the Welcome Center on Hospital Road; (812) 526-1744.

Camp Atterbury also served as a prison camp for Italian and German soldiers during World War II. While there, a group of Italian prisoners of war who were skilled artisans were given permission to build a small chapel that they used for daily worship. Using scraps of brick, cement, and wood, they constructed an 11-by-16-foot building and decorated its floor, ceiling, and walls with intricate hand-painted frescos. Now known as the *Chapel in the Meadow,* it's located just north of today's camp boundaries and can be visited daily, free of charge, during daylight hours.

Write the camp's Welcome Center at PO Box 5000, Edinburgh 46124-5000 for specific directions to all camp facilities and for information about special

events open to the public; call (812) 526-1433 or visit atterburymuscatatuck.in
.ng.mil.

Madison County

On the north side of the little country town of *Chesterfield,* two massive stone
gateposts mark the entrance to the beautiful parklike grounds of *Camp Chesterfield.* They also mark the entrance to another world, for Camp Chesterfield
is one of the major headquarters in this country for spiritualists.

Spiritualists, in case you don't have a dictionary handy, believe that mor-
tals can communicate with the spirits of the dead through a medium. Using
a variety of methods, the mediums at Camp Chesterfield attempt to do just
that. They conduct séances, go into trances, evoke ectoplasms, cause spirits to
materialize, and predict the future. The mediums are carefully screened before
being selected to join the camp's staff, and each has his or her own specialty
and sees clients by appointment in one of the cottages scattered about the
48-acre grounds.

The Visitor Welcome Center is open from 10 a.m. to 4 p.m. daily and at
other times for special events; the beautiful grounds are always open. Fees,
quite reasonable, are charged for private consultations with the staff member
of your choice, but there is no charge to enter the camp, attend services at
the Cathedral in the Woods, view various public demonstrations of psychic
phenomena, walk a replica of the Chartres labyrinth found at the famous
Chartres Cathedral in France, or tour the fascinating art gallery and museum.
The museum houses the memorabilia of the Fox sisters, who are credited with
initiating the modern spiritualism movement.

If you'd like to read up on such subjects as reincarnation, astrology, and
faith healing, you'll find books on these subjects and more in the camp's book-
store. To spend the night, the Western Hotel was built in 1945 and designed
after typical roadside inns of the time. It features both single and twin rooms
with attached baths. The lower level offers a women's dorm that allows for
communal accommodations. It also has a smaller men's dorm. The hotel was
the first fireproof building in the state of Indiana. There are even a few campsites for self-contained recreational vehicles. No tents are permitted. Occasionally, you can take courses in such subjects as the technique of spiritual healing,
handwriting analysis, and trance development. All rates are reasonable.

Lest you scoff, remember that such notables as Sir Arthur Conan Doyle,
creator of Sherlock Holmes, and Thomas Edison dabbled in spiritualism. Even
Sigmund Freud expressed an interest in the movement and said, shortly before
his death, that if he had his life to live over again he "would concern himself

more with these matters." No matter what your beliefs, you will leave here with much food for thought. The camp has also been designated a US Historic Place by the National Park Service, which recognizes cultural resources worthy of preservation. For a schedule of events and other information, write Camp Chesterfield, PO Box 132, Chesterfield 46017; call (765) 378-0235; or visit campchesterfield.net. To make hotel reservations, write the hotel manager at the same address or call (765) 378-0237 or visit campchesterfield.net/hotel/. The camp is located at 50 Lincoln Dr.

Not far southwest of Chesterfield, atop limestone bluffs overlooking the White River, you can study the curious architecture of mound-building Indians. Of the eleven prehistoric earthworks preserved at **Mounds State Park,** the most exceptional is the circular Great Mound (circa 160 BC), nearly 1,200 feet in circumference and 9 feet high. Two other mounds are guitar shaped, yet another is conical, and one is U shaped. Excavations can be seen, and a naturalist is available to explain the cultures of the Adena and Hopewell Indians, who are believed to have built these mounds. The park, steeped in Indian legend, is reportedly home to the Puk-wud-ies, a peaceful tribe of little people who continue to inhabit the forest as they have for time immemorial. Some visitors have reported encountering the blue-gowned dwarves on park trails. In addition to historical tours, the park offers a swimming pool, hiking and cross-country ski trails, modern campsites, and canoeing on the White River. Canoes and ski equipment can be rented in the park. You can reach the park by taking Mounds Road (SR 232) southwest from Chesterfield for about 2 miles. There's a daily vehicle admission fee of $7 for Indiana residents and $9 for out-of-state visitors. Write to Mounds State Park, 4306 Mounds Rd., Anderson 46017; call (765) 642-6627 or visit in.gov/dnr/parklake/2977.htm.

At Anderson University at 1100 E. 5th St. university, you can also visit the **Charles E. Wilson Library,** which contains the archives and personal papers of the man who served as secretary of defense under President Dwight D. Eisenhower. The **Wilson Art Gallery** houses a $250,000 porcelain bird collection donated by Wilson's daughter, and a collection of 1,500 napkin rings that range in variety from a solid gold, jewel-encrusted ring once used by Louis XIV of France to rings made from toilet paper spools in a Japanese prison camp during World War II. **Reardon Auditorium** features an unusual chandelier that holds some 10,000 lightbulbs and a stunning light sculpture in the lobby.

Elsewhere in Alexandria, house painter Mike Carmichael has spent his spare time working on his personal masterpiece. It all began with an accident in the mid-1960s, when Mike accidentally dropped a baseball in some paint. For some inexplicable reason, Mike decided to continue painting his baseball, and he's been at it ever since. Today, that baseball is hanging in a special **Ball** *of Paint Pavilion* next to Mike's home, and virtually everyone in town, from the mayor on down, has added a layer or two of paint to it. When last weighed and measured in 2018, it weighed 6,050 pounds and had about a 492-inch circumference. It then wore 27,039 layers of paint. Mike's wife, Glenda, has added some 9,000 coats herself. Visitors just keep coming and keep painting; so far, they have come from every state and forty foreign countries, including Germany, Italy, Thailand, and Australia.

Mike's project has been officially designated the world's largest ball of paint and is listed as such in the *Guinness Book of World Records*. A few years back, Alexandria was in the news when a 400-pound hairball was found in a town sewer. The *National Enquirer* ran a story about that event. The original hairball eventually dissolved, but local citizens created a replica and even gave it a place of honor in the town's annual Christmas parade. Now city officials hope Alexandria will gain fame as the town of balls.

If you would like to see Mike's ball of paint for yourself, give Mike or Glenda a call at (765) 724-4088 to make an appointment. When you visit, you may be asked to paint a layer and to add your name to the list of painters on the wall. Mike and his ball are located at 10696 N. CR 200 West; admission is free.

Marion County

The magnificent **Soldiers and Sailors Monument** has graced the heart of downtown **Indianapolis** since its dedication in 1902. Adorned by statuary and surrounded by fountains, it is recognized as one of the most unique monuments in the country and is the largest in the nation dedicated to the common soldier. An enclosed observation deck near the top of the 284-foot-tall monument offers a 360-degree view of the surrounding area. It can be reached by elevator for $2 for adults and $1 for children ages 6–17. Veterans and US military ride free. Visitors can climb the stairs for free; the 331 steps are numbered so visitors can keep track of their progress. After the elevator ride, visitors must also climb forty-nine steps to reach the observation levels. Many of the steps have been dedicated to veterans of our country's wars, and you can read about them as you climb. Located at 1 Monument Circle at the intersection of Meridian St. and Market St. Open free of charge from 10:30 a.m. to 5:30 p.m. Wednesday through Sunday from May through October, and from 10:30 a.m. to 5:30 p.m. Friday through Sunday from November through April.

On the lower level of the monument, you can visit the 9,000-square-foot **Colonel Eli Lilly Civil War Museum,** where you can experience the Civil War from home front to battlefield. Display cases exhibit such artifacts as guns, medical kits, letters, personal diaries, and the personal effects of Colonel Lilly, for whom the museum is named. One of the most impressive and thought-provoking exhibits is a large sketch that depicts life in the infamous Andersonville Military Prison in Georgia; its creator was a young Hoosier native named Thomas O'Dea who spent time there as a prisoner of war. Colonel Lilly, a native Hoosier from Greencastle, took the lessons he learned

about medicine during the war and created a business that eventually evolved into the pharmaceutical giant, Eli Lilly and Company. The museum entrance is located on the west side of the monument. Be aware there are no public restroom facilities within the monument.

For additional information about both the monument and the museum, call (317) 232-7615 or (800) 665-9056, or visit in.gov/iwm/2335.htm.

The three-story *Indiana World War Memorial,* built as the centerpiece of a five-block plaza in downtown Indianapolis, pays homage to Hoosiers killed during US wars fought in the twentieth century. Patterned after the Tomb of King Mausolus at Halicarnassus, one of the seven wonders of the ancient world, the building is an architectural marvel. It is the Shrine Room on the top floor, however, that is the glory of the memorial. Massive dark red marble columns surround a marble altar that commemorates fallen war heroes. A 17-by-30 foot American flag, supported by invisible wires, is suspended above the altar. Tiny blue lightbulbs that flicker off and on in the ceiling surround a huge Swedish-crystal light fixture in the shape of a star. Daylight filters through

How to Speak Hoosier

If you'd like to blend in with the natives when visiting Indiana, you might want to learn Hoosier speak. It's almost as unique as the state's Hoosier nickname.

Hoosier speak is a frugal way of talking. Never use more syllables, words, or letters than you need to get your message across. This allows one to quickly move on to more important things in life.

When it's absolutely imperative to say "Indianapolis" rather than "Indy," Hoosiers have found several different ways to condense the name of their capital city. According to author John W. Terhune, they've found twenty-six different ways. To learn them all, try to find a copy of his hilarious book, *Why Hoosiers Can't Pronounce Indianapolis* (no longer published, but available in many libraries). In his book, Dr. Terhune makes this observation: "Hoosiers can't pronounce Indianapolis because Hoosiers have absolutely no use for a six-syllable word."

In addition to their frugality, Hoosiers have a great sense of humor.

twenty-four deep blue glass windows. The memorial also houses a museum that contains such artifacts as a Korean War-era helicopter, a Navy Terrier missile, and some jeeps. On September 21, 2001, an exhibit honoring casualties from our country's latest war was officially dedicated; the display in the building's Grand Foyer honors seven Hoosiers who lost their lives in September 11, 2001, attacks on the World Trade Center and the Pentagon. The War on Terror room on the main floor contains a flag that bears the names of all Hoosier casualties in the conflicts in Afghanistan and Iraq from September 11, 2001, through the summer of 2010. Elsewhere, memorabilia and artifacts from the USS *Indianapolis* relate the story of the World War II ship's sinking after being hit by a Japanese torpedo; only 317 members from a crew of 1,197 survived in the shark-infested waters. A 7-foot long scale model of the ship and a re-creation of the ship's radio room are highlights of the exhibit.

Outside, on the south steps of the memorial, visitors will see a one-of-a-kind statue known as *Pro Patria*. The 24-foot-tall, 7-ton sculpture, cast in bronze in 1929 by a New York City artist, has stood here since the memorial was dedicated in 1930. In 1945, a B-25 crashed into the Empire State Building and sent flaming debris into the artist's nearby studio. The model for *Pro Patria* was destroyed, making the statue impossible to replace.

Located at 55 E. Michigan St., the Indiana World War Memorial is open free of charge from 9 a.m. to 5 p.m. Wednesday through Sunday; call (317) 232-7615 or visit in.gov/iwm.

At 700 N. Pennsylvania St., the **American Legion National Headquarters** houses one of the world's most extensive collections of World Wars I and II posters—more than 800 from World War I and 1,200 from World War II. Approximately forty are on display throughout the American Legion Building, with the rest available for view on a slide collection. A museum on the top floor of the 4-story building exhibits memorabilia from the wars our country fought in the twentieth century. You may tour the building free of charge from 8:30 a.m. to 4 p.m. Monday through Friday; call (317) 630-1200 or (800) 433-3318 for additional information and to make an appointment to view the slide collection. You may also visit online at legion.org.

indiana*trivia*

Actor Clark Gable drove the pace car for the 1950 Indy 500.

If anyone ever compiles a list of national treasures, **The Children's Museum of Indianapolis** should be on it. It is the largest children's museum in the world, and in this case, bigger *is* better. You can ride an early twentieth-century carousel; stand beside a 55-ton, wood-burning locomotive; see a 30-foot-tall glass water clock, the largest in North America; watch a spectacular

"Leggy" Statue Honors Hoosier Icon John Wooden

Some like it. Some don't. Such is the nature of art. But the John Wooden sculpture in downtown Indy is certainly getting plenty of attention and no one disputes that the man depicted is a Hoosier icon.

Located on the reconstructed section of Georgia Street, the bronze sculpture of the basketball legend was created by Jeffrey Rouse, a former Indiana resident living in New York.

Wooden is depicted in a familiar stance—squatting in a courtside huddle grasping his signature rolled-up playbook. Surrounding him are players wearing socks and gym shoes that mark significant eras of Wooden's career. However, only five pairs of legs of the players are seen.

Rouse has said that he used only the legs to keep the sculpture from becoming too cluttered and to maintain the emphasis on Wooden himself. Approaching the sculpture, viewers are on the same eye level as Wooden. Although coaches today usually stand while players sit on the bench for those huddles, Wooden was known for his up-close cluster while he knelt.

Titled **Wooden's Legacy**, the base of the sculpture is encircled with words from Wooden's Pyramid of Success, such as confidence, honesty, initiative, loyalty, cooperation, and enthusiasm. Wooden is gazing toward Bankers Life Fieldhouse where the Indianapolis Pacers and Heat play basketball games.

The reconstructed section of Georgia Street between Pennsylvania Street and Capitol Avenue was unveiled in September 2010 as a pedestrian-friendly streetscape featuring a wide pedestrian mall in its median. It connects Bankers Life Fieldhouse with the Indiana Convention Center and Lucas Oil Stadium and serves as a new downtown gathering place also designed to reflect the character and achievements of Hoosiers.

Born in Martinsville, Wooden played basketball for Purdue University, later coaching at Indiana State University and UCLA. There, he led teams to ten national basketball championships (seven in consecutive years) from 1964 to 1975. He died in 2010 at age ninety-nine.

One of the favorite quotes uttered by Wooden: "Don't let making a living prevent you from making a life."

collection of toy trains in motion; examine real fossils on display; conduct scientific experiments; and so much more.

Budding scientists can explore Corteva ScienceWorks. Children are enthralled by the magic of live theater productions at the Lilly Theater. Playscape offers learning through play for youngsters aged birth to five years old. Walk among fully articulated dinosaurs in Dinosphere; see, hear, and smell them in the 65-million-year-old environment in which they thrived. Presiding over the lobby of the Welcome Center is a 1-ton, 17-foot-tall bumblebee, an acquired prop from the 2007 movie *Transformers*.

A magnificent 43-foot-tall, 3,200-piece tower of brilliantly colored glass, known as *Fireworks of Glass*, rises above a glass ceiling in the museum's central atrium. It is the largest permanent sculpture ever created by world-renowned artist Dale Chihuly. Visitors can sit on a revolving platform below the glass pergola and look up at the more than 1,600 additional pieces of brightly colored glass embedded in the ceiling itself. Bathed in natural sunlight during the day and lit at night during special events, the tower and ceiling form the centerpiece of a hands-on exhibit that demonstrates how ordinary glass can be turned into extraordinary works of art.

An exhibit called Treasures of the Earth, created through a partnership with the National Geographic Society, focuses on three famous archaeological finds from around the world—the tomb of an ancient Egyptian pharaoh, the Terra Cotta Warriors of China's first emperor, and the wreck of Captain Kidd's ship that was discovered in the depths of the Caribbean in 2007. All displays are designed to be touched and explored.

In the Power of Children gallery, learn the stories of Anne Frank, Ruby Bridges, and Ryan White, three extraordinary children who changed the world. In 2021, Malala Yousafzai will be added to the gallery. When a member of the Taliban shot Malala in the head on the way home from school in October 2012, the shooter had no idea that, instead of silencing the young girl, her voice became louder. The fifteen-year-old Pakistani girl made a miraculous recovery, continued to fight for girls' education, and became the youngest-ever Nobel Peace Prize recipient.

It's "game on" in the newest addition at The Children's Museum of Indianapolis in the $38.5 million Riley Children's Health Sports Legend Experience. Opened in March 2018, the 7.5-acre complex combines rich sports history, physical fitness, and health education in twelve immersive outdoor experiences and three new indoor experiences. The new sports utopia features basketball, football, hockey, soccer, golf, baseball, and tennis. Since this is Indy, it also spotlights the Indianapolis Motor Speedway with pedal car racing and a dragstrip with pedal cars. A fitness path boasts several fitness pads and exercise equipment to improve muscle strength, balance, coordination, and flexibility.

For motivation, the Old National Bank Avenue of Champions invites visitors to meet legendary characters, hear their stories of greatness, and learn tips on how to succeed. The avenue features statues of twelve sports legends, including Larry Bird, Reggie Miller, Wilma Rudolph, and Hank Aaron where visitors can pose for photos and learn more about their heroes. Watching over the sporty fun is a 60-foot-tall Fantasy Tree House of Sports where children of all ages can climb inside and explore a hard-to-believe-it-is-not-real tree filled with fantasy and sports.

Big adventures bring on big appetites. A Food Court in the museum offers reasonably priced food such as burgers, pizza, sandwiches, soup, salad, and cookies. The Kohler Pavilion Grab & Go in the sports arena serves ballpark eats like hot dogs, fresh fruit, and ice cream. Visitors also are invited to bring their own lunch and enjoy it at picnic tables.

Check the website for highly discounted days ($5 First Thursdays) to plan-ahead-pricing that ranges from $14 to $40. Admission is free for children under two years old. Carousel rides are $1. Hours vary but are usually 10 a.m. to 5 p.m. for the museum and 10 a.m. to 6 p.m. for the outdoor Sports Experience. The museum and Sports Experience are open daily in the spring and summer; both are closed Mondays in autumn and Outdoor Experience is closed in the winter.

The museum is located directly north of downtown Indianapolis, at the corner of 30th and N. Meridian. The entrance is on Illinois St. (the first street west of Meridian St.) Look for the three huge dinosaurs escaping through a museum wall on one end and two gigantic dinos peeking in on another. Parking is free in the garage and visitors can walk outside or through an enclosed walkway from the garage into the museum. The museum also is a stop on the city's Red Line bus system. Call (317) 334-3322, (317) 334-4000, or (800) 820-6214 or visit childrensmuseum.org.

indianatrivia

Indianapolis native Booth Tarkington (1869–1946) is one of only three authors to win the Pulitzer Prize for Fiction twice. The others are William Faulkner and John Updike.

indianatrivia

Albert Von Tilzer, an Indianapolis native, composed the music for "Take Me Out to the Ball Game." Only two songs are sung more often in this country—"The Star Spangled Banner" and "Happy Birthday."

The *Crispus Attucks Museum* showcases and celebrates the accomplishments of African Americans in Indianapolis, with a special focus on the graduates of Crispus Attucks High School. Back in the 1950s, when Attucks was a consolidated high school for the city's Black youngsters, basketball great Oscar Robertson was a student here. Under his leadership the school's basketball team captured the state championship, the first Black team and the first team from any Indianapolis high school ever to do so. (In 2006, the team was elected en masse to the Indiana Basketball Hall of Fame in New Castle; see

A Woman of Distinction

The world remembers her today as Madame C. J. Walker, but she was born Sara Breedlove. Sara was born on December 23, 1867, the daughter of ex-slaves living in Louisiana. By the time she died in 1919 at the age of fifty-one, she was a self-made millionaire and believed to be the wealthiest Black woman in the country.

Madame Walker's fascinating life story includes being orphaned at age seven, getting married at age fourteen, and becoming a widow with a two-year-old daughter at age twenty. When she and her daughter moved to Denver in 1905, she carried her entire life savings of $1.50. There she met and married a newspaper sales agent named Charles Joseph Walker and created the Walker line of hair-care products for Black women.

In 1910, Madame Walker moved her company to Indianapolis to take advantage of the city's eight railway systems as a means of distributing her products nationally, and she built a sales force of more than 2,000 women who generated annual revenues of $500,000. She also began developing the triangular-shaped Walker Building and Theatre, a project that was completed by her daughter after Madame Walker's death. Today, the **Madame Walker Legacy Center** at 617 Indiana Ave. is a National Historic Landmark and a national model for African American arts.

In recognition of her lifetime achievements, Madame Walker was elected to the National Business Hall of Fame in 1992. She was further honored on January 28, 1997, when the US Postal Service issued a 32-cent commemorative stamp bearing her likeness. The stamp was dedicated in a special ceremony at the Walker Theatre. For additional information about the many special events presented at the Walker Theatre and about tours of the building, call (317) 236-2099 or visit madamewalkerleg acycenter.com.

Henry County in Southeast Indiana.) Visitors can explore some thirty exhibits, including a basketball hall of fame, in four galleries. Although best known for its basketball history, the school has produced many extraordinary graduates. They gained fame as musicians, soldiers, and athletes, and their stories are told through the extensive and still-growing collection of memorabilia and artwork. The museum is located at 1140 N. Dr. Martin Luther King Jr. Dr. on the campus of Crispus Attucks Medical Magnet High School. Named for a Black man and former slave who was the first patriot to die in the American Revolution, Crispus Attucks High School was placed on the National Register of Historic Places in 1989. Open 9 a.m. to 5 p.m. Monday through Friday or from noon to 5 p.m. Saturday; nominal admission fee; call (317) 226-2432.

The ***Indianapolis Museum of Art at Newfields*** (IMA), situated on a bluff overlooking the White River, is far more than a museum. It's a 152-acre art park that includes a sculpture garden, botanical and formal gardens, patches of woodland, a greenhouse, a wildlife refuge, a 152-acre art and nature park, and a restaurant. The 12-foot-high steel sculpture known as *LOVE* occupies a prominent place on the museum's lawn. An iconic work of pop art, it has been replicated in many places around the world, but the one you see here is the original; sculptor Robert Indiana (née Robert Clark) is a native Hoosier. Among the museum's exhibits are the world's largest collection—outside the United Kingdom—of J. M. W. Turner watercolors and prints, a self-portrait of Rembrandt as a young man, and important collections of Asian, African, and neo-Impressionist art. An acquisition of screens and scrolls from the Edo period is the largest single purchase of Japanese art in US history. The museum site was once the private estate of Mr. and Mrs. J. K. Lilly Jr. (of Lilly pharmaceutical fame), and there is also much of architectural interest here. Lilly Pavilion is the original Lilly mansion, formerly known as Oldfields; it's one of the few nineteenth-century American Country Place estates still in existence and the only one in this country to share the grounds of a major art museum. The garage contains a rotating display of cars from the Indianapolis Motor Speedway's Hall of Fame Museum. Many special events and programs are held here. Open 11 a.m. to 5 p.m. Tuesday and Wednesday; 11 a.m. to 8 p.m. Thursday through Saturday; 11 a.m. to 5 p.m. Sunday. Admission: adults $18; children (ages 6–17) $10. The gardens and grounds are open daily from dawn to dusk. Free admission is offered the first Thursday of each month from 4 to 9 p.m. Located at 4000 Michigan Rd.; call (317) 923-1331 or visit discovernewfields.org for up-to-date information.

Tucked away in the basement of the Schwitzer Student Center at the **University of Indianapolis** is a gallery of extraordinary Chinese art. The forty-five exquisite pieces displayed here, valued at $1 million, are the work of Master Au Ho-nien, considered the greatest living traditional Chinese artist. Museums in China, Hong Kong, and Taiwan competed to host the canvases seen on these walls, but the artist chose this location because of his close friendship with one of the school's professors. The collection, which came here in 2004, includes a bust of the artist. Open free of charge 8 a.m. to 5 p.m. daily. To learn more about the **Au Ho-nien Museum,** contact the University of Indianapolis, 1400 E. Hanna Ave., Indianapolis 46227; (317) 788-3368 , (800) 232-8634, or uindy.edu/aumuseum.

Indianapolis has gone wild over its state-of-the-art **Indianapolis Zoo.** Stretching along the west bank of the White River, the innovative 64-acre facility is the first zoo ever to be completely designed around the biome concept. Biomes are simulated natural environments in which animals are grouped by habitats rather than by the continents of their origins. Forest animals from around the world, for instance, share the forest biome, while other animals find appropriate homes in the desert, plains, and aquatic biomes.

Indy Zoo Orangutan Center Helps Endangered Species

Ambling through an open door, Azy the orangutan flops on a large seat and eyes the computer screen in front of him. Watching Dr. Robert Shumaker through a huge observation window in an adjoining room, Azy patiently waits for symbols to appear on the computer screen.

Then the action starts.

The goal in this exercise is for Azy to identify numbers on the screen, arrange them in numerical order, and press a "send" button on the computer to share the answer with Shumaker. For every right answer, Azy gets an apple slice. If wrong, he knows to try again.

However, the purpose is not for visitors just to be impressed by the computer skills of the 11 orangutans at the $26 million **Simon Skjodt International Orangutan Center** at the **Indianapolis Zoo**. Opened on Memorial Day weekend in 2014, the project was designed with a far more important purpose in mind.

"We want to make people care about a species on the verge of extinction," said Shumaker, zoo president. "Hopefully, what people see here will make them feel compelled to protect the future of a species that is on track to become the first great ape species to become extinct."

Destruction of habitat is the main threat to orangutan survival. All the orangutans at the Indy Zoo were born in captivity and could not survive in the wild.

For the computer work, orangutans can choose to participate or not. "The door is always open," Shumaker said. "They can come in and they can leave whenever they want."

After his numbers work, Azy proceeds to object identification on the computer. Shumaker holds up an item like an apple or a cup and Azy correctly identifies it on the computer. When the exercises are over, Shumaker hands Azy a paper bag with the remainder of his apple slice treats. What Azy does next is perhaps the most amazing to me. Azy eats the slices. Then he carefully hands the empty bag back to Shumaker before exiting the computer room.

"That is very important to us," Shumaker explained. "If something were to fall into their area that they shouldn't have, something that might hurt them, we want Azy and the others to know that they should return that item to us."

The overall land area for the new zoo facility is larger than two NFL football fields. Visitors can watch orangutans go through their computer paces, smile for cameras, swing from ladders, and do other acrobatics in their Indianapolis habitat. The animals can move outdoors to an orangutan sidewalk in the sky—a series of cables, bridges, and platforms rising 45–80 feet high. Visitors also can have a close encounter with orangutans over their heads by riding a 1,200-foot-long Skyline on aerial cable cars.

It is thrilling to come face to face with orangutans and realize that they are watching us as much as we are watching them. "Look into the eyes of an orangutan and you see a sentient being looking back," Shumaker said.

Meaning "People of the Forest" in the Malay language, orangutans are capable of learning and using language, as well as solving problems. That is not surprising, Shumaker said, since orangutans and human being share 97 percent of the same DNA.

Looking somewhat like a contemporary church with a steeple, the 150-foot-tall building where the orangutans can be seen has towers where the critters can climb and also can get away for privacy, if so desired.

The centerpiece of the center is the Nina Mason Pulliam Beacon of Hope. A towering 150-foot structure, the Beacon is illuminated each night by lights, the color of which is controlled by the orangutans. Designed as a beautiful addition to the downtown Indy skyline, the Beacon of Hope also serves as a symbol and call to action.

"The future of the endangered orangutans rests with us all," Shumaker said. "If we don't do something, orangutans might not be around for future generations."

Unlike most of its counterparts, the Indianapolis Zoo combines the best elements of a zoo and an aquarium, Visitors can enter the watery world of the zoo's dolphins via an underwater 30-foot-diameter glass dome and watch the dolphins swim over, under, and around them. In one of the country's largest shark touch pools, you can stroke a shark's back. This zoo is one of only five in the world that can accommodate walruses.

The *Tiger Forest* exhibit is home to the stunningly beautiful and rare Amur tigers, separated from onlookers only by a thick glass window; tigers locate their prey by smell, and the glass prevents your scent from reaching them.

At a cheetah exhibit, you can see five of the endangered creatures; the cheetah is the fastest land animal in the world, capable of going from 0 to 60 miles per hour in 3 seconds. For a modest fee, you can run against an array of LED lights that simulate the speed of a cheetah and see how your own running speed compares. You'll also hear a narrative by a guy who knows all about speed; Tony Stewart, a NASCAR driver, Indiana native, and big animal fan, helped fund the exhibit.

In 1998, for the first time in the world, the zoo's two female African elephants delivered healthy calves after being artificially inseminated; since then, more healthy babies have been born here and in zoos worldwide using the method developed here, helping to insure the survival of the species.

Once every other year, the zoo awards $100,000 to an individual who has made extraordinary contributions to animal conservation. It is the largest such prize in the world and has contributed to the zoo's international reputation as a leader in conservation efforts.

Visitors will also find a behind-the-scenes train tour, a carousel, and a family roller-coaster ride.

The zoo is open 9 a.m. to 5 p.m. Monday through Thursday and 9 a.m. to 7 p.m. Friday through Sunday, from Memorial Day weekend through Labor Day; 9 a.m. to 4 p.m. daily from March to the day before Memorial Day weekend and on the day after Labor Day through October; 9 a.m. to 4 p.m. Wednesday through Sunday in November before Thanksgiving, and noon to 9 p.m. after Thanksgiving through December, except Christmas Eve and Day; 9 a.m. to 4 p.m. Wednesday through Sunday in January and February. Admission: adults $25.50; children (ages 2–12) $19.75. Hours and rates may vary, so it's best to contact them before going; call (317) 630-2001 or visit indianapoliszoo.com. The zoo is located just west of the downtown area at 1200 W. Washington St.

Admission to the zoo includes a visit to the adjacent **White River Gardens.** Included in the gardens' 3.3 acres are a glass-enclosed conservatory, water gardens, outdoor design gardens, and an outdoor wedding garden. From spring through Labor Day weekend, the conservatory is filled with more than 1,000 butterflies. Nearly, fifty bronze sculptures of small animals are scattered over the grounds.

In addition to its reputation as the amateur sports capital of the world, Indianapolis is also noted for having the country's most impressive collection of American war memorials outside Washington, DC. The **Congressional Medal of Honor Memorial** at 650 W. Washington St. is the only memorial in the US that honors our nation's most highly decorated war heroes. Of the tens of millions of men and women who have served our country in the military, only some 3,475 have earned the Medal of Honor (76 are from Indiana); more than half were awarded posthumously. Covering 1 acre in White River State Park, the memorial represents fifteen different conflicts, ranging from the Civil War through the wars in Afghanistan and Iraq. Its 27 curved glass walls range from 7 to 10 feet in height and are inscribed with the name of each medal recipient. As beautiful as the memorial is during the day, it is more spectacular at night, when the highlighted glass walls glow green. The outdoor memorial is open free of charge at all times; visitors who come at dusk will hear recorded stories, played over a public address system, of medal winners or of the conflicts in which they fought. Call (317) 261-5447 or visit indianawarmemorials.org/explore/medal-of-honor-memorial.

indianatrivia

Indianapolis is the capital of and largest city in Indiana. As of the 2018 census, its population is 876,862, making it the 17th largest city in the United States, the second-most populous state capital (after Phoenix, Arizona), and the most populous state capital east of the Mississippi River.

Not far away, at 500 W. Washington St., the ***Eiteljorg Museum of American Indians and Western Art*** showcases the arts and crafts of the American West in a building reminiscent of an Indian pueblo that's a work of art in itself. Opened in 1989 primarily to house the collection of the late Indianapolis businessman and philanthropist for whom it's named, the museum is one of only two of its type east of the Mississippi River. Its still-growing collection, currently valued at more than $45 million, includes sculptures by Charles Russell, bronzes by Frederic Remington, and paintings by Georgia O'Keeffe. Special programs breathe life into the exhibits; visitors may, for example, see roping demonstrations or attend a lecture series that offers instructions on how to make a cowboy hat or a lariat. The gift shop features authentic arts and crafts from the southwestern United States, and an on-site cafe offers inexpensive Southwestern cuisine and a view of the city's skyline. Admission: adults $15; senior citizens $12; children (ages 5–17) $8. The museum is open 10 a.m. to 5 p.m. Monday through Saturday and noon to 5 p.m. Sunday; public tours are offered at 1 p.m. on Saturday and Sunday. Closed major winter holidays; (317) 636-9378 or eiteljorg.org.

When the Smithsonian National Museum of the American Indian (NMAI) opened in Washington, DC, in September 2004, it selected the Eiteljorg as its first-ever alliance partner. The partnership allows the Eiteljorg to borrow and exhibit artifacts from NMAI's huge collection.

Indy 500 Roars Every May

The rumble of snarling engines mingles with the thunderous roar of an estimated 100,000 people at Indianapolis Motor Speedway. Resplendent in a spiffy white suit, Carl Fisher drives the pace car, a Stoddard-Dayton roadster, to lead the pack of forty race cars on the first of what would become a Memorial Day tradition.

Amid a haze of heavy smoke from burning fuel and oil, Fisher proudly motors along at 40 miles an hour, then veers to the left near the starting line. From the trackside, Fred "Pop" Wagner waves his red flag and the first Indy 500 on May 30, 1911, is on its way into racing history.

Visitors from around the world arrive in Indianapolis every May to celebrate the running of the Indy 500. And it all started with a crazy idea.

In the early part of the twentieth century, Indiana was the second-largest American automobile manufacturer behind Michigan. But all vehicles then could have used a higher testing standard. What this country needed, Indianapolis auto parts manufacturer Carl Fisher decided, was a good way of testing cars before putting them on the road. The best way to do that, Fisher thought, was to build a racetrack.

He pitched the idea to three friends—James Allison, Arthur Newby, and Frank Wheeler—and the four men bought a 328-acre plot of land northwest of downtown Indianapolis for $72,000. Surfaced with a combination of crushed stone and asphalt, the track opened for its first auto race on August 19, 1909.

The race was a treacherous one. The track's surface broke up from the heat and the traffic before Louis Schwitzer won the first race of the day. To repave the track, sturdy street-paving bricks were used–3,200,000 of them. By the time the project was finished, the track had already been nicknamed "The Brickyard."

To draw the public, Fisher and his partners decided they needed something big, something unheard of, a really spectacular one-day annual event instead of a series of minor races. That's how the Indy 500 was born.

The inaugural Indianapolis 500-Mile Race was announced for Memorial Day 1911. Making it 500 miles was a big deal, meaning the race would last almost a workday between mid-morning and late afternoon. With the speed of cars in those days, it would take about seven hours for racers to run 500 miles.

The race generated big interest from the beginning and spectators weren't disappointed. To put himself in the spotlight, as well as to let spectators get a better look at the competitors, Fisher decided to lead the cars around the track in a parade lap in his Stoddard-Dayton. It was the first known rolling start of a major auto race and the first use of a pace car.

Among the race favorites was Ray Harroun who had come out of retirement to run the first 500. His vehicle was a yellow and black No. 32 Marmon Wasp, which he had designed. Driving the only single-seat car in the race, Harroun didn't have room for a ride-along mechanic as did other cars to watch for danger. Instead, to be aware of passing cars, Harroun devised a four-posted rearview mirror, said to be the first known rearview mirror on an automobile.

Spectators were mesmerized from the get-go. Of the forty starters, only twelve actually ran the full 200 laps. Harroun in his Wasp crossed the finish line with a time of six hours, forty-two minutes and eight seconds. He covered 500 miles with an average speed of 74.59 miles per hour.

Today, the Indy 500 is a month-long celebration leading up to the big moment when gentlemen (and ladies) start their engines and end with the winner kissing the bricks. Most of the track was repaved with asphalt by 1938 and the remainder in 1961. Today, all that remains of the original brick surface is a 36-inch strip at the start/finish line.

The brick kissing tradition was started by NASCAR champ Dale Jarrett after his Brickyard 400 victory in 1996. Jarrett and crew chief Todd Parrott walked to the brick strip to kneel and kiss the bricks as a tribute to the fabled history of the Indianapolis Motor Speedway.

The zoo, the White River Gardens, the Medal of Honor Memorial, and the Eiteljorg Museum lie within the 250-acre **White River State Park,** which borders both sides of the waterway for which it is named in the heart of downtown Indianapolis. The park also includes **Victory Field** (home of the Indianapolis Indians, the city's AAA baseball team), **Military Park,** the popular IMAX 3-D theater, the **NCAA Hall of Champions,** and the magnificent **Indiana State Museum.** Information about the park's attractions is available at the park's visitor center at 801 W. Washington St. Open 9 a.m. to 7 p.m. Monday through Saturday and 11 a.m. to 7 p.m. Sunday from Memorial Day through Labor Day; 9 a.m. to 5 p.m. Monday through Saturday and 11 a.m. to 5 p.m. Sunday the rest of year; hours may vary, so check before going: (317) 233-2434, (800) 665-9056, or whiteriverstatepark.com.

During warm-weather months, you can ride an authentic Italian gondola on Indianapolis's Downtown Canal, complete with a serenade and a history lesson of gondolas in Venice, Italy. **Old World Gondoliers** operates from 340 W. Michigan St. by advance reservation; cruises are offered from late May through early September. Call (317) 340-2489 or visit 4gondola.com for additional information and to make an advance reservation; reservations are accepted starting on April 15. If you prefer, you can walk along the paved, 5.25-mile-long towpath that borders the canal. The August 2005 issue of *Fitness Magazine* named the towpath the fifth-best metropolitan-area hiking trail in the country.

On August 2, 1995, a group of World War II veterans gathered in downtown Indianapolis to witness the realization of a long-cherished dream. They came to dedicate a memorial that would forever honor the memory of their fallen shipmates in one of the nation's greatest wartime tragedies, the sinking of the USS *Indianapolis*. When it was hit by a Japanese torpedo on July 30, 1945, the *Indianapolis* became the last US Navy ship lost in World War II. The heavy cruiser was returning from a top-secret mission—delivering components of the atomic bomb that would be dropped on Hiroshima in early August. Because of the secrecy surrounding the mission, crew members spent five days in shark-infested waters 600 miles west of Guam before being spotted accidentally by a Navy seaplane. Only 317 of the 1,195 crew members survived. The loss of 880 men remains, to this day, the single largest loss of life in American naval warfare history.

Visitors can view the **USS Indianapolis Memorial** in the plaza at the corner of Walnut St. and Senate Ave. in downtown Indianapolis. The south face of the black-and-gray-granite monument is engraved with the names of the ship's crew and on the opposite face with a likeness of the USS *Indianapolis*. Engravings on the limestone base tell the story of the ill-fated vessel. Because

How to Move a Building

In 1930, the Indiana Bell Telephone Company in downtown Indianapolis badly needed additional space. The decision was made to move its eight-story building to an adjacent lot and erect a larger building at the original location. All this needed to be done, however, without an interruption in the company's around-the-clock service.

The move was begun by emptying the basement and attaching flexible hoses to water, sewage, and gas lines. The wires that carried electricity to the building were given some slack. Cables spliced into the telephone circuits added extra length.

A concrete slab foundation was poured on the adjacent site to accommodate the relocated building. The entrance to the building was connected to the sidewalk by a movable steel bridge. A system of jacks, I-beams, and rollers were placed next to each of the building's fifty-nine steel support columns.

With everything in place, the move was begun. The jacks raised the columns 1/4 inch off their foundations, the columns were cut loose, and the weight of the building was transferred to 4,000 steel rollers. The jacks were then simultaneously given six pumps, resulting in a move of about 3/8 inch. Gradually, moving up to 8 feet a day, the building was turned until its east-facing doors faced north. The building was then inched westward to its new site, and there it stood until 1964, when it was finally torn down and replaced.

Throughout the move, phone company employees continued their work inside the building. They felt no movement but could observe the subtle shift of the view outside the windows. Outside, interested spectators were provided with a 300-seat grandstand built specifically for observation of the monumental occasion.

A new high-rise building was erected on the vacated site while workers continued to provide telephone service in the old building. The history-making move was done in this fashion because at the time it was the most cost-effective way to do it.

this is an outdoor site, the memorial, impressive and sobering, can be viewed anytime. For additional information, call (317) 650-9058 or visit indianawar memorials.org/explore/uss-indianapolis-memorial.

Holliday Park would certainly be a top contender for honors as Indianapolis's most unusual park. Located on the west bank of the White River at 6363 Spring Mill Rd., the 94-acre park was initially developed in 1936 as a botanical garden, and the grounds still contain more than 800 species of plants. Children love its nature center and its innovative playground, especially a rope-climbing contraption that resembles a giant spider web and some twisty tube slides.

The park is most famous, however, for its "ruins." Three stone statues that formerly resided on the long-vanished St. Paul Building in New York City now perch on a ledge atop three Doric columns, dominating a setting that is the focal point of Holliday Park. Three times life-size, the kneeling figures represent white, Black, and Asian males who have labored in unity. Just behind the statues is a grotto with a fountain and reflecting pool. Twenty-five 10-foot-tall columns obtained from a local convent when it was razed several years back surround the grotto and contribute to the ruins' effect. Nearby, four statues that once stood atop Marion County's old courthouse adorn the lawn. The collection of statuary is not only eye-catching but also an imaginative contribution to the recycling effort. The park is free and open to the public daily from dawn to dusk; the nature center's hours are 9 a.m. to 5 p.m. Monday through Saturday and 1 to 5 p.m. Sunday. Call (317) 327-7180 or visit hollidaypark.org.

You can learn about the life and times of the only president from Indiana when you visit the ***Benjamin Harrison Presidential Site*** at 1230 N. Delaware St. in Indianapolis. As our twenty-third president, Harrison served just one term, from 1889 to 1893. Although relatively obscure today, Harrison is credited with several notable achievements during his four years in office. Among them are his successful promotion of pensions for war veterans and the Sherman Anti-Trust Act. Six states—North Dakota, South Dakota, Montana, Washington, Idaho, and Montana—were admitted to the Union during his tenure in office, more than in any other administration since George Washington's. He authorized our first two-ocean US Navy, making it a world power; he commissioned the flying of the US flag over schools and government buildings; and he established seventeen national forest reserves totaling 13 million acres, laying the foundation for today's national forest system. The year Harrison took office, he started the still-observed presidential tradition of planting a tree on the White House lawn; his scarlet oak survived for 118 years, finally succumbing to bad weather in 2007. Harrison also advocated civil rights, was the first president to hire a female administrative assistant, and, perhaps of particular interest today, was president when Congress appropriated a $1 billion annual spending budget for the first time in our nation's history. Harrison and his wife, Caroline, an accomplished painter, built their home in 1874; during an informative, 1-hour guided tour, you'll see such personal items as his Whitney home gym and her artwork, as well as their original furnishings and political memorabilia. First Ladies from Martha Washington forward are honored in a special exhibit, and a small gift shop offers china designed by various First Ladies for use in the White House. Admission: adults $12; senior citizens $11; children (ages 5–17) $7. Open 10 a.m. to 3:30 p.m. Monday through Saturday, and noon to 3:30 p.m. Sunday, with tours beginning on the hour and half hour; some holiday closings. Several special events are offered throughout the year; call (317) 631-1888 or visit bhpsite.org.

In the midst of **Lockerbie Square,** a six-block area of late-nineteenth-century homes near downtown Indianapolis, stands an old brick house once occupied by poet James Whitcomb Riley (for information about Riley's birthplace, see Hancock County earlier in this chapter). Riley spent the last twenty-three years of his life here, and his memorabilia are everywhere. Built in 1872, the structure and its contents have been impeccably restored and preserved in keeping with the Victorian era. It is recognized as one of the two best Victorian preservations in the country. This is not a reinterpretation of history. Riley's pen is on his desk, his suits are in the closet, and his hat is on the bed. The carpets are slightly faded, and the upholstery shows signs of wear, just as it did when Riley lived here. A humble, unpretentious man, Riley would have been astounded to learn that his home is now a major tourist attraction. Located at 528 Lockerbie St., the **James Whitcomb Riley Museum Home** is open from 10 a.m. to 3:30 p.m. Tuesday through Saturday; closed major holidays and the first two weeks in January. Admission: adults $10; children (ages 7–16) $1. For additional information, call (317) 631-5885 or visit rileymuseumhome.org. When Riley died in 1916, he was interred in **Crown Hill Cemetery.** His grave, sheltered by an elegant but simple Greek temple, is at the crest of Strawberry Hill, the highest point in Indianapolis. Coins are often left on Riley's grave. The money is given to Riley's Children Hospital in Indianapolis.

Among the other notables buried here are Benjamin Harrison, twenty-third president of the United States; three vice presidents; and the infamous John Dillinger. Ironically, it is Dillinger's grave that commands the most attention. His funeral in 1934 was the only occasion in Crown Hill's history that the cemetery had to close its gates and restrict attendance. Since then it has been necessary to replace his grave marker several times. Souvenir hunters chip away at them relentlessly, and one collector actually carried away an entire tombstone. To be sure that Dillinger's body would not be exhumed by souvenir collectors, Dillinger's father and brother had layers of iron and concrete placed over the outlaw's body.

One of the most touching monuments in the cemetery is the **Hearts Remembered Memorial,** a tribute to 699 children buried without headstones on what is known as Community Hill. The memorial, dedicated in June 2006, consists of three black granite monoliths. A 9-foot-tall center stone houses a bronze sculpture of two children, hand-in-hand, flanked by two 5-foot-tall stones that are engraved with the names of the children. All the boys and girls buried here were abandoned and neglected orphans who died between 1892 and 1980, destined to be forgotten until a charitable foundation decided to remedy the situation. The center stone bears their poignant epitaph: EVERY LIFE TOUCHES SOMEONE, AND NO LIFE SHOULD EVER BE FORGOTTEN, ESPECIALLY THE LIFE OF A CHILD.

Also located here is ***Crown Hill National Cemetery***—a cemetery-within-a-cemetery and the final resting place for nearly 2,000 soldiers, mostly Civil War veterans. The cemetery has set aside a 4-acre tract of land on the north grounds to provide additional burial space for the military; it is also home to the Field of Valor Mausoleum for above-ground burials.

Founded in 1863 on the site of a former tree farm and nursery, the cemetery is a serene and beautiful place in which to wander about in the autumn, when some 4,000 trees of more than 100 species are ablaze in fall color. The main gate at 3402 Boulevard Place is open daily during daylight hours. Before entering, however, you should stop by the office at 700 W. 38th St. and ask for a map and/or directions to the various grave sites; the cemetery covers more than 500 acres and is crisscrossed by nearly 50 miles of roads. The office is open daily 8:30 a.m. to 5 p.m. Monday through Friday and from 8:30 a.m. to 2 p.m. Saturday; the grounds are open daily from 8 a.m. to 8 p.m. April through mid-October and from 8 a.m. to 6 p.m. mid-October through March. Call (317) 925-3800 or (800) 809-3366; crownhillhf.org. Several special guided tours are offered for a nominal fee; reservations should be made in advance.

It began as one man's dream. That dream became a reality in March 1994 when the ***Indiana State Police Museum*** opened its doors to the public. One of only about a half-dozen police museums in the country, it was funded entirely by private donations and is filled with exhibits that will fascinate visitors of all ages.

indianatrivia

Richard Dillinger, half-brother of bank robber John Dillinger, worked as a mechanic for the Indiana State Police. Richard's sister Ethel also worked for the state police as a secretary.

The museum collection features vintage police cars and motorcycles, an aluminum boat used by state police scuba divers, a copper moonshine still, some John Dillinger memorabilia (including the Dillinger death mask), and handcuffs, firearms, and bulletproof vests. The Harger Drunkometer displayed here was developed in the 1920s; Indiana state troopers were the first in the nation to use it. Many of the exhibits are designed for hands-on inspection, and children especially love the two-headed police car (which is actually the front halves from two police cars welded together and facing in opposite directions). Kids can climb inside, turn on the lights and siren, and talk on the radio. There's also a tornado room where visitors can learn what to do when a tornado is approaching—the simulation is very realistic, complete with sound and fury.

The museum is the brainchild of Ernie Alder, the former director of youth services for the Indiana State Police. Located at 8660 E. 21st St., the museum is open 9 a.m. to 3 p.m. Monday through Friday or by appointment. Admission is free, but donations are appreciated. Group tours and educational programs can be arranged by appointment. Call (317) 899-8293 or (888) 477-9688 or in .gov/isp/museum

Visitors of all ages can leave their inhibitions behind and give in to the beat of the music at the **Rhythm! Discovery Center.** Operated by the Percussive Arts Society, which has its headquarters in Indianapolis, the 15,000-square-foot facility contains the world's most extensive collection of percussion instruments and artifacts in four galleries, and visitors will find instruments to play in each of them. The 1926 Wurlitzer organ, one of the five largest in the world, once provided the soundtrack for silent movies at the Paramount Theatre in New York City; you're welcome to try out such sound effects as galloping horses and train whistles. Strike an 8-foot gong drum and feel the vibrations run through your body. Rock out on a drum set, or have a jam session in the hands-on area. You'll see such rare and unusual instruments as an 87-inch-tall slit drum, bamboo bongos, a marimba-like instrument made from meteorites, and the *apentema,* a "talking" drum that mimics human vocal inflections. Admission: adults $12; senior citizens $8; students (ages 17–25) with valid student ID $9; children (ages 5–15) $6. Open Memorial Day through Labor Day on Monday from 10 a.m. to 5 p.m.; Wednesday through Saturday from 10 a.m. to 5 p.m.; Sunday noon to 5 p.m. From September through April, open Monday from 10 a.m. to 5 p.m.; Wednesday from noon to 7 p.m.; Thursday through Saturday from 10 a.m. to 5 p.m.; Sunday noon to 5 p.m. Located at 110 W. Washington St., Suite A, Lower Level; call (317) 275-9030 or visit rhythmdiscoverycenter.org.

The late author Kurt Vonnegut often stated that the happiest years of his life were those he spent in his hometown of Indianapolis. That's where he graduated from Shortridge High School in 1940; he credited the great teachers he had there with giving him a university-caliber education and encouraging him to pursue a literary career. His antiwar novel *Slaughterhouse Five,* regarded as one of the best books of the twentieth century, was born from his experiences as a German prisoner of war during World War II. To celebrate his life and work, the **Kurt Vonnegut Museum and Library** was opened in his hometown on January 29, 2011. Located at 543 Indiana Ave., the memorial includes a replica of Vonnegut's writing space, complete with his rooster lamp and his Smith Corona typewriter; his World War II Purple Heart, some early rejection letters, and some paintings done by the author. His own books and books by his favorite authors can be seen in the library, and souvenirs can be purchased in the gift shop. Admission: adults $8; senior citizens $6; students (ages 6–17) $4. A former museum opened in 2011 until its lease was up in January 2019. After a whirlwind fundraising campaign, an 1882 building was purchased to become a "forever

NCAA Hall of Champions

In the early 1900s, football was literally a deadly sport. Mass formations like the flying wedge where teammates protected the ball carrier by locking arms and gang tackling were resulting in deaths and serious injuries on the field. So disturbing was the situation that President Teddy Roosevelt called college presidents and gave them an ultimatum.

Roosevelt told them to either make the game safer or he would mandate changes to them. Fearing Roosevelt's threat to abolish football, college presidents hastened into action. When the organization that was to become the National Collegiate Athletic Association was founded, their first act was to abolish the flying wedge formation.

To commemorate this act, the Hall of Champions has a full-scale, life-sized sculpture of the menacing formation known as the flying wedge. The purpose is to demonstrate to visitors the NCAA's role in promoting and protecting the student-athlete.

"One human life is too big a price for all the games of a season," James Day, chancellor of Syracuse, said in 1905. His words are now displayed near the flying wedge sculpture.

But the flying wedge sculpture is only part of what you can find at the 25,000-square-foot attraction, located adjacent to the NCAA headquarters in White River State Park in downtown Indianapolis. The building's design is similar to a sports arena. The front doors open to a spacious great hall with a 50-foot ceiling, hung with banners celebrating collegiate sports champions.

From the first championship in 1921, Track and Field, to the modern competitions of Water Polo and Field Hockey, all twenty-four sports and ninety national championships administered by the NCAA are highlighted.

Much of the Hall of Champions is devoted to the concept of what it means to be a champion—with the focus on what it means to be a champion in life, not just in one particular competition.

home" for the museum and library. The new facility opened on November 9, 2019. Open from 10 a.m. to 7 p.m. Sunday through Tuesday; 10 a.m. to 9 p.m. Thursday through Saturday. Call (317) 652-1954 or vonnegutlibrary.org.

Just west of Indianapolis is the ***Indianapolis Motor Speedway,*** where each May the world famous Indy 500 auto race is held. When the course is not being used for competition or test purposes, you can see the track as professional racers see it by taking a bus tour around the 2.5-mile asphalt oval. Your pace, of course, will be much more leisurely, and you'll learn many interesting facts along the way.

A ***Hall of Fame Museum*** inside the track houses a vast collection of racing, classic, and antique passenger cars—including more than thirty past winners of the Indy 500—and some valuable, jewel-encrusted trophies. Perhaps the best-known artifact is the unusual Borg-Warner Trophy, which displays the sculpted, three-dimensional faces of every 500 winners since 1936. You'll also see film clips of old races, a stock car, and the Brickyard 400 trophy. This National Historic Landmark attracts visitors from around the world.

The museum and track, located at 4790 W. 16th St. in the suburb of *Speedway,* are open daily 9 a.m. to 5 p.m. from March through October and 10 a.m. to 4 p.m. November through February except Thanksgiving and Christmas; hours are extended during May. Admission: adults $12; senior citizens $11; children (ages 6–15) $8. Tour information and tickets are available at the museum; call (317) 492-6784 or visit indianapolismotorspeedway.com.

The Indy 500 track owes its existence in part to James Allison, whose legacy in the automotive and aeronautics industry endures in Indianapolis years after his death in 1928. An inventor who was fascinated with speed and racing, he was one of the partners who built the raceway. In 1915, Allison started a company to build auto parts for early 500 race cars, actually engineering the car that won the 1919 race, and expanded into the production of aircraft engines during World War I. The company went through several different affiliations before being sold to Rolls-Royce Aerospace in Indianapolis in 1995; some of the products born of that affiliation can be seen at the *James A. Allison Exhibition Center.* Located at 450 S. Meridian St., the museum displays a Liberty engine from World War I, engines from World War II fighters, an Olympus engine from the Concorde, a second-stage engine from a Titan missile, and many more. Visitors will also see a 1994 Chevrolet Caprice, built with a special gas turbine engine for road testing. Open for viewing free of charge from 9 a.m. to 3 p.m. Monday through Friday; it's most appropriate for those fourteen and older. For additional information, call (317) 230-6516 or visit rolls-royce.com/about/heritage/branches/indianapolisbranch.

The state's first medical center is also the nation's oldest surviving pathology laboratory. Housed in the Old Pathology Building on the grounds of the now-closed Central State Hospital, it remains virtually untouched by time. Known as the *Indiana Medical History Museum,* it features a fascinating collection of some 15,000 medical artifacts, including "quack" devices used in the nineteenth and early twentieth centuries, and an impressive display of brains in jars. The forty-nine brains were taken from mental patients at the hospital. *Medical Landmarks USA,* a travel guide published by McGraw-Hill in 1990, describes it as a "marvelous museum quite simply without peer in the entire country." A Medicinal Plant Garden just south of the building features medicinal plants, trees, shrubs, and vines from the Americas, Europe, Asia, and

Origins of the Circle City

Indianapolis is called "the Circle City," a little boy said, because Indy 500 cars drive in circles for hours. A cute story but the nickname really came from Alexander Ralston's nineteenth-century street layout based on concentric circles.

Alexander Ralston, who had helped Charles L'Enfant design Washington, D.C., was chosen to bring order to the heavily wooded site that would become the capital city. He designed a city modeled after Washington. He laid out Indianapolis in a circular pattern based on a square mile because that was as large as he thought the struggling city would ever become. Ralston's 1821 plan called for four diagonal streets radiating out from the center like spokes on a wagon wheel.

At the center, on a wooded knoll circled by a wide street, would sit the governor's mansion. Completed in 1827, the mansion cost $6,500 during the term of Governor James B. Ray, but the governor's wife refused to move into the home because of its lack of privacy. Having the first family's dirty laundry hung out for all to see on the public square was not a happy prospect. No governor ever lived in the mansion and it was eventually demolished in 1857. Later, Governor's Circle became known as Monument Circle when the magnificent Soldiers and Sailors Monument was completed on the site in 1901.

Africa. Open 10 a.m. to 4 p.m. Wednesday through Saturday. Admission: adults $10; senior citizens $9, college students with valid ID $7; children under age 18 $5. Visitors are taken on 1-hour guided tours that are offered on the hour only, with the last tour beginning promptly at 3 p.m.; group tours of ten or more must be scheduled in advance. The museum, which was placed on the National Register of Historic Places in 1972, is located at 3045 W. Vermont St. in Indianapolis; (317) 635-7329 or imhm.org.

In a small park on Indianapolis's north side, the **Landmark for Peace Memorial** recalls the deaths of Martin Luther King Jr. and Robert Kennedy. Robert Kennedy came to this predominantly Black neighborhood during his presidential campaign in 1968 to deliver a scheduled speech. When he arrived in Indianapolis on April 4, he learned that Dr. King had been assassinated earlier that day. The crowd that awaited Kennedy's appearance had not yet heard of Dr. King's death, so in lieu of his prepared speech, Kennedy delivered the news and asked them to look beyond their grief to continue their quest for the goals of their beloved spiritual leader. Two months later Kennedy was dead, also the victim of an assassin.

More than 100 communities across the country experienced some form of violence as the news of Dr. King's death spread, but there was not one incident of violence in Indianapolis. Robert Kennedy's heartfelt words were credited with maintaining the city's calm. To preserve the memory of what happened to two remarkable men, the city erected the Landmark for Peace Memorial in the Dr. Martin Luther King Jr. Park at 1702 N. Broadway St. The outdoor sculpture, which depicts the two men reaching toward each other with outstretched hands, was created from guns that had been turned in during a gun amnesty program and then melted down. A plaque at the site bears the words of Kennedy's speech. The memorial was formally dedicated by then President Bill Clinton in 1994. Open daily from dawn to dusk; call (317) 327-7418 or visit visitindy.com.

If you've ever had a hankering to drive around in a bright yellow limousine topped with a giant chicken, there's one available in Indianapolis. Inside, up to eight passengers can enjoy a luxurious ride enhanced by three television sets, a minibar with ice coolers at each seat, and a high-quality sound system; outside, the chicken announces its presence to all whom it passes with loud clucks and a thunderous cock-a-doodle-doo. In addition to the Chicken Limo, there's the Hippo Party Bus, and the Dragon Wagon. For additional information, call **Chicken Limo** at (317) 759-4470 or visit chickenlimo.com.

Morgan County

The Hunter family has been producing honey on its farm for more than 100 years. Now run by the fourth generation of Hunters, the Martinsville farm has several hundred hives that produce more than twenty varieties of honey. Visitors will learn how the honey is extracted from a hive, bottled, and turned into such unique products as honey beef jerky, honey chocolate sauce, honey caramel corn, honey-scented soaps and candles, and much more. They're all sold at the on-site gift shop; children especially are fascinated by the see-through hive in the shop that allows them to watch the bees at work. The shop is open from 9 a.m. to 6 p.m. from Monday through Saturday year-round. Guided tours of the farm led by knowledgeable guides are offered at 10 a.m., 1 p.m., and 3 p.m. during summer months for $5.50; call in advance to schedule a tour. As part of the tour, visitors can sample honey, see honey extracting (seasonal), watch a candle dipping demonstration, and try bottling honey. If you visit during the

indianatrivia

John Wooden, a Morgan County native, is one of only two people who have been named to the Basketball Hall of Fame as both player and coach. In 2009, a panel of coaches named Wooden the best coach of all time in any sport.

holiday season, you can also purchase your Christmas tree from the Hunters' tree farm. **Hunter's Honey Farm** is located at 6501 W. Honey Ln.; call (765) 537-9430 or visit huntershoneyfarm.com.

For a special treat, head to the **Martinsville Candy Kitchen** at 46 N. Main St. at Christmastime. That's when the shop is hand-pulling thousands of candy canes in about twenty-five different flavors and four different lengths. Visitors can watch the whole process through large windows in the back of the store. The molten candy batter is first poured onto a marble slab, then worked into a block, hung on a hook, and pulled, colored, and twisted into the familiar cane shape.

Although it's most noted for its candy canes, the shop is almost as famous for its chocolates. The late John Wooden, a Martinsville native, loved their chocolate candy so much that he had it flown to his home in California, where he had gained a reputation as the best college basketball coach of all time when his UCLA team won ten national championships in a twelve-year period.

For hours of operation, call (765) 342-6390. If you go during cane-making season, it's best to call ahead so you'll know when they're pulling cane; tasting a cane while it's still warm is a special treat.

indianatrivia

The first railroad west of the Allegheny Mountains was constructed on the east side of Shelbyville in 1834. The owner couldn't find a locomotive for the short line, which traveled 2.5 miles round-trip, so the cars were pulled by horses.

indianatrivia

When 113-year-old Bertha Fry of Muncie attended the birthday party for 114-year-old Edna Parker in Shelbyville on April 20, 2007, the women set a Guinness World Record. Their combined age of 227 years is more than that of any other known meeting of two people. Edna died on November 26, 2008, at the age of 115 years, 220 days; Bertha died November 14, 2007, at the age of 113 years, 348 days.

Shelby County

The excellent **Grover Museum of the Shelby County Historical Society** contains exhibits that depict the history of the local area. In this respect, it is not unlike other county historical museums. One display, however, is unique. Visitors may view the underwear worn by our nineteenth-century ancestors. Among the many interesting tidbits of knowledge, you'll glean from your visit is the fact that women's crotchless underpants did not originate with Victoria's

A Woman to Look Up to

When the late Sandy Allen of Shelbyville was born on June 18, 1955, she weighed 6.5 pounds and gave no indication of the extraordinary life that awaited her. Through the years, she grew—and grew and grew—until she reached the height of 7 feet, 7.25 inches tall and was recognized by the *Guinness Book of World Records* as the tallest living woman in the world, a title she held for the last sixteen years of her life.

The excessive growth hormone at work in Sandy's body was triggered by a tumor on her pituitary gland. If she had not had surgery when she was a teen to help control her growth, she might have grown even taller.

Sandy sewed most of her own clothes, wore size 22 hand-me-down sneakers provided by players in the National Basketball Association, and slept in an 8-foot-long custom-made bed. She held a few jobs along the way, including one as a secretary in the office of a former mayor of Indianapolis and another as part of the staff at the Guinness Museum in Niagara Falls, New York. She also appeared in the acclaimed Frederico Fellini movie, *Casanova,* in the role of Angelina the Giantess.

As her health declined, Sandy was forced to spend much of her time in a wheelchair. Although she could no longer work and make a living, her spirits remained high. She visited with schoolchildren as often as possible and delivered her message that "It's Okay to Be Different" with great wit and charm.

Eventually it became necessary for her to move into a retirement home in her home-town of Shelbyville, where she met Edna Parker, a fellow resident who was then the acknowledged oldest living woman in the world. Sadly, Sandy passed away at age fifty-three on August 13, 2008, and Edna died soon after on November 26, 2008, at the age of 115 years and 220 days old.

Upon meeting Sandy, it was impossible, of course, not to notice her physical stature, but after leaving her presence, it was her enormous heart that one remembered.

Secret or Frederick's of Hollywood. They were worn for efficiency's sake (all those long skirts and outhouses to contend with, you know) by inventive females in the 1800s. The museum also houses a model railroad layout and re-creations of twenty-six shops from Shelbyville's past that are known collectively as the Streets of Old Shelby. Located at 52 W. Broadway St. in downtown **Shelbyville,** the museum is open from 9 a.m. to 4 p.m. Tuesday through Saturday or by special arrangement. Admission is free; call (317) 392-4634 or visit grovermuseum.org.

OTHER ATTRACTIONS WORTH SEEING IN CENTRAL INDIANA

ANDERSON

Paramount Theatre and Ballroom Tour
1124 Meridian Plaza
(765) 642-1234 or
(800) 523-4658
andersonparamount.org

ELWOOD

House of Glass
7900 SR 28 East
(765) 552-6841
thehouseofglassinc.com

INDIANAPOLIS

Indianapolis Firefighters Museum
748 Massachusetts Ave.
(317) 262-5161
I416.com

Fort Harrison State Park
6000 N. Post Road
(317) 591-0904
in.gov/dnr/parklake/2982.htm

Holcomb Observatory and Planetarium
Butler University
4600 Sunset Ave.
(317) 940-8333 or
(800) 368-6852
butler.edu/holcomb-observatory

Indiana History Center
450 W. Ohio St.
(317) 232-1882
indianahistory.org

Indiana State Museum
650 W. Washington St.
(317) 232-1637
indianamuseum.org

NCAA Hall of Champions
700 W. Washington St.
(017) 916-4255
ncaahallofchampions.org

Scottish Rite Cathedral
650 N. Meridian St.
(317) 262-3110
aasr-indy.org

Tipton County

Jim Richardson loves the 1950s. He loves them so much that he and his wife, Tricia, have created a life-size working 1950s town in their 3-acre backyard. Called **Summer Place,** it is a work in progress, but it already contains a gas station (with a sign advertising gas for 23.9 cents a gallon), a movie theater, a diner, a police station, a fire station that contains a 1955 Mack fire truck, a barbershop, and a train station—all historically accurate. Cars and bicycles from the 1950s are parked around town, and a phone booth stands on the corner. When you enter the town, the sign that greets you reads TOWN OF SUMMER PLACE, POPULATION: MANY HAPPY PEOPLE.

Visitors who yearn for a gentler time when life flowed at a slower pace come from all over the country to enjoy the ambience of this unique and special place; they learn about it from one of the more than twenty-five television shows on which it's been featured. Although Summer Place is not open to the public on a regular basis, it's open by appointment and for the several public charity events the Richardsons sponsor each year. During those events, the diner is open for business, serving up such fare as cheeseburgers, fries, sodas, and banana splits, and the theater offers movies and popcorn. All proceeds and donations go to the Richardsons' foundation, A Home for Every Child, which finds adoptive homes for unwanted children.

Summer Place is located at 4190 N. SR 19 in **Sharpsville.** For a schedule of events and for up-to-date information, call the Richardsons at (765) 963-5943 or visit asummerplace.org.

Places to Stay in Central Indiana

BROWNSBURG

Comfort Suites West
500 W. Northfield Dr.
(317) 852-2000
choicehotels.com

Quality Inn & Suites
31 Maplehurst Dr.
(317) 852-5353
choicehotels.com

CARMEL

Hotel Carmichael, Autograph Collection
1 Carmichael Ln.
(317) 688-1700
marriott.com

DANVILLE

Marmalade Sky
337 N. Washington St.
(317) 507-3993
themarmaladesky.com

FRANKLIN

Ashley-Drake Historic Inn and Gardens
668 E. Jefferson St.
(317) 736-0199
ashleydrakeinn.com

The Flying Frog Bed and Breakfast
396 N. Main St.
(317) 697-3212
theflyingfrogbedand
breakfast.com

FISHERS

Prairie Guest House
13805 Allisonville Rd.
(317) 663-8728
prairieguesthouse.com

FORTVILLE

Ivy House Bed and Breakfast
304 N. Merrill St.
(317) 485-4800
ivyhousebb.com

INDIANAPOLIS

The Alexander
333 S. Delaware St.
(317) 624-8200
thealexander.com

Buck Creek Farm
11944 Southeastern Ave.
(317) 862-0003
buckcreekfarm.com

Conrad Indianapolis
50 W. Washington St.
(317) 713-5000
conradindianapolis.com

Fort Harrison State Park Inn
5830 N. Post Rd.
(317) 638-6000 or
(877) 937-3678
In.gov/dnr/parklake/inns/
fharrison

Harney House Inn
345 N. East St.
(317) 636-7527
harneyhouseinn.com

Hilton Indianapolis Hotel & Suites
120 W. Market St.
(317) 972-0600
hilton.com

Hotel Broad Ripple
6520 E. Westfield Blvd.
(317) 787-2665
hotelbroadripple.com

Inn of Beginnings
6918 W. Thompson Rd.
(317) 695-0954
innofbeginnings.com

Ironworks Hotel Indy
2721 E. 86th St.
(463) 221-2200
ironworkshotelindy.com

**JW Marriott.com
Indianapolis**
10 S. West St.
(317) 860-5800
marriott.com

Le Meridien Indianapolis
123 S. Illinois St.
(317) 737-1600
marriot.com

Looking Glass Inn
1319 N. New Jersey St.
(317) 639-9550
thelookingglassinn.com

Omni Severin Hotel
40 W. Jackson Pl.
(317) 634-6664
omnihotels.com

Nestle Inn
637 N. East St.
(317) 610-5200 or
(877) 339-5200
nestleindy.com

**Old Northside Bed and
Breakfast**
1340 N. Alabama St.
(317) 635-9123 or
(800) 635-9127
oldnorthsideinn.com

Speedway Legacy Inn
1829 Cunningham Rd.
(317) 677-3733
speedwaylegacyinn.com

Stone Soup Inn
1304 N. Central Ave.
(317) 639-9550 or
(866) 639-9550
stonesoupinn.com

PLAINFIELD

**SpringHill Suites by
Marriott**
6014 Gateway Dr.
(317) 279-2394
marriott.com

ZIONSVILLE

Brick Street Inn
175 S. Main St.
(317) 873-1900 or
(855) 873-1900
brickstreetinn.com

Places to Eat in Central Indiana

ALEXANDRIA

Curve Inn
114 S. Park Ave.
(765) 724-2722
thecurveinn.net
Comfort food

Rachel's Hi-Way Cafe
2617 S. Park Ave.
(765) 724-2944
rachelshiwaycafe.com
American

ANDERSON

Burro Loco
21 W. 8th St.
(765) 640-6565
burrolocoin.com
Mexican

The Lemon Drop
1701 Mounds Rd.
(765) 644-9055
American

Ninja of Japan
21 W. 38th St.
(765) 393-2613
ninjaofjapantogo.com
Asian, sushi

BEECH GROVE

**El Mariachi Mexican
Restaurant**
3535 S. Emerson Ave.
(317) 755-2370
elmariachi-bg.com
Mexican

**Fujiyama Steak House of
Japan**
5149 Victory Dr.
(317) 787-7900
fujiyamaindy.com
Hibachi grill/sushi bar

**Napoli Villa Italian
Restaurant**
758 Main St.
(317) 783-4122
napoliindy.com
Italian

1949 Tavern
914 Main St.
(317) 591-9026
1949tavern.com
Bar food

CARMEL

Bub's Burgers
210 W. Main St.
(317) 706-2827
bubsburgers.com
Burgers/fast food

Charleston's Restaurant
14636 Greyhound Plaza
(317) 846-5965
charlestons.com
American

**Convivio Italian Artisan
Cuisine**
11529 Spring Mill Rd.
(317) 564-4670
convivoindy.com
Italian

divvy
71 City Center Dr.
(317) 706-0000
divvycarmel.com
American

DANVILLE

Courthouse Grounds
65 S. Washington St.
(317) 563-3131
courthousegrounds.com
Comfort food

Mayberry Cafe
78 W. Main St.
(317) 745-4067
mayberrycafe.com
Home cooking

FISHERS

Detour American Grille & Bar
10158 Brooks School Rd.
(317) 669-9333
detourgrille.com
American

LouVino Fishers Restaurant & Wine Bar
8626 E. 116th St.
(317) 598-5160
louvino.com
Southern

Peterson's
7690 E. 96th St.
(317) 598-8863
Petersonsrestaurant.com
Steak/seafood

Pure Eatery Fishers
8235 E. 116th St.
(317) 288-0285
pureeatery.com

GREENFIELD

Carnegie's
100 W. North St.
(317) 462-8480
carnegies-restaurant.com
Italian

Dragon Palace
413 N. State St.
(317) 462-4965
dragonpalacegreenfield
.com

Chinese

GREENWOOD

Green Ginger
1675 W. Smith Valley Rd.
(317) 743-8288
greengingergreenwood
.com
Sushi

Stone Creek Dining Company
911 N. S. R. 135
(317) 889-1200
stonecreekdining.com
American

INDIANAPOLIS

Ambrosia
5903 N. College Ave.
(317) 255-3096
ambrosiaindy.com
Italian

Bluebeard
653 Virginia Ave.
(317) 686-1580
bluebeardindy.com
New American

Bakersfield Mass Ave
334 Massachusetts Ave.
(317) 635-6962
bakersfieldtacos.com
Mexican

Bazbeaux
329 Massachusetts Ave.
(317) 636-7662
bazbeaux.com
Italian

Café Patachou
225 W. Washington St.
(317) 632-0765
cafepatachou.com
Eclectic

The Eagle's Nest
1 S. Capitol Ave.
(317) 616-6170
hyatt.com

American

Harry & Izzy's
153 S. Illinois St.
(317) 635-9594
harryandizzys.com
Steak/American

Hollyhock Hill
8110 N. College Ave.
(317) 251-2294
hollyhockhill.com
Home cooking

Iaria's Italian Restaurant
317 S. College Ave.
(317) 638-7706
Iariasrestaurant.com
Italian

Kona Jack's
9419 N. Meridian St.
(317) 843-1609
jacksarebetter.net
Seafood/sushi

Mama Carolla's Old Italian Restaurant
1031 E. 54th St.
(317) 259-9412
mamacarollas.com
Italian

Mesh on Mass
725 Massachusetts Ave.
(317) 955-9600
Meshrestaurants.com
Eclectic/vegetarian/vegan

Morton's The Steakhouse
41 E. Washington St.
(317) 229-4700
mortons.com
Steakhouse

Naked Tchopstix
3855 E. 96th St. A.
(317) 569-6444
nakedtchopstix96.com
Sushi

1913 Restaurant
40 W. Jackson Pl.

(317) 634-6664
omnihotels.com
American

Oakleys Bistro
1464 W. 86th St.
(317) 824-1231
oakleysbistro.com
American

**Rathskeller at the
Athenaeum**
401 E. Michigan St.
(317) 636-0396
rathskeller.com
German/American

Rook
501 Virginia Ave.
(317) 737-2293
rookindy.com
Asian

Saffron Café
621 Fort Wayne Ave.
(317) 917-0131

saffroncafeindy.com
Moroccan

**Shapiro's Delicatessen
and Cafeteria**
808 S. Meridian St.
(317) 631-4041
shapiros.com
Deli/American

Slippery Noodle Inn
372 S. Meridian St.
(317) 631-6974
slipperynoodle.com
American

Spoke & Steele
123 Illinois St.
(317) 737-1616
spokeandsteele.com
American

St. Elmo Steak House
127 Illinois St.
(317) 635-0636
stelmos.com

Steak/seafood

Sullivan's Steakhouse
3316 E. 86th St.
(317) 580-1280
Sullivanssteakhouse.com
Steak/seafood

Thai Taste Restaurant
5353 E. 82nd St.
(317) 578-9722
thaitasteindy.com
Thai

Union 50
620 N. East St.
(317) 610-0234
Union-50.com
American

Vida
601 E. New York St.
(317) 420-2323
vida-restaurant.com
Modern American

SOURCES FOR ADDITIONAL INFORMATION ABOUT CENTRAL INDIANA

**Anderson/Madison
County Visitors Bureau**
6335 Scatterfield Rd.
Anderson 46013
(765) 643-5633 or
(800) 533-6569
visitandersonmadisoncoun
ty.com

**Boone County
Convention and
Visitors Bureau**
101 E. Main St.
Lebanon 46052
(765) 484-8572
boonecvb.com

**Franklin (Johnson
County) Chamber of
Commerce**
370 E. Jefferson St.
Franklin 46131
(317) 736-6334
franklincoc.org

**Greater Greenwood
(Johnson County)
Chamber of
Commerce**
65 Airport Pkwy., Suite 140
Greenwood 46142
(317) 888-4856
aspirejohnsoncounty.com

**Greater Martinsville
(Morgan County)
Chamber of Commerce**
464 S. Main St.
Martinsville 46151
(765) 342-8110
martinsvillechamber.com

**Greater Mooresville
(Morgan County)
Chamber of
Commerce**
4 E. Harrison St.
Mooresville 46158
(317) 831-6509
mooresvillechamber.com

Hamilton County
Convention and
Visitors Bureau
37 E. Main St.
Carmel 46032
(317) 848-3181
Visithamiltoncounty.com

Hancock County
Tourism and
Visitor Center
119 W. North St.
Greenfield 46140
(317) 477-8687
visitinhancock.org

Hendricks County
Convention and
Visitors Bureau
8 W. Main St.
Danville 46122
(317) 718-8750 or
(800) 321-9666
visithendrickscounty.com

Indianapolis Conven-
tion and Visitors Asso-
ciation (Marion County)
200 S. Capitol Ave.,
Suite 300
Indianapolis 46225
(317) 262-3000 or
(800) 323-4639
visitindy.com

Shelby County Tourism
and Visitors Bureau
501 N. Harrison St., Suite C
Shelbyville 46176
(317) 398-9623 or
(888) 303-0244
visitshelbycounty.com

Zionsville Chamber of
Commerce
1100 W. Oak St., Suite 214
Zionsville 46077
(317) 873-3836
zionsvillechamber.org

MOORESVILLE

Gray Brothers Cafeteria
555 S. Indiana St.
(317) 831-7234
graybroscafe.com
Home cooking

MORRISTOWN

**Kopper Kettle Inn
Restaurant**
135 E. Main St.
(US 52)
(765) 763-6767
kopperkettle.com
American

NOBLESVILLE

Aspen Creek Grill
13489 Tegler Dr.
(317) 559-3300
aspencreekgrill.com
Steakhouse

Books & Brews
13230 Harrell Pkwy.
(317) 770-8119
American

**Stone Creek Dining
Company**
13904 Town Center Blvd.

(317) 770-1170
stonecreekdining.com
American

PENDLETON

Catello's Mozzarella Bar
103 E. State St.
(317) 498-5906
catellos.com
Italian

PERKINSVILLE

Bonge's Tavern
9830 W. CR 280
North
(765) 734-1625
bongestavern.com
American

SHELBYVILLE

Fiddlers Three
1415 E. Michigan Rd.
(317) 392-4371
thefiddlersthree.com
American

Just Peachy Café
52 E. Washington St.
(317) 825-0669
justpeachycafe.com
Comfort food

SPEEDWAY

Barbecue and Bourbon
1414 N. Main St.
(317) 241-6940
barbecueandbourbon.com
Barbecue

Dawson's on Main
1464 N. Main St.
(317) 247-7000
dawsonsonmain.com
Steaks/seafood

Union Jack Pub
6225 W. 25th St.
(317) 243-3300
unionjackpubspeedway.com
American/pizza

ZIONSVILLE

Cobblestone
160 S. Main St.
(317) 873-4745
cobblestonez.com
New American

The Friendly Tavern
290 S. Main St.
(317) 873-5772
friendlytavernzionsville.com
American

Northeast Indiana

Perhaps best known as Amish country, northeast Indiana is home to one of the largest populations of Old Order Amish in the world. For the most part, it is a serene and pastoral world, sculpted long ago by the glaciers of the Ice Age. Beyond the scattering of towns and cities, the gentle hills sometimes seem to march on forever. Natural lakes are small but abundant; Steuben County alone is dotted with 101 of them.

Although travelers can hurry north and south on I-69 or east and west on I-80/90 (Indiana's only toll road), those who want to experience the simple charms of this part of the Hoosier State will set out on back roads and byways. It is there that they will discover the essence of this pocket of peace.

Adams County

In the Swiss village of **Berne,** you can visit the ***First Mennonite Church.*** Located at 566 W. Main St. (260-589-3108; firstmennonite.org), the classic Gothic structure is one of the two largest Mennonite churches in North America. The main sanctuary can seat some 2,000 people. Of particular note is the Moeller organ with its 2,281 pipes, which have produced

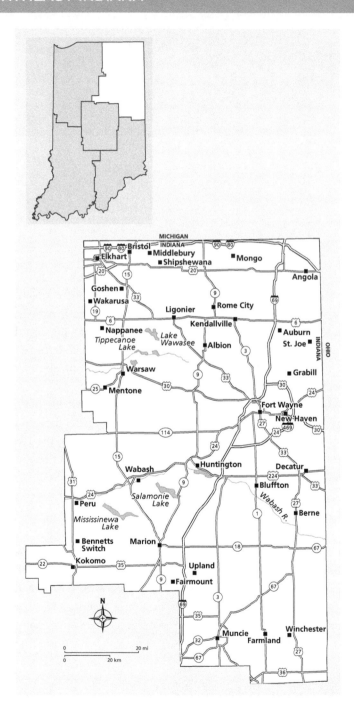

beautiful music since 1914. Visitors come from all over the United States, Canada, and Europe to tour the church and listen to the organ. The church is open to visitors daily from 9 a.m. to 4:30 p.m.; Sunday services are held at 10 a.m.

At the **Swiss Heritage Village and Museum,** you can see twelve restored structures on 26 acres that provide a glimpse of the lifestyle of the Swiss immigrants who settled in this area between 1860 and 1900. A **Heritage Festival** held each September features Swiss singing, stone throwing, historic crafts, and cider making on the world's largest cider press. Built during the Civil War, the gigantic hand-hewn press weighs about 2 tons. The village and museum are open 10 a.m. to 4 p.m. Monday through Saturday June through October, and at other times for special events. Admission: adults $6; senior citizens $5; children (ages 6–12) $3. Located at 1200 Swiss Way in Berne; (260) 589-8007; swissheritage.org.

In further tribute to its Swiss heritage, the town of Berne erected a unique, 160-foot-tall clock tower modeled after the famous Zytglogge clock tower in Bern, Switzerland. Dedicated on July 31, 2010, it features four clock faces and a carillon capable of playing more than 1,000 songs, including "On the Banks of the Wabash," "Back Home Again in Indiana," and tunes by native sons Cole Porter, Hoagy Carmichael, and John Mellencamp. A 7-foot-tall statue known as "Bernard the Bell Ringer" strikes the bell in the cupola at the top of each hour with a clockwork-operated hammer. Each day at 3, 6, and 9 p.m., to the accompaniment of carillon music, twelve animated glockenspiel figurines tell the story of the settlement of Berne as they revolve in and out of the tower wall. The clock tower is the focal point of Muensterberg Plaza public park. The **Muensterberg Plaza and Clock Tower** are located at the intersection of US 27 and SR 218. For up-to-date information, contact the Berne Community Development Corporation, PO Box 27, Berne 46711; (260) 589-3139; berne-clocktower.org.

For information about Berne's unusual shops and stores, many of which cater to the area's 4,000 Amish residents, contact the Berne Chamber of Commerce, 205 E. Main St., Berne 46711; (260) 589-8080; bernein.com.

indianatrivia

In the 1890s, the largest reservoir of oil discovered anywhere in the world up to that time was found in Indiana. Known as the Trenton oil field, it extended under parts of eight counties in the northeast quadrant of the state.

Allen County

John Chapman, better known as Johnny Appleseed, traveled on foot through much of the Midwest, planting seeds that would one day grow into vast apple orchards. In his own time he was much beloved, and he remains a folk hero to this day. What most folks don't realize is that Johnny didn't wander about in all those raggedy clothes because he had to. Johnny was a miser—kindly, but a miser nevertheless—who found free room and board with families along the routes he followed, planted some apple seeds in their fields, and eventually moved on. It was no surprise to those who knew him that his death on March 18, 1845, was due to exposure. He died near **Fort Wayne** and was buried there with honors. His gravesite, open at all times to the public, is located in the 43-acre **Johnny Appleseed Park,** located at 1500 N. Harry Baals Dr.; (260) 427-6000; fortwayneparks.com. A festival held annually on the third full weekend in September since 1974 has grown so much in popularity that it has expanded into adjoining Archer Park to accommodate all the visitors and vendors; (260) 424-3700 or (800) 767-7752; johnnyappleseedfest.com.

AUTHOR'S FAVORITE ATTRACTIONS/ EVENTS IN NORTHEAST INDIANA

Aloha International Hawaiian Steel Guitar Convention
Winchester; July
aisgc.org

Auburn-Cord-Duesenberg Festival
Auburn; September (week before Labor Day)
(260) 925-3600 or (877) 833-3282
acdfestival.org

Auburn-Cord-Duesenberg Museum
Auburn
(260) 925-1444
automobilemuseum.org

Circus City Festival
Peru; July
(765) 472-3918
perucircus.com

Easter Pageant
Marion; Easter weekend
(765) 664-0544
easterpageant.com

Fairmount Museum Days/Remembering James Dean
Fairmount; September
(765) 948-4555
jamesdeanartifacts.com

Grissom Air Museum
Peru
(765) 689-8011
grissomairmuseum.com

International Circus Hall of Fame
Peru
(765) 472-7553 or
(800) 771-0241
visit.circushalloffame.com

Menno-Hof Visitors Center
Shipshewana
(260) 768-4117
mennohof.org

Midwest Museum of American Art
Elkhart
(574) 293-6660
midwestmuseum.org

The 40-acre **Fort Wayne Children's Zoo,** with more than 500 domestic and exotic animals, delights visitors of all ages. Although small, it has been internationally recognized for its landscaping and cleverly designed exhibits. *Travel America* says this is "simply the best children's zoo in the nation," the *New York Times* calls it one of the top five children's zoos in the country, and *Child* and *Parents* magazines have both chosen it as one of the "Ten Best Zoos

indianatrivia

The world's first practical gas pump was invented in Fort Wayne in 1885 by Sylvanus F. Bowser. Fort Wayne is also the home of the first gas pump that could accurately measure the amount of gas dispensed and give the price in dollars and cents; it was offered to the public in 1932.

for Kids." Children love to feed the animals, pet tame deer, and ride the miniature train and the endangered-species carousel. The whole family will love the safari through a recreated African veldt where all animals roam free. An exhibit devoted to Australian wildlife includes a 20,000-gallon Great Barrier Reef aquarium, a 50,000-gallon shark aquarium, and two 500-gallon jellyfish tanks. The Indonesian Rain Forest features a Sumatran elephant skeleton, rare Sumatran tigers roaming in a half-acre re-creation of their outdoor habitat, and endangered Sumatran orangutans. If you want the orangutans to notice you, wear red or pink; they seem to be partial to those colors. Open 9 a.m. to 5 p.m. daily late April through mid-October. Admission: adults $15; senior citizens $12; children (ages 2–18) $10. Located at 3411 Sherman Blvd. in Fort Wayne's Franke Park; (260) 427-6800; kidszoo.org.

One of the most breathtaking sights in downtown Fort Wayne is the **Foellinger-Freimann Botanical Conservatory.** A series of three buildings connected by tunnels, it is one of the largest passive solar structures in the United States. Some 1,300 panels of insulating glass permit the sunshine to enter; moreover, the city passed special zoning laws to ensure that all available sunlight could reach the buildings unobstructed. Visitors will see displays of North American desert plants, rare tropical plants from around the world, a talking tree, a worm tunnel, and changing seasonal exhibits. Admission: adults $5; children (ages 3–17) $3. Open 10 a.m. to 5 p.m. Tuesday through Saturday and noon to 4 p.m. Sunday; hours extended to 8 p.m. on Thursday; closed Monday, Labor Day, Christmas Day, and New Year's Day. Located at 1100 S. Calhoun St.; (260) 427-6440; botanicalconservatory.org.

Anyone interested in architecture will want to see the **Cathedral of the Immaculate Conception,** a Gothic-style church in the center of Fort Wayne. Its Bavarian stained-glass windows are recognized as the finest in the Western Hemisphere, and its hand-carved wood altar is considered one of the finest woodcarvings in the country. Maps are available for self-guided tours of the church, which is open 8:45 a.m. to 4:30 p.m. Monday through Friday; 1 to 6 p.m. on Saturday; and 7:30 a.m. to 6 p.m. on Sunday. Located at 1122 S. Clinton St.; (260) 424-1485; cathedraloffortwayne.org.

Fort Wayne is also home to one of the finest genealogical research facilities in the country. The collection, second in size only to the one in Salt Lake City that's owned by the Mormon Church, is housed in the **Allen County Public Library** at 900 Library Plaza. Included in the materials found here in the library's Genealogy Center are more than 370,000 printed volumes, some 590,000 microforms, military records dating back to the 1700s, city directories, census records, and much more; at this writing, the collection totals more than 961,700 items, as well as an extensive computer database. Each month about 1,500 new items are added to the collection. More than 100,000 visitors use the resources of the genealogy department each year, free of charge. The library is open 9 a.m. to 9 p.m. Monday through Thursday, 9 a.m. to 6 p.m. Friday and Saturday, and 1 to 6 p.m. Sunday; closed Sunday from Memorial Day weekend through Labor Day weekend. For additional information, write the library at PO Box 2270, Fort Wayne 46802; call (260) 421-1200, or visit acpl-cms.wise .oclo.org.

Until the **Lincoln Museum** in Fort Wayne closed in 2008, it was home to the largest private collection of Lincoln memorabilia in the world. Such entities as the Smithsonian Institution in Washington, DC, and the Lincoln Presidential Library and Museum in Springfield, IL, wanted the $20-million-dollar collection, but it was awarded to the state of Indiana. Among the many treasures in the collection are the original photo of Lincoln that's used on our $5 bill, the inkwell Lincoln used to sign the Emancipation Proclamation, and a rare copy of the slavery-abolishing 13th Amendment, one of only three in the world, that bears the signatures of Lincoln and the senators who passed it. The latter has an estimated value of $1.5 million. The Allen County Public Library and the Indiana State Museum in Indianapolis are now the joint stewards of the collection, and the library has begun the process of digitalizing all the materials. It is an ongoing project that will take several years to complete, but you can view numerous photographs that have

indianatrivia

Philo T. Farnsworth, acknowledged as the inventor of electronic television, received a patent for the first television system on August 26, 1930. His company produced television sets in Fort Wayne from 1938 to 1967. Farnsworth was one of four inventors honored in 1983 by the US Postal Service, which issued a stamp bearing his portrait.

ANNUAL EVENTS IN NORTHEAST INDIANA

Wakarusa Maple Syrup Festival
Wakarusa; April
(574) 862-4344
wakarusachamber.com

Cole Porter Festival
Peru; June
(765) 472-1923
coleporterfestival.org

Haynes-Apperson Festival
Kokomo; July 4th weekend
(765) 457-5301
haynesappersonfestival.org

Swiss Days Festival
Berne; July
(260) 589-8080
swissdaysberne.com

Three Rivers Festival
Fort Wayne; July
(260) 426-5556
threeriversfestival.org

Pickle Festival
St. Joe; July
(260) 920 8269
stjoepicklefestival.org

Popcorn Festival
Van Buren; August
(765) 934-4888
popcornfestivalofvanburen.org

Apple Festival
Nappanee; September
(574) 773-7812
nappaneeapplefestival.org

Forks of the Wabash Pioneer Festival
Huntington; September
(260) 359-0176 or (800) 848-4282
pioneerfestival.org

Grabill Country Fair
Grabill; September
(260) 627 5227 or (800) 767-7752
grabillcountryfair org

Johnny Appleseed Festival
Fort Wayne; September
(260) 483 5638
johnnyappleseedfest.com

The Christmas City Walkway of Lights
Marion; late November to late December
(765) 662-9931
walkwayoflights.org

already been digitalized at the library's website: lincolncollection.org. More items are being added all the time, so check back often.

DeBrand Fine Chocolates of Fort Wayne has gained a reputation as one of the world's elite makers of fine chocolates. Donald Trump is a customer; he contracted with DeBrand to stock the luxury suite used by *The Apprentice* candidates with about 3,000 gold- or silver-foil-covered chocolate bars stamped with the name Trump. For $5, you can see and taste why during a tour that includes a video presentation, a tour of the company's three kitchens, and a sampling of the wares. The tour cost includes a rebate of $5 off a $10 or more purchase. If you like what you taste, you can purchase more to take with you at an on-site shop. DeBrand is also noted for its artisan marshmallows; in 2006, the cocoa flavor was named the best in the US by the *Wall Street Journal.* Located at 10105 Auburn Park Dr.; call (260) 969-8333 or visit debrand.com for tour information. Open tours are offered at the Auburn Park Drive shop 10 a.m. and 1 p.m. on Tuesday and Thursday from Memorial Day through Labor Day; they're also offered at 10 a.m. on Tuesday and at 1 p.m. on Thursday year-round. Reservations are required for groups of twelve or more. The shop is open 7 a.m. to 9 p.m. Monday through Friday; 10 a.m. to 9 p.m. Saturday; and noon to 6 p.m. Sunday. DeBrand Chocolates also has shops at 5608 Coldwater Rd., 4110 W. Jefferson Blvd., and 878 Harrison St.

Exhibits at the ***African/African-American Museum*** in Fort Wayne highlight the heritage and culture of African Americans throughout our country's history. You'll learn about prominent Blacks in politics, science, music, and sports. One exhibit describes how Blacks escaped from slavery in the South to freedom in the North via the Underground Railroad. Open 10 a.m. to 2 p.m. Tuesday, Thursday, and Saturday. Docent-led tours are available. Located at 436 E. Douglas Ave. Admission: adults $7; children $5; (260) 420-0765.

For a get-away-from-it-all experience, travel southwest from downtown Fort Wayne to the 605-acre ***Fox Island County Park.*** There, in a 270-acre state nature preserve, you'll see a 40-foot sand dune and an unusual (for Indiana) quaking bog whose surface ripples when you stamp your feet. You may also want to check out the nature center at the park. Located at 7324 Yohne Rd.; (260) 449-3180 or allencountyparks.org/parks/fox-island.

The peaceful little town of ***Grabill,*** located in the center of an Amish farming community northeast of Fort Wayne, is a lovely place to explore crafts and antiques shops. ***H. Souder & Son's General Store*** at 13535 Main St. is an authentic general store steeped in nostalgia; you'll find such old-fashioned delights as penny candies, tin toys, old-time medicines, and rustic housewares. Open Monday through Saturday 9 a.m. to 5 p.m. Call (260) 627-3994 for more information.

Each year in September, the ***Grabill Country Fair*** lures more than 100,000 people from throughout the Midwest. The fun includes contests for seed spitting, frog jumping, chicken flying, and wife calling. Go north from Fort Wayne onto SR 1 to Hosler Road in the town of Leo, then turn east onto Hosler Road. For additional information, contact the Grabill Chamber of Commerce, 13717 1st St., PO Box 254, Grabill 46741; (260) 627-5227, ext. 4, or (866) 939-5227; grabill.net.

Born to Fly

From the moment Margaret Ray Ringenberg took her first airplane ride in 1928 at the age of seven, the little farm girl from Grabill knew that she wanted to spend her life in the air. She succeeded beyond her wildest dreams when she grew up to become one of the most celebrated female pilots of her generation.

After earning her pilot's license at the age of twenty, Margaret applied for admission to the Women Airforce Service Pilots (WASP) program, created during World War II to perform stateside duties that freed up male pilots for overseas combat. She was one of 1,830 women accepted for the program from more than 25,000 applicants and one of only 1,074 who passed the training. She and other WASPs transported personnel, ferried new aircraft from factories to bases, towed targets that were shot at by antiaircraft gunners, and trained male pilots for combat duty.

When the WASPs program was terminated in December 1944, Margaret returned to Indiana and took a desk job at Smith Field Airport near Fort Wayne, where she also gave flying lessons when regular instructors weren't available. In 1946, she married a local banker named Morris Ringenberg and had two children. The couple had a very simple prenuptial agreement: He could play golf whenever he wanted, and she could fly whenever she wanted. Their union endured for fifty-six years until Morris's death in 2003.

In 1957, Margaret began competing in cross-country air races for women and won more than 150 trophies. She competed in an around-the-world air race in 1994; she was seventy-two, the oldest entrant in the race. In 2001, at the age of seventy-nine, she flew in a race from London to Sydney, Australia. She competed in every Air Race Classic (ARC), held each June, since its inception in 1986; she won in 1988, placed second in 2003, and consistently placed in the top ten.

In addition to her racing, she was much in demand as a motivational speaker, sharing her experiences with such audiences as Air Force Academy cadets in Colorado Springs and NASA employees. According to her granddaughter, the latter group let Margaret try out the space shuttle simulator, advising her that almost all pilots who trained on it crashed a few times until they got the hang of it. Margaret landed it perfectly each time she tried.

In June 2008, at the age of eighty-seven, Margaret participated in her last ARC race, finishing in third place. On July 28, 2008, Margaret passed away in her sleep while attending an Experimental Aircraft Association event in Oshkosh, WI. She had logged more than 40,000 miles in the air (she stopped counting after 40,000), more than most airline pilots. Two rooms in her family home bore testament to her extraordinary life; they were filled from floor to ceiling with hundreds of trophies and awards.

Tom Brokaw chose Margaret as one of the World War II heroes he profiled in his 1998 bestseller, *The Greatest Generation.* He expressed great sadness at the news of her death and said that she had been one of his favorite subjects.

Railroad buffs will enjoy a visit to **TrainTown,** located at 15808 Edgerton Rd. in **New Haven,** where some part of railroad history is almost always being taken apart or put back together in a restoration shop by members of the Fort Wayne Railroad Historical Society. One

of the projects was the restoration of the old Nickel Plate 765 steam locomotive, restored piece by piece between 1993 and 2005.

Shop projects are ongoing. Visitors are welcome to lend a hand with whatever restoration program might be under way at the time of their visit. For a fee, a volunteer will show anyone 18 or older how to operate a 44-ton working diesel engine built in 1953. Participants receive instruction on general locomotive operation on the society's trackage. The society also offers excursions on trains they've made roadworthy, including the 765.

Plans in the works include the restoration of the Lake Erie and Fort Wayne six-coupled steam locomotive No. 1. The workshops and the TrainTown museum are open free of charge from 10 a.m. to 4 p.m. on Saturday; fees are charged for the excursions and locomotive operation instructions. Everything here is done by volunteers, so call before visiting to make sure someone will be on hand to show you around. For additional information, write the Fort Wayne Railroad Historical Society, PO Box 11017, Fort Wayne 46855; call (260) 493-0765; or visit fortwaynerailroad.org.

DeKalb County

A rare treat awaits old-car buffs in the town of **Auburn.** Housed in the administration building of the old Auburn Automobile Company is one of the country's finest collections of cars.

The **Auburn-Cord-Duesenberg Museum** and its contents complement each other perfectly. Constructed in 1930, the building is an architectural masterpiece of the art deco style. The automobiles within it are among the most beautiful ever produced—products of a golden age when luxury and power were the gods of the road. Some 140 classic, antique, special-interest, and one-of-a-kind cars dating from 1898 to the present are on permanent display here.

Indiana was once the automobile capital of the world, and Auburn was its heart, the birthplace of twenty-one of America's early motorcars. The Duesenbergs designed and produced here were the costliest domestic automobiles of the 1920s and 1930s—commanding prices of $15,000 to $20,000 even in the midst of the Great Depression. Greta Garbo owned one, as did Gary Cooper, Clark Gable, and many of the crowned heads of Europe. The cars were not only symbols of extravagant wealth but were also supremely engineered machines that could hurtle down the highway at speeds up to 130 miles per hour. Four of them were first-place winners at the Indianapolis 500, and another won the French Grand Prix at Le Mans. Today Duesenbergs are worth hundreds of thousands of dollars as collector cars.

indianatrivia

In 1996, *American Heritage* magazine called the Cord 810 Sedan, built by the Auburn Automobile Company in 1936, "the single most beautiful American car" ever made.

OTHER ATTRACTIONS WORTH SEEING IN NORTHEAST INDIANA

DUNKIRK
Dunkirk Glass Museum
309 S. Franklin St.
(765) 768-6872
dunkirk.lib.in.us

ELKHART
National New York Central Railroad Museum
721 S. Main St.
(574) 294-3001
elkhartindiana.org

Ruthmere Museum
302 E. Beardsley Ave.
(574) 264-0330 or (888) 287-7696
ruthmere.org

FORT WAYNE
Science Central
1950 N. Clinton St.
(260) 424-2400
sciencecenter.org

GREENTOWN
Greentown Glass Museum
112 N. Meridian St.
(765) 628-6206
greentownglass.org

HUNTINGTON
Forks of the Wabash Historic Park
3011 W. Park Dr.
(260) 356-1903
forksofthewabash.org

KOKOMO
Seiberling Mansion
(Howard County Museum)
1200 W. Sycamore St.
(765) 452-4314
hchistory.org

MUNCIE
Minnetrista
1200 N. Minnetrista Pkwy.
(765) 282-4848 or (800) 428-5887
minnetrista.net

WAKARUSA
Wakarusa Dime Store
103 E. Waterford St.
(574) 862-4690 or (877) 715-9821
jumbojellybeans.com

WINONA LAKE
The Village at Winona
700 Park Ave.
(574) 268-9888
villageatwinona.com

Various models of the Cord, more modest than the Duesenberg but still a cut above the rest, and the Auburn are displayed, along with more obscure cars, such as the Locomotive, Rauch-Lang, and McIntyre. The collection includes a flamboyant 1956 Bentley owned by John Lennon in the 1960s. Visitors will also see a 1948 Tucker and a 1981 DeLorean.

The museum, designated a National Historic Landmark in 2005, is open daily year-round, except for major winter holidays, from 9 a.m. to 5 p.m.; hours are extended to 8 p.m. on Tuesday. Admission: adults $12.50; students (ages eighteen and younger) $7.50. Contact the Auburn-Cord-Duesenberg Museum, 1600 S. Wayne St., Auburn 46706; (260) 925-1444; automobilemuseum.org.

Each year on Labor Day weekend Auburns, Cords, and Duesenbergs from all over the US return to the city of their creation for an annual festival. A highlight of the event is the collector-car auction, which has produced many world-record prices; in 2010, a 1932 Model J Duesenberg sold for $1 million. Even for spectators, it's an exciting show, with some 5,000 cars going up for auction each day.

Write the Auburn-Cord-Duesenberg Festival at the museum's address, or call (260) 925-3600; acdfestival.org.

Complementing the Auburn-Cord-Duesenberg Museum is the **National Automotive and Truck Museum of the United States.** The museum, known locally as NATMUS, houses more than 100 post–World War II cars and a truck collection that spans the entire motorized industry. A prize of the collection is the Endeavor, a truck built on a modified International Harvester chassis that set the world land speed record for trucks on the Bonneville Salt Flats of Utah. Thousands of toy model cars and trucks are also on display. NATMUS is located at 1000 Gordon M. Buehrig Place and is open 9 a.m. to 5 p.m. daily. Admission: adults $10; children (ages 5–12) $5. For additional information, write NATMUS at PO Box 686, Auburn 46706-0686, or call (260) 925-9100; natmus.org.

At 2181 Rotunda Dr. in Auburn, the **Early Ford V-8 Museum** is a tribute to the Ford Motor Company and its influence on automotive and American history from 1932 to 1953. Open 9 a.m. to 5 p.m. daily. Admission: adults $10; senior citizens $8; children (ages 7–12) $6. Call (260) 927-8022 or visit fordv8foundation.org.

In the tiny town of St. Joe, you can tour **Sechler's Pickle Factory,** where multitudes of midwestern cucumbers have been transformed into pickles since 1921. Along with the traditional types, the factory produces such unique varieties as candied orange strip, lemon strip, apple cinnamon, and raisin crispy pickles. Now a third-generation family operation, Sechler's is believed to be the only pickle manufacturer that makes an aged-in-wood genuine dill pickle (the same pickle made the same way by the first generation of Sechler pickle producers). Free 30-minute tours are offered by appointment (drop-in visitors can sometimes be accommodated) from 9 to 11 a.m. and 12:30 to 3 p.m. Monday through Thursday and on a limited basis on Friday, April through October. Located at 5686 SR 1; (260) 337-5461 or (800) 332-5461. A salesroom on the premises displays Sechler's plethora of pickles; you can also order them online at sechlerspickles.com. The late Frank Sinatra ordered his favorites, the candied sweet dill strips, a case at a time.

Delaware County

In **Muncie** the winter winds can be fierce, the snows deep, and the temperatures subzero, but in two greenhouses on the campus of **Ball State University** a tropical garden of rare and exquisite orchids blooms all year long. The **Wheeler–Thanhauser Orchid Collection** contains one of the most extensive collections of orchid species in the world. More than 1,800 plants thrive here in a simulated rain forest environment complete with rain, frogs, and a small waterfall, and the collection's species bank was the first such bank anywhere. Open free of charge 7:30 a.m. to 4:30 p.m. Monday through Friday; (765) 285-8839; bsu.edu.

The greenhouses are situated in 17-acre **Christy Woods,** where there's an arboretum, flower gardens, a demonstration wetland area, research facilities, and a nature center that serves as an outdoor laboratory for both Ball State students and the general public. If you come in April or May, you'll also see a profusion of wildflowers. Free admission; open 7:30 a.m. to 4:30 p.m. Monday through Friday and 10 a.m. to 3 p.m. Saturday, April through October. Call (765) 285-2641; bsu.edu.

The **David Owsley Museum of Art,** located in the Fine Arts Building, houses such treasures as paintings by Degas and Rembrandt, illuminated manuscripts, stone carvings from India, and wooden masks from Africa. Free admission; open 9 a.m. to 4:30 p.m. Monday through Friday; 1:30 to 4:30 p.m. Saturday. Hours may vary during spring and winter breaks and in the summer; (765) 285-5242; bsu.edu/web/museumofart.

The entryway to the Ball State Music Instruction Building is home to a stunning light painting by artist Stephen Knapp. Called **First Symphony,** it's a dazzling array of brilliant colors created with 100 pieces of coated glass, polished steel brackets, and a few halogen light bulbs. The unique painting is highly visible, especially at night, through panes of glass, but it's colorful at all times. Its appearance changes depending on the time of day and the amount of light that filters through the windows. This is the only artwork of the Massachusetts-based artist in Indiana. For more information, call (765) 285-5400; bsu.edu/academics/collegesanddepartments/music.

For information about other Ball State University attractions, contact the Ball State Welcome Center in Lucina Hall at 2000 W. University Ave.; (765) 289-1241, (800) 382-8540; bsu.edu.

Nationally recognized for the hands-on experience it provides, the **Muncie Children's Museum** occupies a 24,000-square-foot building at 515 S. High St. Children can burrow through a human-size ant farm, learn how to escape from a building "on fire," join a railroad crew laying track across the country, and climb over, under, through, and on ten separate structures, including an eyeball. Admission: $6 per person; open 10 a.m. to 5 p.m. Tuesday through Saturday and 1–5 p.m. Sunday; closed July 4, Thanksgiving, December 25, and January 1; (765) 286-1660 or munciemuseum.com.

indianatrivia

Ball State University's Bracken Library has the third largest collection of John Steinbeck books in the country. They have been translated into virtually every language and even include a copy of *The Pearl* in Eskimo.

indianatrivia

Director Steven Spielberg chose Muncie as the town portrayed in his 1977 movie *Close Encounters of the Third Kind,* even though he'd never been there.

Muncie became the world headquarters for model aviation in 1994, when the Academy of Model Aeronautics (AMA) moved here from Reston, Virginia. The 1,000-acre AMA complex consists of the **National Model Aviation Museum** and a model-airplane flying field. Visitors to the museum will see the largest collection of model aircraft in the country. The craftsmanship and artistry of the master builders are astonishing. Academy members stage flying competitions on an almost continuous basis from mid-May until the end of September. The events include rocket launches, helicopter meets, jet power contests, air combat, soaring competitions, and a vintage radio control reunion. Museum hours are 8 a.m. to 4:30 p.m. Monday through Friday; weekend hours vary, so call before you visit. Admission to the museum for non-AMA members: adults $5; children (ages 7–17) $2.50. Admission to the flying site is free to the public at all times. The complex is located at 5151 E. Memorial Dr.; (765) 287-1256, (765) 289-4248, or (800) 435-9262; modelaircraft.org.

Elkhart County

One of the best ways to gain insight into the lifestyle of the Amish is through a visit to **The Barns at Nappanee,** formerly known as Amish Acres, an authentic 80-acre restoration of a century-old farming community in **Nappanee** with eighteen restored and historical buildings to explore. Amish farmhouses dot the countryside, flat-topped black buggies wander the roads, farmers plow the fields, livestock graze behind split-rail fences, and women quilt, bake in an outdoor oven, and dip candles. You can see demonstrations of soap making, horseshoeing, and meat preserving; and visit a bakery, a meat and cheese shop, an antique soda fountain and fudgery, a cider mill, a smokehouse, a mint still, and a sawmill. Stage productions are presented in The Round Barn Theatre.

You may want to take a horse-drawn buggy ride or enjoy the excellent Amish cooking at the **LaSalle Farm & Table.** The soup is always on in big iron kettles, and such typical dishes as noodles, spiced apples, and sweet-and-sour cabbage salad are on the menu. Be sure to try the shoofly pie; it was declared the best by the *Chicago Tribune* after a shoofly pie taste test in 139 towns around the country.

Amish Acres is located on US 6, 1 mile west of Nappanee. The restored farm is open Tuesday through Saturday from 10 a.m. to 8 p.m.; 10 a.m. to 5 p.m. on Sunday. Admission: adults $12.95: children $4.95. Special package price for a guided tour is: adults $17.95; children $8.95. Hours may vary, so check before you go. The Barns at Nappanee is located at 1600 W. Market St., Nappanee 46550; or call (574) 773-4188 or (800) 800-4942; thebarnsatnappanee.com. The information center also can assist you in making reservations for an overnight stay in an area farm home.

The area in and around Nappanee abounds with interesting shops and Amish businesses that can be toured. *Time* magazine honored the area in its December 8, 1997, issue by naming Nappanee as one of the top ten small-town success stories in the nation. The Nappanee Area Chamber of Commerce, at 302 W. Market St., Nappanee 46550, will be happy to provide you with additional information; (574) 773-7812; nappanee-chamber.com.

If you stop at the **Elkhart County Visitor Center,** you can pick up maps, brochures, and a free Heritage Trail audio tour CD that will guide you to the attractions along a 90-mile scenic trail through the heart of Amish country. Your route will take you from your starting point in Elkhart on a clockwise loop through the quaint towns of Bristol, Middlebury, Shipshewana, Goshen, Nappanee, and Wakarusa. In September 2010, *USA Today* featured the Heritage Trail as one of the top five themed trails in the country, and the editors of *Life* named it one of our nation's most scenic drives. The visitor center is located at 3421 Cassopolis St. in Elkhart; it's open 8 a.m. to 5 p.m. Monday through

The Beast of 'Busco

In the long-ago spring of 1949, the small Whitley County town of Churubusco was consumed with the tale of the "Beast of 'Busco." Local farmer Gale Harris had reported seeing a turtle as large as a dining room table in a lake on his land, and the hunt was on.

Tales about a 400-pound turtle quickly spread far and wide. Newspaper reporters swarmed along the lake's shoreline, and small planes filled with photographers circled overhead. Divers suited up and plunged into the murky waters. In the course of one day, some 3,000 people tramped through Harris's fields to watch the goings-on. At the height of the search, some 400 cars an hour crept past the lake.

Traps were set but remained empty. Gale Harris tried to drain his lake but was unsuccessful. The huge turtle, dubbed Oscar, was never found, nor was he ever seen again. Experts who heard the story of Oscar speculated that, if the elusive reptile did indeed exist, he was probably a rare, unusually large alligator snapping turtle.

Whatever Oscar might or might not have been, he holds a very special place in the history of Churubusco. A documentary film entitled **The Hunt for Oscar** premiered locally in November 1994. Signs in Churubusco still welcome visitors to "Turtle Town U.S.A.," and each June the community hosts a Turtle Days festival.

You can learn more about the festival that honors Oscar by contacting the Turtle Days Association, Inc., PO Box 187, Churubusco, IN 46723; (260) 693-2229 or turtledays-dot.com.wordpress.com.

Friday and 9 a.m. to 4 p.m. Saturday, but a lobby containing travel information is open 24/7. Call (574) 262-3925 or (800) 250-4827; visitelkhartcounty.com. If you take the drive from Memorial Day weekend through September, you'll see an array of supersized quilt gardens along the way; some 100,000 blooms color the landscape in quilt patterns, and you can explore them for free.

The *Midwest Museum of American Art* would be a gem anywhere, but in the small municipality of *Elkhart* (population 52,367) it is a crown jewel. Noted for its extensive collection of Norman Rockwell lithographs (believed to be the largest collection anywhere), paintings by Rockwell and Grandma Moses, the largest Overbeck art pottery collection in the state, and photographs by such distinguished photographers as Ansel Adams, the museum has become one of Indiana's most important art institutions. Admission: adults $10; children (ages 13–18) $8; children (ages 8–12) $6. Open 10 a.m. to 4 p.m. Tuesday through Friday; 1–4 p.m. Saturday and Sunday. Located at 429 S. Main St.; (574) 293-6660; midwestmuseum.org.

The amazing collection at the ***Hall of Heroes Superhero Museum*** in Elkhart covers the entire history of superheroes in comic books, toys, film, and cartoons from the late 1930s to the present. It's housed in a 2-story building that's a replica of the Hall of Justice from a classic cartoon called *The Super Friends*. Inside, there's a replica of the Batcave, complete with Batpole, from the 1960s *Batman* television series, as well as a full-size Spiderman and the original costume worn by William Katt on *The Greatest American Hero* television show. You'll also find more than 50,000 comic books, many of them original editions; some 10,000 toys, sculptures, and original movie and TV props; and more than 100 pieces of comic book and animation art. Hours are 11 a.m. to 5 p.m. on Monday, Tuesday, Thursday, and Friday; 10 a.m. to 5 p.m. on Saturday; and noon to 5 p.m. on Sunday. Admission: $9 for ages 10 and up; $6 for ages 3–9. Located at 1915 Cassopolis St.; (574) 333-3406; halloftheheroes museum.com.

Elkhart also is home to a museum that will warm the hearts of owners and wannabe owners of recreational vehicles. The ***RV/MH Hall of Fame*** showcases the growth, history, and accomplishments of the RV and manufactured-housing industries. Originally located in Washington, DC, the Hall of Fame was moved to Elkhart, widely recognized as the RV Capital of the World, in 1991. Indiana factories make about 75 percent of the RVs produced in the United States, and more than half of those are made in Elkhart.

Among the exhibits are the first RV ever made (built in 1915), camping trailers of the 1930s, the classic art deco Airstream, and a 1934 motor home custom-built for movie star Mae West. There's even a tiny pink trailer suitable for small pets and some scale models of trailer high-rises. Believe it or not, someone once envisioned building whole communities of vertical trailer parks with twenty stories of single-wide trailers stacked on top of one another. The RV Wall of Fame pays tribute to more than 170 people who are famous in the RV industry.

The museum is open 9 a.m. to 5 p.m. Monday through Saturday and 10 a.m. to 3 p.m. from April 1 to October 21. From November 1 to March 31, open Monday through Saturday 10 a.m. to 4 p.m. Admission: adults $12; senior citizens $10; children (ages 6–16) $9. Located at 21565 Executive Pkwy., just off I-80/90 at exit 96; call (574) 293-2344 or (800) 378-8694; rvmhhalloffame.org.

If you'd like to watch an RV being assembled, take a free plant tour at ***Jayco, Inc.,*** located at 903 S. Main St. (SR 13 South) in Middlebury. Tours are conducted at noon Monday through Thursday. There's also a visitor center at 911 S. Main St. to explore during business hours; open 8 a.m. to 5 p.m. Monday through Friday. Call the factory at (574) 825-5861 or visit jayco.com for additional information.

On the northwest corner of Main St. and Lincoln Ave. in **Goshen** stands an intriguing-looking *limestone booth.* The octagonal structure, complete with gun ports and bulletproof green glass, was erected in 1939 by the Works Progress Administration (WPA) to provide a lookout for local police. At that time, two banks stood at the intersection. A slew of recent robberies in surrounding communities had been widely publicized, and the local citizenry decided to take some precautionary measures. Their jitters apparently were not easily dispelled, because police continued to man the enclosure 24 hours a day until 1969. Since 1983 it has been owned by the Goshen Historical Society, 124 S. Main St.; (574) 975-0033; goshenhistorical.org.

Grant County

The death of James Dean on September 30, 1955, catapulted the popular young actor to enduring fame as a cult hero. Although he made only three movies— *East of Eden, Rebel Without a Cause,* and *Giant*—Dean gave voice through his roles to the restlessness and discontent of his generation. He died at the age of twenty-four, the victim of an automobile accident on a lonely California highway. Dean was speeding along in his silver Porsche when he collided with a car making a left turn across the highway in front of him. Ironically, Dean had been given a speeding ticket a little over 2 hours before the accident that claimed his life. His family brought him home to Indiana to bury him. Today rarely a day goes by—no matter what the weather—that someone doesn't show up in *Park Cemetery* at *Fairmount,* where Dean grew up, to see his grave and mourn his passing.

For ten years after his death, Warner Brothers received as many as 7,000 letters a month addressed to Dean from devoted fans who refused to accept his death. His tombstone in Park Cemetery, defaced by souvenir seekers, was replaced in 1985. Within a few short months it, too, was defaced. A sign that read THIS WAY TO JAMES DEAN'S GRAVE lasted one afternoon, and handfuls of dirt regularly disappear from his burial site. People from as far away as Germany have wanted to purchase a plot here so that they can "be buried near Jimmy." To this day, books are still being written about Dean. When the US Postal Service began issuing its "Legends of Hollywood" stamp series, it was James Dean whose image was chosen for the second stamp in the series. (Marilyn Monroe's stamp, the first, was released in 1995; the Dean stamp was released in 1996.) Between 1986 and 1996, the estate of James Dean amassed more than $100 million from merchandising materials. At this writing, more than 200 companies worldwide market about 1,500 products that bear his name, and his estate continues to earn more than $5 million a year. The *New York Times* Store includes a photo of James Dean in its collection of rare and newsworthy items that was selling for $800 in 2011. In 2005, the editors of *Variety* magazine, a leading publication in the entertainment industry, asked show business professionals and the public to choose the most influential entertainers of the past 100 years; James Dean was seventh on the list, ahead of Marilyn Monroe, Mickey Mouse, and Elvis Presley. The phenomenon of James Dean shows no signs of letting up and can never be fully explained—a charisma that has endured to this day. Park Cemetery, open daily dawn to dusk, is on CR 150E; (765) 948-4040.

The **Fairmount Historical Museum** at 203 E. Washington St. tells the story of Dean's life through a series of exhibits and a display of some of Dean's possessions from a family collection. Each September, near the date of Dean's death, the museum hosts the Remembering James Dean Festival and the James Dean Memorial Service. The museum also honors Fairmount's other favorite son—Jim Davis, creator of "Garfield the Cat." Local artist Olive Rush is also honored in the museum. No admission fee, but donations are accepted. Open 11 a.m. to 5 p.m. every day except Tuesday and Thursday. For information, call (765) 948-4555 or visit jamesdeanartifacts.com.

More Dean memorabilia can be seen at the **James Dean Gallery,** which is devoted exclusively to the late actor. Among the items on display are several dozen movie posters in twenty different languages, as well as hundreds of foreign-language books and magazines that date from the mid-fifties to today— all devoted to Dean. Items from his school days in Fairmount include some early schoolwork and his high school yearbooks. Dean was also considered a talented artist, and some of his watercolor and oil paintings are exhibited here. Open 9 a.m. to 6 p.m. daily year-round except for major winter holidays; admission free, but donations are appreciated. Located at 425 N. Main St. in Fairmount; (765) 948-3326 or jamesdeangallery.com.

A small landscaped park in downtown Fairmount pays tribute to the legendary actor. Known as the **James Dean Memorial Park,** it's located at the corner of Main and Second Streets at 220 N. Main St. A monument topped by a bust of Dean bears a plaque reading, in part: AN AMERICAN ORIGINAL WHO … IN A PERIOD OF FIVE YEARS ROSE TO THE VERY PINNACLE OF THE THEATRICAL PROFESSION AND THROUGH THE MAGIC OF MOTION PICTURES LIVES ON IN LEGEND.

Dean was further honored by his hometown in October 2011, when a 7-foot-8-inch-square mural of the star was hung on the outside wall of the Fairmount Antique Mall at the corner of Washington and Main Streets. Made entirely from different pieces and colors of denim, the unique portrait pays tribute to the man who is credited with making denim a fashion staple. Look closely, and you'll see an image of a denim-clad Dean walking in Fairmount on his last visit home.

Everyone's Favorite Feline

Indiana's most beloved native is arguably Garfield the Cat. Although Garfield is lazy, fat, and selfish, he gets away with it precisely because he *is* a cat. It also helps that he is adorable.

Jim Davis, Garfield's creator, grew up in Fairmount, Indiana, where he and his family shared the family farm with about twenty-five cats. Today, Davis lives and works near the small town of Albany, which lies a few miles northeast of Muncie, Indiana. Davis's company, Paws Inc., is the licensing and merchandising firm for anything created in Garfield's image.

For the curious among you, here are some interesting facts about the cat and his creator:

Davis shares his tubby tabby's love for lasagna.

Garfield is Davis's grandfather's name (the two reportedly share a few traits).

More than 60 million Garfield books have been published worldwide, and Garfield has been the star of several CBS-TV specials. *Garfield,* a movie starring Bill Murray as the voice of Garfield, was released in 2004. Murray was again the voice of Garfield in *Garfield: A Tale of Two Kitties,* a movie that debuted in 2006. A third Garfield movie is set to be released in 2021.

The comic strip that features Garfield is the most widely syndicated strip in the world, read daily by some 200 million people in more than 2,500 newspapers in more than 100 different languages.

A free brochure available at several places in Fairmount guides visitors to ten sites, including his old high school and his boyhood home, that were landmarks in Dean's life.

The nearby town of *Marion,* where James Dean was born, is noted for its extraordinary Easter pageant, presented each Easter morning at 6 a.m. Lauded as the equal of Oberammergau's famous passion play, the pageant draws spectators from all fifty states and from overseas. Free admission; for tickets and information, contact the Marion/Grant County Convention and Visitors Bureau, 505 W. Third St., Marion 46952; (765) 668-5435 or (800) 662-9474; showmegrantcounty.com.

indianatrivia

Harley-Davidson motorcycles were first called "hogs" at the 1920 Marion International Motorcycle Race. The winners celebrated their victory by riding around the track with a pig, and the moniker stuck. The victory lap is still recreated each August at the Hog Daze Motorcycle Rally.

Marion is also home to the **Quilters Hall of Fame,** which celebrates quilting as an art form and honors those who have made significant contributions to the world of quilting. If you ever felt that quilts were uninteresting or boring, you won't after a visit here. The three-story building in which the collection of quilts and associated memorabilia is housed is the former home of the late Marie Webster, an internationally famous maker and designer of quilts who's sometimes called the "first quilt celebrity." A pioneering female entrepreneur, she sold her innovative quilt patterns worldwide through a very successful mail-order business from 1912 to 1942. She was also the author of the first book of quilt history, *Quilts: Their Story and How to Make Them,* published in 1915. The significance of the house and museum was officially recognized in 1992 when it was designated a Landmark of Women's History and a National Historic Landmark by the National Park Service; the latter is the only such landmark that honors a quilter. Each year during the third week of July, the museum hosts a quilting celebration; a variety of classes and lectures are offered, and a new Hall of Fame honoree is inducted.

Admission: adults $4; senior citizens $3. Open from 10 a.m. to 4 p.m. Tuesday through Saturday, July through September; hours may vary, so call before visiting. Located at 926 S. Washington St., (765) 664-9999; quiltershalloffame.net.

Ice cream lovers will want to journey to **Upland,** home of Taylor University, and visit **Ivanhoe's.** When they spy the menu here, they'll think they've died and gone to heaven. Sundae and shake flavors are arranged alphabetically—100 delicious flavors each, plus a special section for extras. If you manage to eat your way through all 100 flavors in either category, your name is enshrined on a special plaque that hangs on the dining room wall. Hoe's, as it's known locally, also serves ice cream sodas, floats, and excellent sandwiches and salads. Located at 979 S. Main St., it's open from 10 a.m. to 10 p.m. Monday through Thursday, 10 a.m. to 11 p.m. Friday and Saturday, and 2–10 p.m. Sunday. Call (765) 998-7261; ivanhoes.info.

Howard County

The world has stainless steel because **Kokomo** inventor Elwood Haynes wanted to please his wife. Well aware of her husband's ingenuity, Mrs. Haynes asked him to perfect some tarnish-free dinnerware for her. And in 1912, he did.

The remarkable Mr. Haynes also invented the first successful commercial automobile. On July 4, 1894, he put his gasoline-powered creation to the test on Pumpkinvine Pike (now known as Boulevard Street) east of Kokomo, speeding along at 7 miles per hour for a distance of about 6 miles. That same car is now on display at the Smithsonian Institution in Washington, DC.

Another of Haynes's inventions is stellite, an alloy used today in spacecraft, jet engines, dental instruments, and nuclear power plants. New applications are still being found for it.

The **Elwood Haynes Museum,** housed in Haynes's former residence, contains a vast collection of Haynes's personal possessions and his many inventions. Visitors particularly enjoy the 1905 Haynes automobile, in which the driver sits in the backseat. Other exhibits reflect Howard County's history during and after the area's great gas boom.

The largest natural gas gusher ever brought into production in this country was struck in 1887 in what is now southeast Kokomo. Almost overnight the town was transformed into a center of industry. Kokomo's many contributions to the industrial growth of America, in addition to Haynes's inventions, have earned it the nickname "City of Firsts." Many of the items first produced here are among those featured in the upstairs rooms of the Elwood Haynes Museum, located at 1915 S. Webster St. Free of charge, it's open 11 a.m. to 4 p.m. Tuesday through Saturday and 1–4 p.m. Sunday; closed holidays. Call (765) 456-7500.

Just to the northwest of the Haynes Museum, at 900 W. Deffenbaugh St., enter **Highland Park** and view the city's most visited attraction, Kokomo's own **Old Ben.** Ben was a crossbred Hereford steer who at the time of his birth in 1902 was proclaimed to be the largest calf in the world, weighing in at 135 pounds. When you see Ben, you won't find it hard to believe. At four years of age, the steer weighed 4,720 pounds, stood 6 feet 4 inches tall, measured 13 feet 6 inches in girth, and was an astonishing 16 feet 2 inches from his nose to the tip of his tail. For many years he was exhibited around the country in circuses and sideshows. He had to be destroyed in 1910 after breaking his leg, and shortly thereafter he was stuffed and mounted. Today he shares a place of honor with another of Kokomo's giant wonders—*the stump of a huge sycamore tree.* The stump—12 feet tall and 57 feet in circumference—is impressive enough, but it only hints at the magnificent mother tree. Originally more than 100 feet in height, the tree grew to maturity on a farm west of Kokomo. Its hollow trunk once housed a telephone booth large enough to accommodate more than a dozen people at a time. When the tree was storm-damaged around 1915, the enormous stump was pulled to the park by a house mover. Old Ben and the stump now occupy a building built specifically to display and protect them. The 83-acre park is also home to the Vermont Covered Bridge. Free admission; open dawn to 11 p.m. daily year-round. Call (765) 456-7275; cityofkokomo.org.

The **Kokomo Opalescent Glass Company,** in operation since 1888, once supplied glass to Louis C. Tiffany. Today this small factory is known worldwide

Kokomo: City of Firsts

Kokomo bills itself as the City of Firsts. Here are a few of the reasons why:

First commercially built auto (road tested locally on July 4, 1894)
First pneumatic rubber tire (1894)
First aluminum casting (1895)
First carburetor (1902)
First stellite cobalt-based alloy (1906)
First stainless steel (1912)
First American howitzer shell (1918)
First aerial bomb with fins (1918)
First mechanical corn picker (early 1920s)
First dirilyte golden-hued tableware (1926)
First canned tomato juice (1928)
First push-button car radio (1938)
First all-metal lifeboats (1941) and rafts (1943)
First signal-seeking car radio (1947)
First all-transistor car radio (1957)

as a leading producer of fine art glass, and visitors can watch the glassmaking process from beginning to end. Tours are offered for $6 per person and $3 for students at 10 a.m. Monday through Friday, except on holidays and in December; at the end of your tour, you will be given a gift. Visitors must wear closed-toe shoes with thick soles for safety. An adjoining retail shop is open 9 a.m. to 5 p.m. Monday through Friday and 9 a.m. to 1 p.m. Saturday. Located at 1310 S. Market St.; to schedule a tour or for additional information, call (765) 457-1829 or (877) 703-4290; kog.com.

Huntington County

One of Indiana's most famous sons, J. Danforth Quayle (better known as Dan), is the fifth Hoosier to serve as our country's vice president. Quayle was born in Indianapolis in 1947, but his family moved to Huntington about a year later, and it is Huntington that Quayle calls home.

When George Bush and Quayle launched their campaign for the White House in 1988, they came to the Huntington County Courthouse to do it. When Quayle and his wife, Marilyn, received their law degrees from Indiana University in Bloomington, they came to Huntington to open a law office. When Quayle first ran for public office in 1976 (as a US Representative), he ran as a resident of Huntington.

In June 1993, **Huntington** demonstrated its affection for Quayle by opening the Dan Quayle Center and Museum, later renamed the **Quayle Vice Presidential Learning Center,** at 815 Warren St. Visitors will see exhibits from every phase of Quayle's life, including a newspaper clipping announcing his birth, a baby footprint taken at the hospital in which he was born, and a photo of the newborn Quayle in a diaper. Of particular interest is Quayle's second-grade report card, boasting all As and Bs. A copy of Quayle's college diploma is missing a few pieces, thanks to a family dog (a photo of the offender, much loved nevertheless, is framed with the diploma). No museum honoring Dan Quayle would be complete without some golf memorabilia; an old golf bag and photos of a teenage Quayle holding trophies won in a junior tournament are among them.

You'll know when you get to Huntington. It would be hard to miss the sign at the city limits that proclaims this to be HUNTINGTON: HOME OF THE 44TH VICE PRESIDENT DAN QUAYLE.

Although the museum bears Dan Quayle's name, it pays tribute to all of our country's vice presidents—the only such museum in the country. Visitors will learn about the history, responsibilities, and contributions of the office of the vice president.

The museum is open 9 a.m. to 1 p.m. Thursday through Saturday. Sometimes it is closed to the public for special school programs, so it's best to call before coming. Admission: adults $3; children (ages 7–17) $1. For more information, call (260) 356-6356 or visit historyeducates.org.

After you've toured Dan Quayle's museum, stop by and see **Hy Goldenberg's Outhouses.** You won't see any signs honoring Hy's outhouses, but the town is fond of them just the same.

Hy purchased his first two outhouses in the 1960s for strictly utilitarian reasons. He and his wife were building a home in a then-isolated spot on the banks of the Wabash River, and they needed a toilet the carpenters could use while working on the house. Because of that experience, Hy came to regard outhouses as an important segment of Americana and collected seventeen of them before his death in 2000.

Although most of the outhouses are variations of the typical square wooden ones, there is also an octagon-shaped concrete one. A three-seater model boasts a child-size seat in the middle for the family that enjoys togetherness. One of Hy's rarest outhouses is a round privy that sports a copper weather vane atop

indianatrivia

The Wabash River flows dam-free for 411 miles from a reservoir near Huntington to the Ohio River near Evansville. It is the longest section of free-flowing water east of the Mississippi.

its roof. Hy paid a whopping $17 for that one. Although most of his outhouses cost $2–3 each, Hy had to bid against someone at an auction before he could call the cherished round privy his own.

Building outhouses was a source of employment for many men during the Great Depression. Although comfort and safety were certainly important considerations, aesthetics also played a role. Many were covered with roses and trellises to please the lady of the house.

After Hy's death, his widow, Lorry, donated part of her husband's collection to the **Huntington County Historical Museum.** Lorry died in 2011. For additional information, contact the museum at 315 Court St. in Huntington; (260) 356-7264 or huntingtonhistoricalmuseum.com. The museum is open from 10 a.m. to 4 p.m. Wednesday through Friday and 1–4 p.m. Saturday. Admission is free, but donations are welcome. The remaining outhouses may be seen free of charge on what was once the Goldenberg's property; it is now the **Tel-Hy Nature Preserve,** a property of the Acres Land Trust. It's located southwest of Huntington at 1429 CR 300 West; for exact directions, call (260) 637-2273 or visit acreslandtrust.org.

Lest you doubt the current value of outhouses to our society, you should know they are still being built, albeit in more modern forms, in areas where it would be environmentally and economically impractical to install water and sewers. The most expensive outhouse in Indiana to date is a four-seat composting toilet in Charlestown State Park in Clark County that set the state back $87,000 when it was built in the mid-1990s. That one, however, is a piker compared to a four-seat outhouse in Glacier National Park in Montana, completed in 1998 at a cost of $1 million.

Kosciusko County

Some towns will do almost anything to get attention. **Mentone** grabbed its share of publicity by erecting a monument unique in the world. There it stands, at the corner of E. Main and S. Morgan Streets—a 12-foot-high, 3,000-pound **concrete egg.** If, when in Mentone, anyone should ask the perennial puzzler "Which came first, the chicken or the egg?" the answer would almost certainly have to be "the egg."

In 1946, when the monument was first "laid," every farmer in the area had a chicken house, and eggs were shipped all over the Midwest. That enterprise declined in the 1950s, but the lives of the town's 950 residents continue to be intertwined with eggs and chickens. Local businesses hatch eggs, provide chicken meat for soup companies, and separate egg whites from the yolks for bakeries. And each June the community celebrates industry, heritage, and monument with an Egg Festival. Food booths sell eggs most any way you like them, while some fun-loving residents dress up in chicken suits and strut about dancing and singing. (Don't knock it—Brad Pitt got his start wearing a chicken suit.) Contact the Kosciusko County Convention and Visitors Bureau, 111 Capital Dr., Warsaw 46582; (574) 269-6060; visitkosciuskocounty.org.

Next to the city park at 210 S. Oak St., just south of SR 25 West in downtown Mentone, you'll find the *Lawrence D. Bell Aircraft Museum.* It contains the memorabilia of Larry Bell, the Mentone native who forsook eggs and instead founded the Bell Aircraft Corporation. Bell produced twenty aviation firsts, including the world's first commercial helicopter, the nation's first jet-propelled fighter plane, the first jet vertical takeoff and landing airplane, and the first aircraft to shatter the sound barrier. Scale models of many Bell aircraft, as well as a Bell-designed Agena space rocket engine that's known as the "workhorse of the space age," are on display, and a 10-minute video presentation describes Bell's life and career. The current museum is a work in progress; future plans include building a hangar that will display each aircraft ever manufactured by Bell. At this writing, the museum owns a "Huey," a type of medical rescue helicopter used in Vietnam (you'll see it sitting in the museum's yard), and a 47G helicopter like those used by MASH units in Korea. Open from 1 to 5 p.m. Sunday, June through September; other times by appointment. Free admission; write the museum at PO Box 411, Mentone 46539, or call (574) 353-7318 or (800) 800-6090; bellaircraftmuseum.org.

One of the finest and the largest of such gardens in the United States, the *Warsaw Biblical Gardens* cover nearly 1 acre in Center Lake Park in *Warsaw.* All plants mentioned in the Bible have been meticulously researched for this project, and thus far some 160 varieties of flowers, shrubs, and grasses have been acquired.

An oasis of tranquility, the gardens are enclosed by a low fieldstone wall. Visitors can meander along stone paths that lead through six distinct plant environs: meadow, crop, orchard, forest, brook, and desert. A plaque for each of the species identifies the plant and its biblical reference. Water lilies, yellow iris, and sweet flag adorn a water garden that's shaded by an umbrella palm. A unique wooden arbor was designed by famous craftsman David Robinson, who served as the first coordinator for the restoration of New York City's Central Park before going into business for

indianatrivia

When the Wisconsin glacier withdrew about 14,000 years ago, its melting ice created the many natural lakes found today in northern Indiana. Indiana's largest natural lake is 3,060-acre Lake Wawasee; its deepest natural lake is 123-foot-deep Tippecanoe Lake. Both are in Kosciusko County.

himself. Grape vines planted when the gardens were dedicated in June 1991 now nearly obscure the arbor, creating a cool, shaded retreat on hot summer days.

The gardens, located at the intersection of SR 15 North and E. Canal St. at 349 N. Buffalo St., are officially open free of charge from dawn to dusk, April 15 to October 10. Guided tours for $2 are offered from May 15 through September 15. For additional information, call (574) 267-6218; warsawbiblicalgardens.org.

LaGrange County

No place in this country has done better by its junk than the tiny hamlet of **Shipshewana**. Each Tuesday and Wednesday from 8 a.m. to 4 p.m. May through September, it puts on what may be the biggest small-town sale in the country. Anything you've ever wanted has almost certainly, at one time or another, been available at the **Shipshewana ("Shipshe" for short) Auction and Flea Market.** The items available at one sale included old beer cans, garden tools, round oak tables, new hats and clothing at discount prices, doorknobs, bubblegum machines, rare books, antique china, long-legged underwear, fence posts, Aladdin lamps, fishing rods, parts for old wagons, extra pieces for a Lionel train set, hand and power tools, quilts, a worn-out butter churn, a half-full can of green-house paint, baseball cards, homemade toy alligators, and—perhaps the most unusual item ever offered here—a used tombstone. Find bargains on home décor, clothing, produce, plants, tools, crafts, books, beauty supplies, vintage items, and almost everything imaginable.

Wednesday is the bigger business day. In addition to the flea market, a livestock sale takes place at 10 a.m. The horse auction is Friday at 10:30 a.m. Plus an antique auction is scheduled every Wednesday from 9 a.m. The vast array of items for sale in the antiques barn keeps auctioneers busy from 9 a.m. to 5 p.m., while in the livestock barn farmers do some hot-and-heavy bidding on cattle, sheep, goats, and pigs from 10 a.m. to 5 p.m. Outside in the flea market yard, nearly 700 vendors display their wares. On average, $200,000 worth of livestock and goods changes hands, not including the several thousand dollars spent at the flea market. Although it would be a compliment to describe some of the merchandise as junk, there are also many valuable antiques and hard-to-find items.

The Shipshe Auction hosts as many as 20,000 visitors each week. License plates reveal they come from across the country and Canada. When winter comes the flea market closes down, but the auctions continue throughout the year.

Each Friday the auction yard is the scene of a horse auction that draws buyers and sellers from all over North America; the Amish draft horses, reputed to be some of the finest in the land, are especially popular. (Shipshewana is in the heart of one of the largest Amish settlements in the United States.)

Since all the people who attend Shipshe's various auctions have to eat, a special Auction Restaurant, operated from one of the sale barns, is open three days a week in the summer. It dishes up delicious and inexpensive Amish food nonstop from 7 a.m. to 5 p.m. Tuesday and Wednesday, and from 7 a.m. to 2 p.m. Friday. Open Wednesday and Friday only during winter months.

With so much to do, shopper and visitors can stay right on the grounds, within walking distance to Shipshewana retail shops at either the Farmstead Inn, their Amish-inspired hotel or the newly expanded Shipshewana RV Park, located adjacent to the Shipshewana Flea Market and Auction grounds.

The auction yards and restaurant are located at 345 S. Van Buren St. (SR 5) at the south edge of Shipshewana. For more details, exact hours, and information about special events, write to the Shipshewana Auction and Flea Market, PO Box 185, Shipshewana 46565; call (260) 768-4129 or (800) 254-8090; shi pshewanatradingplace.com.

To learn more about the Mennonite/Amish/Hutterite lifestyle and heritage, explore the fascinating exhibits at the **Menno-Hof Visitors Center,** located at 510 S. Van Buren St. (SR 5) opposite the Shipshewana Auction grounds. You can explore a seventeenth-century sailing ship and replicas of a nineteenth-century print shop and meetinghouse; in the center's theatre, you'll "feel, see, and hear" a simulated tornado. Admission: adults $7.50; children (ages 6–14) $4. Family admission for two adults and all children is $16. Open 10 a.m. to 7 p.m. Monday through Friday and 10 a.m. to 5 p.m. Saturday June through August; 10 a.m. to 5 p.m. Monday through Saturday the rest of year; closed major winter holidays and Good Friday. Call (260) 768-4117; mennohof.org.

Stretching along the Pigeon River in northeastern LaGrange County and reaching eastward into Steuben County is the 11,500-acre **Pigeon River State Fish and Wildlife Area.** The hauntingly beautiful stream, edged by lush vegetation choked with hyacinths, flows through an outstanding variety of habitats—marshes, meadows, woods, swamps, and bogs. Birders love this area; more than 200 species of birds, many of them rare, have been sighted here. In the spring and early summer, wildflowers run rampant. It's all reminiscent of the Southland's fabled Suwannee River—a fine and private place in which to study nature; canoe; hunt mushrooms, nuts, and berries; hike; fish; pitch a tent; or ski cross-country.

The **Tamarack Bog State Nature Preserve** near the center of the wildlife area contains the largest tamarack swamp in Indiana and harbors such unique plants as the insectivorous pitcher plant and sundew. Contact the

Pigeon River State Fish and Wildlife Area, 8310 E. CR 300 North, Box 71, Mongo 46771; (260) 367-2164 or in.gov/dnr/fishwild/3086.htm.

Miami County

The circus first came to Peru, Indiana, in the late 1800s, and it remains there to this day, the single most dominant force in the community.

It all began with native son Ben Wallace, who owned a livery stable in **Peru.** One winter a broken-down animal show limped into town and found shelter in Ben's stable. When spring came, Ben was left with all the animals in lieu of a fee. Using his Hoosier ingenuity, Ben spiffed things up a bit, started his own circus, and built it into one of the world's finest—the **Hagenbeck-Wallace Circus.** Winter quarters were set up on the vast farm fields just outside town, and other major circuses of the day, lured by the excellent facilities, also came to Peru in the off-season.

Among the show business greats who spent at least part of the year here were Clyde Beatty, the noted animal trainer (like Ben Wallace, a native son); Emmett Kelly, the renowned clown; Willi Wilno, "the human cannonball"; and Tom Mix, who later starred in Hollywood westerns. The late Red Skelton left his home in southern Indiana when he was just a boy to join the Hagenbeck-Wallace Circus and to launch one of the most famous and enduring careers in the entertainment business.

The circus—and Peru with it—flourished for many years before passing into near oblivion, but local folks, many of them direct descendants of stars who brightened the firmament of circus history, decided that their town's unique heritage should be preserved forever. And so each year in mid-July, the circus once again comes to Peru when the community celebrates the **Circus City Festival.**

The performers, who must be residents of Miami County, range in age from 7 to 21 years old, and they are so skilled you'll find it difficult to believe that this is not a professional show. Since many of the children of Peru begin their training in their earliest childhood under the tutelage of some of the finest circus pros in the country, a constant supply of new talent is available. All the components of the old-time circus are here—aerialists, clowns, tightrope walkers, human pyramids, gymnasts, animal trainers, and much more. The whole thing is so authentic and entertaining that NBC-TV once filmed an hour-long documentary about it.

There are several performances during the eight-day festival, as well as a giant parade complete with calliopes, old circus wagons, and the rousing music of the Circus City Band. For additional information, contact the Circus City

Festival Office, 154 N. Broadway, Peru 46970; (765) 472-3918 or perucircus.com. The office shares its quarters with the **Circus City Museum,** which houses artifacts from the city's century-old association with the circus. Its rich heritage is preserved in photos, miniatures, and costumes. Open Monday through Friday from 9 a.m. to 5 p.m. April through September and 9 a.m. to 4 p.m. October through March; hours are extended during festival week. Admission is by donation only.

One of the finest collections of circus relics in the world is housed in Peru's **International Circus Hall of Fame.** One relic, an elaborately decorated circus wagon built in Peru in 1903, is the only one of its kind in the world. There's also a miniature replica of the 1934 Hagenbeck-Wallace Circus, complete with animals, performers, and the circus parade. In 1995 the museum acquired the Italian-made tent of the Big Apple Circus, which played at Lincoln Center in New York. Still under development, the museum currently occupies what used to be the Hagenbeck-Wallace Circus's wagon barn at the 10-acre Old Circus Winter Headquarters, a National Historic Landmark since 1988. The Hall of Fame is located just south of US 24 about 3 miles northeast of Peru; follow signs. Open 10 a.m. to 4 p.m. Monday through Friday and by appointment on Saturday and Sunday (except in July, when it's open 10 a.m. to 4 p.m. on Saturday and noon to 4 p.m. Sunday), May through October; open November through April by appointment. Admission: adults $5; children (ages 6–12) $2.50. All military personnel admitted free with military ID. For further information, contact the Circus Hall of Fame, 3076 E. Circus Ln., PO Box 700, Peru 46970; (765) 472-7553 or (800) 771-0241; circushof.com.

Even in death, Ben Wallace chose to remain in Peru. He is buried in Mount Hope Cemetery on 12th Street, along with another well-known native son, **Cole Porter.** One of the few songwriters who wrote both words and music, Porter penned such classics as "Night and Day," "Begin the Beguine," "I've Got You Under My Skin," and "What Is This Thing Called Love?" Today, Porter is considered one of the greatest songwriters of the first half of the twentieth century. His life and music were depicted in the 2004 movie *De-Lovely,* starring Kevin Kline as Porter and Ashley Judd as his wife, Linda.

In 2006, *Parade* magazine asked its readers to nominate little-known historical sites across the county that deserved special recognition. More than 2,500 people responded, and Cole Porter's birthplace finished in the top ten. Although the home was a private residence at the time, a plaque on the front lawn identified it as the place in which Porter was born on June 9, 1891. Dedicated fans raised money to purchase and renovate it, and on June 9, 2007, the home was opened to the public as a museum that celebrates Porter's life and music.

The sprawling home also serves as a bed and breakfast, the **Cole Porter Inn;** three six-room suites, available for moderate rates, are decorated to reflect the period in which Porter lived there. The suites are musically named the Cole Porter Suite, the Anything That Goes Suite, and the Day & Night Suite. Each suite has a kitchen with microwave and refrigerator, private bathroom, sitting room, sun room, cable TV, and Wi-Fi. The Inn is located at the corner of Huntington and E. 3rd Streets at 19 S. Huntington St.; (765) 469-1917; coleporterinn.com.

At the **Miami County Museum** in Peru, you can see more Cole Porter memorabilia, including his 1955 Fleetwood Cadillac and one of his Grammy awards. Other items of interest include pioneer and Miami Indian artifacts, the bullet-riddled skull of a killer elephant, and the overalls of Robert Wadlow, the world's tallest known man (8 feet, 11.1 inches tall) who died in 1922. Located at 51 N. Broadway St. (765-473-9183) open 9 a.m. to 5 p.m. Tuesday through Saturday. Admission is by donation.

Each year on the weekend nearest June 9, Porter's birth date, Peru honors its native son with a **Cole Porter Festival.** Call (765) 473-9183 or visit coleporterfestival.org for additional information.

A few miles south of Peru along US 31, you'll come upon the **Grissom Air Museum ,** where a still-growing outdoor museum displays historic military aircraft. A B-17 flying fortress; a massive B-47 Stratojet and its midair refueler, the KC-97; a tank-killing A-10 Warthog; and the celebrated EC-135 air command post of Desert Storm fame are among the aircraft that can be seen here. A B-58 Hustler, a supersonic bomber, is one of only six remaining in the world; the one you see here was the first aircraft to drop bombs from both Mach 1 and Mach 2. Grissom is also one of a handful of sites selected by the Navy to permanently display a Navy F-14 fighter jet. It's okay to climb and sit on several of the planes, and visitors are welcome to climb into the cockpit of an F4 Phantom fighter. An indoor museum houses various types of military memorabilia, including bombs, missiles, and survival gear. There's also a display on Virgil "Gus" Grissom, the man for whom the museum is named; the Indiana native from Mitchell was one of the seven original astronauts and the second American in space.

Visitors can climb to the top of a 40-foot-tall Cold War-era security tower to get a bird's-eye view of the museum's historic planes and gaze at sights up to 20 miles away. The museum is open from 10 a.m. to 4 p.m. Tuesday through Sunday from spring through fall months; hours and months sometimes vary, so it's best to call ahead before visiting. Admission: adults $7; senior citizens $6. The outdoor exhibits are open daily from 7 a.m. to dusk. For additional information, contact the Grissom Air Museum, 1000 Hoosier Blvd., Peru; (765) 689-8011 or grissomairmuseum.com.

Noble County

Opened in the summer of 1997, the **Mid-America Windmill Museum** in **Kendallville** is one of only two of its kind in the country. Currently, some fifty windmills have been restored and are on display on a 35-acre plot on Kendallville's southeast side. Plans call for the acquisition and restoration of about fifty more.

The gem of the collection is the Robertson Windmill, a replica of the first windmill built in what is now the United States (circa 1610). It was constructed from a set of blueprints on loan from the Colonial Williamsburg Foundation. Because it's built on a post, the entire structure can be turned to take advantage of the wind's direction.

Kendallville seems a logical place for such a museum because it's in the heart of an area that was once referred to as the windmill store of the nation. In the heyday of wind power, nearly 80 windmill manufacturers were located within a 150-mile radius of Kendallville, and the country's second-largest windmill maker was actually in Kendallville.

In the museum building are models and displays that show the advances in windmill technology around the globe and through the years, beginning with a wind-powered gristmill used in Persia that dates to about AD 200. All windmill restorations are done in this building, and visitors can view the process in various stages.

You'll find the museum at 732 S. Allen Chapel Rd. (CR 1000 East). Admission: adults $5; senior citizens $4; children (ages 7 and up) $3. Open 10 a.m. to 4 p.m. Tuesday through Friday, 10 a.m. to 5 p.m. Saturday, and 1–4 p.m. Sunday, April through November, and by appointment the rest of the year. A Windmill Festival is held here each June. For additional information, call the museum at (260) 347-2334 or visit midamericawindmillmuseum.org.

Black Pine Animal Sanctuary in **Albion** offers a permanent refuge for displaced, captive-raised exotic animals in need. What started out as a backyard menagerie has evolved into a full-time business that is now home to more than eighty animals representing some forty different endangered and exotic species; among them are lions, tigers, bears, chimpanzees, camels, cougars, and a leopard. The nonprofit sanctuary has won kudos from well-known zookeeper Jack Hanna. Located at 1426 W. CR 300 North; open daily 10 a.m. to 5 p.m. from Memorial Day weekend through Labor Day, and Saturday and Sunday after Labor Day through the end of October; by appointment the rest of the year. Tour fees start at $10 and depend upon guest's age and type of tour. Guided tours are not recommended for children under age five. (260) 636-7383 or bpsanctuary.org.

Gene Stratton-Porter, a native Hoosier who became a noted author, nature photographer, and environmentalist, lived among the swamps and wetlands that once covered much of northeastern Indiana. In 1913, she built a cabin on the south shore of Sylvan Lake near Rome City and spent the next six years of her life exploring, photographing, and writing about the natural setting in which she lived. All twenty-six of the books she wrote are still in print today. Several of her books were made into movies, which she herself wrote and produced. One of her best-known books, *A Girl of the Limberlost,* was the first American book to be translated into Arabic. It is also one of the top five favorite children's books of J. K. Rowling, author of the popular Harry Potter books; Ms. Rowling says she rereads it all the time. Today the cabin and the 123 acres of fields, woods, and formal gardens surrounding it are preserved as the **Gene Stratton-Porter State Historic Site.** Ms. Porter, who died in 1924 at the age of sixty-one, and her daughter Jeannette are interred in a mausoleum near the orchard. The site is open from April through November; grounds are open dawn to dusk, and a visitor center is open 10 a.m. to 5 p.m. Tuesday through Saturday and 1–5 p.m. Sunday; closed Monday, Easter Sunday, and Thanksgiving. Guided cabin tours are offered at the hour when the visitor center is open. Admission: adults $8, senior citizens $7; children (ages 3–17) $5. Located at 1205 Pleasant Point; (260) 854-3790 or indianamuseum.org.

Randolph County

At the **Silver Towne Coin Shop** in **Winchester,** all that glitters *is* gold—or silver—and the beautiful antique-decorated showrooms in which the collections are displayed are as dazzling as the shop's wares. The building includes such architectural elements as a 7-by-6-foot Czechoslovakian chandelier containing 7,775 crystals, and leaded stained-glass windows dating to the 1910s. A working mint supplies items to TV shopping networks. Visitors will also see a stunning array of jewelry, sports memorabilia, and collectibles. Open 8 a.m. to 5 p.m. Monday through Friday. Located at 120 E. Union City Pike; (765) 584-7481 or (877) 477-2646; silvertowne.com.

Wick's Pies, Inc., in Winchester bakes 12 million pies a year in huge ovens that hold hundreds of pies at once. Although all its pies are undeniably delicious, Wick's has become nationally known for its sugar cream pies. On National Pie Day in January 2009, the Indiana legislature paid homage to the sugar cream pie by adopting it as the official state pie, and the Indianapolis Colts have adopted the pie as an essential team menu item. Visitors can watch and smell the pies being made on a free tour of the bakery. Don't just drop in,

The Real Bare Naked Ladies

When Randolph County commissioners voted in 2005 to raze the county's rapidly deteriorating courthouse, they had no idea what resistance they would encounter. Residents loved the building's beauty, its majesty, and its historic architecture, a style known as Second Empire that dated to the 1870s.

Members of a bridge club from Farmland were particularly outraged and formulated an unusual plan to save their beloved courthouse from the wrecking ball. Publishing a calendar to raise funds for a community project was not a unique idea, but using naked models who ranged in age from 77 to 94 was.

Seven female members of the club happily stripped down and posed au naturel, smiling for the camera while holding strategically-placed miniature courthouse models. Each woman was featured alone on a page of her own, then posed with the others for group photos for the remaining five months. Their underlying message was that old—whether a woman or a courthouse—can be beautiful, too. Sold for $12.95 each, the resulting 2006 calendar generated publicity throughout North America and raised $45,000 for the courthouse's renovation. A documentary film about their efforts, entitled *Courthouse Girls of Farmland,* has been shown at film festivals and special events across the country, winning many awards.

Sadly, some of the calendar girls have since passed away, but their efforts were not in vain. The county commissioners rescinded their earlier decision, additional funds were raised, the courthouse was renovated, and proudly welcomes visitors and officials.

however; the tours usually fill up a year in advance, so reservations are essential. Located at 217 Greenville Ave.; (800) 642-5880, or wickspies.com. Wick's also operates an outlet store and full-service restaurant nearby.

Near *Farmland,* you can visit the *Davis-Purdue Agricultural Center,* site of the largest and oldest mapped temperate deciduous forest in North America. Every tree in this 126-acre forest has been numbered, mapped, described, and tagged by Purdue University foresters, a task that began in 1926; in 1975, 51 acres of the site were designated a Registered Natural Landmark by the National Park Service. You'll also see a constructed wetland. Open free of charge from 7 a.m. to about 3:30 p.m. daily; located at 6230 N. SR 1, approximately 6 miles north of Farmland; (765) 468-7022 or ag.purdue.edu.

Steuben County

Majestic *Potawatomi Inn,* the only state park inn in northern Indiana, is one of the finest in the system. Resembling an Old English lodge, it sits in a clearing on the shore of Lake James in 1,200-acre *Pokagon State Park* in *Angola.*

Winter is king here, and the main treat is a refrigerated twin toboggan slide, generally open on weekends from Thanksgiving Day through February, that whisks you over the hills and through the woods at speeds of up to 50 miles per hour. In this snowy park tucked into the northeastern corner of the Hoosier State, winter visitors will also find an ice-skating pond, a sledding hill, and cross-country ski trails. Toboggans and cross-country ski equipment can be rented in the park.

After frolicking in the chilly outdoors all day, you can retire to the inn for a sauna and whirlpool bath, do a few laps in the indoor pool, or bask in the warmth of the redbrick fireplace.

The inn features nearly 140 rooms and serves 3 meals daily in its highly rated dining room. The atmosphere is so down-homey that guests often come to eat in their stocking feet

Although Pokagon State Park and its inn have gained a reputation as a winter resort, people also come here in other seasons, when the forests and the sweeping lawns of the inn are a lush green, park lakes are ice-free for swimmers and anglers, and park trails accommodate hikers instead of skiers. Horses can be rented at the saddle barn, and the tennis and basketball courts see heavy use.

The nature center is popular year-round, with naturalists always on hand to interpret each of nature's moods. Bison and elk reside in nearby pens. One park trail leads to the marshes, swamps, and forests of the *Potawatomi State Nature Preserve.* The largest known tamarack and yellow birch trees in the state, the only northern white cedars known to exist in Indiana, and several species of wild orchids grow within the preserve's 208 acres.

For information about either the park or the inn, write Pokagon State Park, 450 Lane 100 Lake James, Angola 46703. The park's phone number is (260) 833-2012; call the inn at (260) 833-1077 or (877) 768-2928 or visit in.gov/dnr/parklake/2973.htm. To reach the park, go west from Angola on US 20 to I-69. Turn north on I-69 and proceed to SR 727; SR 727 leads west from I-69 to the park entrance.

All of Steuben County is noted for its natural beauty. Its combination of 101 lakes and verdant forests has earned it the nickname "Switzerland of Indiana," and no less an impresario than P. T. Barnum once pronounced Lake James "the most beautiful body of water I have ever seen!" What's more, Steuben County contains more dedicated state nature preserves than any other county in the state; you can learn more about them by writing or calling the Department of Natural Resources, Division of Nature Preserves, 402 W. Washington St., Room W267, Indianapolis 46204; (317) 232-0209 or in.gov/dnr/naturepreserve.

Wabash County

In the town of **Wabash, Modoc the Elephant** is the stuff of legend. The huge pachyderm came to town with the Great American Circus in 1942. Shortly after their arrival, she and two other elephants broke loose and headed downtown, perhaps enticed by the smell of peanuts roasting inside a local drugstore. Modoc's two companions were soon rounded up, but Modoc would not be deterred from getting to those peanuts. She squeezed through the front door, ate her fill, and exited through the back door. With her would-be captors hot on her trail, she traipsed around the county for a week, creating havoc and making headlines around the country in the process. A sweet-talking circus trainer with twenty-six loaves of bread finally managed to capture her (the fact that she had a cold and had lost some 800 pounds might have had a bit to do with it, too). Today, the drugstore is Modoc's Market, and elephant statues saunter along the sidewalk outside its door. Visitors can see circus and elephant memorabilia inside the store and view a large mural painted on the wall of a downtown building that commemorates the day Modoc came to town. Modoc's Market is located at 205 S. Miami St.; (260) 569-1281 or modocsmarket.com.

Although the folks in Wabash didn't realize it at the time, Modoc was a very famous elephant who is remembered today for much more than her long-ago jaunt through a small Indiana town. You can read about her remarkable life in a book by Ralph Helfer titled *Modoc: The True Story of the Greatest Elephant That Ever Lived.*

indianatrivia

The city of Wabash became the first electrically lighted city in the world in 1880. One of the original lights is displayed in the lobby of the Wabash County Courthouse.

Wells County

Bluffton native Charles C. Deam (1865–1953) was the Hoosier State's first state forester and an internationally recognized authority in the field of botany. Approximately, 4 miles northwest of **Bluffton,** you can see the **Deam Oak,** a rare hybrid tree named in the forester's honor. The tree, discovered in 1904, is believed to be the first of its kind; its acorns have since been distributed across the country. A natural cross between white and chinquapin oaks, the tree stands at the center of a small tract of state-owned land at the junction of SR 116 and CR 250 North.

You can learn more about Deam and his oak tree at the **Wells County Historical Museum** in Bluffton. Also featured here are the memorabilia of

Everett Scott, another Bluffton native, who played for the Boston Red Sox and the New York Yankees in the 1920s. A baseball autographed by Scott and his friend and sometimes roommate, Babe Ruth, is a highlight of the exhibit. Civil War buffs can read pages from the Civil War diary of William Bluffton Miller, the first child born in Bluffton. The museum is located at 420 W. Market St.; open 1 to 4 p.m. Sunday, Tuesday, and Wednesday in the spring, summer, and fall. In December, an annual Christmas in the Mansion event is presented where visitors can view more than thirty decorated trees and vote for favorites. After this event, the museum is closed until April. Check the website before going: (260) 824-9956; wchs-museum.org. Free, but donations are appreciated.

Places To Stay In Northeast Indiana

ALBION

Brick Ark Inn Bed and Breakfast
215 N. Orange St.
(260) 636-6181 or
(260) 609-6186
brickarkinn.com

ANGOLA

Potawatomi Inn
Pokagon State Park
6 Lane 100 A Lake James
(260) 833-1077 or
(877) 768-2928
in.gov/dnr/parklake/inns/
potawatomi

University Inn
1208 W. Maumee St.
(260) 665-9451
angolauniversityinn.com

AUBURN

Inn at Windmere
2077 County Rd. 40
(260) 925-3303
innatwindmere.com

Whispering Pines Lodge B&B
3190 County Rd. 36
(260) 925-3666
whisperingpinesauburn
.com

BERNE

Clock Tower Inn
1335 US 27 North
(260) 589-8955
berneclocktowerinn.com

Schug House Inn
706 W. Main St.
(260) 589-2303

BLUFFTON

Washington Street Inn
220 E. Washington St.
(260) 824-9070

FAIRMOUNT

Haisley's Hideaway Bed & Breakfast
1457 W. 800 South
(765) 506-1228
haisleyshideaway.com

FORT WAYNE

Courtyard by Marriott
1150 S. Harrison St.
(260) 490-3629
Marriott.com

Don Hall's Guesthouse
1313 W. Washington
Center Rd.
(260) 489-2524

Hampton Inn & Suites
5702 Challenger Pkwy.
(260) 489-0908
Hilton.com

Hilton Fort Wayne at the Grand Wayne Convention Center
1020 S. Calhoun St.
(260) 420-1100
Hilton.com

LaSalle Downtown Inn
517 W. Washington Blvd.
(260) 422-0851

FREMONT

White Pine Lodge
6975 N. Ray Rd.
(260) 495-0137
wildwindsbuffalo.com

GOSHEN

Rose Land Farm Bed & Breakfast
66537 County Rd. 11
(574) 535-4315
roselanefarmbedandb
reakfast.com

HUNTINGTON

The Purviance House Bed & Breakfast
326 S. Jefferson St.
(260) 224-1545
purviancehouse.com

LIGONIER

Solomon Mier Manor Bed and Breakfast
508 S. Cavin St.
(260) 894-3668
smmanor.com

MARION

College Inn Bed & Breakfast
3902 S. Washington St.
(765) 667-9161
collegeinnbb.com

Old Oak Inn
2213 W. 38th St.
(765) 603-6681
oldoakinn.net

MIDDLEBURY

Meadows Inn Bed & Breakfast
12013 US 20
(574) 825-3913
meadowsinnbnb.com

McKenzie House Bed and Breakfast
52215 SR 13
(574) 825-9787
or (877) 825-9787
mckenziehousebnb.com

MUNCIE

Courtyard by Mariott Muncie
601 S. High St.
(765) 287-8550
Marriott.com

NAPPANEE

Amish Inn
1234 W. Market St.
(574) 773 2011 or
(800) 800-4942
theamishinn.com

Countryside Inn
2004 W. Market St.
(574) 773-5999
countrysideinnnappanee

NORTH MANCHESTER

Fruit Basket Inn
116 W. Main St.
(260) 982-2443
fruitbasketinn.com

PERU

Cole Porter Inn
19 S. Huntington St.
(765) 460-5127
coleporterinn.com

ROANOKE

Inn at Joseph Decuis
492 N. Main St.
(260) 672-2356
josephdecuis.com

Joseph Decuis Farmstead Inn
191 N. Main St.
(260) 672-1715
josephdecuis.com

ROME CITY

Mirror Lake Bed and Breakfast
11463 N. 150 West
(260) 854-4675
mirrorlakebb.com

SHIPSHEWANA

Morton House
100 Morton St.
(574) 238-5559
shipshewanalodging.com

Old Carriage Inn Bed and Breakfast
240 Farver St.
(260) 768-7217 or
(800) 435-0888
oldcarriageinn.com

SYRACUSE

Brook Pointe Inn
4906 E. 1200 North
(574) 457-4466
brookpointeresort.com

Oakwood Resort
702 E. Lake View Rd.
(574) 457-7100
oakwoodresort.com

Places to Eat in Northeast Indiana

ANGOLA

The Hatchery
118 S. Elizabeth St.
(260) 665-9957
thehatcheryrestaurant.com
American/Italian

Village Kitchen
109 N. Superior St.
(260) 665-9053
villagekitchenin.com
American

AUBURN

The Deli at Sixth & Main
115 N. Main St. 2nd fl
(260) 333-7200
thedeliauburn.com
Deli

Italian Grille
227 N. Duesenberg Dr.
(260) 925-9400
italiangrille.com
Italian/American

Oriental Gourmet
558 N. Grandstaff Dr.
(260) 927-1788
American/Chinese

Sandra D's Italian Garden
1330 Main St.
(260) 927-7282
sandra-ds-italian-garden
.business.site
Italian

BERNE

Alpine Rose Coffee
Shoppe
206 E. Main St.
(260) 589-2124
alpinerosecoffeeshoppe
.com
Coffee shop

BLUFFTON

Coco China Buffet
2020 N. Main St
(260) 827-0838
cocochinabuffet.com
Chinese

Corner Depot Family
Dining Restaurant
1529 S. Harrison Rd.
(260) 824-4775
cornerdepotrestaurant.com
Comfort food

Tyeger's Pizza Parlour
931 N. Main St.
(260) 827-0700
tyegerspizza.com
Pizza

DECATUR

Back 40 Junction
Restaurant
1011 N. 13th St.
(260) 724-3355
back40junction.com
American

The Galley
622 N. 13th St.
(260) 724-8181
thegalleydecatur.com
Seafood

Soul Pig BBQ
135 S. Second St.
(260) 301-9800
soulpigbbqin.com
Barbecue

ELKHART

Antonio's Italian
Restaurant
1105 Goshen Ave.
(574) 295-8424
antoniositalian.com
Italian

Artisan
505 S. Main St.
(574) 355-3355
artisanelkhart.com
American

Chubby Trout
3421 Plaza Ct.
(574) 264-5700
chubbytrout.com
Seafood

DaVinci's Italian Family
Restaurant
2720 Cassopolis St.
(574) 264-6248
davincisrestaurant.biz
Italian

The Vine
214 S. Main St.
(574) 970-5006
thevineonmain.com
American

FORT WAYNE

Chop's Steak & Seafood
6421 W. Jefferson Blvd.
(260) 436-9115
chopswineanddine.com
Seafood/steak

Cindy's Diner
230 W. Berry St.
(260) 422-1957
American

Don Hall's Hollywood
Drive-In
4416 Lima Rd.
(260) 482-1113
donhalls.com
American

Paula's On Main
1732 W. Main St.
(260) 424-2300
paulasonmain.com
Seafood

Tolon
614 Harrison St.
(260) 399-5128
American

FREMONT

Clay's Family
Restaurant
7815 N. Old 27
(260) 833-1332
claysfamilyrestaurant.com
American

Timbuktoo's
215 E. State Rd.
(260) 495-1658
timbuktoos.com
American

GOSHEN

Maple Indian Cuisine
127 S. Main St.
(574) 533-0000
mapleindiancuisine.com
Indian

South Side Soda Shop
1122 S. Main St.
(574) 534-3790
American

Venturi
123 E. Lincoln Ave.
(574) 485-2985
eatventuri.com
Pizza

HUNTINGTON

Brick House Grill
19 Washington St.
(260) 224-6696
brickhousegrill.org
American

Chava's Mexican Grill
102 Frontage Rd.
(260) 358-4204
Mexican

Hoosier Drive-In
1525 Etna Ave.
(260) 356-7826
American

Nick's Kitchen
506 N. Jefferson St.
(260) 356-6618
nicksdowntown.com
American

LIGONIER

Calvin Street Pizzeria
316 S. Calvin St.
(260) 894-4240
ligonierpizza.com

Fashion Farm Restaurant
1680 Lincolnway West
(260) 894-4498
fashionfarminc.com
Home cooking

MARION

9th Street Café
1802 W. Ninth St.
(765) 664-4851
the9thstreetcafe.com
Comfort food

Yamato Steakhouse
506 N. Baldwin Ave.
(765) 668-8880

yamatosteakhouseonline
.com
Japanese

MIDDLEBURY

**Das Dutchman
Essenhaus**
240 US 20
(574) 825-9471 or
(800) 455-9471
essenhaus.com
Amish/American

41 Degrees North
104 S. Main St.
(574) 358-0314
41degrees-north.com
American

Village Inn Restaurant
107 S. Main St.
(574) 825-2043
American

NAPPANEE

The Barns at Nappanee
1600 W. Market St.
(574) 773-4188 or
(800) 800-4942
thebarnsatnappanee.com
Amish

Hunters Hideaway Inc.
153 S. Main St.
(574) 773-7121
huntershideawaynappane
e.com
American

Ruhe 152
152 W. Market St.
(574) 832-7843
ruhe152.com
Comfort food

U.S. 6 Diner
1103 E. Market St.
(574) 773-2724
us6dinernappanee.com
Comfort food

NORTH MANCHESTER

Main View Inn
141 E. Main St.
(260) 901-5016
American

ROANOKE

**Joseph Decuis
Restaurant**
191 N. Main St.
(260) 672-1715
josephdecuis.com
American

The Parker Grace
138 First St.
(260) 715-6609
theparkergracetearoom
.com
Teahouse

Roanoke Village Inn
190 N. Main St.
(260) 672-3707
roanokevillageinn.com
American

SHIPSHEWANA

Blue Gate Restaurant
105 E. Middlebury St.
(260) 768-4725
thebluegate.com
American/Amish

Millie's Market Café
225 N. Harrison St.
(260) 768-7334
millies-market-café.
business.site
Comfort food

**Shipshewana Auction
Restaurant**
345 S. Van Buren St.
(260) 336-8362
shipshewanatradingplace
.com
American

SOURCES FOR ADDITIONAL INFORMATION ABOUT NORTHEAST INDIANA

DeKalb County Visitors Bureau
1601 S. Van Buren St.
Auburn 46706
(260) 927-1499 or (877) 833-3282
dekalbcvb.org

Berne Chamber of Commerce
205 E. Main St.
Berne 46711
bernein.com
(260) 589-8080

Bluffton/Wells County Chamber of Commerce
211 W. Water St.
Bluffton 46714
(260) 824-0510
wellscoc.com

Elkhart County Convention and Visitors Bureau
3421 Cassopolis St.
Elkhart 46514
(800) 262-8161
visitelkhartcounty.com

Visit Fort Wayne
927 S. Harrison St.
Fort Wayne 46802
(260) 424-3700 or (800) 767-7752
visitfortwayne.com

Huntington County Visitors Bureau
407 N. Jefferson St.
Huntington 46750
(260) 359-8687 or (800) 848-4282
visithuntington.org

Greater Kokomo Visitors Bureau
700 E. Firmin St.,
Suite 100
Kokomo 46902
(765) 457-6802 or (800) 837-0971
visitkokomo.org

Kosciusko County Convention and Visitors Bureau
111 Capital Dr.
Warsaw 46582
(574) 269-6090 or (800) 800-6090
visitkosciuskocounty.org

Shipshewana LaGrange County Bureau
780 S. Van Buren St.
(SR 5 South)
Shipshewana 46565
(260) 768-4008 or (800) 254-8090
visitshipshewana.org

Marion/Grant County Convention and Visitors Bureau
505 W. Third St.
Marion 46952
(765) 668-5435
showmegrantcounty.com

Muncie Visitors Bureau
3700 S. Madison St.
Muncie 47302
(765) 284-2700 or (800) 568-6862
visitmuncie.org

Noble County Convention and Visitors Bureau
110 S. Orange St.
Albion 46701
(260) 636-3602
visitnoblecounty.com

Peru/Miami County Chamber of Commerce
13 E. Main St.
Peru 46970
(765) 472-1923
miamicochamber.com

Randolph County Convention and Visitors Bureau
123 W. Franklin St.
Winchester 47394
(765) 584-3266 or (800) 905-0514
roamrandolph.org

Steuben County Tourism Bureau
130 N. Wayne St.,
Suite 1B
Angola 46703
(260) 665-5386 or (800) 525-3101
visitsteubencounty.com

Visit Wabash County
221 S. Miami St.
Wabash 46992
(260) 563-7171 or (800) 563-1169
visitwabashcounty.com

SYRACUSE

The Channel Marker
5793 E. Pickwick Dr.
(574) 457-5900
channelmarket.net
American

The Frog Tavern
1116 S. Harkless Dr.
(574) 457-4324
sslillypad.com
American

The Pier & Back Porch at Oakwood Resort
702 E. Lake View Rd.
(574) 457-8700
oakwoodresort.com
American

TOPEKA

Tiffany's
414 E. Lake St.
(260) 593-2988
tiffanystopeka.com
Amish

Topeka Auction Restaurant
601 E. Lake St.
(260) 593-2197
topekalivestock.com/
restaurant
American

WABASH

Harry's Old Kettle Pub & Grill
1633 Stitt St.
(260) 563-7317
harrysoldkettle.com
Grill food

Mi Pueblo Mexican Restaurant
810 N. Cass St.
(260) 274-0388
mipueblomexicanrestaurantwabash.com
Mexican

Twenty
111 W. Market St.
(260) 563-0111
charleycreekinn.com
American

WARSAW

La Troje
115 S. Buffalo St.
(574) 376-4234
Mexican

One Ten Craft Meatery
110 N. Buffalo St.
(574) 267-7007
110craftmeatery.com
American

Rua
108 E. Market St.
(574) 267-4730
ruawarsaw
New American & Thai

WINONA LAKE

BoatHouse Restaurant
700 Park Ave.
(574) 268-2179
boathousewinona.com
American

Cerulean Restaurant
1101 E. Canal St.
(574) 269-1226
ceruleanrestaurant.com
Asian

Light Rail Café & Roaster
1000 Park Ave.
(574) 269-1000
lightrailroaster.com
Pizza

WINCHESTER

Coe's Noodles
112 W. Washington St.
(765) 595-8005
mrscoesnoodles.com
Comfort food

Mrs. Wick's Restaurant
100 N. Cherry St.
(765) 584-7437 or
(800) 642-5880
wickspies.com
Home cooking/pies

Northwest Indiana

Northwest Indiana is a land of contrasts. The most heavily industrialized region of the Hoosier State shares the Lake Michigan shoreline with the hauntingly wild and beautiful Indiana Dunes National Lakeshore. Lake County, which covers 501 square miles in Indiana's northwestern corner, is the state's second most populous county—some 496,000 people live within its borders. Not far south lie the rich farmlands of Benton County, whose 407 square miles are inhabited by about 9,000 people, and whose tiny town of Oxford is the birthplace of the famed racehorse Dan Patch.

Two of Indiana's most fabled rivers wend their way through northwest Indiana. The Kankakee River, which flows southwest from South Bend to the Illinois border, and its adjacent wetlands evoke memories of the lush 500,000-acre Grand Kankakee Marsh it once nourished. Indiana's longest waterway, the Wabash River, cuts a swath through four of this region's counties on its 475-mile journey west across the width of the state and then south to the Ohio River.

Visitors travel to and through northwest Indiana on I-80/90, an east–west highway that is Indiana's only toll road; I-65, a north–south route; and several excellent US highways.

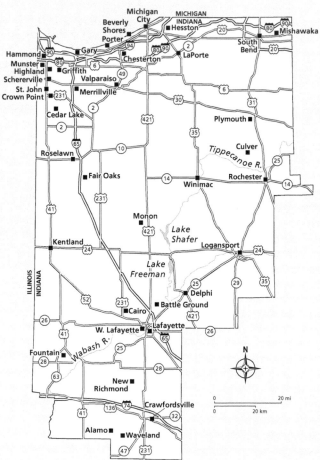

Carroll County

In **Delphi,** you can visit the last water filled portion of the storied Wabash and Erie Canal that is publicly accessible in Indiana. At the time it was built in the mid-1800s, the 460-mile-long waterway was the longest canal in the Western Hemisphere and provided the fastest mode of transportation then available. From a terminus at Lake Erie in Toledo, Ohio, the canal wove its way into northern Indiana, traversed the width of the Hoosier State, and then turned south to the canal's Ohio River terminus at Evansville. Locks along the way allowed goods and people to travel both ways. With the advent of the railroad, the canal gradually fell into disuse and was eventually abandoned. Today, the history of that era comes vividly to life at the **Wabash and Erie Canal Park,** where a 54-foot-long replica canal boat takes visitors for a leisurely 2.5-mile float on the waters of the canal.

Back on land, you can explore the park's interpretive center, where you can guide a miniature boat through a reproduction of a canal lock, and step into the living quarters below the deck of a canal boat. Elsewhere in the park, several historical buildings, including a blacksmith's shop, schoolhouse, cooper, papermaker, and smokehouse, comprise an 1850s pioneer village.

The park also features a trail system that can be hiked or biked; a variety of bicycles can be rented in the park. Some of the trails that run parallel to the canal were once towpaths trod by the mules and horses that pulled the canal boats along their way.

Officially opened in July 2003, the park and towpaths are open daily free of charge from dawn to dusk year-round. A fee is charged for boat rides, which are offered at 1:30 p.m. and 2:30 p.m. Saturday and Sunday from late May through early September; additional rides are scheduled according to demand, from mid-May through mid-October. Months may vary, prices may vary, and water levels may sometime force cancellations, so it's best to call before coming. The Interactive Museum is open from 1 to 4 p.m. Sunday through Friday; 10 a.m. to 4 p.m. Saturday year-round; no admission fee, but donations are appreciated. The park is located at 1030 W. Washington St.; (765) 564-2870; wabashanderiecanal.org.

Cass County

The pride of **Logansport** is its turn-of-the-twentieth-century **carousel** (574-753-8725; casscountycarousel.com). About a century old, it is one of only two all-wood, hand-carved merry-go-rounds still operating in Indiana. (The other is in the Indianapolis Children's Museum.) Delighted riders compete for a mount on the perimeter and the chance to snag the coveted brass ring as the carousel spins round and round. The brightly colored mounts—a mix of thirty-one horses, three goats, three reindeer, three giraffes, a lion, and a tiger—were produced in 1892 by the talented hands of German craftsman Gustav A. Dentzel, who moved to the United States in 1860 and became this country's chief carousel maker.

The carousel is a National Historic Landmark. A ride costs $1 to help offset maintenance costs. You'll find the merry-go-round in ***Riverside City Park,*** located along the south bank of the Eel River at 1212 Riverside Dr.—just follow the sound of music. It operates 6 to 9 p.m. Monday through Friday;1 to 9 p.m. Saturday and Sunday, Memorial Day through mid-August. Contact the Cass County Visitors Bureau, 311 S. Fifth St. Logansport 46947; (574) 753-4856; visit-casscounty.com.

AUTHOR'S FAVORITE ATTRACTIONS/ EVENTS IN NORTHWEST INDIANA

Feast of the Hunters' Moon
Lafayette; September and October
(765) 476-8411 or (800) 872-6648
tippecanoehistory.org/feast.htm

General Lew Wallace Study and Museum
Crawfordsville
(765) 362-5769
ben-hur.com

Indiana Dunes National Lakeshore
Lake, Porter, and LaPorte Counties
(219) 395-1882
nps.gov/indu

Indiana Fiddlers' Gathering
Battle Ground; June
(765) 588-1376
indianafiddlersgathering.org

Kentland Dome
Kentland
(219) 474-5125

Marshall County Blueberry Festival
Plymouth; September
(574) 936-5020 or (888) 936-5020
blueberryfestival.org

Popcorn Festival
Valparaiso; September
(219) 464-8332
valparaisoevents.com

Shades State Park
Waveland
(765) 435-2810
in.gov/dnr/parklake/2970.htm

Studebaker National Museum
South Bend
(574) 235-9714 or (888) 391-5600
studebakermuseum.org

Subaru of Indiana Factory Tour
Lafayette
(765) 449-6250
subaru-sia.com

Wolf Park
Battle Ground
(765) 567-2265
wolfpark.org

Mark Racop fell in love with the Batmobile in 1967 when he was two years old. That's when he first saw the original 1966 *Batman* television series starring Adam West and Burt Ward. He announced to his mom and dad that someday he would build a car like that, and when he was seventeen, he did. Using a 1974 Monte Carlo, four photographs, and a toy Batmobile for reference, he crafted his first car in his father's garage. He couldn't call it a Batmobile, however, because the name was trademarked. That didn't deter him from building more cars, and eventually his passion evolved into a full-time business.

In 2010, after the patent for the Batmobile design had expired, Mark acquired the sole rights from DC Comics to officially call his cars 1966 Batmobile replicas. The full-size, fully drivable, street-legal cars have fully functional gadgets galore, including a Batphone, a detect-a-scope radar screen, a gold antenna grid called the Batbeam, and a rocket exhaust tube that shoots a 2-foot flame out the back of the vehicle. Each car takes six months to build and costs about $150,000; the demand for them requires that three or four be under construction at the same time. Buyers have come from Canada, England, Italy, and all over the United States, and there's a waiting list.

Mark produces his replicas in a small shop called **Fiberglass Freaks** at 602 Erie Ave. in Logansport. If you'd like to visit, contact Mark at (574) 722-3237. Fans will feel like kids in a candy store. There's also a fantastic website at fiberglassfreaks.com that will tell you everything you ever wanted to know about the Batmobile and Mark's company. If you can't come to Mark, you might be able to arrange for Mark to come to you. He has what he calls a "scratch and dent" Batmobile that he sometimes takes to birthday parties and other events. Kids are welcome to climb in and over it; Mark can always build another one if need be.

Four miles west of Logansport off US 24 you'll come upon **France Park** and its picturesque swimming hole. An abandoned limestone quarry, partly hemmed in by precipitous cliffs, it is filled with clear, brisk, spring-fed water that's irresistible on a hot summer day. Scuba and cliff divers like it, too.

Patches of woodland and a mossy, 15-foot waterfall on Paw Paw Creek add touches of beauty to the 500-acre county park. Seven miles of hiking/biking trails include a towpath that follows the remains of the old Wabash and Erie Canal. Visitors will also find a water slide, miniature golf course, some 200 campsites, an Italian bread-baking oven, and, near the entrance, a log cabin (built circa 1839). Winter visitors enjoy cross-country skiing; bring your own or rent them in the park. Admission: Per person $5; children (ages two and under) free. Beach open Memorial Day through Labor Day; park open daily year-round 9 a.m. to 11 p.m. Contact France Park, 4505 W. US 24, Logansport 46947; (574) 753-2928; co.cass.in.us.

Fountain County

It will never give the folks in Utah anything to worry about, but Indiana does have a unique stone arch that's been declared both a National Natural Landmark and a state nature preserve. Through the years the meanderings of a tiny stream in northwestern Fountain County have carved a 30-by-12-foot opening through a massive sandstone formation and created a natural bridge known as **Portland Arch.** Nearby Bear Creek flows through a deep ravine edged by rugged sandstone cliffs. The rare bush honeysuckle grows here, and this is the only known site in the state where the Canada blueberry is found. At times, a cover of mosses and lichens and several species of ferns growing in the crevices of the cliffs create a landscape of green velvet. A quaint pioneer cemetery on the 435-acre preserve contains eleven marked graves, and a portion of the long-abandoned Wabash and Erie Canal touches a corner of the preserve.

ANNUAL EVENTS IN NORTHWEST INDIANA

Redbud Trail Rendezvous
Rochester; April
(574) 223-4436
fultoncountyhistory.org

Mint Festival
North Judson; June
(574) 772-0896 or (877) 733-2736
starkecountychamber.com

Canal Days
Delphi; July
(765) 564-2870 or (866) 374-6813
wabashanderiecanal.org

Pierogi Fest
Whiting; July
(219) 659-0292 or (877) 659-0292
pierogifest.net

Kouts Porkfest
Kouts; August
(219) 766-3312
koutsindiana.org

Scarecrow Festival
Wanatah; September
(219) 733-2183 or (800) 584-1417
scarecrowfest.org

Steam and Power Show
Hesston; September
(219) 872-5055
hesston.org

Trail of Courage Living History Festival
Rochester; September
(574) 223-4436
fultoncountyhistory.org

Elvis FANtasy Fest
Portage; October
(219) 926-2255 or (317) 844-7354
elvisfantasyfest.com

Portland Arch State Nature Preserve is located on the south side of the town of *Fountain.* Signs lead the way to the preserve and two parking lots, each adjoined by a self-guiding trail. The loop trail leading from the first and main parking lot follows a hilly route about 1 mile long to Portland Arch. For additional information, write or call the Department of Natural Resources, Division of Nature Preserves, 402 W. Washington St., Room W267, Indianapolis 46204; (317) 232-4052 or in.gov/dnr/naturepreserve.

Fulton County

Fulton County is peppered with round barns, the legacy of a turn-of-the-twentieth-century fad. Indiana had more round barns than any other state, and Fulton County had more round barns than any other Indiana county. At last count, eight of the original barns, the newest of which was built in 1924, were still standing. They are kept in excellent repair and are both unusual and beautiful to behold. No two are alike. The main idea behind this flurry of round-barn building was to create one centralized feeding station for livestock, thus increasing the efficiency of the farm operation. The idea was eventually abandoned, in part because the mechanization of agriculture was more suited to rectangular barn design.

In 1988, the *Fulton County Museum* near *Rochester* opened its doors to the public. A round barn, rebuilt on the premises and opened in 1990, showcases historic farm tools and machinery. Nearby, a living history village depicts life in a Fulton County farming community from 1900 to 1925; among the buildings you'll see are a cider mill, a stagecoach inn, a windmill, and a round chicken house. Together they offer a glimpse into the county's past and provide information about its unique heritage. Maps are available for a driving tour of the county's barns. Although the barns are not officially open to the public, many owners, if they're at home when you arrive, are happy to show you through their barns. Several barns are also open to the public for one weekend each June when the county celebrates a Round Barn Festival. Admission to the museum is free, but donations are very much appreciated; open 9 a.m. to 5 p.m. Monday through Saturday, May through September. The museum is located at 37 E. CR 375 North, about 4 miles north of Rochester; (574) 223-4436 or fultoncountyhistory.org. The Fulton County Historical Society, which has its headquarters at the museum, founded the National Round Barn Center to keep track of and to help preserve all round barns in the country.

Jasper County (Central Time Zone)

Each fall one of Indiana's most magnificent natural spectacles takes place at the 8,000-acre *Jasper-Pulaski State Fish and Wildlife Area.* During the last week in October and the first week in November, some 15,000 to 20,000 greater sandhill cranes pause here to rest on their annual journey south for the winter. Jasper-Pulaski is believed to be the only place east of the Mississippi River where this unusual species stops en masse during migration.

These beautiful blue-gray birds, which stand about 3.5-feet tall and have a wingspan of up to 7 feet, are as impressive to hear as they are to look at. The best times to view them are at dawn, when they rise up from the misty marshes and call to one another in noisy unison, and again at sunset, when they return to the marsh for the night.

You can pick up literature about the cranes and obtain a free observation permit at the area headquarters, then continue to one of two observation towers.

The cranes also migrate through Jasper-Pulaski between late February and mid-April, but they are usually present in greater concentration in the fall.

Although the sandhills are the main attraction, other wildlife species are here as well. Canada geese, quail, woodcock, and deer live in the wild year-round, and elk and bison roam fenced-in pastures. Part of Jasper-Pulaski serves as a game farm where pheasant are reared as stock for wildlife areas throughout the state. Natural history and wildlife exhibits are maintained in one of the service buildings, and hiking trails wind through the area.

Located in the area's northwest corner is the 480-acre *Tefft Savanna State Nature Preserve,* home to many plants that are extremely rare in the Midwest. The entire fish and wildlife area actually occupies portions of three counties—Jasper, Pulaski, and Starke—but the majority of its 8,000 acres are in Jasper County. It's open daily year-round at all times, and entrance is free. The headquarters office is open 8 a.m. to 3:30 p.m. Monday through Friday, but hours may be extended in certain seasons.

To reach the refuge, go north from Medaryville (in Pulaski County) on US 421 and turn west onto SR 143; proceed 1.5 miles to the entrance on the right side of the road; follow the signs. Write or call Jasper-Pulaski State Fish and Wildlife Area, 5822 N. Fish and Wildlife Ln., Medaryville 47957; (219) 843-4841 or in.gov/dnr/fishwild/3091.htm.

For a day of fun and education for the whole family, head to *Fair Oaks Farms* in the small community of *Fair Oaks.* It's the rural equivalent of Disney World. You'll begin your tour at the Dairy Adventure Barn, where you'll watch a 4-D movie and learn what awaits you. After the movie, you can explore some educational exhibits (one game lets you match your cow-milking skills against those of the experts) while waiting for a cow-patterned tour bus that takes you to the dairy barns. Here, you'll learn how the cows are bred to produce the maximum amount of milk and how their manure produces methane gas that is converted to energy that powers the generators that provide the farm's electricity. Thirty thousand cows live here, so there's a lot of manure! Watch as the cows walk onto a carousel to be milked and then casually walk off 8.5 minutes later after traveling one revolution. With so many cows, there are bound to be a lot of calves. About eighty calves are born here each day, and there's a state-of-the-art birthing barn where you can watch the entire process. A blinking light signals when a birth is imminent (yellow when the calf's hooves are coming out and green when the baby is being born) so you can get to the barn in time.

In good weather, an outdoor play area known as Mooville provides fun for the kids; there's a 25-foot-tall climbing wall shaped like a giant milk jug, a huge pillow to jump on, and a string cheese maze. The little ones can ride the MooChoo train, and young and old alike can experience bungee jumping. Everything is included in the price of admission for $20.

In growing season, walk through the garden adjacent to the birthing barn and, if you like, pick a few fresh vegetables. A seasonal selection of fresh produce is always available for sale in the garden shop.

Before you leave, head to the cheese factory barn and sample the farm's award-winning cheese in its gift shop, eat a grilled cheese sandwich and an organic salad at the cafe, and try the sweet treats at the ice-cream parlor. Located at 856 N. CR 600 East; open 9 a.m. to 5 p.m. Monday through Saturday and 10 a.m. to 5 p.m. Sunday. Call (219) 394-2025 or (877) 536-1194; fofarms.com.

indianatrivia

On July 14, 1936, the temperature in Collegeville rose to 116 degrees Fahrenheit, the hottest temperature ever recorded in the state of Indiana.

Lake County (Central Time Zone)

When the first white settlers came to Indiana, seven-eighths of the state was covered with a forest so dense that the sunlight could barely penetrate the canopy of leaves. The far northwest corner, however, including what is now Lake County, was a sea of grass—grass so tall in places that a rider on horseback could not be seen above it. It was a long time before residents realized the value of saving some remnants of that original landscape, and by then most of it was irretrievably lost.

Two of the finest examples still in existence can be seen in Lake County. *German Methodist Cemetery Prairie* covers just 2.7 acres at the rear of the cemetery for which it's named, but more than eighty rare and vanishing plant species thrive in its rich black soil. In late summer, when most of them are in bloom, it is a place of incredible beauty.

This tiny preserve is probably the most botanically diverse acreage in Indiana. You'll find it in the midst of farm fields on the east side of US 41, 1 mile south of the intersection of US 41 and 141st St. in *Cedar Lake.* The old cemetery is still there and should be respected. Behind it is the prairie, surrounded by a chain-link fence to protect the fragile plant life. For additional information, write or call the Nature Conservancy, Indiana Field Office, 620 E. Ohio St., Indianapolis 46202; (317) 951-8818; nature.org.

Hoosier Prairie, the largest virgin prairie in Indiana, sprawls over 430 acres near *Griffith.* It contains some 300 species of native plants, including grasses that reach 12 feet in height. A trail about 2 miles long leads through some of the preserve's less sensitive areas and permits a look at the diverse habitats. You may even spot a deer along the way. Hoosier Prairie, a state nature preserve, is located west of Griffith on the south side of Main Street; a small parking lot is near the trailhead. Open daily year-round during daylight hours; admission is free. Write or call the Department of Natural Resources, Division of Nature Preserves, 402 W. Washington St., Room W267, Indianapolis 46204; (317) 232-0209; in.gov/dnr/naturepreserve/4698.htm#lake.

The late pastor Win Worley of the *Hegewisch Baptist Church* in Highland gained worldwide fame as an exorcist. He began casting out evil spirits in 1970, and within one year, with no publicity other than word of mouth, more than 1,000 first-time visitors were streaming into the small church annually. At an Exorcism Open House sponsored by the church in 1992, for instance, some 500 people from twenty-eight states and three foreign countries showed up. Now several Deliverance Workshops are held each year, and you are welcome to attend. For additional information, write Hegewisch Baptist Church, 8711 Cottage Grove Ave., Highland 46322; call (219) 838-9410; or visit hbcdelivers.org.

indiana*trivia*

The first American to win the Nobel Prize in Economics was Paul Samuelson, a Gary native who won the prize in 1970. His 1948 book, *Economics,* is the best-selling economics textbook in history.

The *Carmelite Shrines* in *Munster* offer a haven of serenity. On the grounds are many shrines that display Italian sculptures in a grotto studded with crystals and unusual rocks. The overall effect is enhanced by special lighting. You'll also find an arboretum and, in the monastery, a replica of the Vatican's Private Audience Hall. The grounds are open free of charge 9:30 a.m. to 5:30 p.m. from Easter through October, weather permitting; open other days if you call one day before. Building interiors can usually be seen on request. The shrines are located at 1628 Ridge Rd., 0.5 mile west of US 41; (219) 838-7111; carmelitefathers.com.

The collection of life-size sculptures and monuments that dot the landscape at 9710 Calumet Ave. in Munster are vivid reminders of our country's twentieth-century military conflicts. Visitors who follow the brick pathway through the 6.5-acre park can hear prerecorded messages that relate the history of each war. Each monument is inscribed with descriptions of the conflict it depicts and quotations from those who fought them. Known as the **Community Veterans Memorial,** it is realistic, sobering, and affecting. Open daily free of charge from dawn to dusk. Call (219) 836-3392 or visit communityve teransmemorial.org. For additional information and to make appointments for guided tours, contact the Community Foundation of Northwest Indiana, Inc., 905 Ridge Rd., Munster 46321; (219) 934-3845.

An extraordinary spiritual experience awaits visitors to the **Shrine of Christ's Passion** in **St. John.** Forty life-size bronze statues that depict the final hours of Christ's life on earth, beginning with the Last Supper and ending with the Resurrection, border a half-mile long prayer trail. Each statue is an exquisitely crafted work of art that's set in one of the fourteen Stations of the Cross; each station is enclosed in its own grotto and has a taped message that describes the scene you are viewing. More than 150 speakers play background music along the way. The setting of the entire site is designed to be evocative of the landscape as it might have appeared in Jerusalem during Christ's lifetime. Volunteers staff a visitor center and gift shop on-site and, by advance appointment, provide tours via electric carts for visitors who are unable to walk the distance. There is no admission fee, but donations are appreciated. The shrine, visitor center, and gift shop are open from 10 a.m. to 5 p.m. daily year-round. Located at 10630 Wicker Ave. (US 41); (219) 365-6010; shrineofchr istspassion.org.

Crown Point is dominated by the "Grand Old Lady of Lake County," the magnificent **Old Lake County Court House,** which many regard as Indiana's most impressive. Built in 1878, it served as the seat of county government until 1974. Today it houses more than a dozen crafts and specialty shops, as well as the **Lake County Historical Museum.** Don't miss its arched brick ceilings and intriguing hallways. The courthouse is located at the corner of Joliet and Court Streets; its shops are generally open from 10 a.m. to 5 p.m. Monday through Saturday (until 7 p.m. on Friday); hours may vary. The museum is open 1 to 4 p.m. Thursday through Saturday, May through October; other times by appointment. Admission: adults $1; children 50 cents. For additional

John Dillinger Escapes From Jail

Bold headlines shouted the news: John Dillinger had escaped from jail.

Carving a fake gun from a block of wood and staining it with black shoe polish, Dillinger had broken out of the so-called "escape proof jail" in Crown Point on March 3, 1934. Adding insult to injury, Dillinger made his getaway in the sheriff's new V-8 Ford.

The FBI's first "Public Enemy" was on the loose again. But he wouldn't be free for long. Before the year had ended, the thirty-one-year-old Hoosier gangster would be dead.

Born June 22, 1903, in the Oak Hill section of Indianapolis, John Herbert Dillinger, Jr. grew up in a middle-class home. His father was a grocer who tried to steer his son on the straight and narrow path, believing in "spare the rod and spoil the child." Dillinger's mother died shortly before his fourth birthday.

Frequently in trouble with the law for fighting and petty theft, Dillinger quit school at age sixteen and went to work in an Indianapolis plywood mill. Fearing that the big city was corrupting his son, Dillinger's father moved the family to a farm in the tiny town of Mooresville. Dillinger didn't take the move kindly. Small town life was boring to him.

Newsreel footage showed Dillinger arriving in Crown Point to await trial and execution. When the heavily guarded Dillinger landed at Midway Airport in Chicago after his arrest on January 30, 1934, several thousand people turned out to get a glimpse of him. "This is the end of Dillinger," Lake County Prosecutor Robert Estill announced, not knowing that the city's law enforcement would soon become a national joke.

Armed deputies stood atop the jail and other deputies surrounded the car when the handcuffed Dillinger was escorted into the jail. Sheriff Lillian Holley—who had taken over the job just months before when her sheriff husband was killed—swore that Dillinger would not escape from her jail.

Spread in newspapers across America, a photograph showed prosecutor Estill and Sheriff Holley smiling proudly and posing with their prisoner. For a shockingly chummy photo, Dillinger rests his elbow on the shoulder of the prosecutor and Estill has his arm around the alleged murderer.

With the gang safely behind bars, the legal system began its slow paperwork grind to send Dillinger to the electric chair. Trail was set for March 12. But Dillinger didn't wait that long.

Early on the morning of Saturday, March 3, 1934—five weeks after his celebrity arrival at the Crown Point jail—Dillinger made his move. Sticking the wooden gun in a guard's back, Dillinger ordered him to open the door to his cell.

Although Dillinger later told his father that he had used a safety razor blade to slowly carve the fake gun out of the top brace off a washboard, reports still linger that the convict was helped to escape by corrupt police officers and maybe even by his own attorney.

Dillinger seemed to have dropped out of sight. Then the Feds got a huge tip. Afraid of being deported to her native Romania and hoping to pocket reward money, a Chicago prostitute named Anna Sage said she could lead the men to Dillinger. During a heat wave in Chicago, Dillinger, his girlfriend Polly Hamilton, and Sage were going to the Biograph Theatre to cool off on the night of July 22.

To alert the FBI, Sage would wear an orange skirt that would look red under the marquee lights. FBI agent Melvin Purvis would wait outside the theater, lighting a cigar to signal that Dillinger was on his way.

The movie that Sunday was a crime thriller, **Manhattan Melodrama**, starring Clark Gable. The movie ended with the hero walking a last mile to the electric chair. Moments later, wearing a straw hat and gold-rimmed eyeglasses, Dillinger walked a few yards to an ambush death in a nearby alley.

Leaving the theatre with his girlfriend on one arm and Sage on the other at about 10:30 p.m., Dillinger suddenly sensed that something was terribly wrong. Seeing an alley as the nearest escape route, Dillinger turned the girls loose, crouched, and started to run, reaching for the .380 automatic pistols in his right pocket.

He never made it. Brought down in a hail of bullets from almost thirty Feds, Dillinger crumbled to the sidewalk. Pandemonium erupted. Two passing by women had been injured by G-Men gunfire. There were reports of men dipping their handkerchiefs and women the hems of their skirts into the pools of Dillinger's blood as souvenirs of that fateful day.

In his pocket, one of the nation's most successful bank robbers had $7.70. The public was so enthralled with Dillinger that his body was put on display in the Cook County morgue where 15,000 people filed through for a grisly glimpse.

information, call (219) 662-3975 or visit cpcourthouse.org. You can also obtain information from the Lake Court House Foundation, 21 Court House Sq. Suite 200, Crown Point 46307; (219) 663-0660.

In 1896, William Jennings Bryan stood on the courthouse steps and campaigned for the presidency. A then-unknown car designer, Louis Chevrolet, came here to accept the winner's cup for the first major auto race in the United States, a race held in 1909 that was the forerunner of the Indy 500. From 1916 to 1941, the courthouse became famous for its instant marriages; the usual blood test and three-day waiting period were not required here. Among the thousands married at the courthouse during that period were Joe DiMaggio, Red Grange, Colleen Moore, Tom Mix, Muhammad Ali, Ronald Reagan (to Jane Wyman), and, at the height of his career, Rudolph Valentino.

Have you ever wondered how gummies are made? You can find out when you take a fascinating free tour of the **Albanese Candy Factory** in **Merrillville.** Part of the fun of eating a gummi is choosing your favorite shape;

here they make not only the usual bears, dinosaurs, sharks, and worms, but also such novelty shapes as army guys, jet fighters, and butterflies. You can also forget about having only five flavors from which to choose; Albanese has added peach, mango, and banana, with other options to come. At the end of your tour, you'll receive a free gummi, along with a free sample of the company's Gold Label chocolates. If you like what you taste, you can buy some to take with you for cheaper-than-wholesale prices at an outlet store on-site; the store also features a floor-to-ceiling chocolate waterfall. Albanese makes and sells other types of confections, too. The self-guided tours are available without reservation at any time during the store's business hours (except in November through December and March through April, when they're busy filling Santa's and the Easter Bunny's orders); open 9 a.m. to 8 p.m. Monday through Saturday and 10 a.m. to 6 p.m. Sunday. Located at 5441 E. Lincoln Hwy., Merrillville; (219) 947-3070; albanesecandy.com.

Not too long ago, the city of **Gary** was known as Steeltown, U.S.A, but it is perhaps better known today as the birthplace of the late **Michael Jackson.** Michael was born here on August 29, 1958, and grew up with his eight siblings in a small, two-bedroom, one-bath house located at 2300 Jackson St. (named long ago in honor of President Andrew Jackson). Although Michael's personal life took some bizarre turns, he left a legacy of unforgettable music to the world; he sold more than 200 million albums worldwide during his lifetime, and his 1982 album *Thriller* is still the best-selling album of all time. When Michael died in 2009 at the age of fifty, his fans came here from all over the world to see his birthplace and pay tribute to his memory. The house, still owned by the Jackson family, is not open to the public, but it can be viewed from the street. The 7-foot-tall black granite monolith that stands in the fenced-in yard depicts a dancing Michael on one side and is inscribed with the lyrics to his song, "Gone Too Soon," on the back. Michael wrote the song in honor of the late Ryan White, an Indiana teenager who died from AIDS in 1990; Ryan was a hemophiliac who was infected during a blood transfusion. Now the words also serve as an epitaph for Michael.

The **Indiana Welcome Center** in **Hammond** is a tourist attraction in itself. Built at a cost of $6 million in 1999, the structure is domed with blue glass and stainless steel that symbolize the waves of Lake Michigan crashing against the shore to the north. An undulating south wall represents the Kankakee River, which forms Lake County's southern border. Also along the southern portion of the building is a silo that pays tribute to the county's agricultural heritage. An exhibition hall displays artifacts from various Indiana attractions, including an Indianapolis 500 race car and an Amish buggy. Open daily, but hours may vary.

The Welcome Center is located just south of the intersection of Kennedy Avenue and I 80/94 at 7770 Corinne Dr.; (219) 989-7979 or (800) 255-5253; southshorecva.com.

LaPorte County (Central Time Zone)

At the tiny town of **Hesston,** northeast of LaPorte, you can visit the **Hesston Steam Museum** (heston.org). Spread out over a 155-acre site is an assemblage of steam-powered equipment worth several million dollars—trains, cranes, buzz saws, and a boat among them. Among the stationary displays are a restored 1889 Scottish-built locomotive that was used in the movie *Around the World in Eighty Days* and a Czechoslovakian locomotive that was built in 1940 for use by the Germans. You can take a 2-mile ride on a steam train or watch a miniature train, authentic to the tiniest detail, whiz by on a 3.5-inch track. Feel free to toot a horn or ring a bell—it's that type of place.

Open noon to 5 p.m. on Saturday, Sunday, and holidays, Memorial Day weekend through Labor Day, and Sunday only after Labor Day through mid-October. Four events are held here each year—the Whistle Stop Days on Memorial Day weekend; a Civil War skirmish, complete with musket and cannon competitions, in mid-August; the exuberant Annual Labor Day Weekend Steam and Power Show, and the Ghost Train ride in mid-October. The outdoor museum and the on-site Whistle Stop Cafe are located at 1201 E. CR 1000 North, approximately 2.5 miles east of SR 39. Admission is free except on Labor Day weekend; a nominal fee is charged at all times for train rides. Contact the LaPorte County Convention and Visitors Bureau, Marquette Mall, 4073 Franklin St., Michigan City 46360; (219) 778-2783, (219) 872-5055, (800) 634-2650, or michigancitylaporte.com.

In the town of **LaPorte**, you can tour the **LaPorte County Museum.** Among the more than 80,000 exhibits are an auto collection that includes a Duesenberg, a Cord, a Tucker, a DeLorean stainless steel car, a Baker electric car, a 1903 Winton, and an Amphicar that runs on land and water, as well as several early airplanes. The W. A. Jones collection of antique firearms and weapons is recognized as the best collection of its kind in the United States and one of the three best in the world. There's also a display that tells the story of Belle Gunness, LaPorte's Madam Bluebeard, who in the early 1900s lured at least a dozen men to her farm north of town by promising to marry them; once there, the would-be husbands were promptly killed for their money and buried in the farmyard. When Belle's house burned to the ground in 1908, the skeletons of her three adopted children and a headless woman were found in the ashes. The woman's body was much too short to be Belle's, but it was never learned what really happened to her. The museum, located at 2405 Indiana Ave., Suite 1, is open from 10 a.m. to 4:30 p.m. Tuesday through Saturday (closed holidays). Admission: adults $5; senior citizens $4; children (under age eighteen) free. Call (219) 324-6767 or visitlaportecountyhistory.org.

In *Michigan City,* a fishing pier that extends into Lake Michigan offers a view of Indiana's only operating lighthouse. On a clear day, you can also see the Chicago skyline.

The area's natural history is explored at the *Old Lighthouse Museum* in *Washington Park,* Michigan City's 90-acre lakefront park. Situated on Heisman Harbor Road at the park's west entrance, the museum contains a rare fifth-order Fresnel lens, shipbuilding tools, and other maritime artifacts. You'll see exhibits about Lake Michigan shipwrecks, learn about the lighthouse's female keeper, and, if you like, climb into the lantern tower. Open 1 to 4 p.m. Tuesday through Sunday, April through October; closed Monday, January and

indiana*trivia*

Michigan City native Don Larsen pitched the only perfect game in World Series history on October 8, 1956. Larsen, playing for the New York Yankees, achieved his remarkable feat in game 5. The Yankees won the series, defeating the Brooklyn Dodgers 4 games to 3.

The Trail of Death Regional Historic Trail

In 1838, the Potawatomi Indians of northern Indiana were rounded up by federal troops and led on foot to the land on which the government had decreed they should henceforth live. The tribe of Chief Alexis Menominee numbered more than 850 when it started its westward walk. During the 900-mile trek to Kansas, some 150 Potawatomis perished from disease, fatigue, and adverse weather conditions. That fateful journey is recorded in history as the Trail of Death.

From the north bank of Twin Lakes in Marshall County, where the long walk began, the trail leads south to Logansport before turning southwest to follow the banks of the Wabash River to the Indiana-Illinois border. Numerous markers and memorials have been established along the trail, but the most impressive of all is the granite statue of Chief Menominee that stands on the site his tribe once called home.

Visitors will find it on S. Peach Road a little southwest of the town of Plymouth.

Mas-saw, a Potawatomi Indian who survived the Trail of Death, was the great-grandmother of Jim Thorpe. Thorpe, an athlete who excelled at several sports, is generally recognized as the best male athlete of the first half of the twentieth century.

February, and holidays. Admission is $5 for ages fourteen and older: $2 for children under age fourteen: free for preschool children; (219) 872-6133; oldlighthousemuseum.org.

Marshall County

In celebration of its agricultural heritage and a passion for the time-honored culture of quilting, Marshall County has established Indiana's first **Barn Quilt Trail.** Historic barns, family homesteads, and public spaces throughout the county have been adorned with colorful murals in a variety of heirloom quilt patterns. Begun in 2009, the trail features four loops, with nearly seventy murals completed at the end of 2020. They range in size from 4-by-4-feet to 8-by-8-feet square, and no two patterns are the same. Each loop begins at the Marshall County Convention and Visitors Bureau in Plymouth and takes between one and two hours to drive.

Visitors can obtain a free trail map at the Marshall County Convention and Tourism Bureau's office at 220 N. Center St. in Plymouth; (574) 936-1882 or (800) 626-5353. The map can also be downloaded from the bureau's website at visitmarshallcounty.org.

Montgomery County

For sheer natural beauty it's hard to beat **Shades State Park** near **Waveland,** but to fully appreciate its magnificent scenery and outstanding geologic features you'll have to do some hiking. Only by taking to the trails can you see the primeval terrain for which the park is noted. Some first-time hikers do a double take when they see what awaits them—a landscape like this just isn't associated with Indiana.

About 470 acres of the 3,000-acre park have been set aside as the **Pine Hills State Nature Preserve.** Within its boundaries are four narrow rock ridges from 75 to 100 feet tall that are recognized as the finest example of incised meanders in the eastern United States. This observation was made by no less an authority than the National Park Service, which designated the preserve a National Natural Landmark.

Giant hemlock trees, not usually found this far south, rare Canada yews, and native white pine are relics of a long-ago past when this area was much cooler. The arrival of spring is first announced by the flowering of the rare snow trillium, and the coloring of the land continues through May, when the dogwoods and redbuds show off their blossoms. Through it all flows Sugar Creek, the most beautiful stream in the state.

When early European settlers first cast eyes on the lush forests and deep gorges along Sugar Creek, they referred to this place as "the Shades of Death." The long shadows cast by the heavy growth of trees initially appeared ominous to them, but as they became more familiar with the area the nickname was shortened to "the Shades." It remains appropriate to this day since the land has remained virtually untouched by human hands.

Two other impressive features are Silver Cascade Falls, one of eleven waterfalls in the park, and Devil's Punchbowl, a large, circular grotto cut into the sandstone by two small streams.

OTHER ATTRACTIONS WORTH SEEING IN NORTHWEST INDIANA

FOWLER

Benton County Wind Farm Tours
Benton County Economic Development
706 E. Fifth St.
(765) 884-2080
benton4business.com

LAFAYETTE

Columbian Park Zoo
1915 Scott St.
(765) 807-1540
columbianparkzoo.org

LINDEN

Linden Depot Museum
520 N. Main St.
(765) 339-7245
lindendepotmuseum.org

MICHIGAN CITY

Great Lakes Museum of Military History
360 Dunes Plaza
W. US 20
(219) 872-2702 or (800) 726-5912
southshorecva.com

International Friendship Gardens
2500 E. US 12
(219) 878-9885
friendshipgardens.org

Lubeznik Center for the Arts
101 W. 2nd St.
(219) 874-4900
lubeznikcenter.org

SOUTH BEND

The History Museum
897 Thomas St.
(574) 235-9664
historymuseumsb.org

Potawatomi Zoo
500 S. Greenlawn Ave.
(574) 235-9800
potawatomizoo.org

VALPARAISO

Porter County Museum
153 S. Franklin St.
(219) 465-3595
pocomuse.org

WINGATE

Midtown Museum of Native Cultures
208 S. Vine St.
(765) 376-7128
visitmoco.com

WEST LAFAYETTE

Fort Ouiatenon Historical Park
3129 S. River Rd.
(765) 743-3921
tippecanoehistory.org

Canoeists take to Sugar Creek in droves, and if you're into solitude you'll want to avoid a trip on summer weekends. Weekdays in May or June or any day in August or September when the water level is down promises quieter floats. The most scenic stretch, which lies between Shades State Park and Turkey Run State Park (located to the southwest in adjoining Parke County), can be seen in one day. Put in at Deer's Mill Covered Bridge, which spans Sugar Creek along SR 234 on the eastern edge of Shades State Park. For an enjoyable two-day trip, put in at Elston Park in Crawfordsville. Both trips end at West Union Covered Bridge in Parke County. Always check water conditions at park headquarters before starting out, however; the creek can be dangerous at flood stage.

Although most of the park is undeveloped, visitors will find more than 100 primitive campsites, special campgrounds for backpackers and canoeists, and several picnic areas, some with shelters. Bicycles can be rented in the park, and a naturalist is on duty in the summer.

Shades State Park is located along both banks of Sugar Creek in southwestern Montgomery County and spills over into Parke County. The entrance is on CR 800 South, just west of SR 234; look for signs. It's open daily year-round, vehicle admission fee is $7 per day. Write or call the property manager at Shades State Park, 7751 S. CR 890 West, Waveland 47989; (765) 435-2810 or in.gov/dnr/parklake/2970.htm.

Just north of Shades State Park, CR 875 West leads north off SR 234 to the Hoosier State's own **Alamo,** which the town's sixty-six residents hope you'll remember. There, on the outside front of an old-school gymnasium, a local artist has created a series of colorful murals that depict both Alamos—the one in Texas and the one in Indiana.

Another small town in the northwestern corner of the county achieved fame without even trying. When Hollywood came to Hoosierland looking for an idyllic rural area in which to film the principal exterior shots for the movie *Hoosiers,* it chose **New Richmond.** (For readers who missed it, *Hoosiers* is loosely based on the true story of a small-town high school basketball team that defied all odds to win the Indiana state championship.) Now tourists, enthralled with what they saw on the screen, travel here to see the real thing—the storefronts, the main street with its single traffic light, the farm fields bathed in sunset gold. The sign that identifies the community as New Richmond is now embellished with the words WELCOME TO HICKORY (the town's movie name).

For information about Alamo and New Richmond, contact the Montgomery County Visitors & Convention Bureau, 101 W. Main St., Crawfordsville 47933; (765) 362-5200 or (800) 866-3973; visitmoco.com. For additional information about the making of *Hoosiers,* see Ripley County in the Southeast Indiana section.

The Old Montgomery County Jail at 225 N. Washington St. in **Crawfordsville** was the first of only seven rotary jails ever built worldwide and is the only one still operational. Completed in 1882, it remained in daily use until 1973. The cell blocks are arranged in a circle in such a way that the sheriff, with the turn of a crank, could rotate the cells around him and check on his prisoners without ever taking a step. Now known as the **Old Jail Museum,** it's open from 10 a.m. to 5 p.m. Wednesday through Saturday, from May through August; 10 a.m. to 3 p.m. Wednesday through Saturday, from August through May. Tours are conducted on the hour, with the last tour beginning at 2 p.m. Admission: adults $5; children (ages 6 to 11) $3; (765) 362-5222 or rotaryjailmuseum.org.

The campus of **Wabash College,** at the corner of W. Wabash and Grant Avenues in Crawfordsville, is of interest because of the mid-1800s architecture of its buildings and its arboretum of native Indiana trees. Students apparently find the setting conducive to learning. Out of 1,500 colleges and universities in this country, Wabash ranks sixteenth in the percentage of graduates who go on to earn PhDs. Perhaps it's the lack of distraction—Wabash is an all-male college, one of only three in the country. The other two all-male colleges are Hampden-Sydney College in Hampden Sydney, Virginia; and Morehouse College in Atlanta, Georgia. Call (765) 361-6100 or (800) 345-5385; wabash.edu.

Also in Crawfordsville, on the corner of Wallace Avenue and E. Pike Street at 200 Wallace Ave., you'll find a 4-acre park that contains the **General Lew Wallace Study and Museum.** One of Indiana's most fascinating native sons, Wallace was a soldier in the Mexican War, the Union Army's youngest major general during the Civil War, and a state senator. He served as prosecutor during the Lincoln assassination trial, signed Billy the Kid's death warrant, was US Minister to Turkey, and made violins. Nevertheless, Wallace is probably best remembered as the author of the novel *Ben-Hur.* Published in 1880, it was one of the most popular novels of all time, becoming the first book ever to exceed the Bible in annual sales (more than one million copies were sold through the Sears catalog alone). A dramatic version was one of the longest-running plays in history. Hollywood twice made *Ben-Hur* into a movie, once as a silent picture in 1926 and again as a remake in 1959. The latter won eleven Academy Awards, including one for Best Picture. Wallace's eclectic study, a National Historic Landmark designed by Wallace himself, is a mix of French, Byzantine, Romanesque, and Greek styles. The 20-foot-tall bronze statue of Wallace that stands nearby is a replica of one that was unveiled in Washington, DC, in 1910. Open 10 a.m. to 5 p.m. Tuesday through Saturday. Admission: adults $7; military with ID $5; students (ages 13–18) $3; students (ages 7–12) $1. Call (765) 362-5769, or visit ben-hur.com.

Newton County (Central Time Zone)

What is often described as a unique natural feature in Indiana is a peculiar layering of rock near **Kentland** known as the **Kentland Dome.** Elsewhere in the state, layers of rock are almost horizontal, but here many of the layers are vertical. The deformed rocks bear mute testimony to a force of nature so incredible that it folded and fractured layers of rock that lay in a horizontal position 1,800 feet below the surface of the earth and thrust them above the surface in a nearly vertical position.

Currently, two theories exist. The more popular one is that a huge meteorite hit here several million years ago and created the huge crater about 4.5 miles in diameter that is seen today. A second theory is that a sudden, violent explosion of trapped underground gases caused the faulting.

While geologists have been speculating about the cause of the disruption since the 1880s, when the strange formation was first discovered, no geologic

The Governor's Bull

In a lonely field in Newton County, a fading stone monument marks the final resting place of Perfection Fairfax. The occupant of the grave is the grand champion of the 1907 International Livestock Exposition, a prize bull that brought fame and fortune to his owner.

Warren T. McCray brought his prize-winning, perfect bull to his stock farm near Kentland, where the bull became the progenitor of many perfect little bulls and made a tidy sum of money for his owner. When Perfection Fairfax died in 1920, his owner buried him with much pomp and honor.

To see the stone that memorializes McCray's bull, go east from the intersection of CRs 50 East and 1300 South for about 0.33 mile, then turn north for about 0.25 mile. On a clear, sunny day, the stone can be seen from several miles away.

The fortune to which Perfection Fairfax had contributed so much helped propel McCray into Indiana's statehouse, where he served as governor from 1921 to 1924. During his tenure in office, McCray sponsored the amendment to the state constitution that gave women the right to vote, created the state gasoline tax to fund much-needed highway construction, and improved teachers' pensions. Unfortunately, he also earned the dubious distinction of being the only Indiana governor (to date) to go directly from the statehouse to the Big House. Tried and convicted of mail fraud and forgery, McCray was sent to the federal prison in Atlanta, where he resided until 1930, when President Herbert Hoover pardoned him. Some believe the governor was set up because he appointed the attorney who in 1925 successfully prosecuted D. C. Stephenson, grand dragon of the state's then-politically powerful Ku Klux Klan.

evidence yet exists to explain the origin of the Kentland Dome. To this day, it remains a geologic enigma.

Although the formation is on private property, visitors may view it by advance appointment. For further information, write or call the Newton County Quarry, Rogers Group, Inc., 235 US 24 East, PO Box 147, Kentland 47951; (219) 474-5125.

Near **Roselawn,** you can see one of the most unusual sundials anywhere. A 63-foot-long lady's leg, fetchingly posed, accurately tells you the time on any sunny day. You can see it near the entrance to **Sun Aura,** a 309-acre, clothing-optional resort for those over twenty-one that features rental cabins, campsites, an Olympic-size swimming pool (skinny dipping only), hiking trails, and a clubhouse that offers food, entertainment, and a dance floor. No photographic equipment of any kind is permitted. Sun Aura, which has undergone several name changes since its founding in 1933, is the oldest nudist resort in the country. Hours vary so check the website. Contact the resort at 3449 E. SR 10, Lake Village 46349; (219) 345-2000 or sunauraresort.net.

Porter County (Central Time Zone)

Indiana does not have a Grand Canyon or a Yosemite, but it does have some of the largest sand dunes this side of the Sahara. Since 1972, most of them have been part of the 15,000-acre **Indiana Dunes National Lakeshore,** a miracle of survival in the midst of one of the most heavily industrialized regions in the country. In 2011, National Geographic ranked the lakeshore as one of the top ten urban escapes in the country. Its lovely sand beaches along the southern shoreline of Lake Michigan are legendary for miles around, but they are only part of what can be seen and done here.

Mt. Baldy inches away from the lake each year; its name hints at why. Because it has not been stabilized by vegetation, the 135-foot-tall dune is kept in constant motion by wind and water, forcing the dune to take giant steps backward. Climb to the top for a sweeping view of Lake Michigan.

Not all of the landscape is sand and water. There are also grassy hills, patches of prairie, lush wetlands, and cool forests with a canopy so dense that sunlight barely filters through. Miller Woods, Cowles Bog, and Pinhook Bog would be exceptional natural areas anywhere, but their existence in the midst of such pollution, industry, and urban population is incredible.

The Bailly Homestead, dating from 1822, and the Chellberg Farm, built in the late 1880s, contain historical structures that the public can visit. There are hiking, bicycling, and horseback-riding trails to follow; in the winter they're used by cross-country skiers. At least 223 species of birds have been identified here, and many rare plants live among the dunes. Special programs and events are held all year long.

When the Chicago World's Fair of 1933 closed, five homes from the ***"Houses of the Future" exhibit*** were placed on a barge and transported across Lake Michigan to the then-new community of **Beverly Shores.** Plans to make Beverly Shores the ultimate vacation resort were thwarted by the lingering effects of the Great Depression, but the houses are still there, lined up along Lake Front Drive and still of interest. Especially startling is the House of Tomorrow, a twelve-sided structure built like a wedding cake (the top two floors are each smaller in circumference than the floor below). You'll also see a reproduction of Boston's Old North Church; it, too, was carted over from the fair. Guided tours of the homes are offered each fall by advance reservation.

Although the national lakeshore actually lies in parts of three counties—Lake, Porter, and LaPorte—its visitor center is in Porter County, and this is where you should begin your visit. The center is located on Kemil Road, which runs south from US 12 about 3 miles east of the intersection of US 12 and SR 49 near Porter, and is open daily year-round, 8 a.m. to 6 p.m. Memorial Day through Labor Day and 8.30 a.m. to 4.30 p.m. the rest of the year; closed major winter holidays. The park is open daily year-round; hours vary from area to area and are subject to change. Standard hours for general areas are 6 a.m. to 11 p.m. A $6 entry fee per vehicle is charged at West Beach; everything else is free. For additional information, write or call Indiana Dunes National Lakeshore, 1100 N. Mineral Springs Rd., Porter 46304; (219) 926-7561 or nps.gov/indu.

Completely surrounded by the national lakeshore are 2,182 acres that make up **Indiana Dunes State Park.** It offers a microcosm of the features found in its big brother and boasts the highest sand dune along the lakeshore—192-foot-tall Mt. Tom.

When conditions are just right, the drifting sand emits a low, humming sound, soothing to the ear and soul, that is akin to the sound produced by drawing a bow across the strings of a bass viola. The unique phenomenon is known locally as the music of the "singing sands."

Birders will find the park unique because both northeastern and southern bird species are found here. One, the Kirtland's warbler, is the rarest songbird in the nation and one of the rarest on earth; fewer than 2,000 exist worldwide.

The 1,500-acre **Dunes State Nature Preserve,** which lies within park boundaries, contains more species of trees than any other area of comparable size in the Midwest; from one spot alone you can identify thirty different

Diana of the Dunes

The story of Diana of the Dunes is one of the most enduring in Indiana lore. Born Alice Mable Gray, she was given the name by which she is remembered in legend when she rejected civilization in 1915 to move into an abandoned fisherman's shack nestled in the wilderness of Porter County's dune country.

Diana, a Phi Beta Kappa from Chicago, was believed to have been inspired by the poetry of Byron, who wrote in his poem "Solitude" that "in solitude we are least alone." It is reported that, when weather permitted, she was often seen wandering over and among the dunes sans clothing.

Diana later married and shared her solitude with Paul Wilson, another lover of solitude who sought out Diana after reading about her unique lifestyle. The public, however, would not permit them their privacy, and when a man's charred body was found near their shack, many people believed the two were guilty of murder.

In 1925, Diana died and was buried in an unmarked grave in a nearby cemetery. Her grieving husband packed up and moved away. It is reported even today that her ghost can sometimes be seen at twilight flitting among the dunes she loved.

varieties. In the summer the myriad of rare flowers and ferns found here create a near-tropical appearance. Recreational facilities include a modern campground, a nature center, a swimming beach, and trails for hiking, bicycling, and cross-country skiing. To reach the park, proceed north from I-94 on SR 49 for about 2 miles. The park is open year-round; a nominal vehicle admission fee is charged from spring through fall. Contact Indiana Dunes State Park, 1600 N. CR 25 East, Chesterton 46304; (219) 926-1952 or in.gov/dnr/parklake/2980.htm.

The **Hoosier Bat Company** produces more than 50,000 custom-made baseball bats each year for such teams as the Seattle Mariners, Chicago White Sox, Baltimore Orioles, Cleveland Indians, and Milwaukee Brewers. Sammy Sosa of the Chicago Cubs used one to break his batting slump in 1998, then went on to become that year's National League Most Valuable Player and the first player in history to hit more than sixty home runs in consecutive seasons (1998 and 1999). The bat he used to hit his 69th home run in 1998 is now in the Baseball Hall of Fame. Owner Dave Cook says his company's bats are harder and more durable than typical bats; his patented design is made of three woods: ash in the handle, hickory in the hitting area, and maple on the barrel end. He also says that no cork is used in any of his bats. Visitors can buy a regulation or mini-size bat personalized with the buyer's name. Open Monday through Friday from 9 a.m. to 4 p.m.; Sat by appointment. tours are free, but

Corn Off the Cob

The word **popcorn** and the name "Orville Redenbacher" have become virtually synonymous in the minds of snack lovers all over the world. An Indiana native and a graduate of Purdue University in West Lafayette, Orville began his rise to fame when he and a friend purchased a small agricultural company in Valparaiso. The unassuming entrepreneur dreamed of giving the world a fluffier, higher-quality popcorn, and the world is grateful for his efforts.

Originally marketed as red bow popcorn (a blending of Redenbacher and the name of his partner, Charles Bowman), it is now known as Orville Redenbacher's Gourmet Popping Corn. The two changed the name on the advice of a marketing firm, and sales soared. Perhaps in deference to his roots, one of Orville's trademarks was his red bow tie.

In later years, Orville's company was sold to Hunt-Wesson, Inc., and moved to California. However, until his death in 1995 at the age of eighty-eight, Orville never forgot his Indiana roots, returning to the state almost every year for the annual Valparaiso Popcorn Festival in September.

Today, Orville Redenbacher's Gourmet Popping Corn remains the top-selling microwave popcorn and is the only popcorn sold at Disney World in Florida and Disneyland in California.

an advance appointment is necessary; for safety reasons, no child 7 or under is allowed on the tour. Hoosier Bat is located at 1556 W. Lincolnway, Suite 2 in Valparaiso; call (877) 711-0410, or visit hoosierbat.com.

In October 2011, MSN's Local Edition featured ten arboreta in the United States that "may well leave you speechless." **Taltree Arboretum** in **Valparaiso** was one of them. More of a nature preserve than an array of manicured gardens, Taltree is a 360-acre mix of woodlands, wetlands, prairie, formal gardens, and some three miles of walking paths.

The arboretum began with a dream of creating a lush green oasis in the midst of an area that was rapidly giving way to Chicago's encroaching bedroom communities. In the spring of 1998, staff and volunteers planted more than 7,000 oak and hickory trees to lay the groundwork for the arboretum seen today. One themed display, an area known as Oak Islands, showcases more than forty different oak species from around the world and contains the largest collection of oak trees in the state.

The latest addition to Taltree is its still-developing Railway Garden. The first of three planned phases, devoted to the steam era of railroading, opened in May 2011. Entered through a circa 1920s train depot, the 1-acre garden is traversed by model trains that race across thirty bridges and pass through a simulated variety of landscapes that include canyons, mountains, and prairies. Nine historical vignettes throughout range from a buffalo wallow to a limestone quarry to a recreation of Lincoln's funeral train at a stop in Richmond, Indiana; each is enhanced by miniature plantings appropriate to the scene.

Taltree Arboretum is open daily from 8 a.m. to 7 p.m. April through October, 9 a.m. to 4 p.m. in November and January through March, and 9 a.m. to 8 p.m. in December. The Railway Garden is open daily from 10 a.m. to 5 p.m. April through October; also open the rest of the year, but hours vary; trains run year-round as weather permits. Admission is $10 per car. Located at 450 W. 100 North; (219) 462-0025; pnw.edu.

Pulaski County

Motorcycle aficionados from around the world beat a path to the tiny rural town of **Winimac** to visit the **World of Motorcycles Museum.** They come to see a world-class collection of more than 100 machines from eight different countries that span nearly nine decades of motorcycle history. Among the vintage bikes exhibited here are a 1931 Indian four-cylinder, a 1916 Harley-Davidson Model J, and a 1926 Harley-Davidson BA; every bike in the collection is kept in running condition.

The idea for the museum grew out of a young boy's passion for all things mechanical. One of his first experiments involved combining a motorcycle frame with the motor from his mother's washing machine, despite the fact that his mother was still using her Maytag washer. A forbearing mother allowed her son to keep the motor, and today that same boyhood invention, dubbed the Simpletag, is on display in Kersting's museum. Admission is $5 per person. Open same hours as Kersting's Cycle Center. Call ahead if you plan to visit (574) 896-3172.

Should a visitor be inspired to buy his own motorcycle, he'll find a shopping nirvana in the adjoining **Kersting's Cycle Center,** where both new and used machines, along with all the accessories and clothing any enthusiast could desire, may be purchased or just admired. A cigar-store Indian is on hand to greet you. Open 10 a.m. to 6 p.m. Tuesday through Thursday; 10 a.m. to 8 p.m. Friday; and 10 a.m. to 5 p.m. Saturday; closed Sunday and Monday. The museum and store are located at 8774 W. 700 North; (574) 896-2974 or (877) 537-7846; kerstingscycles.com.

St. Joseph County

From nearly every vantage point in **South Bend,** you can see the renowned golden dome that tops the administration building of the **University of Notre Dame.** A walking tour of the 1,250-acre campus will take you to such places as the Grotto of Our Lady of Lourdes, an exact reproduction of the original in France; the Sacred Heart Church, an awe-inspiring Gothic structure that contains one of North America's oldest carillons; the Snite Museum of Art, which houses rare religious artworks and masterpieces by such noted artists as Chagall, Picasso, and Rodin; and the Notre Dame Memorial Library, a huge, fourteen-story building noted for its rare-books room and the 132-foot-high granite mural of Christ raising his arms in benediction that adorns its outer wall on the south side. The mural, which can be seen from the north goal post on the university's football field, has been nicknamed "Touchdown Jesus" by football fans; the nickname has become so popular that few know the mural's true name, *Word of Life*. To reach the university, go north from South Bend on US 31/33 to Angela Boulevard and turn east; call (574) 631-5000 for general information, (574) 631-5726 for tour information; nd.edu.

Another name that's famous around South Bend is Studebaker. Clement Studebaker began his career as a wagon maker, supplying the Union Army during the Civil War and later the thousands who trekked west. As he progressed from wagons to carriages to automobiles, he kept a collection of company vehicles. They are housed today in the **Studebaker National Museum** at 201 S. Chapin St. Among the exhibits are a Conestoga wagon, the last Studebaker produced, the Studebaker carriage in which Abraham Lincoln rode to Ford's Theatre the night he was assassinated, a 1934 Bendix car, and a 1956 Packard Predictor Car of the Future. The museum is open from 10 a.m. to 5 p.m. Monday through Saturday and noon to 5 p.m. Sunday; closed major holidays Hours may vary, so call before visiting. Admission: adults $10; senior citizens $8.50; children (ages 6 and up) $6; call (574) 235-9714 or (888) 391-5600, or visit studebakermuseum.org.

By 1888, Studebaker had become a wealthy man, and he built himself a forty-room mansion worthy of his station, complete with twenty fireplaces and 24,000 square feet of space. Its massive stone walls, turrets, and irregular roofs gave it the appearance of a feudal castle. Today the historic mansion is called **Tippecanoe Place** and houses a fine gourmet restaurant that serves continental cuisine. Tours are available outside of dining hours; reservations are strongly advised for both meals and tours. Located at 620 W. Washington St.; (574) 234-9077 or tippe.com.

Knute Rockne and "The Gipper"

Clustered close to radios around the world, listeners heard the words emanating from South Bend, Indiana, on April 4, 1931. For the first time in the history of broadcasting, a funeral was being covered by an international radio hookup.

Broadcast live coast to coast on CBS Radio and sent by shortwave to Europe, South America, and Asia, the service marked a world coming together in grief at the death of one man. How could a college football coach have inspired such devotion that his death at age forty-three would bring about such unprecedented press coverage?

At the end of the 1930 football season, Knute Rockne was on his way to Los Angeles aboard a Transcontinental-Western flight from Kansas City. The plane encountered a storm shortly after takeoff and crashed in a rural area near Bazaar, Kansas. All eight on board were killed. Legend says that the passengers and crew were aware of their fate. When a rescue crew recovered Rockne's body, it was said the coach had a rosary clutched in his hand.

The Knute Rockne story started on March 4, 1888, when the baby was born in Voss, Norway. A carriage maker, his father moved the family to Chicago when Knute was five. Neighborhood youngsters would spend long evenings playing sandlot baseball and football. Afraid he would be injured in the rough sport, Knute's parents forbade him to play football. Knute, of course, slipped away to the neighborhood football field whenever he could. A short scrawny kid, Knute took more than his share of knocks.

At Chicago's North West Division High School, Rockne ran track and played football for a short time. Dropping out of school, Rockne had a series of odd jobs and at age nineteen got a job as a postal clerk. When he heard that a couple of his buddies were headed to Notre Dame college, Rockne decided to give it a try. Although he knew nothing about Notre Dame, Rockne quickly discovered that the college had a football team and that scored it for him. Passing an entrance exam, the twenty-two-year-old Rockne enrolled at Notre Dame in 1910.

"I went to South Bend with a suitcase and $1,000," he later wrote, feeling the strangeness of being a lone Norse Protestant invading a Catholic stronghold." He converted to Catholicism in 1925.

Still seeking its place in the sun, Notre Dame was a small college surrounded by farms and gently rolling Hoosier countryside. At only 5-foot-8 and 160 pounds, Rockne wasn't built like a powerhouse football player but he made it on the team and played fullback and end. When the 1911 season started, Notre Dame began experimenting with a football play called the forward pass.

Spectators were not used to seeing a football thrown in the air. After all, footballs were made for kicking. But Rockne made an art of throwing and an art of receiving the football. When the 1913 Notre Dame team suited up with Rockne as captain under new coach Jesse Harper, they were ready to make gridiron history.

Only a small crowd turned out for the Army versus Notre Dame game. It was a foregone conclusion that the mighty Army would win. Notre Dame was just a blip on the Army game schedule. Imagine the amazement when Notre Dame defeated Army 35-13.

Graduating with honors and a bachelor's degree in chemistry and pharmacology in 1914, Rockne considered going to medical school in St. Louis. But he decided to stay at Notre Dame to teach chemistry and be a football assistant coach. In Rockne's four years as assistant, Notre Dame lost only five games. He took over as head coach at Notre Dame in 1918 when Harper resigned.

Rockne's record as a coach is one of the most remarkable that any coach of any sport has ever compiled. His 1918 and 1919 teams went unbeaten. Perhaps, his greatest teams were in 1920, 1924, 1929, and 1930. Called by Rockne, the "greatest player Notre Dame ever produced," George Gipp was attending Notre Dame on a baseball scholarship when he caught Rockne's attention and joined the Fighting Irish.

Nominated as the first Notre Dame player in history to make the All-America first team, Gipp came down with a throat infection which turned deadly serious. A few weeks after the close of the 1920 season, "the Gipper" was dying with Rockne by his bedside. As lore has it, Gipp spoke these words to Rockne from his deathbed on December 14, 1920:

"I've got to go, Rock. It's all right. I'm not afraid. Some time, Rock, when the team is up against it, when things are wrong and the breaks are beating the boys—tell them to go in there with all they've got and win just one for the Gipper. I don't know where I'll be then, Rock. But I'll know about it, and I'll be happy."

As Gipp requested, those words were used to inspire the team in the November 1928 game against Army. And they did "win one for the Gipper."

Not surprisingly, Hollywood came calling, wanting to make a movie of Rockne's life. Troubled by phlebitis in his leg, Rockne was advised by his doctors to take it easy but he decided to make the flight. On March 31, 1931, Rockne met his five fellow passengers and two pilots at the Kansas City airport.

A light snow was falling as the plane took off shortly after 9 a.m. In eastern Kansas, the plane became enveloped in a thick fog. Near the tiny town of Bazaar, some ranchers working with their cattle saw the plane emerging from a big cloud nearly 90 degrees off course. Suddenly, the plane lost part of its left wing and plunged toward the snow-covered prairie. No one survived the violent wreck. Rockne was laid to rest two miles from the Notre Dame campus in Highland Cemetery.

Almost a decade later, the Hollywood film for which Rockne had taken his last flight was released. ***Knute Rockne: All-American*** starred Pat O'Brien as Rockne and future president Ronald Reagan as George Gipp. More than half century after his death, Rockne became the first coach in any sport to be honored with a commemorative stamp. The day the 1988 stamp was issued, President Reagan delivered a speech at Notre Dame before a capacity crowd of 10,000—many of whom hadn't even been born when Knute Rockne died.

Studebakers Start Building Wagons

On a cold day in February 1852, the Studebaker brothers, Clem and Henry, opened their new wagon building/blacksmith business. Then they waited. Their only customer that first day was a man who wanted his horse shod with two shoes. The brothers did a quick and excellent job. They earned 25 cents. That was it for the whole day.

After all, blacksmiths and wagon builders were common in those times. Setting up shop in the Hoosier city of South Bend may have seemed like a good idea but many other entrepreneurs had come to the area hoping to make a living, as well.

Within a few days, though, more customers came to the new Studebaker shop. The man who had his horse shod had spread the word that the Studebakers did good work and charged a fair price. It took weeks, however, before the first customer appeared inquiring about having a wagon built.

The man wanted a simple farm wagon. The Studebakers obliged. A week later, the buyer plunked down $175 and drove off in a green and red wagon that made folks stop and stare in admiration. Painted on the sides and back in yellow was the name Studebaker.

That was the beginning of a company whose name and products would span the centuries. From the horse-drawn era to the roaring automobiles, the Studebaker name would mean quality on wheels. The Studebaker brothers lived up to their motto of delivering more than promised.

Back then, of course, such horseless contraptions as automobiles were far from people's minds. Wagons were the way to go and the Studebakers quickly gained a reputation for producing the best in the business. At their shop, the Studebakers saw wagon trains coming from the east and going west, many of them heading to California and its promise of strike-it-rich gold.

In 1857, the brothers made their first fancy carriage. South Bend was no longer a pioneer town. Women and their families now wanted spiffy carriages for church and social events. When the Civil War hit, the US Army needed even more wagons.

But the travel tide was turning. Horseless carriages were the way to go. In 1902, Studebaker started building electric automobiles, soon switching to gasoline power.

By 1915, Studebaker was building more than 45,000 cars annually, fueled by a growing public passion for the contraptions. The primitive motorcars were expensive, but they were catching on. The wagons were now only a sideline. Within a few short years, the wagons would be gone altogether. The last Studebaker wagon was built in 1920.

For many years, Studebaker manufactured cars that consumers liked, such as the bullet-nosed 1953 Starliner and Starlight coupes and the 1963 Avanti Sports coupe. By the mid-1950s, however, Studebaker didn't have the resources of its Big Three competitors.

In December 1963, Studebaker shuttered its South Bend plant. The company's Canadian facilities remained in operation until March 1966 when Studebaker closed its doors for the final time after 114 years in business.

The only artificial whitewater course in North America and one of only three in the world is located in the heart of downtown South Bend. Called the *East Race Waterway,* it's a 2,000-foot-long channel that bypasses the South Bend Dam across the St. Joseph River. The elite of whitewater paddlers from around the globe come here each summer to take part in national and international competitions. Because the flow of water can be controlled, the waterway can generate the churning rapids and 6-foot-tall waves needed for athletic events or can present a surface calm enough for whole families to paddle on. It's open to the public for rafting, kayaking, and other water sports, under the watchful eyes of a well-trained rescue team, from noon to 5 p.m. Saturday and 1 to 5 p.m. Sunday. The many adjacent walkways and bridges provide landlubbers with a close-up view of waterway happenings. Located east of the St. Joseph River, along the west side of Niles Ave., and between Jefferson Blvd. on the south and Madison St. on the north. For additional information about competitive events and watercraft rental, contact the East Race Waterway Corp., 126 N. Niles Ave., South Bend 46617; (219) 233-6121; or the South Bend Parks Department, 321 E. Walter St., South Bend 46614; (574) 299-4765; eastracewatersway.gr8.com.

indianatrivia

New Carlisle is the unofficial snow capital of Indiana. It gets an average of 95 inches of snow a year.

During March and August through November, the East Race Waterway also functions as a fish ladder, one of four such ladders on the St. Joseph River. Steelhead trout and coho salmon are able to detour around four dams and travel freely along the 63-mile stretch of river between Mishawaka and Lake Michigan. Some 300,000 of those fish are reared annually at the *Richard Clay Bodine State Fish Hatchery* in *Mishawaka.* Visitors can take a free, self-guided tour of the facilities daily between 8 a.m. and 3:30 p.m. Monday through Friday. Located at 13200 E. Jefferson Blvd.; (574) 255-4199; in.gov/dnr/fishwild/5459.htm.

indianatrivia

Gangster Al Capone enrolled in Notre Dame in 1937 to study science. He later changed his major to commerce but left in 1938 due to "poor scholarship."

To sample one of Indiana's most delicious diversions, stop by the factory where the *South Bend Chocolate Company* makes its delectable treats (5,000 pounds daily and twice that around the holidays) and take a free 20-minute tour. It's a good thing free samples are provided at the end of the tour because you'll be salivating by then. A chocolate museum displays the world's largest

The Taking of Oliver

On the evening of December 24, 1889, friends and relatives gathered at the Matthew Larch farmstead near South Bend to celebrate the Christmas holiday. It was pitch black when eleven-year-old Oliver Larch was sent outside to fetch water from the well.

A few minutes later, Oliver's screams of pure terror reached the ears of those in the house. When they rushed outside to investigate, they clearly heard Oliver's voice from somewhere high above their heads proclaiming "Help! They've got me!" Horrified and helpless, people could only listen as Oliver's cries trailed off into the darkness.

The boy's footprints on the snow-covered ground simply ended. The oak bucket he had carried with him lay on the ground beside his trail. When questioned later by investigators, everyone present, including a local minister and a judge, told identical stories.

Oliver Larch was never seen again.

collection of chocolate-related artifacts, including a 1,300-year-old Mayan chocolate pot. Located at 3300 W. Sample St. in South Bend; tours are offered hourly 9 a.m. to 4 p.m. Monday through Friday and 9 a.m. to 3 p.m. Saturday; large groups are asked to call ahead. Call (574) 233-2577 or (800) 301-4961, or visit sbchocolate.com for additional information and to make reservations.

Landscape architect Shoji Kanaoka went to Florida and designed the grounds at Epcot Center. He also came to Indiana and designed **Shiojiri Niwa,** a lovely 1.3-acre Japanese strolling garden located in the Merrifield Park Complex at 1000 E. Mishawaka Ave. in Mishawaka. Among the garden's many pleasures are Oriental plantings, bridges, a tea garden, and dry waterfalls and streams. Visitors can sample its serenity at any hour of any day. Admission is free. Call the Mishawaka Parks and Recreation Department at (574) 258-1664; mishawaka.in.gov/shojiriniwa.

On the campus of Bethel University in Mishawaka, you can visit the **Bowen Museum.** Dr. Otis Bowen, a physician from Bremen, Indiana, entered politics in 1952. After serving six years as Marshall County Coroner, he was elected to the Indiana House of Representatives, a post he held for fourteen years. Bowen was elected as Indiana's forty-second governor in 1972 and was reelected to a second term by a then-record high margin, the first Indiana governor to serve eight consecutive years. In 1985, at the request of then president Ronald Reagan, Bowen became the first physician ever to fill the position of the US Secretary of Health and Human Services. The museum honors the life of one of Indiana's most revered statesmen through displays of personal items, mementos, and official documents. Located in the Bowen Library at 1001 W.

McKinley Ave. on the campus of Bethel College; open by appointment. Admission is free, but donations are welcome. Call (574) 807-7000 for additional information or visit betheluniversity.edu.

Tippecanoe County

The tiny town of **Cairo** is home to the **Operation Skywatch Memorial,** a limestone statue honoring civilian volunteers in the Korean War. Because there was no national radar system during that conflict, the US Air Force commissioned a nationwide system of observation towers that were manned around the clock by the Civilian Ground Observation Corps. Approximately ninety volunteers from the Cairo area worked in shifts, scanning the skies for enemy planes. The life-size figures of a man, woman, and child, faces turned upward, stand atop the base of the monument, which is inscribed with the words THEY ALSO SERVE WHO STAND AND WATCH. Nearby, the wooden observation tower still stands, alongside a state historical marker that tells the story of what happened here. Located in Memorial Park at the junction of CRs 850 N. and 100 W.; open during daylight hours. For additional information, contact the Indiana Historical Bureau, 140 N. Senate Ave., Room 130, Indianapolis 46204; (317) 232-2535; in gov/history/markers/317.

On November 7, 1811, William Henry Harrison, then governor of the Indiana Territory, led his men in battle against the last all-Indian army to be assembled east of the Mississippi River. The Indians, representing a confederacy of tribes organized by Tecumseh and his brother, the Prophet, went down in defeat, ending any organized Indian resistance to the Europeans' settlement of the Northwest Territory. In later years, Harrison's victory was a decisive factor in his successful bid for the presidency of the United States.

You can see an impressive 85-foot-tall monument and stroll the 96-acre grounds where the battle was actually fought at the **Tippecanoe Battlefield State Memorial** near the town of **Battle Ground.** A scenic trail leads past several trees that stood during the battle; musket balls are still found in the older trees when they fall. The park is also a peaceful and lovely spot for a picnic—except on three days in late June when players of dulcimers, guitars, mandolins, and more hold all-day, all-night jam sessions during the annual **Indiana Fiddler's Gathering.** The park is open daily, free of charge, year-round during daylight hours. A museum on the grounds presents the history of the battle from both sides' points of view. Open 10 a.m. to 5 p.m. daily except Wednesday year-round; closed major winter holidays and during severe weather conditions. Admission: adults $5; senior citizens $4; children (under age sixteen) $2. For additional information or to schedule a tour, call (765)

567-2147 or visit tippecanoehistory.org. The park and museum are located on Prophet's Rock Road just west of Battle Ground; follow the signs.

Nearby **Prophetstown State Park** can be viewed from the Tippecanoe Battlefield site. The 3,000-acre park is home to the Farm at Prophetstown, a real working farm. Guided tours are available for $5 per person. Online self-guided tours also are available. The farm's barn chores are done each day at 8 a.m. and 3 p.m.; visitors are invited to help feed the livestock, collect eggs, and milk the cows. Historic Prophetstown is open daily from 8 a.m. to 5 p.m. April through October and at other times for special events; (765) 567-4700 or prophetstown.org.

Prophetstown State Park features some 900 acres of prairie restoration containing plants native to Indiana, campsites, and hiking and bicycle trails. An outdoor Aquatic Center features a 30-foot tube slide, body flume, lazy river float area, adventure channel, zero-entry pool, and an aquatic activity area with basketball, plus a concessions area. Admission fee is $5 per person with children ages three and younger free. Admission to Prophetstown State Park is a single fee of $8 per vehicle with Indiana license plates and $10 for out-of-state license plates. For additional information, contact Prophetstown State Park, 4112 E. SR 225, West Lafayette 47906; (765) 567-4919; in.gov/dnr/parklake/2971.htm.

On certain nights, full moon or not, you can join a howling at Battle Ground's **Wolf Park.** The eerie but beautiful voices of the resident wolf pack drift through the air and send chills up and down your spine. If you like these misunderstood creatures, it is an experience you will never forget.

This unique wildlife park is a research facility, and you can visit during the day to watch scientists at work. Docents are on hand to tell you each wolf's name and rank order in the pack, and you can see the wolves interact with human beings whom they've come to accept as members of their "society." At 1 p.m., each Sunday from May through November, predators (wolves) and prey (bison) are placed together to demonstrate that a healthy animal has nothing to fear from wolves.

The park is operated by the nonprofit North American Wildlife Park Foundation. A guided walking tour costs $10 for adults, $8 for children ages 6–13, and free for children age five and younger. Advance reservations are required for the wolf howls which cost $12 for adults, $10 for children age 6–13, and free for children age five and younger. Other tours also are available. The park is open 1 to 5 p.m. Tuesday through Sunday from the first weekend in May through November; howls are held at 7:30 p.m. on Saturday year-round and also at 7:30 p.m. on Friday from April through November (weather permitting). To reach the park, go north from Battle Ground on Harrison Road for about

1 mile; Wolf Park signs point the way to the park. Write Wolf Park, c/o North American Wildlife Park Foundation, 4004 E. 800 North, Battle Ground 47920; call (765) 567-2265; or visit wolfpark.org.

In *Lafayette* the 20-acre *Clegg Botanical Gardens* perch on the high bank of Wildcat Creek. Wander along a mile of marked trails that lead past ancient white oaks, sugar maples, and dogwoods. Daffodils bloom in the spring; hybrid daylilies unfold their petals in June and July, followed by resurrection lilies in August and Japanese anemones in September. From Lookout Point, you can see the Indiana countryside for miles around. Open dawn to dusk daily; free. Located at 1782 N. CR 400 East; call (765) 423-1325 or (800) 872-6648; homeofpurdue.com.

indianatrivia

Purdue University is known as the "Cradle of Astronauts." As of 2020, the university has produced twenty-five NASA astronauts, including Gus Grissom, the second American in space; and Neil Armstrong, the first person on the moon.

The *Red Crown Mini-Museum* in downtown Lafayette can be viewed only from the outside in. Housed in a restored 1928 Standard Oil gas station, one of only seven remaining Standard Oil Products buildings in the nation, the museum exhibits gas station memorabilia and antique cars. Everything can be seen free of charge through windows. In 2018, Indiana's first 24-hour library was installed in the museum. The fully automated library resembles a cross between an ATM and a vending machine. The library is filled with about 340 books, audiobooks, and movies on glass-enclosed shelves. The machine works as a self-checkout and a book return. Library users can scan their library cards, select an item, and pick up the item which has been dropped into a bin. Located at 605 South St.; (765) 742-0280 or (800) 872-6648; homeofpurdue.com.

On a free tour of *Subaru of Indiana*, visitors walk along catwalks above the production lines and observe workers, robots, and some gigantic machines assemble complete automobiles. The plant currently produces three Subaru models—the Legacy, Outback, and Tribeca—and, under contract with Toyota, the Toyota Camry. According to the company, this plant was designed with tours in mind. Tours are generally offered at 9 a.m.; reservations must be made at least 2 weeks in advance by calling (765) 449-6250. Participants must be at least ten years old. The plant is located at 5500 SR 38 East in Lafayette; for additional information, call (765) 449-1111; subaru-sia.com.

In 1936, when our country was in the depths of the Great Depression, Frank Lloyd Wright developed an architectural style he called Usonian (an abbreviation for "United States of North America"). The innovative style reflected Wright's desire to create a distinctly American style that was affordable for the "common people." To control costs, Usonian homes had no attics, no basements, and very little ornamentation, but they still displayed the unique beauty of a Wright design.

One of the most pristine examples of this style can be seen today at 1301 Woodland Ave. in West Lafayette. Known as **Samara,** the house was built

The Greatest Pacer of Them All

Long before Hoosier basketball fans fell in love with the Indiana Pacers, Hoosiers and the rest of the world fell in love with another pacer. To this day, Dan Patch remains a legend in harness racing.

Born near Oxford in Benton County on April 29, 1896, the mahogany-colored colt was at first a great disappointment to his owner. Dan's sire had been an outstanding pacer, and Dan's owner had hoped the son would inherit his father's greatness. When Dan was born bow-legged and awkward, that hope dimmed, but the ugly duckling grew into a swan.

Dan began racing in 1900 at age four and won every race he entered. By July 1902, there was no one left who wanted to match his horse against Dan, so Dan began racing only against the clock in exhibitions. At the 1906 Minnesota State Fair, Dan paced a mile in 1 minute, 55 seconds, a world record. Although unofficial, the record was generally accepted and remained unbroken for thirty-two years.

During his lifetime, the charismatic Dan Patch became one of the most successfully merchandised sports figures in history. His name and likeness were used to endorse thirty products, including china, stopwatches, livestock feed, tobacco, washing machines, toys, and manure spreaders. There was a Dan Patch automobile that sold for $525. People danced the Dan Patch Two-Step to the song of the same name. Hollywood immortalized him in a 1949 movie called **The Great Dan Patch.** A Dan Patch thermometer, originally a promotional giveaway, was on sale at an Indiana antiques store in 1998 for $3,000.

Dan is still remembered in his hometown, too. Beginning in 1901, Oxford has honored its famous son with an annual event known as Dan Patch Days. The humble white barn near Oxford in which Dan Patch was born proudly bears the words "DAN PATCH 1:55" in large letters on a green-shingled roof.

Dan had more than one owner in his lifetime. His final owner, M. W. Savage of Minneapolis, cherished and provided well for his champion horse. Dan traveled around the country in a private railroad car adorned on each side with his portrait. The huge Minnesota barn in which Dan was stabled was so elaborate it was nicknamed the "Taj Mahal." It was in this barn that Dan died on July 11, 1916, at the age of twenty. His owner died 32 hours later.

On September 14, 1999, **USA Today** featured its choices for the eight great animal athletes of the century. Among them was Dan Patch, described by the newspaper as probably the greatest pacer of all time.

for John and Catherine Christian, who still occupy it and maintain it in accordance with the architect's exacting standards. Wright personally supervised every detail of the home's construction in 1956, designing and specifying all aspects of the furnishings and landscaping. Today, by advance reservation, visitors can admire Wright's innovative creation from April through November during a guided tour. Admission: adults $10; college students $3; children (ages 17 and under) free. Call (765) 409-5522 or visit samara-house.org.

indianatrivia

Purdue University's airport in West Lafayette, opened in 1932, was the first university airport in the nation.

Places to Stay in Northwest Indiana

CHESTERTON

At Home in the Woods Bed and Breakfast
898 N. CR 350 East
(219) 720-1325
athomeinthewoodsbb.com

DunesWalk Inn at the Furness Mansion
1491 N. Furnleigh Ln.
(219) 728-6393
duneswalkinn.com

Riley's Railhouse
123 N. Fourth St.
(219) 395-9999
rileysrailhouse.com

WaterBird Lakeside Inn
556 Indian Boundary Rd.
(888) 957-3529
waterbirdinn.com

CRAWFORDSVILLE

The Queen & I Bed and Breakfast
2710 SR 32
(765) 910-4077
thequeenandibnb.com

Yountsville Mill Inn
3941 SR 32 West
(765) 307-7565
yountsvillemill.com

LAPORTE

Arbor Hill Inn
263 W. Johnson Rd.
(219) 362-9200
arborhillinn.com

Blue Heron Inn
1110 Lakeside St.
(219) 362-5077
blueheronlaporte.com

Serenity Springs
5888 SR 35
(219) 861-0000
serenity-springs.com

LOGANSPORT

Inntiquity, A Country Inn
1075 SR 25 North
(574) 721-9805
inntiquityacountryinn.com

MICHIGAN CITY

Al & Sally's Motel
3221 W. Dunes Hwy.
(219) 872-9131
alandsallysmotel.com

The Brewery Lodge & Supper Club
5727 CR 600 West
(866) 625-6343
brewerylodge.com

Bridge Inn
510 E. Second St.
(219) 561-0066
bridgeinnmc.com

Duneland Beach Inn
3311 Pottawattomie Trl.
(219) 874-7729 or
(800) 423-7729
dunelandbeachinn.com

4411 Inn & Suites
4411 US 12 Hwy.
(219) 249-4411
4411innandsuites.com

Kings Inn
201 W. Kieffer Rd.
(219) 878-8100
kingsinnmichigancity.com

MISHAWAKA

Beiger Mansion
317 Lincolnway East
(574) 255-6300 or
(700) 437-0131
beigermansion.com

MONTICELLO

Black Dog Inn
2390 Untalulti Dr.
(574) 583-8297
blackdoginn.webs.com

The Lighthouse Lodge Bed and Breakfast
4866 N. Boxman Place
(574) 583-9142
thelighthouselodge.com

PORTER

At Home in the Woods Bed and Breakfast
898 N. 350 East
(219) 728-1325
athomeinthewoodsbb.com

Places to Eat in Northwest Indiana

BATTLE GROUND

TC's Restaurant
109 N. Railroad St.
(765) 567-2838
American

Spring House Inn
303 N. Mineral Springs Rd.
(219) 929-4600 or
(866) 386-3700
springhouseinn.com

SOUTH BEND

Aloft South Bend
111 N. Main St.
(574) 288-8000
marriott.com

The Avanti House
900 Thomas St.
(607) 296-0486
avantihouse.com

The Inn at Saint Mary's
53993 SR 933
(574) 232-4000
innatsaintmarys.com

Innisfree Bed & Breakfast
702 W. Colfax Ave.
(574) 318-4838
innisfreebnb.com

Morris Inn
1399 N. Notre Dame Ave.
(574) 631-2000
morrisinn.nd.edu

The Oliver Inn Bed and Breakfast
630 W. Washington St.
(574) 232-4545 or
(888) 697-4466
oliverinn.com

CEDAR LAKE

Cedar Lake Kitchen
10325 W. 133rd Ave.
(219) 374-8888
cedarlakekitchen.com
American

Frank's Backyard BBQ
13106 Wicker Ave.
(219) 552-1275
franksbackyardbbq.com
BBQ

VALPARAISO

Inn at Aberdeen
3158 S. SR 2
(219) 465-3753 or
(866) 761-3753
innataberdeen.com

Pikk's Inn
62 W. Lincolnway
(219) 476-7455
pikkstavern.davinci-group
.com

Songbird Prairie Bed and Breakfast
174 N. CR 600 West
(219) 759-4274 or
(877) 766-4273
songbirdprairie.com

Valparaiso Inn Bed & Breakfast
301 Washington St.
(219) 242-8934
valpoinn.com

WINAMAC

Mill Creek Gardens
1351 E. 250 South
(574) 216-9070
themillcreekgardens.com

Tortuga Inn
2142 N. CR 125 East
(574) 946-6969
tortugainnbb.com

Harry O's
13226 Wicker Ave.
(218) 374-3403
harryoscl.com
American

Lighthouse Restaurant
7501 Constitution Ave.
(219) 374-9283
cedarlakelighthouse.com
Steak/seafood

Sandbar Grill
13118 Lake Shore Dr.
(219) 374-5777
thesandbargrill.com
American

COVINGTON

**Beef House Restaurant
& Dinner Theatre**
16501 N. SR 63
(765) 793-3947
beefhouserolls.com
Steak/American

Benjamin's Restaurant
225 Eleventh St.
(765) 793-7274
Comfort food

Hilltop Restaurant
1120 Liberty Dr.
(765) 793-4455
hilltop1120.wixsite.com
Comfort food

**Maple Corner Restau-
rant & Pub**
1126 Liberty St.
(765) 793-2224
maplecornercovington
.com
Home cooking

CROWN POINT

Court St. Burritos
930 S. Court St.
(219) 226-4427
court-st-burritos.business
.site
Mexican

Jax's Crown Town Grill
107 N. Main St.
(219) 661-1955
jaxscrowntowngrill
Grill food

Lelulo's
13 N. Court St.
(219) 226-4599
lelulosvegan.com
Vegan

**Lucrezia Italian
Ristorante**
302 S. Main St.
(219) 001-5829
lucreziacafe.com
Italian

CULVER

Cafe Max Eatery & Tap
113 S. Main St.
(574) 842-2511
American

The Lakehouse Grille
620 E. Lake Shore Dr.
(574) 842-2234
thelakehouseculver.com
American

Original Root Beer Stand
824 E. Lake Shore Dr.
(574) 842-2122
Fast food

Papa's
824 N. Lake Shore Dr.
(574) 842-3331
indianasbestpizza.com
American

GARY

Beach Café
903 N. Shelby St.
(219) 938-1100
millerbeachcafe.com
American

Kelly's Soul Kitchen
5025 W. Fifth Ave.
(219) 951-0662
kellyssoulkitchen.business
.site
Soul food

Tequila and Tacos
642 S. Lake St.
(219) 939-7136
tequilatacoworld.com
Mexican

**Thai Chhimski's Egg
Rolls & Stir Fry**
4121 Cleveland St
(219) 344-8213
thaichhimskiseggrolls.com
Thai

HAMMOND

Asian Kitchen
6412A Calumet Ave.
(219) 803-0074
asiankitchen.com
Asian

Cavalier Inn
735 Gostlin St.
(219) 933-9314
cavalierinn.net
Polish

Freddy's Steak House
6442 Kennedy Ave.
(219) 844-1500
freddyssteakhouse.net
Steak

Johnel's Restaurant
4145 Calumet Ave
(219) 931-7000
johnelsrestaurant.com
American

**The Wheel Family
Restaurant**
7430 Indianapolis
Blvd.
(219) 845-0277
thewheelrestaurant.com
American

HEBRON

Pav's Restaurant
642 N. Main St.
(219) 996-7287
eatatpavs.com
American

WANA Pizza
628 Front St.
(219) 996-9262
wanapizza.com
Pizza

HOBART

Café 339
339 Main St.
(219) 940-9644
cafe339.com
Comfort food

Montego Bay Grille
322 Main St.
(219) 940-3152
montegobaygrille.com
Caribbean

New Hong Kong Restaurant
7814 E. Ridge Rd.
(219) 962-3992
newhkrestaurant.com
Chinese

KOUTS

Birky's Bakery & Coffee Shop
205 S. Main St.
(219) 766-3851
birkyfarms.com
Sandwiches/baked goods

Brisket and Bones Smokehouse
105 S. Main St.
(219) 766-3555
brisketandbones.com
Barbecue

LAFAYETTE

Arni's
2200 Elmwood Ave.
(765) 447-1108
meetyouatarnis.com
American

Bistro 501
501 Main St.
(765) 423-4501
bistro501.com
Provincial French

Dog-n-Suds Drive-In
601 Sagamore Pkwy.
(765) 447-5457
Dognsudsgreaterlafayette
.com
Hot dogs/root beer

East End Grill
1016 Main St.
(765) 607-4600
eastendmain.com
American

Mountain Jacks Steakhouse
4211 South St.
(765) 448-1521
mountainjackslafayette.com
Steak/seafood

Nine Irish Brothers
3520 SR 38 East
(765) 447-0999
nineirishbrothers.com
Irish/American

Pepe's Mexican Restaurant
2625 Sagamore Pkwy.
South
(765) 448-1888
pepes.com
Mexican

Sergeant Preston's of the North
1204 6 N. 2nd St.
(765) 742-7378
sgtprestons.net
American

The Tick Tock Tavern & Eatery
1816 N. Ninth St. Rd.
(765) 742-9425
theticktocktavern.com
American

LAPORTE

Christo's Family Dining
1462 W. SR 2
(219) 326-1644
christosfamilydining.com
American

Four Seasons Asian Fusion
701 Lincolnway
(219) 369-6358
4seasonsasianfusion.com
Asian

Trattoria Enzo
601 Michigan Ave.
(219) 326-8000
trattoriaenzo.com
Italian

LOGANSPORT

Amelio's On The River
431 S. Fourth St.
(574) 753-3589
ameliosontheriver.com
Comfort food

Boardwalk Cafe
501 E. Broadway St.
(574) 753-0378
American/pizza

El Arriero
3415 E. Market St.
(574) 753 8331
Elarrierologansport.com
Mexican

Silver Lake
2430 E. Market St.
(574) 753-0281
silverlakefamilyrestaurants
.com
American

LOWELL

George's Family Restaurant
1910 E. Commercial Ave.
(219) 696-0313
georgesfamilyrestaurant.com
American

Gold Star Café and Catering
1336 E. Commercial Ave.
(219) 690-3487
goldstarcafeandcatering.com
American

The Mason Jar
241 N. Liberty St.
(219) 225-5222
themasonjarlowell.com
Comfort food

McVey's Restaurant
312 E. Commercial Ave.
(219) 696-7784
mcveysrestaurantlowell.com
Comfort food

MICHIGAN CITY

Holly's Restaurant & Pub
3705 Franklin St.
(219) 879-5124
hollysrestaurant.com
American

Patrick's Grille
4125 Franklin St.
(219) 873-9401
patricksgrille.com
American

Shoreline Brewery & Restaurant
208 Wabash St.
(219) 879-4677
shorelinebrewery.com
American

Swingbelly's
3101 E. US 12
(219) 874-5718
swingbellys.org
American

MILLER BEACH

Miller Bakery Cafe
555 S. Lake St.
(219) 938-2229
International

MISHAWAKA

Corndance Tavern
4725 Grape Rd.
(574) 217-7584
corndance.com
American

Doc Pierce's Restaurant
120 N. Main St.
(574) 255-7737
cocpiercesrestaurant.com
American

Jesus Latin Grill & Tequila Bar
122 N. Hill St.
(574) 318-4983
jesus-latin-grill.com
Latin

Nedderman's Steak Place
3223 Grape Rd.
(574) 217-8458
thesteakplace.com
Steak

Zing Japanese Fusion
206 N. Main St.
(574) 259-8888
zingmishawaka.com
Japanese

MONTICELLO

Cazadores Mexican Restaurant
111 N. Main St.
(574) 297-5075
cazadoresdowntown.com
Mexican

The Oakdale Bar & Grill
11899 W. Oakdale Dr.
(574) 965-9104
oakdalebarandgrill.com
American

Sportsman Inn
12340 N. Upper Lakeshore Dr.
(574) 583-5133
sportsmaninn.com
American

Sublette's Ribs
924 N. Sixth St.
(574) 583-7427
sublettesribs.com
Barbecue

MUNSTER

Bombers BBQ
435 Ridge Rd.
(219) 836-2662
bombersbbq.com
Barbecue

Café Borgia
10018 Calumet Ave.
(219) 922-8889
cafeborgia.com
Italian

Giovanni's Restaurant
603 Ridge Rd.
(US 6)
(219) 836-6220
giosmunster.com
Italian

Mishkenut Mediterranean Cuisine
221 Ridge Rd.
(219) 836-6069
mishkenut.com
Mediterranean

NEW CARLISLE

Carlisle Coffee and Sweets
203 E. Michigan St.
(574) 988-0219
carlislecoffeeandsweets.com
Coffee shop

Kate O'Connor's Irish Pub
415 E. Michigan St.
(574) 654-8114
kateoconnors.com
Irish pub

PLYMOUTH

The Brass Rail Bar and Grill
225 N. Michigan St.
(574) 936-7004
thebrassrailbar.com
American

PORTAGE

Cappo's
6656 W. US 6
(219) 762-5563
capposcasualdining.com
Italian

El Salto Mexican Restaurant
6295 Ameriplex Dr.
(219) 734-6463
elsaltorestaurant.com
Mexican

Shenanigans
6121 US 20
(219) 762-0509
Italian

RENSSELAER

Fenwick Farms Brewing Company
219 W. Washington St.
(219) 866-3773
fenwickfarmsbrewing
company.com
American

The Station at Embers
230 W. Washington St.
(219) 869-9537
embersvenue.net
American

ROCHESTER

Evergreen Eatery
530 Main St.
(574) 223-3837
evergreeneatery.com
Comfort food

Jarrety's Place
701 Main St.
(574) 223-7101
jarretysplace.com
Comfort food

Streamliner Central
201 E. 9th St.
(574) 223-4656
streamlinerrestaurant.com
American

Uncorked Beer and Wine Bar
527 Main St.
(574) 223-9866
rochesteruncorked.com
Cuban

SCHERERVILLE

Giuseppe's Pizza
1000 Eagle Ridge Dr.
(219) 322-0011
giuseppespizza.net
Italian

Pepino's Restaurant
2410 Ontario
(219) 365-9680
pepinosindiana.com
Italian

Teibel's Family Restaurant
1775 US 41
(219) 865-2000
teibels.com
Chicken/fish

Tyler's Tender Railroad Restaurant
350 E. US 30
(219) 322-5590
tylerstender.com
Comfort food

SOUTH BEND

Barnaby's
713 E. Jefferson Blvd.
(574) 288-4981
barnabys-pizza.com
Pizza

Café Navarre
101 N. Michigan St.
(574) 968-8101
cafenavarre.co
Global fare

Carmela's Restaurant
214 N. Niles Ave.
(574) 280-4824
carmelassouthbend.com
Italian

East Bank Emporium Restaurant
121 S. Niles Ave.
(574) 234-9000
eastbankemporium.com
American

Tippecanoe Place Restaurant
620 W. Washington St.
(574) 234-9077
tippe.com
American

VALPARAISO

China House
120 E. Lincolnway
(219) 462-5788
chinahousein.com
Chinese

Don Quijote
119 E. Lincolnway
(219) 462-7976
donquijotevalpo.com
Spanish

Furin Japanese Restaurant & Bar
21 Lincolnway
(219) 286-6648
furinvalpo.com

Meditrina Market Café
24 Washington St.
(219) 707-5271
meditrina-market-café.com
Mediterranean

Radius
15 E. Lincolnway
(219) 299-2551
radiusvalpo.com
American

Sage Restaurant
157 W. Lincolnway
(219) 464-7243
sagerestaurant.net
Italian

SOURCES FOR ADDITIONAL INFORMATION ABOUT NORTHWEST INDIANA

**Greater Lafayette/
West Lafayette Con-
vention and Visitors
Bureau (Tippecanoe
County)**
301 Frontage Rd.
Lafayette 47905
(765) 447-9999 or (800)
872-6648
homeofpurdue.com

**Greater Monticello
Chamber of Commerce
& Visitors Bureau**
105 W. Broadway St.
Monticello 47960
(574) 583 7220
monticelloin.com

**Visit Michigan City
LaPorte**
4073 S. Franklin St.
Michigan City 46360
(219) 872-5055 or (800)
634-2650
michigancitylaporte.com

**Cass County Visitors
Bureau**
311 S. Fifth St.
Logansport 46947
(574) 753-4856 or (866)
753-4856
visit-casscounty.com

**Marshall County
Tourism**
201 N. Michigan St.
Plymouth 46563
(574) 936-1882 or (800)
626-5353
visitmarshallcounty.org

**Montgomery County
Visitors & Convention
Bureau**
101 W. Main St.
Crawfordsville 47933
(765) 362-5200 or (800)
866-3973
visitmoco.com

**Newton County
Chamber of Commerce**
503 N. Seventh St.
Kentland 47951
(219) 474-6050

Indiana Dunes Tourism
1215 N. SR 49
Porter 46304
(219) 926-2255 or (800)
283-8687
indianadunes.com

**Visit South Bend
Mishawaka**
(St. Joseph County)
101 N. Michigan St.
South Bend 46001
(800) 519-0577
visitsouthbend.com

**South Shore Con-
vention and Visi-
tors Authority (Lake
County)**
7770 Corinne Dr.
Hammond 46323
(219) 989-7770 or (800)
255-5253
southshorecva.com

**Tippecanoe Place
Restaurant**
620 W. Washington St.
(219) 234-9077
tippe.com
Continental

WEST LAFAYETTE

8Eleven Bistro
201 Grant St. Suite 100
(765) 496-5126
8elevenbistro.com

Blue Nile Restaurant
117 Northwestern Ave. #2
(765) 269-9980
bluenilein.site
Mediterranean

Maru Sushi
102 N. Chauncey Ave. D
(765) 743-2646
maru-sushi.us
Japanese

Panchi's Tacos
2415 Sagamore Pkwy.
South
(765) 838-8729
Tacos

**Triple XXX Family
Restaurant**
2 N. Salisbury St.
(765) 743-5373
triplexxxfamilyrestaurant.com
Burgers/American

WHITING

King Chop Suey
1730 Indianapolis Blvd.
(219) 659-3508
kingchopsuey.com
Chinese

Purple Steer Restaurant
1402 Indianapolis Blvd.
(219) 659-3950
purplesteerwhiting.com
American/Italian

Southeast Indiana

Beauty and history exist side by side in southeast Indiana. Although I-70 on the north, I-65 on the west, and I-74 in between carve the landscape into two pie-shaped wedges, the land between those ribbons of the highway is some of the loveliest the state has to offer. This is also the land where history began in Indiana, sweeping in on the waters of the beautiful Ohio River. The first settlers found woodlands so dense, it is said, that a squirrel could make its way across the state without ever once having to touch the ground.

Today a scenic highway winds along the banks of the Ohio, taking those who will spend the time on a voyage of discovery. Antiques lovers may think they've died and gone to heaven. History buffs will find museums galore, with unique treasures tucked away in their corners.

Bartholomew County

According to an article that appeared in the *New York Times Magazine* in recent years, "there is really no equivalent to **Columbus** anywhere." In its December 2005 issue, *Smithsonian Magazine* featured the city in an article that called Columbus the sixth most architecturally significant city in the country, just behind Chicago, New York, San Francisco, Boston, and Washington, DC. In its November/December 2008 issue, the *National Geographic Explorer* magazine named Columbus the number-one historical travel destination in the United States and number eleven in the world. In 2009, the website AOL Travel ranked Columbus among eleven US "places to see before you die" on a list that included such entities as the Grand Canyon and Yellowstone National Park. These are just a few of the many tributes this town of 47,543 people has received from around the world in recognition of its architecture. More than sixty public and private buildings make up the most concentrated collection of contemporary architecture on Earth, and the names of the architects, artists, designers, and sculptors who created them are right from the pages of *Who's Who*. Where else, for instance, can you walk out of a church designed by Eliel Saarinen, cross the street, pass a Henry Moore sculpture, and enter a library designed by I. M. Pei?

One of the most visually striking buildings is the **North Christian Church,** designed by Eero Saarinen (Eliel's son). A low, hexagon-shaped building, it has a sloping roof centered by a 192-foot-tall needlelike spire that's topped by a gold-leaf cross; the American Institute of Architects selected it as one of the thirteen most outstanding American buildings of the last fifty years. The multilevels of **Smith Elementary School,** created by John M. Johansen, are connected by several brightly colored, tube-shaped ramps—pure delight for the children who use them. **Clifty Creek Elementary School** was designed by Richard Meier, the architect who also designed the spectacular J. Paul Getty Fine Arts Center that sprawls atop a Brentwood, California, hilltop. The sanctuary of **St. Peter's Lutheran Church,** topped by a 186-foot-tall, copper-clad steeple, rises in Byzantine-like splendor above its surroundings—beautiful at any time, but especially so when touched by the sun. Just east of town, the sprawling **Otter Creek Clubhouse,** designed by Harry Weese, lies adjacent to one of the finest public golf courses in the country; the late Robert Trent Jones, who laid out the course, once said its 13th hole was the single best hole he'd ever designed.

The beauty of the downtown area is enhanced by a sprawling white structure that serves as the world headquarters of **Cummins, Inc.,** Columbus's oldest and leading firm. Outside, graceful fountains feed shallow ponds and fingers of vines meander up the walls. Inside, within the glassed-in lobby, a diesel engine—the product that first brought fame to the company—is displayed as an abstract sculpture known as the "exploded engine." Each component of a diesel engine, down to the tiniest nut and bolt, has been deconstructed and suspended in midair by a floor-to-ceiling wire to demonstrate how all the parts fit together. The lobby's mini museum also houses antique cars and Indy 500 race cars—with diesel engines, of course. Located at 500 Jackson St.; open free of charge from 9 a.m. to 5 p.m. Monday through Friday year-round.

Not all of these buildings will knock your socks off at first sight. To fully appreciate them, you should learn something about the innovative functions and attention to details that lie behind the facades. The **First Christian Church,** built in 1942, could just as easily have been built yesterday.

Columbus also has its share of renovated and historical buildings, but it is the modern architecture that has brought this small-town fame as the "Athens of the Prairie." In 2001, six of the city's buildings were designated National Historic Landmarks, a rare honor because five of the six did not meet the usual criterion of being more than fifty years old.

One of those National Historic Landmarks is one of the city's newest attractions. Built in 1957, the **Miller House** served as the private residence for the late industrialist and philanthropist J. Irwin Miller and his wife, Xenia, for more than fifty years. Miller, who was the CEO and driving force behind Cummins, Inc.'s rise to international prominence, was also the visionary who was primarily responsible for making Columbus the architectural mecca it is today. When the 6,700-square-foot home he and his wife built for their family was opened for guided tours in May 2011, it was described by *Travel and Leisure* magazine as "the most significant modernist residence in America" and received mention in the *New York Times,* the *Wall Street Journal,* and *Architectural Digest.* The flat roof of the single-story home is supported by glass and stone walls, and the open, flowing interior is filled with vibrant colors. Among the special features are a fixed dining table with a fountain in the middle, a sunken conversation pit in the living room, and a freestanding fireplace that provides 360 degrees of heat. The home sits in the midst of 13 acres of gardens that were described by a British landscape critic as one of the fifty most beautiful gardens in the world.

When the Miller home was first opened to the public, the *CBS Sunday Morning Show* came to Columbus to record the event as part of its annual design show (visits the prior two years had been to the Biltmore Estate in North Carolina and the Hearst Castle in California). After viewing the home and seeing other aspects of Columbus, Charles Osgood, the show's anchor, stated, "Columbus is unique. And I was trained to never use the word *unique* unless you absolutely mean alone in the universe."

You can make a reservation to tour the Miller home and gardens at the Columbus Area Visitors Center, housed in a nineteenth-century home at 506 Fifth St.; (812) 378-2622 or (800) 468-6564; columbus.in.us. You'll find interactive exhibits that call up images of all the area's best-known architecture, including a special child-oriented section, a 15-minute video presentation about the city's architectural heritage, and an eye-catching yellow neon chandelier that highlights a two story bay window.

Measuring 9 feet high by 6 feet across and weighing 1,200 pounds, the chandelier is the creation of world-renowned glass artist Dale Chihuly. The unique work of art contains 900 pieces of handblown glass in four shades of yellow and 50 feet of neon tubing. Chihuly, who studied glassblowing in Italy, is the first American glassblower ever permitted to work on the island of Murano, a carefully guarded and isolated Italian glassmaking center that dates from the thirteenth century. Former president Bill Clinton gave smaller Chihuly pieces as gifts to world leaders when he traveled.

You can also pick up brochures, maps, and other materials for self-guided tours of the city or make advance reservations for a two-hour minibus guided architecture tour at $25 for adults and $20 for students. Check the website for dates and hours of tours. The center is open daily 9 a.m. to 5 p.m. Monday through Saturday; noon to 5 p.m. Sunday; closed major winter holidays.

There's nothing contemporary about *Zaharako's Ice Cream Parlor and Museum* in downtown Columbus—It's pure nostalgia. Located at the same address since October 1900, the store is now a Columbus institution. Its fixtures carry you back to the beginning of the twentieth century—Mexican onyx soda fountains purchased from the St. Louis World Exposition in 1905, a full-concert mechanical pipe organ brought here from Germany in 1908 that mimics the sounds of 182 instruments as it rings out with tunes of the Gay Nineties, an exquisite Tiffany lamp, and accessories of carved mahogany. Amid these ornate surroundings you can enjoy homemade ice cream, fountain treats, and an assortment of candies, as well as sandwiches, soups, and salads. The adjoining museum features such rare 1800s artifacts as a restored 1870s orchestrion, syrup dispensers, and the largest collection of pre-1900 marble soda fountains on public display in the country. You'll find Zaharako's at 329 Washington St.; (812) 378-1900; zaharakos.com. Open 8 a.m. to 8 p.m. Monday through Friday; 9 a.m. to 8 p.m. Saturday and Sunday.

At 309 Washington St., the three-story *Kidscommons Children's Museum* is a learning and fun center that offers a state-of-the-art computer center, a 17-foot-tall climbing wall, and a bubble room. You can also flush your children down a giant toilet (aka a slippery slide): Kids climb in, the toilet flushes, and away they go; you can pick them up on the floor below. Open 10 a.m. to 5 p.m. Tuesday through Saturday and 1 to 5 p.m. Sunday; closed Monday and major holidays. Admission is $7 per person; free for children under eighteen months old. Flush your kids down the toilet as many times as you like at no extra charge. For more information, call (812) 378-3046; kidscommons.org.

AUTHOR'S FAVORITE ATTRACTIONS/ EVENTS IN SOUTHEAST INDIANA

Canaan Fall Festival and Pony Express Mail Run Celebration
Canaan; September
(812) 265-2956
visitmadison.org

Falls Fossil Festival
Clarksville; September
(812) 280-9970
fallsoftheohio.org

Falls of the Ohio State Park
Clarksville
(812) 280-9970
fallsoftheohio.org

Historic National Road Yard Sale
US 40 (Richmond to Terre Haute);
August
(765) 478-4809
oldstorefrontantiques.com

Indiana Basketball Hall of Fame
New Castle
(765) 529-1891
hoopshall.com

National Muzzle Loading Rifle Association National Championship Shoot
Friendship; June and September
(812) 667-5131
nmira.org

Navy Bean Fall Festival
Rising Sun; October
(812) 438-2750 or (888) 776-4786
navybeanfestival.org

Old-Fashioned Christmas Walk
Metamora; weekends from
late November through late December
(765) 647-6522 or (866) 647-6555
metamoraindiana.com

Scottish Festival
Columbus; September
(812) 378-2622 or (800) 468-6564
scottishfestival.org

Squire Boone Caverns
Mauckport
(812) 732-4381
squireboonecaverns.com

Wayne County Historical Museum
Richmond
(765) 962-5756
wchmuseum.org

Whitewater Canal State Historic Site
Metamora
(765) 647-6512
indianamuseum.org/whitewater-canal-state-historic-site

Wilbur Wright Birthplace Festival
Millville; September
(765) 332-2495
wwbirthplace.com

Zimmerman Art Glass Factory
Corydon
(812) 738-2206 or (888) 738-2137
thisisindiana.org

Across the street from Zaharako's and Kidscommons is Columbus's ultra-modern shopping mall and performance center. Sprawled over 56,000-square-feet, the 2-story **Commons** was dedicated in June 2011. It houses the community's beloved *Chaos I,* a 7-ton, 30-foot-tall, in-motion sculpture crafted out of scrap metal by Swiss artist Jean Tinguely; the piece becomes more intriguing the longer you look at it. The sculpture towers next to an innovative indoor children's playground, free of charge, that is divided into three segments for different age groups that range from six months to twelve years old. Designed to be energy efficient, the building is topped by rooftop gardens that aid interior climate control; they occupy an outdoor terrace accessible to visitors from both inside and outside the Commons. Open 7 a.m. to 9 p.m. Monday through Thursday, 7 a.m. to 10 p.m. Friday and Saturday; 10 a.m. to 8 p.m. Sunday; closed Christmas Day; (812) 376-2681; thecommonscolumbus.com.

On the north side of Columbus is the city's municipal airport, originally built during World War II as the Atterbury Air Base. The **Atterbury-Bakalar Air Museum** at the airport pays tribute to military aviators who served their country from 1942 to 1970. Among the memorabilia are uniforms, flight jackets, and scale models of vintage aircraft. Homage is also paid to one of the least-known units of World War II—the pilots who flew the 6,000 gliders known as the "Silent Wings." Towed aloft by C-47s, the engineless planes were cut loose to silently infiltrate enemy territory and deliver their cargoes of infantrymen and munitions. The US Army trained the pilots to fight on the ground as well, but each flight was obviously a one-way mission, and casualties were high.

The museum also honors the famous Tuskegee Airmen, a special unit of Black Americans that was composed of graduates of the Tuskegee Institute in Alabama. During World War II, some of those men trained at Atterbury Air Base in B-25 bombers. Their combat record was unblemished—no bomber flown by a Tuskegee Airman was ever lost to the enemy. In addition to an indoor exhibit, the airmen are memorialized in an outdoor monument that stands on Bakalar Green just south of the airport terminal. The museum is located at 4742 Ray Boll Blvd.; admission is free. Open 10 a.m. to 4 p.m. Tuesday through Saturday; call (812) 372-4356 or visit atterburybakalarairmuseum.org.

Clark County

Along the banks of the Ohio River in **Clarksville** lies a 400-million-year-old fossil bed that is one of the world's greatest natural wonders. Its rare and unusual formations date back to the Devonian age and have for decades attracted sightseers and scientists from around the world. Once the reef was covered by the Falls of the Ohio, a raging, 2-mile stretch of water below

Louisville in which the Ohio River dropped 22 feet over limestone ledges. Now the Ohio has been reduced to a series of pools by a string of dams, and the controlled water levels have left the reef high and dry. Its fossil corals archaeological sites are among the best in the country, and the variety of its migratory bird life is unparalleled at any other inland location.

For years efforts have been underway to preserve this area. The first step in realizing that dream occurred in October 1984, when the US Senate approved funding for the creation of the *Falls of the Ohio National Wildlife Conservation Area.* In 1990, 68 acres of land were dedicated as an Indiana state park. Although relatively small itself, the *Falls of the Ohio State Park* lies within the 1,404 acres of the federally protected conservation area, providing lots of wide-open space to explore.

A 16,000-square-foot interpretive center, perched atop a bluff overlooking the fossil beds, opened to the public in January 1994. The building's exterior features horizontal bands of Indiana limestone alternating with bands of earth-toned bricks, creating a layered look reminiscent of the geological treasure that sprawls below it.

Indiana Fried Chicken?

Few people know that Col. Harland Sanders was born in the tiny southern Indiana town of Henryville. As a matter of fact, few people who live in Henryville knew it until recently. Young Harland loved to cook even as a boy, a skill that served him and his family well. Harland was just five years old when his father died in 1895, and his mother had to go to work to support her family. It fell to Harland to take care of many of the household chores, including much of the cooking. One of his specialties was fried chicken.

When he was barely into his teens, the young man went to work as a farmhand and then as a streetcar conductor in New Albany before enlisting in the army as an underage recruit (easy to do in those days). He later sold insurance in Jeffersonville; started a ferry company that ran boats across the Ohio River between Jeffersonville and Louisville, KY; and worked as a secretary for the Columbus, IN, Chamber of Commerce. There he also launched a manufacturing company that went belly-up when his firm's product became obsolete. Off Harland went to Kentucky, where he progressed from tire salesman to gas station manager to restaurant owner. Finally, it seemed, Harland had found his niche. Kentucky Fried Chicken became one of the most successful food franchises in history.

Harland also knew talent when he saw it. During a visit to a Fort Wayne franchise, he was impressed with the work ethic of a young man who worked there and predicted that the industrious employee would someday amount to something. Indeed, the young man did. Dave Thomas moved on to found Wendy's.

Inside, exhibits lead visitors back through the millennia to a time when ancient Indiana lay about 20 degrees south of the equator beneath the warm waters of a tropical sea. An orientation video employs the latest laser technology to portray the history of the falls. The use of underwater oceanic photography to re-create a 400-million-year-old tropical sea is a first in the film industry. In a wildlife observation room, visitors can view some of the area's 265 species of avian visitors in a small garden area. Elsewhere, the center offers panoramic views of the Ohio River, a historic railroad bridge, the McAlpine Dam and Locks, and the fossil bed itself (best seen from August through October, when the river is at its lowest level).

Low-water periods also provide the best opportunity to explore the fossil bed. More than 600 fossil species have been identified, and two-thirds of those were discovered here for the first time anywhere in the world. Visitors may walk among the eroded rock slabs and search for fossils freed from the bedrock by the powerful waters of the river. Handling of the fossils is encouraged, but they must be returned to their original locations. Collecting is strictly forbidden.

Other activities include fishing, picnicking, and hiking along park trails. A log cabin in the park is a historically accurate reconstruction of the nineteenth-century home of Gen. George Rogers Clark, the Revolutionary War hero who founded Clarksville. Built on the site of Clark's original home, the cabin sits atop a hill overlooking the foot of the Falls of the Ohio. It is open for tours on summer and fall weekends, but hours vary, so check before going.

The park is located on the south side of Riverside Drive, about a mile west of US 31. Visitors to the park alone pay a $2 nominal parking fee. Admission: (ages twelve years and older) $9 (ages 5–11 years) $7 fee for the interpretive center includes free parking. The center is open 9 a.m. to 5 p.m. Monday through Saturday and 1–5 p.m. Sunday; the park is open daily from dawn to dusk. For additional information, write or call Falls of the Ohio State Park, 201 W. Riverside Dr., Clarksville 47129; (812) 280-9970; fallsoftheohio.org.

The Falls of the Ohio area played a major role in the national celebration of the bicentennial of the Meriwether Lewis and William Clark expedition of 1803. It was here that the two explorers and their Corps of Discovery assembled at the home of Gen. George Rogers Clark, William's older brother, before departing on their epic journey. The explorers traveled westward to the Pacific Ocean, mapping the area included in the Louisiana Purchase of earlier that year that doubled the size of the country at that time. As part of the remembrance, Clarksville dedicated its **Lewis and Clark Park** on November 5, 2006, 200 years after the expedition's return to this spot. Located at 1240 Harrison Avenue across from the George Rogers Clark homesite, the park features interpretive

Indiana's Rosie

When the men of our country went off to fight overseas in World War II, women were critically needed to join assembly lines at defense manufacturing plants and produce the ships, tanks, and planes so crucial to the war effort. Many of the women who responded to the call operated rivet guns, and the alliterative name "Rosie the Riveter" was born.

One of those women was Rose Will Monroe, who worked at a Michigan plant that produced B-29 and B-24 bombers. In 1942, Walter Pidgeon, a popular actor of the era, came there to make a film that would promote the purchase of US War Bonds to help finance the war. He noticed Rose on the assembly line and felt she was the right person to personify Rosie the Riveter in his picture. When he found out that her real name was Rose, it seemed like destiny, and they made several promotional films together. Images of other Rosies subsequently appeared on posters and magazine covers, but Rose Monroe is today recognized as the original Rosie.

When the war ended in 1945, the men returned to reclaim their old jobs, and the women were no longer needed. Rose Monroe moved to Clarksville, IN, and worked such jobs as a taxi driver, a school bus driver, a seamstress, and a beauty shop operator. After a stint as a real estate agent, she founded Rose Builders, a construction company that specialized in building luxury homes.

She passed away in Clarksville on May 31, 1997, at the age of seventy-seven and was interred in the Abundant Life Cemetery in New Albany. The only inscription that appears on her headstone is ROSIE THE RIVETER, WW II, followed by the dates of her birth and death. She left behind two daughters, many grandchildren and great-grandchildren, and the legacy of a new image for women.

panels chronicling Lewis and Clark's journey. For additional information, contact the Clarksville Parks and Recreation Department, 2000 Broadway St., Clarksville 47129; (812) 283-5313; clarksvilleparks.com.

Presiding over Clarksville is the town's own version of London's Big Ben. The main building of the former **Colgate-Palmolive plant** at State and Woerner Streets is topped by the second-largest clock in the world, which is a monstrous 40 feet in diameter and has a 16-foot-long hour hand that weighs 500 pounds. (The largest clock in the world, 50 feet in diameter, sits on the former site of a Colgate plant in Jersey City, New Jersey.) No one in Clarksville gets away with saying he doesn't know the time—the electric-powered clock is said to be accurate to within 15 seconds a month, the clock's face can be read from a distance of 2.5 miles, and the clock is illuminated at night by red neon tubes.

Until 1931, the Howard Shipyards were in *Jeffersonville.* During their 107 years in business, the yards produced some 3,000 steamboats, reported to be the finest ever to ply the waters of North and Central America. The *J. M. White,* the most luxurious steamboat in history, was built here, as were the *Glendy Burke,* which inspired the Stephen Foster song of the same name; the *City of Louisville,* the fastest steamboat ever built; and the *Cape Girardeau,* captured on film for all time in *Gone with the Wind.*

The steamboat era was flourishing in the 1890s when construction began on the elaborate twenty-two-room Howard mansion at 1101 E. Market St. that today houses the **Howard Steamboat Museum.** A striking late-Victorian structure, the house features stained- and leaded-glass windows, a Moorish-style music room that contains its original Louis XV furniture, and intricate embellishments that were hand-carved from fifteen types of wood.

You can see all this today, plus a priceless collection of relics that played a role in the golden era of steamboating, miniature models of Howard-built steamboats, and rooms furnished like staterooms on the finest turn-of-the-twentieth-century boats. Open 10 a.m. to 3 p.m. Tuesday through Saturday; 1–3 p.m. Sunday; closed Monday and major holidays. Admission: adults $10; senior citizens $8; students (age six through college) $5. For further details, write the Clark County Historical Society at PO Box 606, Jeffersonville 47131; call (812) 283-3728 or (888) 472-0606; howardsteamboatmuseum.org.

An old-fashioned candy store complete with soda fountain and tin ceiling, **Schimpff's Confectionery** in Jeffersonville, open since 1891, is one of the oldest continuously operated family-owned candy businesses in the country. Its cinnamon red-hot squares are a particular favorite, ordered through the mail by people from around the world. All candies are handmade, just as they were a century ago. They're all scrumptious, and the ice cream's good, too! There's even a free candy museum to explore. Open 10 a.m. to 5 p.m. Monday through Saturday; a lunch counter serves soups, sandwiches, and homemade pies. from 11 a.m. to 3 p.m. Monday through Friday and 11 a.m. to 2 p.m. Saturday. Located at 347 Spring St.; (812) 283-8367; schimpffs.com.

Something's always going on at the 550-acre Huber Farm near **Borden.** Officially billed as the **Huber Orchard, Winery, and Vineyards,** it's open to the public year-round. Strawberries are ripe for do-it-yourself picking from mid-May through mid-June. Twelve varieties of apples are in season from late summer through December. You can select your own pumpkin right from the patch in the fall and cut your own Christmas tree in December. If you don't have time to do your own picking, you can buy fresh produce at the Hubers' Farm Market. Cider made on the farm each fall is available for purchase at any time.

ANNUAL EVENTS IN SOUTHEAST INDIANA

National Maple Syrup Festival
Medora; March
(812) 966-2168
nationalmaplesyrupfestival.com

Madison Regatta
Madison; July
(812) 265-5000 or (800) 559-2956
madisonregatta.com

Swiss Wine Festival
Vevay; August
(812) 427-9463 or (800) 435-5688
swisswinefestival.org

Lanesville Heritage Weekend
Lanesville; September
(812) 952-3091 or (888) 738-2137
lanesvilleheritageweekend.org

Madison Chautauqua
Madison; September
(812) 571-2752
madisonchatauqua.com

Tree City Fall Festival
Greensburg; September
(812) 663-3111
treecityfallfestival.com

Oktoberfest
Seymour; weekend near October 1
(812) 522-3681
seymouroktoberfest.com

Canal Days
Metamora; October
(765) 647-6512
historicmetamora.net

Ethnic Expo
Columbus; October
(812) 376-2520 or (800) 468-6564
ethnicexpo.org

Brothers Gerald and Carl Huber, along with their families, also produce commercial wines, and thus far they've garnered more than 100 awards for their efforts, including "Best of Show" at several Indiana State Fairs. Visitors can sample their many varieties and tour the winery. The Hubers also make cheese on their farm, and visitors can watch this process as well. You can buy the makings for a picnic lunch, as well as ready-made sandwiches and cheese trays, right on the farm. There's also a bakery, a petting zoo, a cafe, an ice cream factory, and Indiana's first distillery.

The Farm Market is open 9 a.m. to 6 p.m. daily May through October; also open 10 a.m. to 6 p.m. Monday through Saturday and noon to 6 pm. Sunday November through April. The winery is open 10 a.m. to 6 p.m. Monday through Saturday year-round; also open 11 a.m. to 6 p.m. Sunday May through October and noon to 6 p.m. Sunday, November through April. Call (812) 923-9463 or (812) 923-9813 for additional information, or write the Hubers at 19816 Huber Rd., Starlight 47106. You can also visit the Hubers online at huberwinery.com.

OTHER ATTRACTIONS WORTH SEEING IN SOUTHEAST INDIANA

CAMBRIDGE CITY

Huddleston Farmhouse Inn Museum
838 National Rd. (US 40)
(765) 478-3172
visitrichmond.org

CHARLESTOWN

Charlestown State Park
12500 SR 62 East
(812) 256-5600
in.gov/dnr/parklake/2986.htm

CORYDON

Corydon Capitol State Historic Site
202 E. Walnut St.
(812) 738-4890
indianamuseum.org/corydon-capitol
-state-historic-site

MADISON

Madison Railroad Station and Jefferson County Historical Society Museum
615 W. 1st St.
(812) 265-2335
jchshc.org

NEW ALBANY

Carnegie Center for Art and History
201 E. Spring St.
(812) 944-7336
carnegiecenter.org

Culbertson Mansion State Historic Site
914 E. Main St.
(812) 944-9600
indianamuseum.org/Culbertson-mansion
-state-historic-site

RICHMOND

Gaar Mansion and Farm Museum
2593 Pleasant View Rd.
(765) 966-1262 or (800) 828-8414
thegaarhouse.com

RISING SUN

Ohio County Historical Museum
212 S. Walnut St.
(812) 438-4915 or (888) 776-4786
ohiocountymuseum.org

SALEM

Beck's Mill
4433 S. Beck's Mill Rd.
(812) 883-5147
becksmill.org

John Hay Center and Stevens Memorial Museum
307 E. Market St.
(812) 883-6495 or (812) 883-4303
johnhaycenter.org

VEVAY

Life on the Ohio River Museum
208 E. Market St.
(812) 427-3560
switzcotourism.com

Switzerland County Historical Museum
210 E. Market St.
(812) 427-3560
switzcotourism.com

If, after visiting Gerald and Carl's farm, you're ready for a hearty meal, ask for directions to their late cousin Joe's restaurant just down the road. The home-cooked meals at *Joe Huber's Family Restaurant* are served country style, and the restaurant is often rated as one of Indiana's ten best. The 360-acre farm on which it's located offers several family activities and special events as well. Visitors can pick their own fruits and vegetables in season. The restaurant is open daily 11 a.m. to 7 p.m. Located at 2421 Engle Rd.; call (812) 923-5255 or (877) 563-4823, or visit joehubers.com.

Dearborn County

Atop a wooded hillside overlooking the village of *Aurora* stands a splendid yellow frame house filled with the memories of a bygone era. It was built in the 1850s by Thomas Gaff, a wealthy industrialist and shipping magnate whose steamboats regularly plied the waters of the Ohio River far below.

Gaff's love for the river ran deep, and that love is reflected in his home, *Hillforest Mansion,* whose architectural style is often referred to as "steamboat Gothic." And indeed it does resemble a steamboat in part, with its rounded front porticoes and cupola, coupled columns, and suspended interior staircase—all features that were typical of the "floating palaces" that graced the nation's rivers in the heyday of river transportation.

indianatrivia

Indiana's first skyscraper was a three-story brick building erected in Lawrenceburg in 1819.

Now restored and filled with antique furniture, the entire mansion can be toured, from its wine cellar up to the observatory at the top of the house. The view of the Ohio River is just as beautiful as it was when Thomas Gaff himself stood here. Around the one-of-a-kind home are 10 acres of grounds laid out in the grand manner of an Italian villa. Open 11 a.m. to 3 p.m. Tuesday through Sunday, April through December 30. Admission: adults $10; students (over age thirteen) $4. Located at 213 5th St.; (812) 926-0087; hillforest.org.

Decatur County

It's easy to tell the visitors from the hometown folks in *Greensburg*—the visitors are all looking up. Up, that is, at a tree that's growing where we've all been led to believe trees can't grow—on a roof. Eye-catching, to be sure.

The tree adorns the tower that tops the *Decatur County Courthouse.* When the first tree appeared here in 1870, local authorities, who knew a tree's proper place, grubbed it out. Five years later a second tree appeared. The amazed citizenry, admiring its tenacity, merely stood by and watched this time. That tree thrived until 1929, when it failed to leaf and was removed to the local Decatur County Museum for preservation.

At the time of its removal, another tree had already started growing on the opposite side of the tower. Other trees appeared through the years, growing without any apparent nourishment (although local comedians conjecture that they are fed by the springs in the tower's clock). The current tree is the eleventh offspring of the original. The townsfolk have long since made their peace with this peculiar situation, and they even celebrate each September with a Tree City Fall Festival.

What type of tree had implanted itself on the courthouse roof? For years, no one could agree on the answer, and finally scientists at the Smithsonian Institution in Washington, DC, were consulted. They declared the trees to be large-toothed aspens. For additional information, contact the Greensburg-Decatur County Visitor Center, 211 N. Broadway St., Greensburg 47240; (812) 222-8733 or (877) 883-5447; visitgreensburg.com.

Fayette County

The ***Whitewater Valley Railroad,*** the longest steam railroad in Indiana, travels thirty-two scenic miles between ***Connersville*** and Metamora each Saturday, Sunday, and holiday from May through October. All the sights and sounds of old-time steam travel have been re-created to transport you back in time, and places of interest, including some of the original locks of the old Whitewater Valley Canal, are pointed out along the way. Two rare Baldwin locomotives, vintage 1907 and 1919, pull New York Central and Erie Stillwell passenger cars over tracks laid along the canal's towpath. At Metamora (see Franklin County) there's time to disembark and explore a restored canal town.

Both round-trips and one-way trips, as well as caboose rides and special themed runs, are available. Round-trips, which are approximately 5 hours long, originate at the Connersville Station, located 1 mile south of town on SR 121; a gift shop sells railroad-related memorabilia, including a wide range of Thomas the Tank Engine items. The train also offers Twilight Limited Train to Dinner when the train departs the Connersville Station at 6 p.m. on the first and third Friday and travels to Laurel Hotel for dinner. For a schedule and additional information, write the Whitewater Valley Railroad, Inc., 455 Market St., PO Box 406, Connersville 47331; call (765) 825-2054; whitewatervalleyrr.org.

Seven miles southwest of Connersville on CR 350 South is the ***Mary Gray Bird Sanctuary,*** a 684-acre wildlife preserve owned and operated by the Indiana Audubon Society. These peaceful surroundings are crisscrossed by several miles of hiking trails, and a full-time naturalist is on hand to answer your questions. A small museum depicts local flora and fauna. The preserve is open daily, free of charge, from dawn to dusk. Write the sanctuary at 3499 S. Bird Sanctuary Rd., Connersville 47337; call (765) 827-5109; indianaaudubon.org.

Franklin County

Not too long ago, **Metamora** was a dying town, its days numbered by the end of the canal era. That was before the state of Indiana decided to restore a 14-mile section of the old **Whitewater Canal,** originally a 76-mile waterway constructed in the mid-1800s. Now the small village hums with activity.

An 80-foot-long covered wooden aqueduct in Metamora was built in 1848 to carry the canal 16 feet above Duck Creek. Believed to be the only such structure in existence, it was once featured on *Ripley's Believe It or Not.*

A horse-drawn canal boat takes visitors for a leisurely 30-minute cruise through the aqueduct and a restored lock. Occasionally the Whitewater Valley Railroad's steam train chugs by, carrying passengers between its Connersville Station (see Fayette County) and Metamora.

Many of the town's fine arts, crafts, and specialty shops are housed in pre–Civil War buildings that cling to the banks of the canal; others occupy reconstructed and reproduced buildings elsewhere in a section known as Old Metamora. An aged brick gristmill still grinds and sells flour, cornmeal, and grits. The total effect is that of a country village suspended in the 1830s.

Of the many special events scheduled throughout the year, the loveliest is the Christmas Walk that's held evenings on the first weekend after Thanksgiving. Some 3,000 lights line the banks of the canal, roads, and walkways. Carolers stroll through the streets; horses clippity-clop along, pulling carriages behind them. The aroma of hot spiced cider perfumes the air. Quite a show for a town that has a population of 188 permanent residents!

If while in Metamora you experience a bit of déjà vu, it may be because you've seen the movie *Rain Man*. Dustin Hoffman and Tom Cruise came here to shoot part of the film.

Most shops are open 10 a.m. to 4 p.m. Tuesday through Friday and 10 a.m. to 5 p.m. Saturday, Sunday, and holidays, from mid-April to late December, while some are open only on weekends. Head for the shops flying bright yellow flags; that's Metamoraese for "Come on in! We're open!" For additional information, write or call the Metamora Visitor Center, PO Box 117, Metamora 47030; (765) 647-2109; metamoraindiana.com.

The canal boat operates on the hour from noon to 4 p.m. Wednesday through Sunday, May through October (by reservation only on May weekdays); a nominal fee is charged. Write or call the Whitewater Canal State Historic

Site, 19083 N. Clayborn St., PO Box 88, Metamora 47030; (765) 647-6512; india namuseum.org/whitewater-canal-state-historic-site.

Oldenburg is another architectural and historical gem that has dwelt in the past since it was founded in 1837. Known as the "Village of Spires" because of its many soaring steeples, Oldenburg is the home of the **convent and academy of the Sisters of St. Francis,** an order that originally came here from Austria. The peaceful grounds, which invite leisurely strolls, include a cemetery reserved for the sisters. In warm-weather months, the cemetery is a stunning mosaic in green and white—paths edged by low-cut green hedges, emerald lawns shaded by the sprawling branches of ancient shade trees, and row on row of small, white, identical stone crosses. The convent itself, renowned for its ceiling frescoes, basilica-like chapel, iron stairways, and solid oak woodwork, can be toured by appointment. Call (812) 934-2475; oldenburgfranciscans.org.

Elsewhere in the picturesque community are houses and storefronts adorned with the ornate tinwork of master craftsman Gasper Gaupel. The lovely tree-lined streets bear German names, ranging from the mundane Haupstrasse (Main Street) to the lyrical Schweineschwantz Gasse (Pigtail Alley). Every so often the aroma of brats and sauerkraut escapes from a local eatery. If you'd like to sample some German cuisine, just follow your nose.

Harrison County

A few miles south of **Corydon** is a peaceful valley laced with subterranean caverns and edged by forested hills. Squire Boone first saw this area in the late 1700s while hunting with his older brother, Daniel, and eventually returned here to settle down, building a home for his family and a gristmill that provided their means of support. When he died in 1815 he was buried at his own request in the cave that today bears his name, and the walnut coffin that contains his remains can be seen on a guided tour.

Cave Saves Squire Boone's Life

Native Americans were hot on his heels when Squire Boone remembered a cave he and his older brother had discovered years earlier. Grabbing a stout hanging vine, Boone swung into the cave near present-day Mauckport, Indiana. Covering the entrance with branches, Boone prayed earnestly that he would not be found.

He wasn't.

Native Americans stomped around above the cave but evidently did not know it was there or that Boone was hidden right below their feet. Ever after that day in 1790, Boone believed the cave was Holy Ground. And he vowed to bring his family there someday.

Boone also chose the small cave for his final resting place. Through a series of luck and perseverance, that is where the famed frontiersman is buried today. It's a weird feeling to come upon the simple walnut coffin and tombstone in the cave that now bears Squire Boone's name. The story of how Boone's remains came to be found there might be even stranger.

Squire Boone and Daniel Boone were brothers. A skilled gunsmith, Squire crafted Daniel's famous "Tick Licker" rifle as a gift. That's one reason, it is said, that Daniel was such a great shot. The gun Squire had made him was so accurate and good.

In 1787, the brothers were exploring an area near what is now southern Indiana. Climbing a hillside, they saw a spring gushing torrents of water. Searching for the water source, the two discovered a cave entrance. This cave would one day save Squire Boone's life.

After his 1790 close encounter with the Native Americans, Squire would often return to the cave to pray, meditate and carve designs and verses of gratitude in the cave. In 1804, Squire moved his wife, daughter, and four sons to the area, where they built a village and a gristmill. Squire spent the last eleven years of his life here—the longest he ever stayed in one place.

As his death neared—Squire suffered from dropsy or heart failure—he began constructing his own coffin from walnut trees growing near the cave. On his deathbed, he asked his sons to bury him in the cave where the Lord had spared his life. On August 15, 1815, Squire's four sons fulfilled their father's final request. Squire was buried in his beloved cave, with a boulder sealing the entrance.

More than 150 years passed. In 1973, the large cave behind the waterfall was named **Squire Boone Caverns** and opened to the public. Modern conveniences such as concrete walkways, handrails, and indirect lighting were installed. The project was immense and slow moving since everything had to be carried into the cave.

Thousands of visitors came to visit the cave. Like the Boones, they were thrilled by the roaring underground streams and waterfalls, the dazzling cave formations, and the massive pillars of stone. The first year the cave was open, a visitor mentioned to the guides that he had visited the burial cave as a child. He recalled seeing the coffin and the cave carvings.

Two of the guides, brothers Rick and Allen Conway, decided to dig out the section of the cave, which was filled with silt and debris, and find the carvings. Instead, in the summer of 1974, they found Squire himself.

First, the brothers uncovered small bones, then larger ones. And finally a skull. Experts determined the bones, marked with old injuries—such as a tomahawk hole in the skull and a shorter right arm from a break that never mended correctly—did indeed belong to Squire Boone.

A new walnut coffin was created and a Boone family descendant knitted a shroud for the bones. Squire Boone's remains were placed in the coffin, the lid was sealed with wax, and the coffin was carried deep into Squire Boone Caverns.

It now rests in front of several long benches where tour visitors like to stop to listen to Squire's story and pay their respects.

Squire Boone Caverns offer a wondrous mix of colorful stalactites and stalagmites, underground streams, waterfalls, twisted helictites, massive pillars of stone, and the world's largest travertine dam formation. Cave crickets, blind crayfish, isopods, amphipods, and a few bats live in the cave's deepest recesses. The tour guides are extremely well informed about this cave and about caves in general. At one point along the way, in the belly of the cave, all lights are turned out—an eerie experience that gives new meaning to the word *black.* This is not the largest cave around, but it is certainly one of the most dazzling. Visitors should be aware that the subterranean temperature is a constant 54 degrees, and there is a steep spiral staircase to climb at the end of the 55-minute, 0.33-mile tour.

Topside, you can visit an operating gristmill rebuilt on the original foundation used by Squire Boone, watch the miller at work, and buy his products. A cluster of log cabins near the cave's entrance houses various crafts shops, an art gallery, a homemade-candy store, and a bakery; the craftspeople who work here are as authentic as the log cabins that shelter them. Children can get acquainted with farm animals at a petting zoo, uncover fossils at the Fossil Dig, pan for gold and gems, and learn something about earth science at the Rock Shop.

To reach Squire Boone Caverns and village, go south from Corydon on SR 135 for about 10 miles, then turn east onto Squire Boone Caverns Road for another 3 miles; look for signs. Guided 1-hour-long cave tours start every 30 minutes from 9 a.m. to 5 p.m. daily from Memorial Day weekend through Labor Day; tours start every 2 hours from 10 a.m. to 4 p.m. daily the rest of the year; call ahead during bad weather (includes heavy rains); closed major winter holidays; admission fee. Village hours are 10 a.m. to 5 p.m. Memorial Day weekdays to June 30; weekends from 10 a.m. to 6 p.m.; from July 1 through mid-August, 10 a.m. to 6 p.m. daily; from mid-August through Labor Day weekdays from 10 a.m. to 5 p.m. and weekends from 10 a.m. to 6 p.m. Tours: adults (ages 12–59) $21; senior citizens $19; children (ages 4–11) $12. The gristmill, which lies just outside the cave-village complex, is open, free of charge, when the village is open. Write Squire Boone Caverns, 100 Squire Boone Rd. SW, Mauckport 47142, or call (812) 732-4381; squireboonecaverns.com.

O'Bannon Woods State Park, named for the late governor Frank O'Bannon, is nestled within the 26,000-acre Harrison-Crawford State Forest. The park is home to a working 1850s-era haypress, an Indiana invention developed during the country's industrial revolution to compress super-sized bales of hay weighing upward of three hundred pounds. One of only seven known to exist, the hay press in this park is the only one that is operational and publicly displayed. Visitors can watch the oxen-powered hay press at work on a pioneer homestead staffed by reenactors during summer months. The park also offers an Olympic-size swimming pool, a nature center, camping, horseback and hiking trails, and canoeing on the Blue River, Indiana's first natural and scenic river. Park headquarters is located at 7234 Old Forest Rd. Southwest near Corydon; (812) 738-8232; in.gov/dnr/parklake/2976.htm.

Back in Corydon at **Zimmerman Art Glass** you can observe a process that is now nearly extinct. Kerry Zimmerman handblows every piece of glassware he makes, and no two pieces are identical. Kerry specializes in paperweights—clear crystal balls, large and small, that enclose unfolding blossoms—but will try just about anything that tickles his fancy. His glass menagerie includes trays of glass fruits, sugar bowls and creamers, and an assortment of baskets, lamps, vases, and perfume decanters—some clear, some in exquisite color.

Many customers order items made to their specifications. An example is the lady from Australia who dropped by to describe the lamp she wanted and asked that it be sent to her home—the shipping charges cost more than the lamp.

Although small, the company is internationally known, and its artistic wares are displayed in many museums, including the Smithsonian Institution. You're welcome to drop in and watch Kerry breathe life into molten glass. Zimmerman Art Glass is located at 300 E. Chestnut St. Open Tuesday through Saturday 9 a.m. to 5 p.m.; (812) 738-2206; thisisindiana.org.

State Capital Originally in Corydon

In late 1824, a wagon train left southern Indiana bound for the new state capital in a fledgling city known as Indianapolis. For eight years, Corydon had been the capital of Indiana and the move—only 125 miles away—took an arduous fourteen days. The goal was to have the new capital settled so the legislature could meet there in January of 1825.

"I could not ride in the wagon as it was covered and made me sick," Mary Anderson Naylor recalled. "I walked the eleven miles of our first day's journey."

Mary was just a young girl when her family moved. Her sister Lydia was married to a lawyer named Samuel Merrill who had been appointed state treasurer. The family lived in the state capital of Corydon at the time so when the capital moved to Indianapolis, state officials had to move, too. They also had to transport all the records, books, treasury, and other items that the new government had accumulated for state business.

"The road was laid with rails or logs for miles, then covered with water that seemed bottomless," Mary wrote in an historical account. "When the horse and wagon would go down, it seemed they might have reached China."

Roads were so bad, she recalled, that one day the group traveled only two and a half miles. "The water lay in the road too deep to venture in and trees had to be felled to make a road around."

So why did folks decide that the capital no longer should be in Corydon? That's a fairly easy answer. The hard question is why it was in Corydon in the first place.

Turn back the clock more than 200 years ago. Corydon was laid out in 1808 by Henry Heth on land bought from William Henry Harrison—the man who went on to win the Battle of Tippecanoe in 1811 and became president of the United States in 1841.

Back in 1808, Harrison was governor of the Indiana Territory. He had named the settlement Corydon for the young shepherd boy who died in Harrison's favorite hymn, "The Pastoral Elegy," which was in the popular songbook, *Old Missouri Harmony*.

It was in Corydon that Indiana delegates met to draft the first state constitution on June 10, 1816. Other towns had initially been under consideration for the new capital and no one seems to know why Corydon was picked since it was in the southern part of the state and was difficult to reach.

Only 40-foot square, the little two-story limestone courthouse which had recently been built was getting quite warm and crowded so the forty-three representatives moved their work outside to the shade of a huge elm street. Standing about 200 yards northwest of the courthouse near Big Indian Creek, the sheltering tree became known as "Constitution Elm." Legend says that the men kept their jugs of fortifying drink cooling in the creek.

The group drafting the state document was composed of twenty-three lawyers, five ministers, veterans of the Battle of Tippecanoe and quite a few farmers. It is said that the writing of the 12-article constitution took only eighteen days because the new lawmakers had to get back to the business of farming. On June 29, the document was finished, largely copied from the US Constitution and the constitutions of surrounding states.

As the state grew, however, it became apparent that Corydon was a bit out of the way to be state capital. Commissioners were charged with finding a better location. They chose a place almost precisely in the geographic center of the state—Indianapolis.

Now the state legislature had to choose a name for the new capital. That honor went to Judge Jeremiah Sullivan who invented the name by joining "Indiana" with "polis" the Greek word for city.

Corydon also went on to prosper. Located less than 30 miles west of Louisville, Corydon is a lovely county seat that proudly preserves its heritage. In the central square stands the limestone building used by the early legislators.

As for that shady elm tree where Indiana's constitution was drafted, it became the most photographed tree in Indiana and a trademark of Corydon. At its peak, the tree was 50-feet-tall with a trunk diameter of five feet and a spread of 132 feet. When a bad spate of Dutch elm disease hit Indiana, Constitution Elm began to show signs of dying. Despite efforts to save it, the tree died in the summer of 1924. In August 1925, all the dead limbs were removed and only the large massive trunk was left standing. The stump was preserved and a brick shrine was built over it.

The wood of the giant elm was saved for posterity. Cross sections from its massive limbs were given to museums, colleges, universities, and libraries throughout Indiana. Bits were also sold as souvenirs, including gavels so Constitution Elm still lives on in many places.

Henry County

In Indiana it's known as "Hoosier Hysteria"; to the rest of the world it's known as basketball. Almost anyone, after spending about 5 minutes in Indiana, can tell you that basketball holds a special place in the hearts of Hoosiers. It is not unheard of, for instance, for whole towns—gas stations, restaurants, and shops included—to shut down totally so that everyone can go to the local high school basketball game. After a short visit to the state, former CBS news anchor Dan Rather was heard to remark that "a ball and a net would make a perfect state flag" for Indiana. The world's record attendance for an indoor basketball game occurred in 1984, when 67,596 persons attended an exhibition game between the National Basketball Association All-Stars and the US Olympic team in Indianapolis. In 1990 two Indiana teams playing for the state championship set a national record for attendance at a high school basketball game—41,046 persons showed up to cheer on their favorites. Nine of the ten largest high school gyms in the country are in Indiana.

It should therefore surprise no one that there is an *Indiana Basketball Hall of Fame;* the citizenry would have it no other way. Previously located in Indianapolis, the Hall of Fame moved to newer and roomier quarters in *New Castle* in 1990. Within its walls, visitors can see multimedia presentations, use computers to research the basketball history of state schools, play a trivia game, try to outwit a mechanical guard, attempt to make the winning shot as a clock counts down the last 5 seconds of a game, hear a locker room pep talk by legendary coach John Wooden (a Hoosier native), and learn basketball lore in abundance. The museum is at 1 Hall of Fame Court. Admission: adults and teens $5; children (ages 5–12) $3. Open 10 a.m. to 5 p.m. Monday through Saturday and 1–5 p.m. Sunday; closed major winter holidays and Easter. Call (765) 529-1891; hoopshall.com.

The *Henry County Historical Society Museum* in New Castle occupies the Italianate-style home of former Civil War general William Grose; it was constructed in 1860 under the supervision of New Castle architect Thaddeus Coffin. After an accident one year later in which he lost all the fingers on his left hand, Coffin began building a remarkable desk that took thirty-five years to complete and can be seen in the museum today. It consists of 56,978 separate inlaid pieces of wood and includes 324 varieties of wood from around the world; one drawer alone contains 2,367 pieces and tells the history of the Coffin family in Morse code. Also found here is a Hoosier Kitchen Cabinet room, devoted to a popular, all-in-one workstation that combined cooking and storage space; the cabinets were manufactured in New Castle in the early 1900s and are prized by

Hoosier Birthplace of Flight Pioneer, Wilbur Wright

More than a century ago, Wilbur and Orville Wright "slipped the surly bonds of earth" and took to the skies. It was December 17, 1903, at 10:35 a.m. in Kitty Hawk, North Carolina.

The engine was started. The securing rope was slipped. The "plane" moved forward. After a 40-foot run along the rail, the flimsy craft rose slowly into the air. In the words of Wilbur, "The age of flight had come at last."

Many people know about Kitty Hawk and about Dayton, Ohio, where the Wright brothers had their bicycle shop. But a lot of people don't know that Wilbur Wright was born right here in Indiana.

In the midst of vast corn and soybean fields in Henry County stands the birthplace of Wilbur Wright. Along with the restored Wright home is a life-size replica of the Wright Flyer, a large museum featuring family artifacts, an exhibit of the Kitty Hawk campsite, a Main Street set in the year of the flight, an actual F-84 Jet, numerous newspaper clippings about the Wrights, a gift shop, shelter house, community center, and picnic area.

The peaceful rural setting of Milltown in East Central Indiana, just west of Hagerstown, also has an airstrip for the Henry County Wright Flyers. The state of Indiana owned and operated this site from 1020 to 1995 but it is now owned by a local volunteer group, the Wilbur Wright Birthplace Preservation Society, a nonprofit organization.

Wilbur Wright was born April 16, 1867, in the small farmhouse on five acres that his parents had bought almost two years earlier. He was the third of seven children born to Milton and Susan Wright. Welcoming the new baby home were older brothers Reuchlin, 5, and Lorin, 4.

Milton was a minister in the United Brethren Church, a professor of theology, editor of his church newspaper, and an elected bishop in his church. Susan excelled in literature, science, and math at Hartsville College and had a knack for building things.

None of the Wright children were given middle names. Wilbur was named for Wilbur Fiske and Orville for Orville Dewey, two clergymen that their father admired. When Wilbur was less than two years old, the Wrights moved to Hartsville, near Columbus, where Milton taught theology and was pastor of the college chapel there.

From there, they moved to Dayton, Ohio, where Orville was born on August 19, 1871. Sister Katharine was born three years later. Twins Otis and Ida were born in 1870 but died in infancy.

In 1878, their father brought home a toy "helicopter" for his two younger boys. Based on an invention of French aeronautical pioneer Alphonse Penaud, the footlong plane was made of paper, bamboo, and cork with a rubber band to twirl its rotor.

Wilbur and Orville played with it until it broke and then built their own. In later years, the boys pointed to their experience with the toy as the first spark of their interest in flying.

The boys were excellent students and always dressed for success. Their father insisted that when they were in public, they had to wear a suit. That's why they both had on suits in Kitty Hawk for that first flight. People are often surprised when they see photographs of them dressed like that for the flight.

Wilbur originally planned to be a teacher and wanted to go to Yale University. However, in the winter of 1885, Wilbur was accidentally hit in the face by a hockey stick during an ice-skating game with friends. The blow knocked out his front teeth. Although his injuries weren't severe, the formerly athletic young man began to withdraw and did not attend Yale as planned.

Instead, Wilbur stayed home and cared for his mother who was terminally ill with tuberculosis. Orville dropped out of high school after his junior year and started a printing business in 1889. With Wilbur's help, Orville designed and built his own printing press and the two brothers published a weekly Dayton newspaper.

Then their interest was captured by the bicycle craze sweeping the nation. In 1892, the brothers opened a repair and sales shop in Dayton. In 1896, they began manufacturing their own brand of bicycle. But they never lost their interest in flight. They began their own aeronautical experimentation.

In 1900, the brothers journeyed to Kitty Hawk for their manned gliding experiments. Wilbur chose the location because the Atlantic coast offered regular breezes and a soft sandy landing surface.

On that historic December day, the brothers made two flights each from level ground into a freezing headwind gusting to 27 miles per hour. The first flight by Orville covered 120 feet in 12 seconds at a speed of only 6.8 miles per hour.

The flight was recorded in a famous photograph with Orville at the Flyer's levers and Wilbur running next to the wing. The brothers were now in the aviation business. And in the history books.

In 1912, Wilbur contracted typhoid fever and died May 30. He was forty-five years old. Orville sold his interest in the Wright Company in 1915 and spent the remaining thirty-three years of his life as an aviation elder statesman.

Orville died of a heart attack on January 30, 1948, at the age of seventy-six. The brothers are buried in a family cemetery plot in Dayton. Orville and Wilbur never married and have no direct descendants.

collectors today. Located at 606 S. 14th St. Admission: adults $3; students $2. Open 1 to 4:30 p.m. Tuesday through Friday; Saturday by appointment only; (765) 529-4028; henrycountyin.org.

At the **Wilbur Wright Birthplace and Museum**, tour guides humanize the brothers with fascinating true stories about their personal lives. Among them are anecdotes about their numerous failed business ventures, Orville's proclivity for practical jokes, and Wilbur's attempts at cooking.

The Legend of the Raintree

It is a legend carved from dreams, a tale of a mystical tree that poets have sung about in every language in every land. Ross Lockbridge Jr. wrote about it in his classic Civil War novel, **Raintree County:** "Luck, happiness, the realization of dreams, the secret of life itself—all belong to he who finds the raintree. Stand beneath its rain of golden blossoms and discover love."

   The beautiful and exotic raintree about which he wrote, it is said, grows somewhere in Indiana's Henry County, but its exact location remains a mystery. Its seed may have been brought here by Johnny Appleseed, who wandered the Midwest in the first half of the nineteenth century planting apple orchards in what was then wilderness. With him, he carried one special seed—the seed of the golden raintree—searching for the one place where the seed might take root and flourish. Somewhere in Henry County, as legend has it, he found that place, and somewhere in Henry County, it endures to this day.

To reach the birth site, go east from New Castle on SR 38 to Wilbur Wright Road, turn north, and follow the signs. It's open from 10 a.m. to 5 p.m. Tuesday through Saturday, April 1 to November 1. Admission: adults $10; children $2.50. For additional information, write or call the Wilbur Wright Birthplace and Museum, 1525 N. CR 750 East, Hagerstown 47346; (765) 332-2495; wwbirthplace.com.

Jackson County

The heavenly aroma that sometimes tantalizes the nostrils in **Brownstown** is a vanilla bean on its way to becoming vanilla extract. This metamorphosis takes place each working day at the **Marion-Kay Spices** plant, which turns out an array of spices, herbs, extracts, and seasonings. You can learn about the whole process, as well as the history of the company and its spices, at the Marion-Kay plant and outlet store at 1351 W. US 50 on the western edge of town. Just inside the building's entrance is a hall lined with exhibits that showcase the various spices and other flavorings that have been produced during the company's eighty-nine year history. One of them, no longer available, was a special chicken seasoning used for several years by Col. Harlan Sanders of Kentucky Fried Chicken fame in his restaurants. Another favorite was the Miss America Katie Stam Seasoning. Miss Stam is a Jackson County resident who was named Miss America in 2009; she is the only Indiana contestant to ever win the Miss America crown. New flavorings are constantly being developed. Open 8:30

a.m. to 4:30 p.m. Monday through Thursday. Staff members conduct free tours by advance reservation, and those who participate will receive a discount on any spices purchased; (812) 358-3000; marionkay.com.

Indiana's **Skyline Drive** meanders across a series of knobs for some 6 miles through the **Jackson-Washington State Forest** and offers spectacular hilltop vistas. The poorly surfaced road is narrow, hilly, and treacherous, so plan on taking your time. A clearing at its peak 929-foot elevation offers picnic facilities and a panoramic view that extends into four counties. If you climb the fire tower that you'll see along the way, you'll see seven counties. To reach the drive, head south from Brownstown on S. Poplar St. and follow the signs. Write the Jackson-Washington State Forest, 1278 E. SR 250, Brownstown 47220, or call (812) 358-2160, for information about the drive and the many recreational opportunities elsewhere in the 18,000-acre forest; in.gov/dnr/forestry/4820.htm.

Vallonia was established circa 1811, making it Jackson County's oldest community. Its longevity may be attributed in part to the fact that it has its own guardian angel.

Made of French marble and soaring to a height of more than 15 feet, the **Angel on Angel Hill** has stood atop a pedestal in a small family cemetery just south of town since 1887. The daughter of a prominent local businessman, who wanted to memorialize her father with a very special monument, had the sweet-faced angel shipped from Paris to New York. There she was placed aboard a train to Seymour and then carted on a log wagon to her permanent home in Vallonia, where she has been a curiosity ever since for both tourists and locals.

The cemetery over which she stands guard, wings unfurled and right arm extended, is atop a small rise in the midst of a soybean field along SR 135 South. A narrow path leads through the field to the graveyard and its angel.

Two notable covered bridges can be seen in Jackson County. Both of them span the East Fork of the White River. To view what's billed as the longest three-span covered bridge in the country, head east from Medora for 1 mile on SR 235. The 434-foot-long span, built in 1875, is certainly the longest in Indiana. It carried traffic across the river until 1974, when it was bypassed by a new bridge. Now listed on the National Register of Historic Places, the old **Medora Bridge** was slowly falling into decay until the funds to preserve it recently became available; a ribbon-cutting ceremony was held in July 2011 to celebrate the completion of the needed repairs.

The **Shieldstown Covered Bridge,** constructed in 1876, is 355 feet long. To visit it, go southwest from Seymour on US 50 for about 6.5 miles, then turn northwest onto a country road leading to Crane Hill and proceed about 1 mile; look for signs along the way.

A third bridge, the 325-foot-long **Bell's Ford Bridge,** collapsed into the White River, a gradual process that culminated in 2006. It was the only triple-burr-arch covered bridge in Indiana and the only known Post truss bridge in existence anywhere. Erected in 1869, the Post truss represented a period when bridges were evolving from all-wood into all-metal or concrete structures. Its sides and floor featured iron rods and straps covered with wood. Funds are being raised to restore it. The bridge was located on SR 258, 3 miles west of Seymour.

For additional information about the county's bridges, write or call the Jackson County Visitor Center, 100 N. Broadway St., PO Box 607, Seymour 47274; (812) 524-1914 or (888) 524-1914; jacksoncountyin.com. You might want to also ask for information about the county's two round barns.

When rock star **John Mellencamp** penned his popular song "Small Town," he was describing his hometown of **Seymour.** Tourism officials in this still-small community say that scarcely a day goes by that they don't receive inquiries about John, so they've created a CD titled *The Roots of an American Rocker* that features a self-guided driving tour of fourteen landmarks associated with the town's most famous native son. The CD, which includes some of Mellencamp's music and narration by his family members and close friends, is available for purchase at the Jackson County Visitor Center (see previous paragraph for contact information).

One of the stops is the **Southern Indiana Center for the Arts** (SICA), home to the only permanent exhibit of John's oil paintings. John comes by his artistic ability naturally. He was exposed to art throughout his life because his late mother, Marilyn, was a painter; her paintings are also displayed at the center. A garden on the grounds is dedicated to the memory of John's grandmother, Laura. There's also a crafts barn with a resident potter who helps visitors take a turn on the pottery wheel.

One of SICA's attractions is the **Conner Museum of Antique Printing.** A working print shop that employs period presses from the 1800s, the hands-on museum showcases the history of printing from cave drawings to bookbinding. Visitors can feel different types of papers and take-home examples of type. A display of rare fragments of Bibles spanning six centuries includes a 1476 Scripture printed in Venice, Italy. Special tours can be arranged. Admission is free. SICA is located at 2001 N. Ewing St.; (812) 522-2278; soinart.com. Open noon to 5 p.m. Tuesday through Friday; 11 a.m. to 3 p.m. on Saturday.

Wildlife lovers will want to stop at **Muscatatuck National Wildlife Refuge,** located 3 miles east of Seymour on the south side of US 50. Covering more than 7,700 acres, it was established primarily as a sanctuary for wood ducks. Each spring and fall thousands of migrating waterfowl pause to rest on the open water and are occasionally joined by flocks of sandhill cranes. White-tailed deer, wild turkeys, and several hundred river otters make their homes here all year long. Once extinct in Indiana, the bald eagle has begun returning to the Hoosier State; this majestic bird can occasionally be seen nesting here. Rare whooping cranes pass over and sometimes pause for a bit during fall and spring migrations between Wisconsin and Florida. The refuge is open daily year-round, from dawn to dusk. The Refuge Visitor Center is open Tuesday through Saturday from 8:30 a.m. to 4:30 p.m. There is no entrance fee to the refuge. Write or call the Muscatatuck National Wildlife Refuge, 12985 E. US 50, Seymour 47274; (812) 522-4352; fws.gov/midwest/muscatatuck/.

Jefferson County

The late Charles Kuralt once wrote: "the princess of the rivers . . . is unquestionably *Madison,* Indiana. It is the most beautiful river town in America." The curator of a Michigan museum, when he first saw Madison, said, "Put a fence around the entire town and don't let anyone touch anything in it!" During World War II the Office of War Information selected Madison as the "typical American town" and made movies of it in thirty-two languages to distribute around the world to remind our troops what they were fighting for. *Life* magazine chose Madison as the most pleasant small town in the country in which to live. Its nineteenth-century architecture, a mix of several styles, has been praised as the most beautiful in the Midwest, and its setting on the banks of the Ohio River, against a backdrop of wooded hills and limestone bluffs, is equally lovely. In 2006, the entire town was designated a National Historic Landmark District. Obviously, if you're going to tour Indiana, Madison is one place you shouldn't miss.

Once Madison was a thriving river port and the largest town in the state. When railroads arrived on the scene, the river traffic departed, and Madison, in keeping with the times, built its own railroad. What no one foresaw was that nearly everyone would get on the train and leave town. For many years, no one came to replace the populace that had moved on, and 133 blocks of buildings thus survived an era when it was fashionable to tear down anything old and replace it with something new in the name of progress. It is this legacy of architectural splendor that can be seen today.

The most notable building is the *Lanier Mansion* at 601 W. 1st St. (812-265-3526; indianamuseum.org/lanier-mansion-and-state-historic-site), a palatial home built in the 1840s for about $50,000—quite a chunk of money in those days. Its owner, James Lanier, was an astute banker whose loans to the state government during the Civil War helped Indiana avert bankruptcy. Facing a broad lawn that rambles down to the Ohio River, the Lanier Mansion is an outstanding example of the Greek Revival style. Its two-story portico is supported by tall Corinthian columns and hemmed in by wrought-iron grillwork. Inside, a spiral staircase climbs three stories, unsupported except by its own thrust, and each of the rooms is decorated with period furniture and accessories. Now a state historic site, the 5-acre estate is open year-round from Wednesday through Sunday from 10 a.m. to 5 p.m. Admission: adults $11; senior citizens $9; children $6; children (under age three) free. The gardens and grounds are open daily free of charge from dawn to dusk.

Among the other attractions in Madison's historic district are the *office and private hospital of Dr. William Hutchings* at 120 W. Third St., (812) 265-2412, with all the original medications and possessions of the late-nineteenth-century doctor still intact and the *Francis Costigan House* at 408 W. Third St., (812) 273-5269, home of the architect who designed Lanier Mansion. The restored *Schroeder Saddletree Factory Museum* at 106 Milton St., (812) 265-2967, a living museum of industry complete with operable antique machinery, is the only museum in the country that explores the saddletree maker's craft. Everywhere in Madison you'll see elaborate ornamental ironwork reminiscent of New Orleans but forged locally (as was much of New Orleans's ironwork).

Maps and guides for walking tours are available from the Madison Visitors Center at 601 W. 1st St.; (812) 265-2956 or (800) 559-2956; visitmadison.org.

Railroad buffs will want to take a look at one of the world's steepest non-cog train tracks. Cut through limestone bluffs in 1835, the track rises 413 feet in elevation in little more than a mile. Eight-horse teams drew the first trains up the incline but were eventually replaced by a wood-burning steam engine The tracks can be viewed from a bridge on SR 56 (Main Street) at the west edge of town.

Not far west of Madison via SR 56 at 1650 Clifty Hollow Rd., you can stay at the *Clifty Inn* at Clifty Falls State Park. Rates for its guest rooms range from moderate to expensive; some rooms have private balconies that overlook the Ohio River valley. The dining room serves three meals a day for reasonable rates. Call (812) 265-4135 or (877) 925-4389, or visit in.gov/dnr/parklake/inns /clifty/.

Noted for its natural beauty, *Clifty Falls State Park* sprawls over 1,360 hilly acres. The prettiest area, *Clifty Canyon State Nature Preserve,* is accessible only on foot. The great boulder-strewn canyon is so deep that sunlight can penetrate it only at high noon. Mosses, lichens, and ferns cling to the precipitous cliffs along Clifty Creek. In the spring, when the water is running fast, there are spectacular waterfalls; Big Clifty Falls, the granddaddy of them all, drops 60 feet. The park also offers an Olympic-size swimming pool, a modern campground, a nature center, an exercise trail, and breathtaking views from atop a 400-foot bluff. Admission is $7 for Indiana residents and $9 for out-of-state visitors. Write or call Clifty Falls State Park, 1501 Green Rd., Madison 47250; (812) 273-8885; in.gov/dnr/parklake/2985.htm.

Canaan's annual Fall Festival, held the second weekend in September, features a potpourri of such events as a frog-jumping contest, a bucksaw woodcutting contest, a greased-pole climbing contest, and the Chief White Eye painting contest. It is the unique *Pony Express Run,* however, that has made the festival famous far and wide. Mail is specially stamped at Canaan, packed in authentic pony express mailbags on loan from the Smithsonian Institution in Washington, DC, and delivered to the Madison post office by a rider on horseback. For further information, write or call Visit Madison (601 W. 1st St., Madison 47250; 812-265-2956 or 800-559-2956; visitmadison.org).

For years, few people knew the story behind the three-story stone structure that sits atop a hill in rural Jefferson County. When the building was first erected by abolitionists in 1848, it was known as *Eleutherian College,* and what went on there was illegal.

The educational institution was quietly set up in the rural community of *Lancaster* to offer college-level courses to all, regardless of race or gender. As such, it was the first school in Indiana to offer a higher education to African Americans. The name it was given attested to its purpose. Eleutherian is a Greek word meaning "freedom and equality."

After falling into a period of decay, Historic Eleutherian College, Inc., was formed as a nonprofit organization to purchase and restore the structure and to research its history. Remnants of cupboards and benches remained, along with a couple of long-abandoned pianos, but a cast-iron bell in the belfry rang as true as the first day it was placed there. One bit of lore claims that two of the children born to Thomas Jefferson and Sally Hemings attended school here. An important first step in the preservation effort was to have the college designated a National Historic Landmark, an honor that was bestowed upon it at a dedication ceremony in October 1997. A visitor center features exhibits depicting the history of the area's ties to the Underground Railroad.

Eleutherian College is located at 6927 W. SR 250, about 10 miles northwest of Madison. Open 10 a.m. to 4 p.m. Monday through Saturday; call (812) 748-2540 to make an appointment for a guided tour; eleutherian-college.org. A donation is required for admission.

Jennings County

Each week from mid-April to mid October, visitors trek to tiny **Commiskey** to enjoy the pleasures of **Stream Cliff,** Indiana's oldest herb farm. They come to wander through the flower gardens, to enjoy the salads, sandwiches, and teas served at the Twigs & Sprigs Tearoom, and to sample the wines at the farm's winery. They browse through the arts-and-crafts shops. They sit beneath a shaded arbor or watch the goldfish glide by in the farm's two ponds. If they're so inclined and register in advance, they can take one of the many classes offered here. Various experts demonstrate such things as the uses of different herbs and how to create craft items. Whatever you choose to do, you will find a quiet and serene retreat in which to do it. Hours vary according to the season so check the website for current hours. Located at 8225 S. CR 90 West; (812) 346-5859; streamclifffarm.com.

In 2006, the Army National Guard officially took over nearly 1,000 acres in southern Indiana to build the Muscatatuck Urban Training Complex (MUTC), established to train military and civilian agencies on how to respond to emergency events in urban settings. In doing so, it displaced the sprawling Muscatatuck State Developmental Center, a Jennings County hospital that had served the mentally disabled from thirty-five southern Indiana counties since 1920. Because the treatment center had meant so much to so many in the region, the Guard promised to preserve its history. That promise was fulfilled in April 2011 when the Guard, in conjunction with the Jennings County Historical Society, opened the **Muscatatuck Museum** in one of the hospital's original buildings near **Butlerville.** Visitors will learn about the evolution of mental health care through the years by viewing the hundreds of artifacts on display and watching a video presentation. The museum is open from 9 a.m. to 3 p.m. Monday through Friday. Visitors must make an appointment to visit because it is a military base. Admission is free, but donations are appreciated. For additional information and exact directions to the museum building, contact the MUTC Public Affairs Office at (317) 247-3300, ext. 41610. You may also contact the Jennings County Historical Society, 134 E. Brown St., PO Box 335, Vernon 47282; (812) 346-8989; jenningscounty.org.

Ohio County

In the small Ohio River community of **Rising Sun,** you can visit **Rees Harps Inc.** and watch as William Rees and his son Garen design and construct fine hardwood harps. William Rees, a nationally known harp builder who makes concert lever harps used by Grammy-winning harpists, also is the inventor of the Harpsicle; a smaller, more affordable, lighter-weight harp that sounds full-size, the Harpsicle has become the shop's best-selling instrument. He, his wife, Pamela, and their children moved to Rising Sun from California a few years back, lured by the town's charm and its growing reputation as an arts center. Now the business is run mainly by Garen and his wife Melissa. You can also purchase Celtic music, jewelry, and other gift items here. Rees Harps is located at 222 Main St. Open 9 a.m. to 5 p.m. Tuesday through Friday; call (812) 438-3032 or visit reesharps.com.

Not long ago, the red wolf was tottering on the brink of extinction, with only twelve of the species surviving. Today, thanks to captive breeding and education, the red wolf is making a comeback. Paul Strasser, a former zoo-keeper, used the rare wolf as a symbol when he established his **Red Wolf Sanctuary** in 1979. In addition to providing a permanent home for some of the wildlife seen here, the refuge also serves as a rehabilitation center for sick and injured wildlife from all over the country. Paul and his wife, Jane, nurse their wild charges back to health, returning those who fully recuperate to their natural habitats and adding the others to their growing "forever family." At this writing, the latter includes seven grey wolves, a red wolf hybrid, three black bears, nine coyotes, a cougar, four bobcats, seventeen red foxes, one arctic fox, one elk, one striped skunk, two opossums, and an assortment of raptors. Wetlands on the Strassers' property are home to beaver and otter; bald eagles and waterfowl sometimes stop by to visit.

The sanctuary, located at 3027 SR 262 near Rising Sun, occupies 452 picturesque acres. Guided tours last about 2 hours; a cart is available for visitors so that no one has to walk the whole time, but dress for the weather and wear comfortable shoes. Admission and tours are by appointment only; (812) 438-2306; redwolf.org. Tours: adults $20; teens $10; children $5. Guided photography tours also are available. Prices for photography tours depend on the number of people. For example, groups of 1–3 people cost $50 per hour while groups of 13–15 people cost $300 per hour. Photography tours usually last 2–3 hours. Donations are applied to the upkeep of the sanctuary and are very much appreciated.

Ripley County

Visitors traveling through **Versailles** often stop to stare in wonderment at the unusual looking church on the corner of Tyson and Adams Streets at 326 W. Tyson St. Known officially as the **Tyson United Methodist Church** and unofficially as the Tyson Temple, it is a continuous flow of rounded corners, arches, columns, windows, and roof lines. Its striking spire is a rounded, inverted conc of openwork aluminum. Inside, the altar is framed by columns that duplicate those in the Taj Mahal. The rounded ceiling above the pews is painted with the stars and constellations that appear over Indiana in October. To enhance the effect of a nighttime sky, the ceiling is illuminated by light reflected from wall fixtures. The dome over the choir loft is covered with gold leaf from Germany. Pulpit furnishings come from Italy, and the windows are from Belgium. The grand but small Tyson Church (it seats only 200 people) draws visitors from across the country. Free tours are offered by appointment; call (812) 689-6976 or visit tysonumc.org.

The Milan Miracle

The score is tied, 30-30. Seconds remain. Bobby Plump crouches, pumps, his right arm thrusts. The ball arcs through the air amid a roar of screaming and crying fans. He scores.

And tiny Milan High School, one of the state's smallest, makes history as the 1954 Indiana state basketball champions. The small-town high school with an entire student body of 161 has toppled the powerhouse defending champ, Muncie Central High School, with its enrollment of 2,200.

More than half a century later, that ultimate David versus Goliath story—inspiring the movie *Hoosiers*—is still the heartbeat of Hoosier Hysteria. Youngsters tossing hoops in barnyards and makeshift basketball courts are reared by it. It has put the ordinary town near the meandering Ohio River on the map and changed the lives of that amazing team forever.

Sports Illustrated named the Milan team one of the top twenty teams of the century. Indiana sports writers chose it as the No. 1 sports story in all of Indiana history. But the heart-stopping last-second win that put a quiet rural town at the top may never come again.

Back then, no attendance classifications separated the largest schools from the smallest in the state tournament. In a state where basketball is king, all competed as equals. In 1997, Indiana ditched its one-classification basketball tournament and divided the schools into four classes.

But, back in 1954, basketball boosters turned their eyes to the Mighty Men of Milan as the team beat its way to the finals. Among their victims was Oscar Robertson's high school team—Crispus Attucks High School in Indianapolis. The "Big O" later went on to be regarded as one of the greatest players in NBA history and was inducted into the National Basketball Association Hall of Fame.

Still Milan romped past Oscar Robertson and Crispus Attucks. For the final game, Hinkle was packed to the rafters with an estimated 15,000 people. Consider that the whole population of Milan was only 1,150.

The fourth quarter of the game is said to be the most famous eight minutes of schoolboy basketball in history. Muncie was ahead. Then Milan. Then Muncie. Then a tie. Plump had the ball with just 18 seconds remaining. The crowd was on its feet screaming as Plump dribbled the ball down court. Plump glanced at the clock. Six seconds left. Time to make his move. Faking left, then right, Plump edged up to the free throw line, jumped, and shot. Fans who saw it said the large orange orb seemed to arch up and drop in slow motion.

The ball whooshed through the net with three seconds remaining. Milan was the new state champs. Pandemonium erupted. Mobbed by well-wishers and media, Plump and the players needed almost two hours to get back to the locker room. Just as he had promised, Indianapolis motorcycle policeman Pat Stark closed off Monument Circle and escorted the newly crowned champions boys in a celebratory drive backward to their Pennsylvania Hotel rooms around Indiana's best-known landmark.

The next morning, the squad did what it usually did at home. Since it was Sunday, they went to church. Afterward, they headed home. As the caravan got closer to Milan, the team began to see hastily erected congratulatory signs. Thousands of cars were now lined bumper to bumper for at least 13 miles along cornfields to Milan. Both sides of the road were crowded with jubilant people waiting for their champs.

It may never come again to a small Indiana town, but the Milan Miracle is the stuff from which dreams are made, the passion that drives young Hoosiers, and the rallying cry for every small school in the state.

The tiny town of **Milan** (population 1,895) is arguably the sports mecca of Indiana. In 1954, its high school basketball team, playing in what was then a single-class state championship tournament, defeated a mighty Muncie Central team 32–30 when Bobby Plump sank a last-minute jump shot. Milan walked away with the championship and walked into sports history. Also in 2004, *Hoosiers* was voted the top sports movie of the last twenty-five years for the first time by the viewers of ESPN, cable television's sports channel, and it remains at the top of that list today. Perhaps the greatest award bestowed upon the movie, however, was its listing by the Library of Congress as an American icon, an honor bestowed upon only a few movies.

The David-over-Goliath victory is still referred to as the Milan Miracle by basketball fans everywhere, and the town honors its heroes at the **Milan '54 Museum.** Visitors will see such memorabilia as photos of the players (then and now), most of their black-and-gold letter jackets, and an autographed hunk of the old maple gym floor on which the championship game was played. A blackboard with a diagram of Bobby Plump's final shot stands in a corner. Other exhibits include twelve lockers decorated with items from each player, Bobby Plump's satin warm-ups, Coach Marvin Wood's good-luck ties, an Indiana All-Star jersey, and hundreds of other items, such as posters, newspaper stories, and pictures.

The museum is located at 201 W. Carr St. in Milan. The museum is open Wednesday through Saturday 10 a.m. to 4 p.m.; Sunday by appointment. Call (812) 654-2772. You can learn more at the museum's excellent website, milan54 .org, where you can watch actual footage from the championship game and compare the "real story" to the "reel story."

Roselyn McKittrick founded the museum and devoted her life to collecting museum memorabilia before her death on March 16, 2019. Thousands of visitors find their way each year to this little off-the-beaten-path town, all lured by the feel-good story of the scrappy little team that pulled off the biggest upset in Indiana basketball history. They visit both the museum and Milan High School, where a display case holds the 1954 game ball and the championship trophy.

When the late Carl Dyer moved to **Friendship** in 1982, he thought he was retiring from a long career of moccasin making, but relentless customers who demanded his products drew him back into the business. He also discovered that he loved his craft too much to give it up.

Dyer never advertised his mostly mail-order business—he didn't have to. Even people from abroad somehow obtained his phone number and called to place their orders.

The son of an accomplished boot maker (his father crafted the aviation boots that Charles Lindbergh wore on his historic flight across the Atlantic), Dyer learned his trade early. Today, although Dyer himself is gone, the business, known as **Carl Dyer's Original Moccasins,** continues to produce several thousand pairs of handmade moccasins in eight different styles each year. The double-soled, heavy leather, waterproof moccasins range in price from approximately $296 to $616.

Customers include celebrities and Fortune 500 company executives, all of whom rave about the molded-to-your-feet comfort. Interestingly, one order was from Charles Lindbergh's grandson, who was unaware that he was ordering his moccasins from the same family that had made his grandfather's boots.

The shop is located at 5961 E. SR 62. Because hours vary, call before visiting; (812) 667-5442 or (800) 638-6627. You can also visit online at carldyers .com.

Wayne County

Every state has one, and in Indiana it's in Wayne County. The distinguished (at least to Hoosiers) spot sits in the middle of a bean field and is marked by a pile of rocks with a stick in it. Officially known as **Hoosier Hill,** it soars to 1,257 feet above sea level and is the highest point in Indiana.

It's a lonely site. In a good year, it lures about 200 visitors from around the country. Many are members of the National Highpointers Club, a group dedicated to visiting the highest point in each of the United States.

The current high point has not always been the highest point in Indiana. Originally that honor belonged to a spot approximately 200 yards to the southwest. But when that spot was resurveyed by satellite a decade or so ago, it was discovered that the original high point had shrunk. The popular belief is that it was done by the repeated attacks of a manure spreader. That fate will not soon befall the current high point.

Getting to Hoosier Hill is an adventure in itself. The noted landmark is located in the northeastern corner of Wayne County, not far from the small town of **Bethel.** From Bethel, go north on SR 227 for about 1.25 miles to Randolph County Line Road (also known as Bethel Road) and turn west. Go west 1 mile and turn south onto Elliot Road. Proceed about 1.25 miles to an access road on the west. Park on the access road, climb over the adjacent fence on a stile provided by some Highpointers Club members, and walk about 100 feet along a rock-lined path to the top of the hill. There you'll find a picnic table and maybe a sign that identifies this as Indiana's Highpoint; the sign keeps getting stolen. There also may or may not be a visitor's sign-in book in a waterproof box hanging from a tree. The book is sometimes stolen, too. For additional information, write or call the Richmond/Wayne County Convention and Tourism Bureau, 5701 National Rd. East, Richmond; (765) 935-8687 or (800) 828-8414; visitrichmond.org.

Although it may seem an unlikely location for such an enterprise, **Richmond** once boasted one of the largest rose-growing industries in the world. **Hill Floral Products, Inc.,** pioneers in greenhouse rose growing from 1881 until closing in 2007, annually shipped more than 30 million cut roses to midwestern and southern states. During its years in business, the Hill family developed nearly 80 percent of all rose varieties grown in the United States, including the famed American Beauty Rose.

The luxurious **Hill Memorial Rose Garden** in Glen Miller Park, which displays more than 1,600 rosebushes, was established in tribute to the Hills and the local flower industry. Located at 2500 National Rd. East, the park is also the site of the All-America Rose Garden and the German Friendship Garden. Peak blooming periods are June and September. Admission is free; the park is open 6 a.m. to 11 p.m. daily. Call (765) 962-1638; waynet.org/nonprofit /rosegarden.

At the **Hayes Regional Arboretum,** a 466-acre botanical preserve, you can view regional plant species—all labeled—on a 2-mile auto tour. Also on the grounds are Indiana's first solar-heated greenhouse, a fern garden, a wild bird sanctuary, 10 miles of hiking trails (one of which passes an Indian mound), and a nature center housed in a barn close to two centuries old, where a telephone line permits you to eavesdrop on a colony of bees busily at work making honey. Open 9 a.m. to 5 p.m. Tuesday through Saturday. A nominal fee is charged for the auto tour; otherwise, admission is free. East Side Trails are open daily from dawn to dusk. Write or call Hayes Regional Arboretum, 801 Elks Rd., Richmond 47374; (765) 962-3745; hayesarboretum.org.

The **Wayne County Historical Museum** is generally recognized as one of the best county museums in the state. Its diverse collection ranges from vintage cars made in Richmond to a Japanese samurai warrior's uniform, from a nineteenth-century general store to a 3,000-year-old Egyptian mummy (X-rays of the mummy taken by two local physicians can be seen by visitors). A collection of jazz memorabilia pays tribute to Richmond's contributions to this uniquely American music genre. Open 9 a.m. to 4 p.m. Monday through Friday and 1–4 p.m. Saturday and Sunday; closed Sunday in January and February and major holidays. Admission: adults $7; senior citizens $5; children (ages 6–17) $4. Write or call the Wayne County Historical Museum, 1150 N. A St., Richmond 47374; (765) 962-5756; wchmuseum.org.

Although every other sport takes a backseat to basketball in Indiana, the state has also produced some football heroes. They're all honored in the **Indiana Football Hall of Fame,** located at 815 N. A St. Among the inductees are O. J. Simpson, Bart Starr, and Jim Thorpe, all of whom once played football in the Hoosier State; Knute Rockne, the legendary coach of Notre Dame; Tom Harmon (the father of actor Mark Harmon), who is the only Indiana native to ever have won the Heisman Trophy, and Weeb Ewbank, a local great who coached the Baltimore Colts and New York Jets. Tony Hulman, whose name is synonymous with the Indianapolis 500, is remembered here as an All-American end on the undefeated Yale University team of 1923. Open 11 a.m. to 5 p.m. Tuesday through Saturday; other times by appointment. Closed the first two weeks of January and national holidays. No admission fee, but donations are greatly appreciated; (765) 966-2235; indiana-football.org. A number of archives from this museum are also exhibited at Lucas Oil Stadium in Indianapolis, home of the Indianapolis Colts professional football team.

Earlham College, located on the south side of US 40 just west of downtown Richmond, is the home of the **Joseph Moore Museum of Natural History.** Such wonders as a prehistoric mastodon, an extinct giant beaver, and authentic *Allosaurus* skeletons are displayed, along with Ordovician fossils, arthropods, live snakes, Indiana birds of prey, and an Egyptian mummy. The free museum is open from 1 to 5 p.m. Monday, Wednesday, Friday, Saturday, and Sunday; other times by appointment. Admission is free, but donations are appreciated.

All That Jazz

The sounds emanating from the small town of Richmond in the 1920s were some of the sweetest on earth. Musicians from all over the country came here during that decade to a tiny recording studio perched on the banks of the Whitewater River.

Our country was in the throes of the Jazz Age then, and many now-legendary jazz artists signed their first recording contracts at Gennett Studios. Among them were Fred "Jelly Roll" Morton, Bix Beiderbecke (his Rhythm Jugglers featured Tommy Dorsey on the trombone), King Oliver, Duke Ellington, and the incomparable Louis Armstrong.

Hoagy Carmichael made the first recording of "Stardust" here, but it was nearly lost to posterity when a Gennett employee almost threw it in the trash. Thankfully, the error was caught in time. Although that original version was recorded in an upbeat dance tempo, "Stardust" has evolved into a more mellow rendition that the world now regards as one of the most beautiful love songs ever written.

Blues musicians also recorded at Gennett, and the recordings of a young Gene Autry introduced old-time country music to the world. Billy Sunday, a popular preacher of the day, and poet James Whitcomb Riley, a native Hoosier, added the spoken word to Gennett's repertoire. The company also produced copies of William Jennings Bryan's famous 1896 "Cross of Gold" speech; they were taken to Tennessee and sold outside the courthouse where Bryan was participating in the 1925 Scopes "monkey" trial.

From 1916 to 1934, the studio produced thousands of recordings, featuring any recorded sound that had or could have a market. All this was accomplished despite the fact that the studio had no electricity until 1926 and had to halt recording every time a train came by on the adjacent railroad track.

Unfortunately, like many other businesses of the day, the Gennett label was done in by the Great Depression, but Richmond has not forgotten its rich heritage as the "cradle of recorded jazz." Visitors can currently learn more about the Gennett studio at the Wayne County Historical Museum.

Additionally, the city has created a *Walk of Fame* near the former location of the Gennett Studio. Located along S. 1st St. near its intersection with Main St., the Walk of Fame consists of three-dimensional cast-bronze and mosaic-tile markers shaped like 78-rpm phonograph records embedded in the pavement. Each marker features an artistic rendering of the musician it represents, and a smaller bronze plaque installed next to each describes the accomplishments of that musician. For additional information, contact the Starr-Gennett Foundation, 33 S. 7th Street, Richmond 47374; (765) 962-2860; starrgennett.org.

Write or call Earlham College, 801 W. National Rd. (US 40), Richmond 47374; (765) 983-1303; earlham.edu/museum.

The *Whitewater Gorge Trail,* which borders the Whitewater River in the heart of Richmond, is one of only two known places in the United States where fossiliferous limestone of the Ordovician period is exposed to the surface.

Geologists, paleontologists, and amateur collectors have been coming to this unique site for more than a century to examine the abundance of fossils in the gorge's 425 million-year-old rock formations. A paved footpath that leads through the gorge is accessible from three trailheads: the South Trailhead on Test Road, the Central Trailhead at the high school parking lot on Hub Etchison Parkway, and the North Trailhead at the Starr Gennett building on the corner of Main and S. 1st Streets. Trail maps and additional information can be obtained by contacting the Richmond Parks and Recreation Department, Administration Office, 2200 E. Main St., Richmond 47374; (765) 983-7275; richmondindiana.g ov or the Richmond/Wayne County Convention and Tourism Bureau, 5701 E. National Rd., Richmond 47374; (765) 935-8687 or (800) 828-8414; visitrichmond .org. You can also obtain information about where you can legally collect fossils.

Fountain City is the home of the *Levi and Catharine Coffin State Historic Site House,* known as "the Grand Central Station of the Underground Railroad." Levi and Catharine Coffin, Quakers who were opposed to slavery, opened their 1839 Federal-style home to approximately 2,000 fugitive Black slaves during the Civil War era. The History Channel listed this National Historic Landmark as one of the top twenty-five most historic sites in the United States. The house, located at 201 US 27 North, is open to the public from 10 a.m. to 5 p.m. Wednesday through Sunday. Admission: adults $10; senior citizens $8; children (ages 3–17) $5. For more information, write the Levi Coffin House State Historic Site, PO Box 77, Fountain City 47341; call (765) 847-2432 or (765) 847-2076; or visit indianamuseum.org/levi-and-catharine-coffin-state-historic-site.

Abbott's Candy Shop, the oldest continuously operating business in *Hagerstown* (circa 1890), uses old family recipes to turn out a cornucopia of confections that are sold at its store at 48 E. Walnut St. and by mail throughout the country. Its specialty and most popular sweet is the caramel, but many other varieties await visitors, too. Open 9 a.m. to 4 p.m. Monday through Friday. Call (765) 489-4442 or 877-801-1200 to arrange a free tour (yes, free samples are included); abbottscandy.com.

The redbrick storefront in *Dublin* gives little hint of the treasure trove inside. Owner Patricia McDaniel is an antiques dealer extraordinaire. She is also one of Hollywood's aces-in-the-hole.

It all began in 1987, when movie director John Sayles needed some props for *Eight Men Out,* a baseball movie that was filmed partly in Indiana. McDaniel was able to supply them; the word spread, and Hollywood has beat a path to her door ever since. Her period props, many of them hard to find elsewhere, have appeared in about sixty major movies, including *Legends of the Fall, Avalon, This Boy's Life, A League of Their Own, Munich, The Good Shepherd, The Notebook,* and *Charlotte's Web.*

Levi Coffin and the Underground Railroad

Clutching her baby, the escaped slave arrived at the home seeking a place to hide and food to eat. Levi Coffin didn't turn her away. He and his wife Catharine had sheltered hundreds of runaway slaves on the Underground Railroad. The woman and child stayed several days at the Coffin home in Newport, Indiana.

It wasn't until years later that Coffin discovered the slave's identity and her important place in the struggle to abolish slavery. The woman he had helped was the real Eliza Harris of *Uncle Tom's Cabin* fame. She was the slave who crossed the Ohio River on the drifting ice with her child in her arms. Eliza's story was graphically told by author Harriet Beecher Stowe in the book that was said to have helped start the Civil War.

The stories are founded on facts that really occurred. Only the names of characters in the book were changed to protect real people, such as those who ran the Underground Railroad. In *Uncle Tom's Cabin,* Coffin and his wife were named Simeon and Rachel Halliday, a Quaker couple who helped Eliza in her escape.

Years later, in 1854, Coffin and his wife were visiting Chatham, Canada. At the close of a meeting at one of the Black churches, a woman came up, grasped his wife's hand, and exclaimed, "God bless you!"

Although the Coffins didn't recognize the woman, she knew them and thanked them for their kindness in sheltering her and her baby for several days during her escape. That woman was Eliza Harris, Coffin recalled in the book *Fleeing for Freedom*.

Born in 1798 in New Garden, North Carolina, Levi Coffin was brought up to be a farmer and a Quaker like his father. As a child, Coffin saw white owners abusing their Black slaves. He dates his own personal conversion to abolitionism to an incident that occurred when he was only seven years old. Chopping wood with his father, Coffin saw a group of slaves handcuffed and chained together being herded along the roadside for sale to another plantation.

In answer to his father's question about why they were chained, Coffin heard the answer—the men were bound so that they could not escape and return to their wives and children. It was inconceivable to the young boy that his own father could ever be taken away from him like that.

That moment, Coffin later said, was the awakening of a deep sympathy in him for the oppressed and a hatred of oppression and injustice of any kind. By the time he was fifteen, Coffin and his cousin Vestal Coffin had frequently helped slaves on their way North. Runaways knew that they could find refuge in the fields surrounding the Coffin farm. Going about his chores, young Coffin would share his own food with the hiding slaves and warn them when they should stay hidden and when it was safe to venture on.

On October 28, 1824, Levi Coffin and his childhood friend Catharine White were married. The Coffins set up housekeeping in Newport, Indiana (now Fountain City) in 1826. The Coffins offered their home as a shelter and it soon became well known to escaping slaves. It is estimated that the Coffins helped over 2,000 fugitives during their twenty years in Newport and another 1,100 while at Cincinnati.

The Levi Coffin House in Fountain City, Indiana, is now a National Historic Landmark and is open to the public. Bought by the state of Indiana in 1967, the house has been well preserved and restored to the period when Levi and Catharine Coffin lived there and welcomed so many escaping slaves to their home.

McDaniel's store is amazing to behold. Something appears to occupy every centimeter of shelf space and very nearly all of the floor space. Yet McDaniel knows her stock. She always knows where something is, even if she's not sure what it is. A case in point is an item called Stop and Go. She originally thought it was a laxative but later learned it was a vitamin.

McDaniel's shop, called *Old Storefront Antiques,* is located at 1837 Main St. (US 40). Store hours are by chance or appointment; for additional information call (765) 478-4809 or visit oldstorefrontantiques.com.

McDaniel also conceived the idea of a *Historic National Road Yard Sale.* The first sale in 2003 included a portion of the National Road (also known as US 40) in Indiana. By 2006, it was such a success that the sale passed through six states (Maryland, West Virginia, Pennsylvania, Ohio, Indiana, and Illinois) and stretched more than 800 miles in length. In 2010, it attracted so many people that some of the restaurants along the way ran out of food. The event now covers 824 miles from Baltimore to St. Louis. The popular annual event is generally held in mid-August during daylight hours. McDaniel will be happy to provide details; her phone number and website appear in the previous paragraph. You can also obtain up-to-date information at the Old National Road Welcome Center, 5701 E. National Rd., Richmond 47374; (765) 935-8687 or (800) 828-8414; visitrichmond.org.

indianatrivia

Cruise control was invented in 1945 by Ralph Teetor, a blind inventor and mechanical engineer from Hagerstown. The first car equipped with Teetor's system was the 1958 Chrysler Imperial.

PLACES TO STAY IN SOUTHEAST INDIANA

AURORA

Tuggles' Folly
9377 Holmes Hill Rd.
(812) 438-9399
tugglesfolly.com

BATESVILLE

Mary Helen's Bed, Breakfast & Fine Dining
13296 N. Coonhunters Rd.
(812) 934-3468
maryhelensplace.com

The Sherman
35 S. Main St.
(812) 934-1000 or
(800) 445-4939
the-sherman.com

BROOKVILLE

The Hermitage Bed and Breakfast
650 E. 8th St.
(765) 647-5182

COLUMBUS

Hotel Indigo Columbus Architectural Center
400 Brown St.
(812) 375-9100
ihg.com

Inn at Irwin Gardens
605 5th St.
(812) 376-3663
irwingardens.com

CORYDON

Kintner House Inn
101 S. Capitol Ave.
(812) 738-2020
kintnerhouse.com

GREENSBURG

Nana's House Bed and Breakfast
3126 E. Base Rd.
(812) 663-6607 or
(877) 669-3870
nanashousebb.com

JEFFERSONVILLE

Market Street Inn B&B
330 W. Market St.
(812) 285-1877 or
(888) 284-1877
innonmarket.com

MADISON

2 Sisters Bed & Breakfast
618 E. Second St.
(765) 430-4676
2sistersbandb.com

2nd St Carriage House and Inn
308 W. Second St.
(219) 508-9644
2ndstreetcarriagehouse
.com

Azalea Manor
510 W. Main St.
(812) 274-4059
theazaleamanor.com

Clifty Inn
Clifty Falls State Park
SR 56 West
(812) 265-4135 or
(877) 925-4389
in.gov/dnr/parklake/inns/
clifty/

Dugan Hollow Log Cabins & Suites
1708 E. Dugan Hollow Rd.
(704) 315-8273
duganhollow.com

Iron Gate Inn
708 E. Main St.
(812) 273-8959
irongateinn.com

Madison Vineyards Estate Winery and Bed & Breakfast
1456 E. CR 400 North
(812) 273-6500 or
(888) 473-6500
madisonvineyards.com

MAUCKPORT

High Ridge Log Cabin Rentals
9100 Cabin Ln. Southwest
(812) 595-8088
highridgecabins.com

METAMORA

The Metamora Inn
19049 Wynn St.
(765) 647-2176
the-metamora-inn.business
.site

NEW ALBANY

The Pepin Mansion Historic Bed & Breakfast
1003 E. Main St.
(812) 725-9186
thepepinmansion.com

NEW CASTLE

Steve Alford All-American Inn
21 E. Executive Dr.
(765) 593-1212 or

RICHMOND

Philip W. Smith Bed and Breakfast
2039 E. Main St.
(765) 966-9972 or

(800) 966-8972
pwsmithbnb.com

RISING SUN

Anderson's Riviera Inn
119 Industrial Dr.
(812) 438-2121 or
(888) 243-6446
andersonsrivierainn
.embarqspace.com

Rising Star Casino Resort
777 Rising Star Dr.
(800) 472-6311
risingstarcasino.com

VEVAY

Ogle Haus Inn
1013 W. Main St.
(812) 427-2020
belterracasino.com/stay/
ogle-haus-inn

Schenck Mansion Bed and Breakfast
206 W. Turnpike St.
(812) 427-2787
(877) 594-2876
schenckmansion.com

Vevay Swiss Inn
100 E. Main St.
(812) 221-1041
vevayswissinn.com

Places to Eat in Southeast Indiana

AURORA

Combs Pizza
329 2nd St.
(812) 926-3273
combspizza.net
Pizza

**Third and Main
Restaurant**
223 3rd St.
(812) 655-9727
thirdandmain.com
American

**Woody's On the Hill
Bar & Grille**
170 Country Club Rd.
(812) 926-1747
dearborncc.net
American

BATESVILLE

**Izzy's Restaurant and
Catering**
850 N. Walnut St.
(812) 932-4999
izzysathillcrest.com
American

**Lil' Charlie's Restaurant &
Brewery**
504 E. Pearl St.
(812) 934-6392
Lilcharlies.com
American/pizza

Randy's Roadhouse
151 Batesville Shopping
Village
(812) 934-4900
randysroadhouse.com
American

The Sherman
35 S. Main St.
(812) 934-1000 or
(800) 445-4939
the-sherman.com
German

Snikkers & Peanuts
101 N. Main St.
(812) 934-2201
snikkersandpeanuts.wixsite
.com
Comfort food

BORDEN

**Joe Huber's Family Farm
& Restaurant**
2421 Engle Rd.
(812) 923-5255
joehubers.com
Home cooking

BROOKVILLE

El Reparo
819 Main St.
(765) 647-6000
Mexican

Pizza Pete
534 Main St.
(765) 647-4176
pizza-pete.com
Pizza

Third Place
734 Main St.
(765) 547-1700
thirdplacebookville.com
Comfort food

CENTERVILLE

Americana Pizza
215 E. Main St.
(765) 855-2601
americanapizza.biz
Pizza/pasta

CLARKSVILLE

**Kansai Japanese
Steakhouse**
1370 Veterans Pkwy.
(812) 218-9538
kansaisteakhouse.com
Japanese

**Naila's Caribbean
Cuisine**
1370 Veterans Pkwy.
(812) 725-0399
nailascc.com
Caribbean

COLUMBUS

Amazing Joe's Grill
2607 Central Ave.
(812) 378-2130
amazingjoes.com
American

Apna Kitchen
1609 Cottage Ave.
(812) 376-7000
apnakitchenrestaurant.com
Indian

The Garage Pub and Grill
308 4th St.
(812) 418-8918
thegaragepubandgrill.com
American

Henry Social Club
423 Washington St.
(812) 799-1371
henrysocialclub.com
New American

Joe Willy's Burger Bar
1034 Washington St.
(812) 379-4559
joewillysburgers.com
American

The Savory Swine
410 Washington St.
(812) 657-7752
thesavoryswine.com
Lunch/sandwiches

Taku Steak House
305 4th St.
(812) 799-7956
takusteakhouse.com
Japanese

Thai Connection
527 Washington St.
(812) 657-3790
thaiconnection.biz
Thai

Yee Kee Restaurant
3984 25th St.
(812) 376-8575
yeekeetogo.com
Chinese

Zaharako's Ice Cream Parlor & Museum
329 Washington St.
(812) 378-1900
zaharakos.com
Sandwiches/salads/soups

FLOYDS KNOBS

Carr's BBQ & Market
3700 Paoli Pike
(812) 728-8106
carrsbbqandmarket.com
Barbecue

Yellow Cactus
3620 Paoli Pike
(812) 903-0313
theyellowcactusindiana
.com
Steak/Mexican

GREENSBURG

Mayasari Indonesian Grill
213 N. Broadway St.
(812) 222-6292
mayasarigrill.com
Indonesian

Storie's Restaurant
109 E. Main St.
(812) 663-9948
storiesrestaurant.com
American

Tarouya
201 E. Main St.
(812) 222-0332
tarouyagreensburg.com
Japanese

JEFFERSONVILLE

Buckhead Mountain Grill
707 W. Riverside Dr.
(812) 284-2919

buckheadmountaingrill.com
American

Cast Iron Steakhouse
1207 E. Market Dr.
(812) 590-2298
castironsteak.com
Steak/seafood

Geraldine's Kitchen
402 Wall St.
(812) 924-7707
geraldineskitchen.com
Breakfast/lunch

Mai's Thai Restaurant
1411 E. 10th St.
(812) 282-0198
maisthai.com
Thai

Pearl Street Taphouse
407 Pearl St.
(812) 285-0890
pearlstreettaphouse.com
American

Portage House
117 E. Riverside Dr.
(812) 913-4250
eatportagehouse.com
American

The Red Yeti
256 Spring St.
(812) 288-5788
redyetijeff.com
Pub food

Town Neighborhood Pub
415 Spring St.
(812) 285-1777
townneighborhoodpub.com
American

MADISON

Crystal & Jules
709 W. Main St.
(812) 274-1077
crystalandjules.com
New American

Diego's Mexican Grill
2455 Lanier Dr.
(812) 265-0065
diegosmexgrill.com
Mexican

Hoboken Eddie's
2840 Wilson Ave.
(551) 486-5522
hobokeneddies.com
Comfort food

Hong Kong Kitchen
102 E. Main St.
(812) 273-6633
hongkongkitchenmadison
.business.site
Chinese

Key West Shrimp House
117 Ferry St.
(812) 265-2831
keywestshrimphouse.com
Seafood

The Red Pepperoni
842 W. Main St.
(812) 274-0111
theredpepperoni.com
Comfort food

METAMORA

The Martindale House
19038 75 Main St.
(765) 309-6913
the-martindale-house-rest
aurant.business.site
Comfort food

MILAN

Hog Rock Café
101 E. Carr St.
(812) 654-2221
hogrock.org
Barbecue

The Reservation
1001 N. Warpath Dr.
(812) 654-2224
thereservationrestaurant
.com
American

SOURCES FOR ADDITIONAL INFORMATION ABOUT SOUTHEAST INDIANA

Franklin County Convention, Recreation, and Visitors Commission
18 West 10th St.
Brookville 47012
(765) 647-6522 or (866) 647-6555
franklincountyin.com

Clark/Floyd Counties Convention and Tourism Bureau
Southern Indiana Visitor Center
300 Southern Indiana Ave.
Jeffersonville 47130-3218
(812) 280-5566 or (800) 552-3842
gosoin.com

Columbus/Bartholomew County Visitors Center
506 5th St.
Columbus 47201
(812) 378-2622 or (800) 468-6564
columbus.in.us

Fayette County Chamber of Commerce
504 N. Central Ave.
Connersville 47331
(765) 825-2561
fayettechamber.com

Dearborn County Convention, Visitor, and Tourism Bureau
320 Walnut St.
Lawrenceburg 47025
(812) 537-0814 or (800) 322-8198
visitsoutheastindiana.com

Decatur County Tourism
211 N. Broadway St.
Greensburg 47240
(812) 222-8733 or (877) 883-5447
visitgreensburg.com

Harrison County Convention and Visitors Bureau
310 N. Elm St.
Corydon 47112
(812) 738-2138 or (888) 738-2137
thisisindiana.org

Henry County Convention and Visitors Bureau
3205 S. Memorial Dr.
New Castle 47362
(765) 593-0764 or (800) 676-4302
henrycountyin.org

Jackson County Visitor Center
100 N. Broadway St.
PO Box 607
Seymour 47274

(812) 524-1914 or (888) 524-1914
jacksoncountyin.com

Madison/Jefferson County Convention and Visitors Bureau
601 W. 1st St.
Madison 47250
(812) 265-2956 or (800) 559-2956
visitmadison.org

Richmond/Wayne County Convention and Tourism Bureau
5701 National Rd. East
Richmond 47374
(765) 935-8687 or (800) 828-8414
visitrichmond.org

Ripley County Tourism Bureau
220 E. US 50
PO Box 21
Versailles 47042
(812) 689-7431 or (888) 747-5394
ripleycountytourism.com

Rising Sun/Ohio County Convention and Tourism Bureau
217 N. High St.
Rising Sun 47040
(812) 438-4933 or (888) 776-4786
enjoyrisingsun.com

NEW ALBANY

Bella Roma
134 E. Market St.
(812) 725-9495
orderbellaromamenu.com
Italian

Brooklyn and The Butcher
148 E. Market St.
(812) 590-2646
brooklynandthebutcher
.com
Steakhouse

Dragon King's Daughter
129 W. Market St.
(812) 725-8600
dragonkingsdaughter.com
Asian fusion

Habana Blues Tapas Restaurant
320 Pearl St.
(812) 944-9760
habanabluestapasrestaura
nt.net
Tapas

Mark's Feed Store
3827 Charlestown Rd.
(812) 949-7427
marksfeedstore.com
Barbecue

Tomo Japanese Restaurant
4317 Charlestown Rd.
(812) 941-0200
tomofriends.com
Japanese

NORTH VERNON

Grateful Grubb
412 S. Madison Ave.
(812) 346-0004
gratefulgrubb.com
Comfort food

NV China Buffet
1599 N. State St.
(812) 352-9888
no1nvchinabuffet.com
Chinese

OLDENBURG

Brau Haus
22170 Wasserstrasse
(Water Street)
(812) 934-4840
oldenburgbrauhaus.com
German

Wagner's Village Inn
22171 Main St.
(812) 934-3854
American

RICHMOND

Firehouse BBQ and Blues
400 N. 8th St.
(765) 488-0312
firehousebbqandblues.com
Barbecue

Galo's Italian Grill
107 Garwood Rd.
(765) 973-9000
galositalian.com
Italian/Mediterranean

Gulzar's Indian Cuisine
4712 E. National Rd.
(765) 939-7401
gulzarsindiancuisine.com
Indian

Little Sheba's
175 Fort Wayne Ave.
(765) 962-2999
littleshebas.com
American

Taste of Szechuan
4710 National Rd. East
(765) 935-4575
jadehouserichmondin.com
Chinese

Old Richmond Inn
138 S. 5th St.
(765) 962-2247
oldrichmondinn.com
American

SCOTTSBURG

Roadhouse USA
519 Beatrice Ave.
(812) 752-9272
roadhouseusa.com
American

SEYMOUR

El Nopal Mexican Cuisine
1863 E. Tipton St.
(812) 523-3399
elnopalonline.com
Mexican

The Fish Stand
423 N. Ewing St.
(812) 522-1526
thefishstandrestaurant.com
Seafood

Larrison's Diner
200 S. Chestnut St.
(812) 522-5523
larrisonsdiner.net
Comfort food

The Pines
4289 N. US 31
(812) 522-4955
thepinesonline.com
Buffet/American

Townhouse Cafe
206 E. 4th St.
(812) 522-1099
townhousecafein.com
American

VERNON

Linda's Log Cabin Inn
59 E. SR 3 and 7
(812) 346-7272
American

VEVAY

Boondoggle's Pub and Grub
212 Ferry St.
(812) 226-6087
boondoggles-pub-and
-grub.business.site
Sports bar

Ferry Street Fudo
314 Ferry St.
(812) 226-6046
ferry-street-fudo.business
.site
Comfort food

Patron Grille
307 Ferry St.
(812) 226-6600
patron-grille.business.site
Tex-Mex

Southwest Indiana

Generally described as the most beautiful part of the Hoosier State, southwest Indiana is filled with uninterrupted stretches of dense forests, jutting cliffs, and clear streams. Scenic highways wind through hills lush with greenery in the spring and summer and blazing with color in the fall. Where the Wabash River, which forms much of the state's western border, meets the Ohio River, which bounds the state on the south, there are misty bayous and cypress swamps reminiscent of the Deep South.

The banks of the Ohio River are dotted with small towns in which historic sites and nineteenth-century architecture have been carefully preserved. Beneath the earth's surface lies Indiana's world-famous limestone belt, laid down by an ancient sea 300 million years ago.

This is the land that shaped a young Abraham Lincoln. It is the place the founders of New Harmony viewed as Utopia. In the 1920s and 1930s, movie stars and gangsters came here to relax and rejuvenate themselves in the waters of the region's abundant mineral springs. It is still a place where life plays out in its own sweet time, a place that invites the visitor to explore and discover.

Brown County

Things don't change much in Brown County. Each morning the mists rise from hills still draped with forests. Log cabins, hemmed in by split-rail fences, nestle in isolated hollows. Like as not there's a woodpile in the yard, and on cool days fingers of wood smoke spiral up from stone chimneys. Narrow, twisting country roads lead to picturesque places with picturesque names—Gnaw Bone, Bean Blossom, Scarce O'Fat Ridge, Bear Wallow Hill, Milk-Sick Bottoms, Slippery Elm Chute Road, and Booger Holler. No billboards mar your view along the way—they're not allowed in Brown County. No air pollution muddies the landscape and offends your nostrils—Brown County has no industry. And if you're in a hurry, you're out of luck—Brown County doesn't cater to people in a hurry.

Nashville, the county seat and largest town in the county, normally has a population of about 1,000 people, but on October weekends that figure swells to more than 100,000. Brown County is best known for its dazzling fall color. Most folks head for **Brown County State Park,** some 15,000 acres of natural beauty near Nashville. **Yellowwood State Forest** in western Brown County and a portion of the **Hoosier National Forest** in the southern part of the county offer equally spectacular and less-crowded panoramas.

In spring Brown County is glorious when its redbud and dogwood trees and myriad wildflowers are abloom. In summer the woods offer a cool green retreat, and for wintertime visitors there are cross-country ski trails.

Brown County first gained fame as a mecca for artists and craftspeople, who have been inspired by the peace and beauty of these hills since the 1870s. Today many open their studios to the public. The **Brown County Craft Gallery,** the **Brown County Art Guild,** and the **Brown County Art Gallery,** all in Nashville, are among the galleries that exhibit some of their works.

Nashville is the hub of activity in Brown County—a potpourri of some 300 shops, galleries, studios, and restaurants. Craftspeople make and sell their wares. At many shops, you can watch the artisans at work. A variety of live entertainment is presented at the **Brown County Playhouse** at 70 S. Van Buren St. For a schedule and show times, call (812) 988-6555, or visit browncounty playhouse.org. Opened in 2019, the **Brown County Music Center** is less than a mile from the heart of Nashville, nestled on the banks of Salt Creek at 200 Maple Leaf Blvd. The 2,107-seat live

indiana trivia

Jerry Garcia, the founder of the Grateful Dead, was a bluegrass fan. He visited Brown County in 1964 and made tapes of Bill Monroe and his Bluegrass Boys.

Artists of Brown County

When Chicago painter Adolph Shulz visited Brown County in the early 1900s, he wrote that "a sense of peace and loveliness never before experienced came over me." Shulz and his wife Ada quickly made the unique hill country their home, along with other celebrated artists such as T. C. Steele.

Today, that "Peaceful Valley" is filled with artisans seeking the same inspiration, tranquility, natural beauty, and genuine hospitality that their predecessors found. The century-old Art Colony of the Midwest boasts award-winning artists in a wealth of mediums. An unofficial estimate notes that at least 100 artists live in Brown County.

Long known for its tradition of handicrafts, Brown County is home to artisans who seem able to create something beautiful from almost anything. That's part of the hill heritage of "using up, making do, or doing without." Unique crafts can be found in many shops, studios, and festivals throughout the area.

Name it—paintings, ceramics, holography, photography, braided rugs, candles, blown glass, hammered copper pots, wrought iron, quilts, furniture, dolls, dollhouses, toys, birdhouses, stained glass, corn fiber brooms, rag rugs, leatherworks, mountain dulcimers, jewelry, carving, pottery, weaving—somebody here makes it.

The four-square-mile county seat of Nashville, with a population of about 1,000, might boast a higher percentage of artisans than any other town in America. Spectacular in every season, Brown County offers a return to a quieter time and a chance to see what gifted artists can create in a spectacular setting.

More than a century ago, legendary artists discovered the natural beauty of Brown County. By hiking or by horse and buggy, artists were drawn to the scenic wonder of the hills and hollows, the quant log cabins, and the stalwart friendly people. In 1907, painter T.C. Steele first established residence in Brown County, with many friends and colleagues soon following his example. Steele's "House of the Singing Winds" is now a state historic site welcoming the public.

By October 1926, the first art gallery was opened in Nashville. It was an immediate success. A heavy stream of traffic raised such dust on the rough roads that drivers kept their headlights on to prevent collisions, local lore says. Folks who had heard about the tranquil splendor of Brown County began making pilgrimages to see the hills, forests, and streams and buy the artists' works. Road began to develop. So popular did it become that by 1949 Nashville was being hailed as the most important art colony between New England and New Mexico.

Today, visitors come to the place that holds dear its legendary past. Painters, photographers, writers, and other artisans have continued to find their inspiration here.

They speak in hushed awe of the "blue haze" that settles over the hills. The dramatic mix of light and mist casts a soft glow that beckons painters, photographers, and nature lovers to pull off the path and enjoy the magical scene.

entertainment venue hosts world-class rock, blues, country, pop, jazz, oldies, and more. For more information, call (812) 988-5323 or visit the website at browncountymusiccenter.com.

What started as a hobby for Adrian Lee and his wife Nichole turned into a popular business known as *Salt Creek Winery*. Established in 2010 by the Lees, the winery is located at 7603 W. CR 925 N. in Freetown. But many people discover the delicious wines by visiting the Nashville tasting room at 26 N. Honeysuckle Lane. Using minimal processing, the Lees produce grape wines as well as fruit wines such as blueberry, strawberry, cherry, plum, raspberry, blackberry, and blackcurrant.

AUTHOR'S FAVORITE ATTRACTIONS/ EVENTS IN SOUTHWEST INDIANA

Antique Auto Hill Climb
Newport; first Sunday in October
(765) 492-4220
newporthillclimb.com

Bluegrass Hall of Fame and Museum and Uncle Pen Day Festival
Bean Blossom; September
(812) 988-6422 or (800) 414-4677
billmonroemusicpark.com

Brown County State Park
Nashville
(812) 988-6406
in.gov/dnr/parklake/2988.htm

Lilly Library of Rare Books and Manuscripts
Indiana University, Bloomington
(812) 855-2452
libraries.indiana.edu/lilly-library

Limestone Heritage Festival
Bedford; June
(812) 849-1090 or (800) 798-0769
limestonecountry.com

New Harmony (entire town)
(812) 682-4488 or (800) 231-2168
visitnewharmony.com

Parke County Covered Bridge Festival
Rockville; October
(765) 569-5226
coveredbridges.com

Red Skelton Festival
Vincennes; June
(812) 886-0400 or (800) 886-6443
visitvincennes.org

Spirit of Vincennes Rendezvous
Vincennes; May
(812) 886-0400 or (800) 886-6443
spiritofvincennes.org

Tulip Trestle (Greene County Viaduct)
near Solsberry
(765) 749-0321
visitgc.com

Turkey Trot Festival
Montgomery; September
(812) 486-3649 or (800) 449-5262
montgomeryruritanclub/turkeytrot.htm

West Baden Springs National Historic Landmark
West Baden
(812) 936-3418 or (866) 309-9139
visitfrenchlickwestbaden.com

The Lees also have a lovely Wine Loft above their Nashville tasting room. Located in the heart of downtown Nashville, the Wine Loft offers a bedroom, bathroom, full kitchen, and living room with queen sleeper sofa. Check the website for hours of operation or call (812) 497-0254; saltcreekwinery.com.

A complex of authentic nineteenth-century buildings just northeast of the courthouse in Nashville is known collectively as the *Brown County Pioneer Village.* Carding, spinning, and weaving are demonstrated in an old log barn. You'll also see a country doctor's office, a blacksmith's shop, and a log cabin home, all complete with furnishings, and an unusual log jail that claims the distinction of being the only one in the state that ever permitted a prisoner to be his own keeper. While serving a sentence for bootlegging, the prisoner went wherever he wanted to during the day, locked himself up at night, acted as a guide for tourists, and once aided the sheriff in making an arrest. Pioneer Village can be toured from May through October from 11 a.m. to 4 p.m. Saturday and Sunday. The buildings can be viewed free of charge at all times from the outside. Across the street and adjoining Pioneer Village is the new *Brown*

ANNUAL EVENTS IN SOUTHWEST INDIANA

Shoals Catfish Festival
Shoals; July
(812) 247-2828 or (812) 617-0200
visitmartincounty.com

Jasper Strassenfest
Jasper; first weekend of August
(812) 482-6866
jasperstrassenfest.org

Knox County Watermelon Festival
Vincennes; August
(812) 882-6440 or (800) 886-6443
knoxcountychamber.com

Schweizer Fest
Tell City; August
(812) 547-7933 or (888) 343-6262
tellcityschweizerfest.org

Amish Quilt Auction
Odon; Saturday of Labor Day weekend
(812) 254-5262 or (800) 449-5262
daviesscounty.net

Lyles Station Corn Maze
Lyles Station; October
(812) 385-2534
lylesstation.org

Native American Days
Evansville; September
(812) 853-3956
indianamuseum.org/historic-sites/angel
-mounds

Lotus World Music and Arts Festival
Bloomington; September
(812) 336-6599
lotusfest.org

Persimmon Festival
Mitchell; September
(812) 849-4441
persimmonfestival.org

Chocolate Walk
Nashville; November
(812) 988-7303 or (800) 753-3255
browncounty.com

County History Center whose centerpiece is a log cabin interior that has been recreated inside the large center. The log cabin contains antique furnishings and other items from the 1800s. For a $2 donation, the History Center can be toured March through October, Tuesday through Saturday from 11 a.m. to 4 p.m. Winter hours for the History Center are Tuesday and Friday from 11 a.m. to 4 p.m. Both are operated by the Brown County Historical Society, 70 Gould St.; (812) 988-2899; browncountyhistorycenter.org.

To bluegrass music fans, the late Bill Monroe is the father of bluegrass and Bean Blossom is a bluegrass mecca. Monroe held annual festivals on his sprawling Bean Blossom property starting in the mid-1960s, making this the locale of the oldest continuous-running bluegrass festival in the world. The thousands of devotees who still come here from all over the country and beyond say the bluegrass festivals at the *Bill Monroe Memorial Music Park* have an ambience unlike any other in the world. When professional musicians aren't playing on stage, amateur musicians in the audience are playing in their own impromptu groups. It's a rare moment when there's no music to be heard anywhere. If you love the sound of bluegrass, there is no better place to be.

Most people stay on the festival grounds for the three or four days a festival is held. A campground on the property offers both modern and primitive campsites. Several rustic log cabins may be rented by advance reservation. In 1992, Monroe brought his extensive collection of bluegrass and country music memorabilia to Bean Blossom and opened the *Bluegrass Hall of Fame and Museum.* Monroe accumulated his collection throughout more than 60 years of entertaining.

One of the fourteen rooms in the 5,000-square-foot museum is filled with Bill Monroe's personal mementos, including items once owned by Johnny Cash, Porter Wagoner, Loretta Lynn, George Jones, Dolly Parton, and Dottie West. On the grounds near the museum is a cabin that was moved here log by log from Nashville, Tennessee. Known as Uncle Pen's Cabin, it belonged to a relative who took young Bill Monroe into his home when Monroe's parents died. Fans will recognize the name from a song Monroe wrote about his uncle. (It was recorded by Ricky Skaggs and Porter Wagoner.)

Originally home to two annual bluegrass festivals, the park has expanded its offerings to include some eight music festivals each year, including the popular John Hartford Memorial Festival in September. The park is located at 5163 SR 135 North in Bean Blossom, about 5 miles north of Nashville. Open daily spring through fall; hours may vary. For additional information, call (812) 988-6422 or (800) 414-4677, or visit billmonroemusicpark.com.

East of Nashville on SR 46 is the northern entrance to Brown County State Park, accessible via Indiana's only divided, two-lane covered bridge (circa

1838). Enjoy 27 miles of scenic roads, hiking and bridle trails, a nature center, campgrounds (including one for horseback riders), an archery range, an Olympic-size swimming pool, a lodge with a restaurant, and a 12,000-square-foot indoor aquatic center, and rustic rental cabins. The park's 25-mile mountain bike trail system has garnered international accolades; in 2011, it was named an Epic Trail by the International Mountain Bicycling Association, an honor it has accorded to only fifty-seven different trail systems around the world over a ten-year period. Additionally, in 2009, *Bike* magazine named the park's trail system one of the thirty-three best in North America. You can also climb the 100-foot-tall fire tower atop Weed Patch Hill, the state's second-highest point (1,058 feet), for a panoramic view. A nature trail leads through 41-acre ***Ogle Hollow State Nature Preserve,*** noteworthy for its rare yellowwood trees; the ***Ten O'Clock Line Nature Preserve,*** open to hikers and equestrians, covers more than 3,300 acres and is the largest in the state. Open year-round during daylight hours; there's a $7 vehicle entrance fee for Indiana licensed vehicles and $9 for out-of-state vehicles. Write or call Brown County State Park, PO Box 608, Nashville 47448; (812) 988-6406; in.gov/dnr/parklake/2988.htm. For lodge and cabin reservations, write or call Abe Martin Lodge, 1405 SR 46 W, Nashville 47448; (812) 988-4418, (877) 265-6343 for information, or (877) 563-4371 for reservations; in.gov/dnr/parklake/inns/abe.

Continuing east from the park on SR 46, you'll come to SR 135, which leads south into a secluded and untrammeled part of Brown County. Follow SR 135 to an area referred to locally as ***Stone Head,*** so called because of the unique monument by the side of the highway that serves as a road sign—a white Stone Head atop a stone pillar. Every once in a while a prankster makes off with the carving, as was the case in 2016 when someone smashed Stone Head and carted the head away. Only the base remained. A local carver created what looks like a gravestone with the engraving "Stone Head, 1851-2016, carved by Henry Cross." Folks still hope that Stone Head may someday return.

Proceed on SR 135 to the tiny community of ***Story.*** Virtually unchanged since its founding in the 1850s, the peaceful hamlet exudes the charm of a long-ago Brown County whose rural serenity and beauty first lured artists and craftspeople to these forested hills. Here, amid a cluster of tumbledown buildings that bear mute testimony to old dreams, the ***Story Inn*** offers food and shelter so pleasing that the Indiana Division of Tourism bestowed its Best Bed and Breakfast in the state award on it. On the outside, the tin-faced, tin-roofed building, complete with two vintage gas pumps, resembles the general store it once was. On the inside, antiques and knickknacks line the walls of the dining room, and a potbellied stove stands ready to serve on cold winter days. The food, however, is pure gourmet. Guests can stay in one of the inn's

When All Else Fails, Try eBay

Owen County Commissioners had a parcel of land they needed to get off the tax rolls, so they tried auctioning it off at county tax sales. When no one expressed any interest, the commissioners decided to post it on eBay, where it immediately attracted interest worldwide. Prospective buyers were intrigued by the idea of owning a property that measured exactly 0.0000000159 of an acre, more popularly described as 1 square inch.

Inquiries came from such places as Australia, Israel, and Japan, but the winning bid of $1,752 was made by a real estate developer in Michigan. His firm bought not only the land but also the right to brag that it owns the most expensive piece of real estate in the history of the world. A full acre of land at the purchase price for that one square inch would cost $10,993,428,864.

The history of the tiny piece of land dates back to the 1960s. At that time, a nearby private lake could be used only by people who owned land along its shores, and one landowner deeded the square inch to his grown child so that child could have access to the lake. When the landowner later sold the main parcel, the square inch remained on the tax rolls as a separate property. No taxes were paid on it, which led to its eventual appearance on eBay in October 2005 and its sale to the highest bidder for a price that included back taxes, interest, and fees.

The new owner has yet to visit his property, however, perhaps because no one knows for sure exactly where on the larger plot the square inch is situated. County officials believe they have identified its location within a couple of yards, but to be sure the owner would have to pay for a land survey. That option is on hold while the owner contemplates what to do with his prized property. Humorists have been quick to offer the following suggestions:

- Rent it to an inch worm.
- Stage a flea circus.
- Establish a safe haven for a little green army man.
- Bury your dead goldfish—vertically.
- Grow a green onion.
- Open a nanotechnology research center.
- Sell satellite flyover and mineral rights.
- Collect a fee from people who step on your inch.
- Declare it an independent country and demand a seat at the United Nations.

upstairs bedrooms or in one of the renovated village cottages nearby; a full country breakfast is included in the rates. All rooms have private baths and air-conditioning but no television, telephone, radio, clock, or Internet access; it's also unlikely that your cell phone will work. If you stay in the Blue Lady Room and you're lucky (or unlucky, depending on your point of view), you may see the Story Inn's resident ghost; she supposedly can be summoned by turning on the blue light next to the bed. The inn's gourmet restaurant offers varied menus; check the website to see what is available. Advance reservations are recommended for meals and are required for overnight accommodations. A Patio Grill serves burgers, barbecue, and more, plus the Tavern offers beer, wine, and cocktails. The inn also sponsors many special events throughout the year. Hiking and mountain biking trails are available in the Hoosier National Forest and Brown County State Park, whose boundaries meet nearby. For additional information, contact the Story Inn at 6404 S. SR 135, Nashville; (812) 988-2273 or (800) 881-1183; storyinn.com.

To experience a bit of splendid solitude and delve into a mystery that has defied explanation for decades, continue southwest from Story on Elkinsville Road to **Browning Mountain.** The journey is an adventure in itself. The paved road soon gives way to a gravel one. Hills and ridges rise above you, and Salt Creek meanders across the valley floor. The road becomes rougher, the bridges narrower. Eventually, you'll drive through rather than over dry creek beds. Then, approximately 4 miles after leaving Story, at the juncture of Elkinsville and Combs Roads, the mountain appears before you. Turn left onto Combs Road and pass by a house with a split-rail fence; the trailhead is just past the fence.

The mountain, of course, is actually a hill, but once you have ascended the steep path that leads to its summit you'll understand why it has come to be popularly known as a mountain. Atop the hill is the mystery you are seeking—Indiana's own version of Stonehenge (the world-famous site near Salisbury, England, where huge stone blocks arranged in an orderly fashion have stood for nearly 1,000 years). No one is sure how the enormous slabs at Stonehenge could have been transported there so long ago, just as no one is sure how the scattering of giant hunks of limestone atop Browning Mountain made their way there. One theory is that a bed of limestone was laid down long ago when Brown County was covered by an ancient sea, then broken up and tossed about by natural forces when the sea waters receded. Another theory is that the stones once marked a place sacred to Native Americans. It is true, however, that these huge rocks must weigh many tons each, and some look as though they might have been cut to size and placed in some sort of significant arrangement.

Over the years, attempts were made to quarry the stones, but so many accidents occurred that all further attempts were abandoned. This gave rise to the legend of an Indian spirit watcher who makes sure no one disturbs the stones and to tales of the ghosts of men who died when they disturbed this spot and were condemned to roam the area forever.

If you still can't solve the mystery, you're in good company. A few years ago, a group of scientists journeyed here from South America to examine these stones, but they couldn't come up with a plausible explanation either. Even if you come away from Browning Mountain with more questions than answers, the journey that takes you there, through one of the most beautiful and unspoiled areas of Indiana, will likely be so rewarding you won't mind at all.

Privately owned until a few years ago, Browning Mountain Trail is now part of the Hoosier National Forest. For additional information, contact the Forest Supervisor at 811 Constitution Ave., Bedford 47421; (812) 275-5987 or (866) 302-4173; fs.usda.gov/hoosier.

Another mystery has recently come to light in Brown County. It was discovered by a hunter who was tracking a wild turkey in Yellowwood State Forest on a cold February morning in 1998. He found his turkey in a most unlikely spot—perched atop a huge, refrigerator-size rock that was cradled in the limbs of a chestnut oak tree about 80 feet above the ground.

Any explanation as to how the rock got there or how long it had been there is purely speculative. No heavy equipment could have placed it there. The area is so remote and so densely forested that any activity involving heavy equipment would be easily spotted. Another theory is that the rock might have been flung there by blasting in a nearby area, but there has been no nearby blasting. Perhaps the most logical suggestion thus far is that a tornado deposited the rock in the branches, but there's no sign of any tornado damage anywhere else in the vicinity. And of course, there are a few people who hint at UFO involvement. Whatever the explanation, *Gobbler's Rock,* as it was officially named, was firmly entrenched in its treetop perch until the tree was uprooted in 2006. The rock now lies on the ground, entangled in the oak's branches, but you can still visit the site and ponder the mystery.

Since the discovery of Gobbler's Rock, the mystery has deepened. Hikers sighted two more giant sandstone boulders sitting in the top limbs of two sycamores growing about 100 yards apart in a remote area of the 23,000-acre forest. In intervening years, four more treetop rocks have shown up. Locals have dubbed the rocks URBs (Unexplained Resting Boulders). Word of the strange phenomena has spread, and the forest office has been getting inquiries about their exact locations. If you would like to view the rocks yourself and are willing to walk a bit to see them, stop by the forest office and ask for directions. You'll likely need a GPS to locate them. The office is located at 772 S. Yellowwood Rd.; take SR 46 west from Nashville for about 6 miles and turn north at the Yellowwood State Forest sign; call (812) 988-7945 for office hours; in.gov/dnr/forestry/4817.htm.

For more information about Brown County and its attractions, contact the Brown County Convention and Visitors Bureau, 211 S. Van Buren St., PO Box 840, Nashville 47448; (812) 988-7303 or (800) 753-3255; browncounty.com.

While in Nashville, buy a copy of the **Brown County Democrat,** which has been honored as Indiana's finest weekly newspaper more times than anyone can remember. The "Sheriff's Log" therein is a Brown County classic. You'll find such entries as:

> *Man called and said he just put on a pot of coffee if*
> *   any officers are in the area and want coffee.*
> *Girl at restaurant requests a conservation officer.*
> *   An owl is sitting on the pizza oven.*
> *Trouble reported at the city dump. Someone abandoned a person there.*
> *A coon is asleep on the shelf [of a local shop] with a teddy bear.*
> *Man wants deputy [any deputy] to meet him so*
> *   that he can borrow $5 or $10.*
> *Man requests Nashville town marshal go to restaurant and*
> *   check the stove to see if he left a pot of beans on.*
> *Caller says someone has been cow tipping. His cows were*
> *   asleep in the field and someone tipped them over.*
> *Woman reports that a white space ship with an El Camino on the*
> *   back of it has been going into her neighbor's house. The man*
> *   driving the space ship has been dead for several years.*
> *Man wants to know if the sheriff would like to come watch his snakes eat.*
> *Cancel burglar alarm. A grouse flew through a window,*
> *   setting off the alarm, but the house cat ate the grouse.*
> *Wild cow reported in Fruitdale.*
> *Three UFOs hovering over house near Bean Blossom.*
> *   Keep changing colors and shapes.*
> *Woman wants to know what she has to do to get arrested so she*
> *   can spend Thanksgiving weekend in jail with her sister.*
> *Man says a naked woman walked into his house.*

Like the mythical sheriff's office in Mayberry, NC, made famous by a television series, this one's run with a lot of heart. Follow the newspaper at bcdemocrat.com.

Clay County

Folks from Wisconsin have munched on cheese curds for years, but they're a relatively new treat for most Hoosier palates. At the *Farm Connection,* not only can you purchase these delectable treats; you can also watch them evolve from start to finish on a free tour. Among the things you'll learn is that a 1,500-pound batch of milk yields 160–180 pounds of cheese. You can also purchase the curds and more conventional types of cheese at an on-site store. Owners Alan and Mary Yegerlehner are not content to rest on their cheese curd laurels, however. They also make and sell butter, grass-fed meat products, and two dozen flavors of ice cream.

To keep their cows on fresh grass year-round, the Yegerlehners rely on rotational grazing. Each March and December, their cows are moved from one pasture to another; they feed on an 80-acre pasture during winter months and on a 200-acre tract the rest of the year. Because the pastures are 3.5 miles apart, the cattle are walked from one to the other; the Yegerlehners believe it's less traumatic than a truck ride. The Farm Connection cheese shop and the farm on which it's located are at 1363 E. CR 550 South, not far north of Clay City. Open noon to 5 p.m. Monday, Thursday, Friday, and 9 a.m. to 3 p.m. Saturday, April through December 23; 10 a.m. to 3 p.m. Saturday, January through March; other times by appointment. Tours must be scheduled in advance; call (812) 939-3027; thefarmconnection.grazecart.com.

At the **Exotic Feline Rescue Center** in **Center Point,** visitors can see more big cats than they would at most zoos. At this writing the center is the "forever home" to more than 230 exotic felines; they include lions, tigers (including two rare white tigers), bobcats, mountain lions, leopards, ocelots, servals, and lynxes. An overnight adult-only guest facility for two overlooks two large tiger enclosures. Founder Joe Taft, who operates the nonprofit center, takes in animals that have been abused or whose owners can no longer care for them. The center is located at 2221 E. Ashboro Rd.; the admission fee of $10 for adults and $5 for children includes a guided tour. Open daily 10 a.m. to 4 p.m. To schedule a tour or make an overnight reservation, call the center at (812) 835-1130 or visit efrc.org.

Items sold at an online gift store include two books that tell the story of the center: *Real Stories of Big Cat Rescues*, published in 2010, and *Saving the Big Cats,* published in 2006; a portion of the funds from each sale will be donated to the center.

Crawford County

Marengo Cave, a National Natural Landmark, was discovered in 1883 by a young brother and sister exploring a sinkhole. The cave, a comfortable 52 degrees at all times, has been open to the public ever since, and its beauty has been acclaimed throughout the world. Concerts were once held in a subterranean room noted for its acoustics, and an early day evangelist preached

OTHER ATTRACTIONS WORTH SEEING IN SOUTHWEST INDIANA

BLOOMINGTON

Eskenazi Museum of Art at Indiana University
Fine Arts Plaza
1133 E. 7th St.
(812) 855-5445
artmuseum.iu.edu

WonderLab
308 W. 4th Street
(812) 337-1337
wonderlab.org

CLAY CITY

Clay City Pottery Tour
(by advance notice)
510 E. 14th St.
(812) 939-2596 or (800) 776-2596
claycitypottery.com

EVANSVILLE

Evansville Museum of Arts, History, and Science
411 SE Riverside Dr.
(812) 425-2406
emuseum.org

FERDINAND

Monastery Immaculate Conception
802 E. 10th St.
(812) 367-1411
thedome.org

JASPER

Indiana Baseball Hall of Fame
Vincennes University
851 College Ave.
(812) 482-2262 or (800) 968-4578
indbaseballhalloffame.org

Saint Joseph Church
1029 Kundek St.
(812) 482-1805 or (800) 968-4578
saintjosephjasper.org

LINTON

Goose Pond Fish and Wildlife Area
13540 W. CR 400 S.
(812) 512-9185
in.gov/dnr/fishwild/3094.htm

NASHVILLE

T. C. Steele State Historic Site
4220 T. C. Steele Rd.
(812) 988-2785
indianamuseum.org/sites/tcst.html

TERRE HAUTE

Terre Haute Children's Museum
727 Wabash Ave.
(812) 235-5548
thchildrensmuseum.com

Native American Museum
Dobbs Park
5170 E. Poplar Dr.
(812) 877-6007
terrehaute.in.gov/departments/parks/city
-parks/dobbs/NAM

Sheldon Swope Art Museum
25 S. 7th St.
(812) 238-1676
swope.org

VINCENNES

Indiana Military Museum
715 S. 6th St.
(812) 882-1941
indymilitary.com

his fiery message from Pulpit Rock. Underground weddings and dances were regular occurrences throughout the years.

A 0.33-mile cave tour is highlighted by a visit to Crystal Palace, acknowledged by speleologists as one of the ten most beautiful cavern rooms anywhere. The 1-mile Dripstone Tour through a different part of the cave features totem pole stalagmites, a cavern that looks big enough to build a highway through. Physically fit visitors may opt to explore two different undeveloped sections of the cave. Above the cavern is a 122-acre park, complete with camping cabins, campsites, and trail rides atop horses from the park's stables and such special activities as rock climbing, gemstone mining, and a simulated cave maze crawl. There's a separate fee for each tour, as well as special combination rates. The cave is open daily year-round, except Thanksgiving and Christmas: 9 a.m. to 6 p.m. weekdays and 9 a.m. to 6:30 p.m. weekends Memorial Day through Labor Day, and 9 a.m. to 5 p.m. the rest of the year. Marengo Cave is just northeast of the town of Marengo; go east from Marengo on SR 64/66 and follow the signs. Write or call Marengo Cave Park, 400 E. SR 64, PO Box 217, Marengo 47140; (812) 365-2705 or (888) 702-2837; marengocave.com.

Children Discover Marengo Cave

Blanche Hiestand tucked some candles in her pocket, grabbed her younger brother Orris, and headed off to the local cemetery to search for a rumored cave. Working as a cook at a boarding school, Blanche had overheard a group of schoolboys talking about a hole they had found not far from the academy.

The boys planned a trip to see if the hole would lead to a big cave. But Blanche beat them to the discovery. Hurrying home after work, fifteen-year-old Blanche and her reluctant eleven-year-old brother slipped away before their parents noticed and found a deep sinkhole hidden in a grove of trees.

Cool air was streaming from the opening as Blanche crawled down into the small crevice. Quickly, Blanche was able to raise up on her hands and knees. Yelling for her brother to join, Blanche and Orris carefully climbed down a steep slope of broken rock.

The rock was slick and water was dripping from numerous small openings in the ceiling. But soon the two were able to stand. Then they heard water falling from the ceiling and saw sparkling formations ahead in the darkness. Even in the dim candlelight, the beauty of the huge chamber was dazzling.

More than a century has passed since the two Indiana kids found *Marengo Cave* on September 6, 1883. And visitors have been flocking ever since to the US National Landmark for a glimpse of one of the Midwest's finest natural wonders.

The cave has had a colorful and checkered history. It was an early destination of railroad excursions and the site of band concerts and many community functions, including dances and concert. Churches services as well as weddings have been held in the cave. Even during the depths of the Great Depression, the cave remained open because it was a tradition for many families to pay a visit. Several movies have been filmed in the cave, including *Madison* in 2001 and *Fire From Below* in 2009.

Marengo Cave also has sort of a reverse wishing well. Instead of tossing coins into a fountain, visitors to Marengo Cave for years have been flipping pennies at the ceiling.

Of course, one reason cave goers do that is to see the coins stick above their heads. Instead of bouncing back down, the air-borne pennies adhere to a thin layer of mud clinging to the cave ceiling. The money sticks in the half-inch-thick layer of soft clay on the ceiling, which stays eternally moist due to the cave's 100 percent humidity.

The result is a metallic ceiling, slowly turning blue-gray over the years.

Once every decade or so the ceiling must be cleared of its coin cover. If not, the new coins wouldn't stand a chance of finding a muddy spot to stick. During its last cleaning, more than 90,000 coins, totaling $3,855.56 were collected. The money was donated to the Nature Conservancy, which is actively involved in protecting southern Indiana cave country and the Blue River.

Some generous visitors tossed more than pennies at the ceiling. No one knows if they couldn't tell the difference between a penny and a nickel or a dime or a quarter in the dark or if they just felt like tossing larger change. The total included 5,750 quarters, 12,218 dimes, 11,806 nickels, and 60,596 pennies. The total weight of the money was nearly 500 pounds.

In addition, several hundred coins from foreign countries were taken off the ceiling. Most of the foreign money came from Canada but other major foreign contributors were Germany, Britain, France, Japan, and Korea.

Twisting its way southward through Crawford County is the lovely, spring-fed **Blue River,** Indiana's first officially designated natural and scenic river and an ideal canoe stream. Several outfitters offer trips, ranging from 7 to 58 miles; on longer trips you spend the night on the river. Depending on the trip you take, you'll float quiet waters and shoot rapids; pass caves, springs, limestone bluffs, and walls of trees; or make your way around rock gardens and through narrow gorges. The fishing is some of the best in the Midwest, producing catches of bass, crappie, bluegill, and catfish, and the serenity can be well-nigh incredible. In its lower stretches, just before it joins the Ohio River, the Blue River turns sluggish—perfect for tubing. Rates for canoeing include paddle, life jacket, and shuttle service; there are special rates for children. The season is usually April through October, but water levels are best for canoeing before mid-July. For names of outfitters in the area, write or call the Crawford County

Tourism Center, 6225 E. Industrial Ln., Leavenworth 47137; (812) 739-2246 or (888) 775-2282; crawfordcountyindiana.com.

About 6 miles south of **Milltown** at 3826 S. Devils Hollow Rd, is one of Indiana's most curious landmarks—a tree known locally as the **Shoe Tree,** where hundreds of pairs of shoes of all shapes, sizes, and colors can be seen dangling from its branches. Local legend says that even Indiana basketball legend Larry Bird has a pair of shoes hanging from the tree. No one seems to know exactly when the custom started, but it's generally believed to date back to the early 1960s. Local folks speculate that someone thought of his shoes as longtime friends that had served him faithfully and well, and deserved a better fate than to be unceremoniously dumped in the garbage, so he decided to display them in a permanent place of honor.

Although old shoes hang from many places these days, the folks in Milltown, who refer to the tree as the town's "branch office," will tell you that their Shoe Tree is the original. In fact, they claim, they've even copyrighted it. A white oak that was the first recipient of the discarded shoes was damaged by lightning in 2005; the speculation is that all the steel-toed boots within its branches attracted the lightning. Since then, folks have substituted the branches of a nearby hickory. To reach the fabled tree and its successor, head south from Milltown on CR 23 to its intersection with CR 30, a distance of about 6 miles. The shoe-laden hickory tree and the still-standing oak tree dominate the landscape at the junction of these two roads.

Daviess County

Along about 1972 the local folks decided they needed a unique attraction to put Daviess County on the map, and their idea brought them fame that exceeded their wildest expectations. They combined Indiana's best-known event, the Indianapolis 500, with Daviess County's best-known product—turkeys—and gave birth to the **Turkey Trot Festival.**

Come September, turkeydom's finest make their way to Ruritan Park in **Montgomery** for four days of the most laughable racing imaginable. Because there are about forty turkeys to every human being in Daviess County (with a noticeable but temporary change in the ratio just after the Thanksgiving and Christmas holidays), there can be a lot of birds to face off. This requires many preliminary heats, and only the cream of the crop survive the grueling schedule to race in the final championship run.

On the last, fateful day, anxious jockeys lead their tethered birds to the starting line, eager to put weeks of training to the test. Some raw talent is always on hand, too, since many owners believe that training a bird with a brain the size of a thumbnail is a waste of time. Onlookers cheer their personal favorites—such racing greats as Dirty Bird, White Lightning, and Turkey Lurkey.

On signal, the turkeys head down a 213-foot-long straightaway track toward a finish line that, for a top turkey trotter, is approximately 20 seconds away. Alas, prima donnas are inevitable. Some refuse to start at all. The more befuddled go sideways or backward. Still others tire along the way and pause to peck at whatever turkeys like to peck at. Some even take to the air, disdainfully rising above it all. Eventually, however, one galloping gobbler manages to cross the finish line and is declared the grand champion.

Another big event is the best-dressed turkey contest, which inspires elaborate costumes. One winner devastated the judges when she modeled her stunning powder-blue bikini, then further charmed them by coyly batting her false eyelashes.

And if you think they don't take all this seriously in Daviess County, consider the fact that these are the only turkey races in the world sanctioned by the National Turkey Federation. The races have received national attention from the day of their inception, and stories about them have been translated into a half dozen languages and printed all around the globe. Spectators come from all over.

Although the turkeys are obviously the main attraction, the festival also features mud volleyball, a demolition derby, tractor pulls, and entertainment by top country music stars. Admission for adults is $10 for Thursday and Sunday, and $20 for Friday and Saturday. Admission for children is $5 daily which includes free unlimited carnival rides. For additional information, write or call the Daviess County Visitors Bureau, 1 Train Depot St., PO Box 430, Washington 47501; (812) 254-5262 or (800) 449-5262; montgomeryturkeytrot.com.

Montgomery is located in the heart of southern Indiana's Amish country, a fact that until a few years ago was little known beyond the borders of Daviess County and its immediate neighbors. To celebrate this heritage, the 92-acre *Gasthof Amish Village* has been constructed near Montgomery. Visitors will find a restaurant that features authentic Amish cooking; a gift shop that sells items handmade by Amish craftspeople; an outdoor flea market (Tuesday, Wednesday, and Saturday, May through October); an inn; and shops that house various Amish businesses. Located just north of Montgomery on CR 650E; hours vary; call (812) 486-4900 or (800) 449-5262; gasthofamishvillage.com.

Gibson County (Central Time Zone)

Henager's Memories and Nostalgia Museum in *Buckskin* (population 80, give or take a few people) is the type of place for which the word eclectic was invented. When James Henager first opened his nonprofit museum in 1996, he planned to use it as a repository for family memorabilia that focused on his family's long history with woodworking. He then decided to add his own collection of artifacts related to his boyhood hero, Roy Rogers. Like any collector, Henager has kept on collecting through the years; unlike many collectors, his interests are not focused on one specific area. His museum now contains more than 30,000 items that contain something of interest to most anyone.

Among the exhibits you'll see here are artifacts related to Gene Autry, Marilyn Monroe, and Vivien Leigh; a tribute to American music that includes thousands of records and a 1952 Seeburg jukebox; an Americana collection that features such icons as Smokey Bear and a 1930 Model A Ford; and an authentic woodworking shop with live demonstrations. There are antique toys, items related to scouting, and some 500 movie posters. The donated baseball lockers seen here were used in the movie *A League of Their Own,* filmed in Evansville. A display honoring Abraham Lincoln, who lived in Indiana during most of his childhood years, contains more than 300 items, and there are papers from several presidential libraries as well. Bob Hope's family has also contributed some items. Classic movies are shown in the small theater area. And that's just the tip of the iceberg.

As the museum's fame grows, the collection grows, thanks in part to the many unique items that are sent here from companies and individuals all across the country. Henager now has so many items that he's run out of room to display them all, so he plans to expand the museum in the future. He also is devoted to another project—a National Veterans Memorial of America that he opened in 2015 and a Veterans Food Bank of America that he started in 2016. Future plans include offering the museum and memorial as a retreat for veterans dealing with post-traumatic stress disorder and Gold Star families. Beyond that, Henager hopes to construct a replica 1940s Main Street, complete with retail stores, a theater, filling station, and soda shop.

You'll find Henager's Museum at 8837 S. SR 57 in Buckskin, about 5 miles north of I-64. Open 8 a.m. to 7 p.m. Monday through Thursday; 8 a.m. to 5 p.m. Friday; and 8 a.m. to 4 p.m. Saturday. Admission: adults $6; children $3, which provides admission to both the museum and the memorial. For more information, call (812) 795-2230, (812) 795-2237, (888) 390-5825, or henagermuseum.com, veteransmemorialofamerica.org., and veteransfoodbankofamerica.org.

In **Princeton,** you can explore the history of Toyota from its origin as a small Japanese loom company to the international automotive manufacturer that it is known as today. The 4-million-square-foot **Toyota Manufacturing Plant** at 2000 S. Tulip Tree Dr. was the birthplace of the Tundra full-size pickup truck (now built in Texas). Today the plant produces sports utility vehicles and minivans; visitors can take a free tour aboard a tram and watch the entire manufacturing process from beginning to end. Tour times vary and are by advance reservation only; call (812) 387-2266 or (888) 696-8211, or visit tourtoyota.com/#/indiana.

A state-of-the-art visitor center features a disassembled 2008 Tundra suspended from the ceiling; all 180 parts are frozen in place as if ready to come together to make a completed pickup truck. You'll also learn about the rich automotive history of southwest Indiana and see some interactive exhibits. Generally open from 1 to 7 p.m. Tuesday and 9 a.m. to 3 p.m. Wednesday through Friday, but hours vary; check before coming.

Toyota is also creating a forest of tulip, walnut, birch, and pecan trees on the 1,140-acre campus that surrounds its manufacturing plant. The first planting in 2008 included some 22,000 trees, with an end goal of planting a total of 131,000 trees. Mission accomplished.

A few miles west of Princeton, you can visit the tiny town of **Lyles Station,** Indiana's first Black settlement and the only one still standing today. First settled in the 1840s by freed and runaway slaves, the town thrived until a devastating flood in 1913 left much of the town under water. Residents who had lost everything moved away, and the town went into decline. Today, only a handful of families remain, but they have worked to preserve the heritage of their hometown. The Wayman Chapel A.M.E. Church still holds Sunday services, and the old schoolhouse has been restored as the **Lyles Station Historic School & Museum ,** a historical museum. One gallery is devoted to telling the story of Alonzo Fields, a native son who became the first African American chief butler at the White House and served in that capacity under Presidents Hoover, Franklin D. Roosevelt, Truman, and Eisenhower. He later wrote a book about his experiences entitled *My 21 Years at the White House.*

The work of the Lyles Station Historic Preservation Corporation, which spearheaded the restoration of the school building, was honored in 2010 when it was named Indiana's Outstanding Historical Organization by the Indiana Historical Society. In 2011, the Smithsonian Institution announced that it would include the story of Lyles Station in its National Museum of African American History and Culture, set to open in 2015 on the National Mall in Washington, DC.

The schoolhouse museum, located at 953 N. 500 West, is generally open from 1 to 4 p.m. Tuesday through Saturday and other times by appointment; hours may vary. Admission: adults $5; senior citizens $4; children (under age seventeen) $3. Call (812) 385-2534 or visit lylesstation.org.

Greene County

Art and nature combine to provide a unique experience at the 30-acre ***Sculpture Trails Outdoor Museum*** in **Solsberry.** Visitors are welcome to walk a woodland trail a little over 1 mile in length and view large-scale metal sculptures created by artists from around the world. All sculptures are created on-site during workshops generally held May through June; materials include cast iron, aluminum, and bronze. The furnace that melts the metal is one of the largest and hottest in the country. Artists and the general public alike are welcome to participate in any of the workshops, which are conducted by sculptor and museum owner Gerard Masse.

The trail is open daily free of charge from 10 a.m. to sundown or by appointment; maps are provided at the head of the trail or can be printed online. Surveillance is provided around the clock to protect both visitors and the collection. Because the sculptures are for sale or lease, the number varies, but at this writing they totaled more than sixty pieces. Fees are charged to participate in the workshops and to purchase materials. Located at 6764 N. Tree Farm Rd.; for information and directions, call (502) 554-1708 or visit sculpturetrails.com.

No matter what you've read or been told, there is no way to fully prepare you for your first glimpse of the ***Tulip Trestle*** (sometimes called the Greene Country viaduct). One minute you're driving along an isolated rural road that winds through wooded hills and hollows; the next minute you're suddenly confronted with an open valley and the massive railroad trestle that spans it—one of the most spectacular sights in the state. Completed in 1906 as part of the Illinois Central Railroad line, the trestle is 157 feet high and 0.5 miles long—the third longest in the world. You can observe it from the road below, but the land around it is privately owned and off-limits to visitors.

The trestle is located just south of a road that links Solsberry and the hamlet of Tulip. Head west from Solsberry on the country road that parallels the railroad tracks. After driving about 5 miles, you'll come to CR 480 East, which turns off to the south and leads beneath the trestle.

It's best to stop at ***Yoho General Store*** at 10043 E. Tulip Rd. (yohogeneralstore.com; 812-825-7834) in Solsberry and ask for exact directions. Roads are not well marked hereabouts, and besides, it's great fun to listen to the yarns being spun by any occupants of the store's "liar's bench." Maybe they'll tell you the one about the man wearing gum rubber boots who fell off the trestle while it was being constructed and bounced for three days. He finally had to be shot to keep him from starving to death. Yoho General Store also serves breakfast, lunch, and dinner. Try the Hoosier favorite, a fried tenderloin sandwich and save room for a slice of the pie of the day. For additional information, write or call the Bloomfield Chamber of Commerce, 6 E. Main St., PO Box 144, Bloomfield 47424; (812) 384-7250 or visit bloomfieldchamberofcommerce.com.

In the vast, dense forest that covered most of Indiana during the past century, there grew a huge sycamore that was the largest tree in the eastern half of the United States. Naturalists and historians advised everyone to go to **Worthington** and see this wonderful tree, which stood 150 feet high, spread its branches to a length of 100 feet, and measured more than 45 feet in circumference at 1 foot above the ground.

In 1920 a storm toppled it, and the town of Worthington decided to preserve one of its limbs in a place of honor. That limb, more than 23 feet in circumference and larger than the trunks of most trees in Indiana today, can be seen in Worthington's City Park at the north end of town. You can't miss it—it's the only tree in the park with a roof over its head.

The town of **Linton** was the birthplace of the late bandleader and show business personality Phil Harris, who never forgot his Indiana roots. Older folks will remember him for his bits on Jack Benny's radio and television shows. Younger folks will remember him as the resonant baritone voice heard in various Disney movies (Little John in *Robin Hood,* Baloo the Bear in *The Jungle Book,* and Thomas O'Malley in *The Aristocats*). For many years, Harris and his late wife, movie actress and singer Alice Faye, returned to Linton for the annual Phil Harris Festival. Alice Faye reportedly loved this small town, and she and Harris donated their collection of numerous show business memorabilia to his boyhood home. A virtual history of show business, the **Harris-Faye collection** includes photographs, awards, scrapbooks, letters, and trophies. Also seen here are souvenirs from well-known personalities in the fields of entertainment, sports, and government, including an array of autographs signed by such stars as Bing Crosby, Shirley Temple, Clint Eastwood, and Larry Bird. The collection is housed in the **Carnegie Heritage and Arts Center** at 110 E. Vincennes St.; open 10 a.m. to 4 p.m. Wednesday through Friday and by appointment on Saturday; (812) 847-0165 or (812) 847-4500 or visitgc.com.

indianatrivia

Southern Greene County is home to the only cave in Indiana where ice is found year-round. Ice caves are generally found only in much colder areas.

Knox County

Vincennes, Indiana's oldest city, has a colorful history, and the town abounds with monuments to its past. George Rogers Clark came here during the

American Revolution to battle the British, and his deeds are memorialized in the 24-acre **George Rogers Clark National Historical Park,** located at 401 S. 2nd St. (open 9 a.m. to 5 p.m. daily, except major winter holidays). Within a magnificent round granite structure are seven murals depicting Clark's military campaigns. Living-history programs, featured on some summer weekends, re-create camp life with military drills and firearm demonstrations. The memorial building and the visitor center are free admission; (812) 882-1776, ext. 110; nps .gov/gero.

At the **Vincennes State Historic Sites,** at the corner of 1st and Harrison Streets on the western edge of the **Vincennes University** campus, is a two-story white frame building that served as the **Indiana Territory Capitol** from about 1805 to 1813. Nearby is the **Western Sun** *Print Shop,* where the territory's first newspaper was published on July 4, 1804; the wooden printing press seen by today's visitors is the same type as the original. Legend has it that Abe Lincoln, a faithful reader of the *Sun,* came here as a young man to study a printing press in operation and actually helped print the Saturday, March 6, 1830, edition of the paper on the day of his visit. Other sites related to the rich history of this area are scattered throughout the area, and you can learn about all of them at the log cabin visitor's center. Open 10 a.m. to 5 p.m. Wednesday through Sunday; Admission: adults $7; senior citizens $6; children (ages 3 to 17) $5. For information, write or call Vincennes State Historic Sites, 1 W. Harrison St., PO Box 81, Vincennes 47591; (812) 882-7422; indianamuseum.org/historic-sites/vincennes/.

Grouseland was the home of William Henry Harrison when he served as the first governor of the Indiana Territory. (He later became the ninth president of the United States and was the grandfather of the 23rd.) As part of his official duties, he once invited Indian chief Tecumseh to his home to discuss their differences. Tecumseh refused to come inside, saying he preferred to sit on the Earth, his mother, and so the two men held council in a walnut grove on the front lawn. Located at 3 W. Scott St.; (812) 882-2096; grouselandfoundation.org. Open Monday through Saturday 10 a.m. to 5 p.m.; Sunday noon to 5 p.m. March through December, except Thanksgiving and Christmas. Closed until the end of February on Sunday and Monday. Admission: adults $7; senior citizens $6; children $5.

The boundaries of the Indiana Territory first encompassed the present-day states of Indiana, Illinois, Michigan, and Wisconsin and part of Minnesota, and later the lands included in the 1803 Louisiana Purchase. So tiny Vincennes, with Harrison at its helm, was for a while the seat of government for most of the US territory from the Alleghenies to the Rockies.

Harrison also served as one of the first trustees of Vincennes University. Founded in 1801, it is the oldest university west of the Alleghenies.

Grouseland: Hoosier home of President William Henry Harrison

If not for bad aim, the nation might have lost its ninth and 23rd presidents all in one fatal shot. A bullet hole in the shutter of the William Henry Harrison mansion in Vincennes recalls that almost deadly incident.

The story goes that William Henry Harrison was walking the floor with his infant son, John Scott Harrison, when someone took a shot at him. The shooter missed. The son that William Henry Harrison was carrying went on to have a son who would become our 23rd president.

Of course, William Henry Harrison went on to become the nation's ninth president. He is also known for serving the shortest time as president and for being the first president to die while in office.

He was in office for only thirty-one days. He gave one of the longest inauguration speeches ever—one hour and forty-five minutes, 8,445 words, and it had been edited and shortened by Daniel Webster. He gave his speech outside in the cold rain without a hat, overcoat, or gloves. He caught a cold that developed into pneumonia.

Harrison was inaugurated on March 4, 1841. He died on April 4, 1841.

Situated on a knoll above the Wabash River, the mansion known as Grouseland was built by Harrison from 1802 to 1804 when he was governor of the Indiana Territory.

The son of a prominent Virginian planter and politician, Harrison had distinguished himself on the battlefield in the Northwest Indian War, while serving under General "Mad" Anthony Wayne at the Battle of Fallen Timbers.

As governor of Indiana Territory, the twenty-seven-year-old Harrison was in charge of a vast area composed of what are now Indiana, Illinois, Michigan, Wisconsin, and southern Minnesota. The capital of the Indiana Territory was at the former French settlement of Vincennes.

When he arrived in Vincennes in January 1801 with his wife Anna and their two small children, Harrison set about building an elegant mansion. The house took two years to complete at a cost of $20,000, an extravagant amount at the time.

William Henry Harrison loved to hunt and he named his home after the abundant game bird, the grouse. William Henry Harrison had ten children. Four were born in the house.

The Federal-style mansion, called the "White House of the West," was the first brick home in the Indiana Territory. Not only was it the seat of territorial government and the Harrison family home, the house was always open as a gathering place and safe house for local settlers. It is often called the birthplace of Hoosier hospitality.

Brute Library Honors 'Most Learned Man of His Day in America'

A treasure house rests behind St. Francis Xavier Cathedral in Vincennes, Indiana. The modern redbrick building gives little clue of what wealth it holds: the Brute Library. The oldest library In Indiana, the Brute contains more than 11,000 rare books and documents. The library was named in honor of Bishop Simon Brute (1779-1839), the first bishop of Vincennes.

Born in France, Brute came to Vincennes in 1834. Brute was an artist, a doctor, a priest, a scholar, and a collector of books.

During the French Revolution Reign of Terror, the Brute home sheltered priests who tutored twelve-year-old Simon since most schools had been forced to close. Brute often took communion to the prisons where priests and other people were awaiting execution for their faith.

If caught, Brute and his family would have been guillotined. It is thought those experiences helped Brute decide to become a priest. He had seen so many suffer and die for their faith.

President John Quincy Adams called Brute "the most learned man of his day in America." The Bible that St. Elizabeth Seton was holding when she died is also displayed. Brute's body is buried in a crypt beneath the sanctuary of St. Francis Xavier Church.

St. Francis Xavier Cathedral, dating back to 1702, is the oldest Catholic church in Indiana. The present redbrick building is actually the fourth church to stand on this site; its first two predecessors were built of logs, while the third, also a brick structure, was built in 1826 and rebuilt later the same year after a storm nearly destroyed it. Rich, dark cedars shelter the serene grounds of the **Old French Cemetery** adjacent to the cathedral, where priests, parishioners, natives, soldiers, and African slaves lie buried, many in unmarked graves. The first interment was in 1741, the last in 1846. The cathedral is located at 100 S. 3rd St.; open 9 a.m. to 3:45 p.m. daily. Call (812) 882-5638 or (800) 886-6443; stfrancisxaviervincennes.com.

Behind the cathedral, housed in a modern redbrick building at 207 Church St., is **Brute Library,** the oldest library in Indiana, containing more than 11,000 rare books and documents. Bishop Simon Brute (1779–1839), the first bishop of Vincennes, assembled the collection in France and brought it with him to the wilderness that was the Indiana Territory.

A papal bull of Pope John XXII, dated 1319 and written on heavy parchment, is the oldest manuscript in the library. The oldest book, dated 1476, glows with the lustrous colors of hand illumination, and the parchment still bears the holes made by the pins that held the pages in place while the illuminating was done. Another interesting volume contains the Lord's Prayer in 250 different languages. In addition, there are old maps, letters, and a certified copy of a license issued on March 6, 1833, to Abraham Lincoln and William Berry, permitting them to operate a tavern in New Salem, Illinois. There's a nominal admission fee. The library is open 1 to 4 p.m. daily, Memorial Day through Labor Day; (812) 882-7016.

Vincennes honors native son Red Skelton

"If by chance some day you're not feeling well and you should remember some silly thing I've said or done and it brings back a smile to your face or a chuckle to your heart, then my purpose as your clown has been fulfilled."

-Red Skelton

Selling newspapers on a corner, the redheaded kid was asked by an out-of-towner what there was to do in the tiny Indiana burg of Vincennes.

Gesturing across the street to a theater, the nine-year old answered that a famous comedian was going to appear that night. When the stranger asked if the boy would be in the audience, the youngster said that he didn't have the money and had to finish selling his papers.

Upon hearing that, the stranger bought the remainder of the papers—paying $1 for three newspapers that sold for three cents each at the time. He also said he would talk to the theater manager about getting the child in free for the show. The boy ran home, gave the money to his mother, and hurried back to the theater where a balcony seat was waiting for him.

When the show began and the performer walked out from behind the curtain, the boy was shocked. The star of the show was *Ed Wynn*—the stranger who had bought his newspapers.

During intermission, the performer invited the boy backstage and held him up to peer through the curtains. That was Red's first look at an audience. He would often reminisce later that was when he fell in love with the audience.

Born July 18, 1913, Richard Skelton got his nickname because of his red hair. The Hoosier boy grew up to become one of the most beloved entertainers of his era. Skelton's radio show debuted in 1941, and ten years later *The Red Skelton Show* premiered on NBC.

Skelton spent twenty consecutive years on NBC and CBS. Skelton starred in more than thirty movies and wrote 5,000 musical pieces and several children's books. Later in life, he started painting and his clown portraits sold for more than $80,000 each.

In 2006, the *Red Skelton Performing Arts Center* at Vincennes University was dedicated. On his 100th birthday in 2013, Skelton's widow Lothian and daughter Valentina officially dedicated the *Red Skelton Museum of American Comedy* at the performing arts center. Lothian donated almost $5 million in mementoes for the museum.

As visitors walk through the museum, they see costumes, film clips, exhibits about Skelton's famous characters, a biographical film in the museum theater, a timeline of Skelton's life, and his interpretation of the "Pledge of Allegiance." A museum entry wall is filled with Skelton's artwork. His widow donated about 200 of his original paintings.

Skelton began painting early in life but, as a self-taught artist, he kept his works private for many years. After his television show ended in 1971, he became a prolific artist. He painted and sketched hundreds of original pieces.

In addition to his paintings and comedy routines, Skelton also composed numerous short stories and musical pieces. Although the specific subject matter of the works varied greatly, they shared common themes such as patriotism, loyalty, and altruism.

Skelton was creative until the end of his life. He died of pneumonia on September 17, 1997, in a Palm Springs, California, hospital. Red Skelton never forgot his hometown. And his hometown never forgot him.

Built about 1806, the ***Brouillet French House*** at 509 N. 1st St. is one of the few remaining upright log-and-mud houses in North America. Inside are the original fireplace and warming oven, along with authentic period furnishings. An Indian museum is located behind the house; hours vary seasonally. Nominal admission fee. Call (812) 882-7422 or (800) 886-6443; vincennescvb.org.

The late **Red Skelton,** the beloved comedian, was born in Vincennes at 111 W. Lyndale Ave. A sign in front of the house, which is owned by Vincennes University, commemorates the occasion.

When Red was just ten he joined the Hagenbeck-Wallace Circus (which wintered in Peru, Indiana) as a clown. That was the beginning of his illustrious career, which included the starring role in some thirty movies, hosting his own television show for twenty years, and performing for eight US presidents.

In February 2006, the 63,000-square-foot ***Red Skelton Performing Arts Theater*** opened at 20 W. Red Skelton Blvd. on the campus of Vincennes University just across the street from Red's birthplace. His widow, Lothian, said Red, who died in 1997, would have been thrilled because it was a lifelong dream of his to have a theater of his own.

The Red Skelton Museum of American Comedy is part of the theater complex. It houses a collection of the comedian's memorabilia, donated by Red's widow, that's valued at almost $5 million. The museum is open from 10 a.m. to 5 p.m. Tuesday through Saturday; noon to 5 p.m. on Sunday. The museum is

The Marrying Man

Until his demise on June 10, 1997, at the age of eighty-eight, Glynn "Scotty" Wolfe was acknowledged to be the world's most married man. Reportedly, until the day he died, he was still chasing women at the nursing home in which he was living—even though he was by then confined to a wheelchair.

Wolfe, who lived in California at the time of his death, was a native of Knox County. Between 1927 and 1996, he married twenty-nine times. His longest marriage lasted six years, his shortest just nineteen days. The flamboyant Wolfe claimed that he left one of his wives because she ate sunflower seeds in bed and walked out on another because she used his toothbrush.

According to the man himself, his colorful life included stints as a Baptist minister, a pilot in Britain's Royal Air Force, a sailor on the USS *Arizona* (before it was bombed and sunk at Pearl Harbor), and a bodyguard for Al Capone.

At the time of his death, Wolfe was survived by his several children (believed but not confirmed to be nineteen in number) and his twenty-ninth wife—Linda Essex-Wolfe of Anderson, IN, who had been married twenty-three times and was the world's most married woman. She passed away at the age of sixty-nine on December 27, 2010, without ever marrying again.

also open on Monday from 10 a.m. to 5 pm. in June, July, and August. Admission: adults $8; senior citizens $7; students (kindergarten through college) $5. A *Red Skelton Festival,* which debuted in 2006, is an annual July event.

For additional information about the theater, call (812) 888-4039 or visit vinu.edu/red-skelton. For information about the museum, call (812) 888-4184 or visit redskeltonmuseum.org.

Lawrence County

For more than 170 years, many of the great public edifices in this country and elsewhere have been constructed with Indiana limestone. Architects favor it because it lends itself easily to carving and the most delicate tracery when first quarried, then becomes hard and durable when exposed to atmospheric agents. Just a few of the structures that are built at least partly of Oolitic limestone (so called because of its granular composition, which suggests a mass of fish eggs) from the Bedford area are the Empire State Building and Rockefeller Center in New York City; Washington National Cathedral (eighty-three years in the making, it was completed on September 29, 1990, when a crane placed a 1,000-pound chunk of intricately carved Indiana limestone atop one of the church's towers); the Pentagon; the Lincoln and Jefferson Memorials; the US

Holocaust Memorial Museum in Washington DC; Chicago's Merchandise Mart; the new Yankee Stadium, the Biltmore Estate in Asheville, NC; and the University of Moscow.

The *limestone quarries* are quite impressive to see—great gaping cavities in the earth from which are extracted immense blocks of stone that average 4 feet in thickness, 10 feet in width, and from 50 to 100 feet in length. Before being removed from the quarry floor, they're broken into small blocks for easy transportation to a processing mill. You can view many attractions related to the limestone industry by following a limestone heritage trail in Lawrence and nearby counties; a free brochure entitled *Experience Indiana Limestone* is available at the Lawrence County Visitors Center (see contact information at end of Southwest chapter) and at area businesses.

indianatrivia

Elliott Stone in Bedford is the only underground limestone quarry in the world.

To view some quarries from the road, go north from Bedford on SR 37 through Oolitic; the quarries are about 0.5 mile north of Oolitic. When you pass through *Oolitic,* stop and meet one of the town's residents—the limestone *statue of Joe Palooka,* which stands in front of the town hall on Main Street. A famous comic strip character from the not-too-distant past, Joe was at the peak of his popularity in the 1940s. A paragon of good, Joe was an earthbound Superman of sorts who championed democracy and decency and was an inspiration to the youth of his day. He was also a boxer, and he is depicted—7 feet tall and weighing more than 10 tons—wearing trunks and boxing gloves. When World War II came along, Joe gave up boxing to enlist in the Army, adding to his reputation as the ultimate American hero. The comic strip was created in 1928 and became so popular that Joe's name became part of the American vernacular; to call someone a "real Palooka" was a compliment of the highest order. Although the strip was canceled in 1984, Joe's statue, a little worse for the wear, still stands at the ready to fight for truth and justice. The town of Idaho Springs, CO, was so impressed by the statue that it paid the Indiana Limestone Company $12,000 to carve a statue of Steve Canyon, a comic book icon of a later era; that statue was dedicated in Idaho Springs in 1950.

Bedford stone, another name for local limestone, is sometimes used for gravestones, and many fine examples can be seen in *Green Hill Cemetery* at 1202 18th St. in *Bedford;* (812) 275-5110; greenhillbedford.com. The monument for Louis Baker, a twenty-three-year-old apprentice stonecutter who died suddenly in 1917, was carved by his grieving fellow workers; they reproduced his workbench, fully detailed and to actual size, exactly as he had left it. The statue of Michael F. Wallner preserves his doughboy uniform down to the most minute crease. Also seen in the cemetery are some of the tree-trunk carvings that were popular around the turn of the twentieth century, including one adorned with high-button shoes and a straw hat that memorializes a seven-year-old girl who died in 1894. These and other Green Hill monuments have been featured on several national television shows. Free walking-tour maps of the cemetery are available from the Bedford Area Chamber of Commerce at 1116 16th Street; (812) 275-4493; bedfordchamber.com or at the Lawrence County Visitors Center in Mitchell (see end of Southwest chapter for contact information). The cemetery is open from 9 a.m. to 5 p.m.

Southwest of Bedford, the longest navigable underground river in the United States flows through a startling subterranean world. More than 20 miles of passageways have been explored at ***Bluespring Caverns,*** one of the world's ten longest, and most of those miles are wet ones—inundated by a system of underground streams. Visitors descend a stairway into a sinkhole entrance room, then venture 4,000 feet into the yawning depths aboard flat-bottomed boats that glide silently through a world of total darkness. The rare white fish and crayfish that live in these waters are blind, having adapted themselves over the years to a habitat where sight is of no use. Lights mounted on the bottom of the tour boat create shifting shadows on fluted walls and provide unique glimpses of water-sculpted formations on the mirror-like surface of the stream. By prior arrangement you can also participate in a "wild tour," which includes exploring some of the dry portions of the cave, crawling, climbing, and viewing an underground slide show. Overnight stays in the caverns are offered on Friday and Saturday evenings from October through April; make reservations early, as many dates are filled up as much as ninety days ahead.

Above ground, you can visit the ***Bolton Natural Area*** via a 0.5-mile-long trail that circles the state's largest sinkhole, a behemoth that covers more than 10 acres; you'll see the surface effects of the caverns forming below.

To reach Bluespring Caverns Park from Bedford, go southwest on US 50 for about 6 miles, then turn west on CR 4505 for about 0.5 mile; signs point the way. Open daily 9 a.m. to 4 p.m. A boat tour costs $20 for adults and $12 for ages 4–15. The overnight adventure is $40 per person. Campsites with water and electricity are available in the park. Bluespring Caverns Park is located at 1459 Bluespring Caverns Rd.; (812) 279-9471; bluespringcaverns.com.

The many attractions at ***Spring Mill State Park*** span a time period from the early 1800s to the threshold of the space age. As a boy growing up in nearby Mitchell, Virgil I. "Gus" Grissom loved this park. Grissom grew up to become one of the seven original astronauts and, in 1965, the second American in space. Two years later he was dead—one of three astronauts killed in

Astronaut Gus Grissom's Hoosier Home

In this small bedroom in Mitchell, a young boy dreamed of flying and yearned to be a pilot. Against all odds, that's exactly what he did. Virgil I. "Gus" Grissom grew up to become one of the most famous aviators in the world.

The native Hoosier was one of the seven original astronauts in the NASA program. Grissom made aviation history as the first man in space to actually steer a space vehicle from the cockpit. Commanding the Gemini 3 capsule with John Young, Grissom made his historic flight on March 23, 1965.

Today, the boyhood home is owned by Virgil I. Grissom Inc., a group dedicated to the preservation of the astronaut's legacy in his Hoosier hometown. The home is pretty much as it was when the Grissoms lived here. The family moved here when Gus was about two years old and his parents lived here until their deaths. No one else has lived here since 1927 except the Grissom family.

With no roped-off areas or barriers, the home looks as though the Grissom family has just stepped out for Sunday church and will soon return for dinner.

Hanging over Gus's boyhood bed is a rifle he bought as a teen with money he earned working with his dad at the railroad. On a nearby desk is a dog-engraved knife that Gus made in shop class in school. His father's heavy work boots wait beside the front door.

Virgil Ivan Grissom was born to Cecile and Dennis Grissom at 8 p.m. on April 3, 1926. The Grissoms had three other children—Norman, Lowell, and Wilma. After graduating in 1944, Grissom joined the US Army Air Corps because he didn't have the money to go to college. He also married his high school sweetheart, Betty Moore, and they had two sons, Scott and Mark.

Grissom then enlisted in the US Air Force and flew 100 missions as a jet fighter pilot during the Korean War. He returned to the states to become a test pilot. When NASA called the best 100 pilots in the nation to pick Apollo's seven astronauts, Grissom was one of them. On July 21, 1961, Grissom rode the Liberty Bell 7 to an altitude of 118 miles, flying at 5,130 miles per hour.

However, when the space capsule splashed down in the Atlantic Ocean, the craft's hatch blew prematurely and Grissom was forced to exit as water poured into the Mercury capsule.

Grissom nearly drowned and the capsule containing valuable scientific data sank to the bottom of the sea. NASA concluded that Grissom was not at fault. The 7-foot capsule was recovered thirty-eight years later. Four years after Liberty Bell 7, Grissom commanded the Gemini 3.

Grissom gave his life to the space program, along with his crew, Ed White and Roger Chaffee, on January 27, 1967, when a fire broke out from an electrical malfunction on the Apollo spacecraft they were testing.

a tragic spacecraft fire at Cape Kennedy. A Gemini III capsule like the one he once piloted now rests, along with his spacesuit and other items related to space travel, in the *Virgil I. "Gus"* Grissom Memorial Museum located adjacent to the gatehouse at the park entrance at 3333 SR 60 in Mitchell. Open daily free of charge 8 a.m. to 4 p.m. year-round; closed major winter holidays. For more information about the Grissom Memorial Museum, call (812) 849-4129 or visit in.gov/dnr/parklake/2968.htm.

Nestled in a small valley among Spring Mill State Park's wooded hills is a *pioneer village* that was founded in 1814. Its sawmill, meetinghouse, apothecary, hatmaker's and weaver's shops, water-powered gristmill, general store, tavern, distillery, post office, and log cabin homes have all been restored, and from April through October the village is alive with inhabitants who go about their daily routine just as their long-ago counterparts did. You can purchase cornmeal ground at the old gristmill and products from the weaver's looms, and, on occasion, you can participate in candlelight tours of the tiny settlement.

Plants in the *Hamer Pioneer Gardens* are the same as those grown by the village's original occupants; some were used for medicine, some for cooking, and some simply to add beauty to a life that was often harsh. Uphill from the village is a pioneer cemetery that dates back to 1832. The stone markers provide a genealogical history of the town below.

During the spring and summer, nearly every variety of wildflower and bird indigenous to Indiana is found here, and to protect some of the 1,300-acre park's finest natural features the state has set aside two areas as nature preserves. A 2.5-mile-loop hiking trail, the most beautiful in the park, winds through *Donaldson's Woods State Nature Preserve,* an outstanding 76-acre virgin forest dominated by giant tulip trees and white oaks. Six acres surrounding the mouth of *Donaldson Cave,* reached by another trail, have also been designated a state nature preserve. The scene that meets your eye here—a small stream flowing from the cave's entrance and through a gorge whose slopes are thick with hardwood trees—is one of the loveliest in the state.

At *Twin Caves*, you can take a short ride on an underground river while a naturalist tells you about the tiny blind cavefish swimming beneath you. Other park facilities include bike rentals, a nature center, a swimming pool, campsites, and a lodge. To reach the park, go east on SR 60 from Mitchell for about 3 miles; the park is on the north side of SR 60—signs point the way; there's a vehicle admission charge. Write or call Spring Mill State Park, 3333 SR 60 East, Mitchell 47446; (812) 849-3534; in.gov/dnr/parklake/2968.htm.

The greatest concentration of Indiana's several earthquake faults is located in Posey County in the southwestern corner of the state, but the longest fault occurs in south central Indiana. Known as the *Mt. Carmel Fault,* it extends

50 miles southeastward from the Morgan-Monroe county line into Washington County. One of the few places in the state where a fault can actually be seen on the surface of the land is alongside SR 446, 2.5 miles south of the Monroe-Lawrence county line, where ancient movements along the Mt. Carmel Fault have uplifted the land. (It may be reassuring for visitors—and nearby residents—to know that no movement of this fault has been recorded in modern history.) For additional information, visit the *Indiana Geological and Water Survey* (IGS) at 6420 N. Walnut St. in Bloomington, where detailed maps showing the location of the Mt. Carmel Fault are on open file. The IGS also can provide information about other faults in Indiana; it's open from 8:30 a.m. to 4:30 p.m. p.m. Monday through Friday; (812) 855-7636; igws.indiana.edu.

Martin County

There's silver in them thar hills, if legend be truth! Since the first Europeans came to these parts, tales have abounded about the lost Indian treasure cave of *McBride's Bluffs*. For nearly 100 years, the Choctaw Indians lived in the bluffs area north of *Shoals*, taking shelter in one particular cave during severe weather. Absalom Shields, one of the first white settlers, told of the time when the natives blindfolded him and took him to this cave, where he was shown a fabulous amount of silver crudely molded into bricks. Shortly after their disclosure to Shields, the natives were forced to flee the area so hastily that they could not take the silver with them. They did, however, seal the entrance to the cave. When one of their tribe was later sent to claim the treasure, the trees he was to use as landmarks to guide him to the cave had been cleared away, and he was never able to find the silver. Since then a few isolated bars of silver have been found above ground, but the whereabouts of the cave remains a secret to this day. It's not for lack of trying, though—people still search for the silver.

The precipitous cliffs known as McBride's Bluffs, which soar 175 feet above the East Fork of White River, are riddled with small caves. Because country roads may be unmarked, it's best to ask locally for exact directions to the bluffs, which lie approximately 5 miles north of Shoals. Start out from Shoals going northwest on US 50/150, then turn north onto SR 450. Continue north to a side road about 1.5 miles north of Dover Village and turn east toward the White River; a single-lane gravel road winds along the riverbank at the base of the bluffs.

Martin County is one of the best places in the state for shunpiking (driving the back roads). Meandering country lanes lead past little-known havens of beauty—rugged hills, dense woodlands, sheer sandstone cliffs—that are even more beautiful when wildflowers color the spring landscape and trees don their autumn hues.

Jug Rock, a striking sandstone monolith that is the focal point of a state nature preserve, is a product of centuries of erosion; it is the country's largest freestanding table rock formation east of the Mississippi River. Although it stretches to a height of 60 feet and is more than 15 feet in diameter, it is difficult to see when the surrounding trees are heavy with foliage. The bottle-shaped rock stands on the north side of US 50/150 a little to the northwest of Shoals, about 1 mile beyond the White River bridge and some 200 yards downhill from the Shoals Overlook Rest Park. Stop at a small roadside pull-off on a high point along the highway and look for a large, flat slab that tops this unusual formation. To gain a better perspective of Jug Rock's dimensions, walk to its base along a 60-yard-long woodland path. For additional information, write or call the Division of Nature Preserves, Indiana Department of Natural Resources, 402 W. Washington St., Room W267, Indianapolis 46204; (317) 232-4052; in.gov /dnr/4571.htm.

Directly west of Shoals you can see the 210-acre **Bluffs of Beaver Bend State Nature Preserve,** noted for the rare species of ferns that cling to the cliff and grow nearby. Beaver Bend is a sharp curve in the East Fork of White River where Beaver Creek flows into it. These cliffs reach their loftiest height at Spout Spring, where water emerges from a pipe driven into the solid rock wall. The honeycombed cliff that overhangs the spring is layered with ocher and yellow rocks that soar 400 feet into the air. Bald eagles are sometimes seen in the trees that line the riverbank. For further information and directions, contact the Indiana Division of Nature Preserves (see contact information in previous paragraph).

Hoosier National Forest, just east of Hindostan Falls, occupies the southeast corner of Martin County. A drive along forest roads reveals a seemingly endless panorama of some of nature's most stunning handiwork: huge rock bluffs, woods, waterfalls, streams, and box canyons. For additional information, write or call Hoosier National Forest Headquarters, 811 Constitution Ave., Bedford 47421; (812) 275-5987 or (866) 302-4173; fs.usda.gov/hoosier.

Northeast of Shoals, bordering the north side of US 50, is *Martin State Forest,* one of the nicest surprises in the state forest system. Within its 6,132 acres you can climb a fire tower, visit an arboretum, or tour one of five demonstration areas to learn about forest management practices. The most spectacular hike in the forest takes you over a rugged 3-mile trail that leads to Tank Spring State Nature Preserve, where water tumbles down 150 feet over moss-covered sandstone; come here in the spring when the greens are newborn and lustrous. Shady campsites atop a breezy ridge make this a great place to spend warm-weather days. The forest is open at all times; admission is free. Write or call Martin State Forest, 14040 Williams Rd., PO Box 599, Shoals 47581; (812) 247-3491; in.gov/dnr/forestry/4822.htm.

Monroe County

The late Thubten J. Norbu, a retired Indiana University (IU) professor and the older brother of Tibet's exiled spiritual leader, the Dalai Lama, was the driving force behind the founding of the *Tibetan Mongolian Buddhist Cultural Center* (TMBCC) in 1979 in *Bloomington.* In 1987, the Dalai Lama came to Bloomington to consecrate the then-new *Jangchub Chorten,* the only Tibetan chorten in the United States at that time and the cornerstone of the TMBCC. Rising 35 feet above its pastoral surroundings, the copper-topped, white, concrete monument to peace memorializes Tibetans who have died in a struggle to gain their country's freedom from Chinese rule, imposed when China took over Tibet in 1959. Sealed within the chorten are such religious artifacts as

The Puzzlemeister from Indiana

In 1974, Indiana University (IU) in Bloomington awarded what was believed to be the world's first degree in enigmatology. The young man upon whom it was conferred, a native of Crawfordsville, IN, designed the degree himself through IU's Individualized Major Program. When he first approached his adviser with the idea for such a degree, she was lukewarm, but the young man persisted and was eventually given the go-ahead to pursue the degree of his dreams. In 1993, at the age of forty-one, that man became the youngest puzzle editor ever at the *New York Times,* a job he still holds today. His passion also led to a second job as star of the puzzle-master segment that airs Sunday morning on National Public Radio (NPR).

Although Will Shortz went on to earn a law degree from the University of Virginia, he never practiced law. Instead, he went straight to an editing job at a puzzle magazine and by 1989 was editor of *Games* magazine. Then it was on to the *Times* and NPR.

Shortz has also authored or edited more than twenty books of puzzles, founded and served as director of the American Crossword Tournament, and founded the World Puzzle Championship. He lives in New York City and collects—what else?—puzzles and puzzle magazines. Among his prized possessions is the first "word-cross" puzzle ever invented; it was published in the December 21, 1913, *New York World,* a Christmas gift for the ages.

In 2006, Shortz was featured in a documentary film entitled *Wordplay.* He shared screen time with such puzzle aficionados as former president Bill Clinton and television personality Jon Stewart. Puzzle fans everywhere owe a debt of gratitude to those folks at IU who allowed Shortz to pursue his dream.

Buddhist scriptures, bits of clothing worn by ancient monks and saints, and hair clippings from thirteen Dalai Lamas (the current Dalai Lama is the fourteenth). Just prior to another visit by the Dalai Lama in 1999, a second monument was added to the center. Known as the **Kalachakra Stupa,** it is dedicated to world peace and harmony. The Dalai Lama returned again in September 2003 to bless the **Chamtse Ling Temple,** a new interdenominational peace temple. The chorten, stupa, and temple, located on the TMBCC's 90-acre property at 3655 S. Snoddy Rd., can be seen free of charge during daylight hours. A nearby building houses a museum, library, and workshop. The Dalai Lama also visited the center in May 2010 for teaching programs at IU. Four retreat cottages deep in the center's woodlands, built to resemble Mongolian yurts, are available for rental. For further information and a schedule of special cultural events sponsored by the TMBCC, write or call the center at 3655 S. Snoddy Rd., Bloomington 47401; (812) 336-6807; tmbcc.net.

Among the more unusual facilities on the IU campus is the **Lilly Library of Rare Books and Manuscripts,** a repository of about 460,000 books, including one of the world's largest collections of miniature books (some the size of the head of a pin), more than seven million manuscripts, and some 120,000 pieces of sheet music. Among its acquisitions are the original scripts from the popular television shows *Star Trek* and *Star Trek: The Next Generation.* One recent donation of note is the personal collection of more than 30,000 comic books from Michael Uslan, a former college professor who taught the world's first college course on comic books at IU in the 1970s and later produced Batman films. Another donation of more than 30,000 mechanical puzzles and 4,000 puzzle-related books was made in 2006; puzzle enthusiast Jerry Slocum chose the Lilly Library over the Smithsonian as the repository for his collection. The library draws on its vast holdings to set up a series of changing exhibits throughout the year, but such treasures as a Gutenberg Bible, George Washington's letter accepting the presidency of the United States, Thomas Jefferson's copy of the Bill of Rights, four Shakespeare folios, a double elephant folio of *Audubon's Birds of America,* and a major Lincoln collection are on permanent display. Admission is free; open Monday through Saturday, but hours vary with the seasons. Located at 1200 E. 7th St. When this book went to the printers, the library was closed until summer 2021 for renovations. To check on the reopening call (812) 855-2452 or visit libraries .indiana.edu/lilly-library.

Although IU's School of Music is world renowned, Bloomington-born songwriter **Hoagy Carmichael** earned a law degree here. Music was always his passion, however, and passion would eventually have its way. One night in 1926, while sitting alone on a spooning wall at the edge of campus thinking of the two girls in his life, Carmichael looked up at the starry sky and began whistling a tune. Unable to get the song out of his mind, he dashed over to use the piano at a local hangout. A few minutes later the proprietor closed up and tossed Hoagy out. Fortunately for the world, the song remained on Hoagy's mind—it ultimately became "Stardust," one of the most recorded American pop songs ever. More than 2,000 versions have been performed by hundreds of artists. An Indiana State Historical Marker stands on the sidewalk at 114 S. Indiana Ave., denoting this as the location of the now-closed hangout in which an inspired Hoagy began his classic composition. On the IU campus, a life-size bronze statue of Hoagy, seated at his trademark Steinway piano, can be seen in the midst of a garden along the northeast side of the IU auditorium; if you choose, there's room on the bench to sit with Hoagy awhile.

Hoagy died in 1981 at age eighty-two and is buried in Rose Hill Cemetery on Bloomington's west side. In 1986, Hoagy's family donated a large collection of the composer's memorabilia to IU, and the school established a **Hoagy Carmichael Room** in which to display it. The composer's piano, a jukebox, photographs of Carmichael with numerous Hollywood stars, and both of the original manuscripts of "Stardust" (one without orchestration and the other with scores for each instrument), both signed and dated by the composer, are just a few of the mementos visitors will see. Located in Room 006 of the **Archives of Traditional Music** in Morrison Hall, the Hoagy Carmichael Room is open free of charge by appointment. Other rooms of the archives—the largest university-based ethnographic sound archives in the country—house such varied holdings as tapes of 350 spoken languages from around the world, the music of the Tupi Indians of Brazil, and recordings of blues artists of the 1940s. The public is welcome to visit the archives free and listen to its collections. Hours vary so check the website or call. Call the Hoagy Carmichael Room at (812) 855-4679; libraries.indiana.edu/hoagy-carmichael-room.

indianatrivia

The first color television set in America was manufactured at the RCA plant in Bloomington in 1954.

While on campus, you also might want to visit another of Morrison's Hall's famous occupants—the world-famous **Kinsey Institute.** The late Alfred Kinsey established the institute in 1947 to conduct his groundbreaking studies of human sexuality. Its collection of art, photographs, and various artifacts in the art gallery can be seen free of charge by appointment; guided tours of the institute, library, and exhibition room are available by advance reservation. Call the institute at (812) 855-7686 or visit kinseyinstitute.org; you'll find the institute on the third floor.

Actor Liam Neeson visited here to research Kinsey's work in preparation for his portrayal of Kinsey in the acclaimed movie of the same name, released in 2004.

You can obtain more information about the facilities of IU by contacting the IU Visitor Information Center at 900 E. 7th St. in Bloomington; (812) 856-4648; visitorcenter.indiana.edu. Open 9:30 a.m. to 5:30 p.m. Monday through Friday, 10 a.m. to 2 p.m. Saturday, and noon to 3 p.m. Sunday. Campus tours are offered on Sunday.

If the IU campus looks familiar, it may be because you saw the award-winning movie *Breaking Away*. It was filmed in Bloomington in 1978 and featured the university's Little 500 Bicycle Race, the largest collegiate bike race in the country, held here each April. The movie launched the careers of two then-unknown actors, Daniel Stern and Dennis Quaid. Billed as "The World's Greatest College Weekend," the Little 500 is modeled after the Indianapolis 500 with bike riders competing in four-person teams around a quarter-mile cinder track at Bill Armstrong Stadium. The men's race is 200 laps (50) miles and the women's race is 100 laps (25 miles). The Little 500 was started in 1951 as a way to raise scholarship money for IU undergraduate students working their way through college. Since that first race, the IU Student Foundation has given more than $2 million to deserving undergrads. For additional information, visit the website of the IU Student Foundation at iusf.indiana.edu/little500. You can drive by the house featured in the film; it's located at 756 S. Lincoln St. on the northwest corner of Lincoln and Dodds streets. The swimming hole seen in the movie was an abandoned water-filled limestone quarry south of Bloomington known as the Empire Quarry; it provided the stone for the exterior of New York City's Empire State Building.

On the western edge of Bloomington lies beautiful **Rose Hill Cemetery**—as much a sculpture garden as a graveyard. Many of the memorials that mark its graves are works of art. In the oldest part of the cemetery are stones adorned with carvings of weeping willows, a symbol of grief that was popular when these markers were carved in the period from 1830 to 1865. These earlier tombstones are made primarily of marble, brought here from Vermont before the growth of the Indiana limestone industry. The image of willows and the use of marble to create them appear to have lost favor about the time the Civil War ended, replaced by the striking tree trunk memorials carved from the more enduring limestone. Other materials have gained favor in later years, but the limestone markers of Rose Hill still stand today as visible reminders of a unique art that once brought worldwide fame to this part of Indiana.

The cemetery serves as the final resting place for some of Bloomington's most renowned citizens, including Hoagy Carmichael and Alfred Kinsey. The university's first president also lies here, along with a former governor of the

Beautiful Charms of Bloomington

When night spreads its velvet cloak over Bloomington and stars shine their brightest, it's easy to see how composer Hoagy Carmichael was inspired to write his lovely classic "Stardust."

Tucked among the rolling hills of southern Indiana, Bloomington is a pleasant combination of cosmopolitan charm and small-town Hoosier hospitality. From Tibetan monks to Big Ten sports, from the state's largest manmade lake to historic limestone buildings, Bloomington is a favorite with group tours. Offering a vibrant arts scene, natural beauty, one-of-a-kind shops, and eclectic restaurants, Bloomington has attractions that visitors may not expect to find in Indiana.

Founded in 1824 as the first college west of the Alleghenies, *Indiana University* offers top-notch attractions like the *Mathers Museum of World Culture*, *Eskenazi Museum of Art*, *Lilly Library*, *Kinsey Institute Gallery*, and *IU Jacobs School of Music Opera and Ballet Theater*, said to be acoustically perfect.

Among its treasures, the Lilly Library has a vast collection of first editions, letters and other material relating to Edgar Allan Poe, including a lock of Poe's hair that he sent in a love letter to his fiancé. It is believed to be the only surviving piece of Poe's hair cut while he was still alive.

With its local limestone architecture and shady trees, the university campus is recognized as one of the five most beautiful collegiate campuses in the country by Thomas A. Gaines's book "The Campus as a Work of Art." Take a limestone tour of the campus and look for a special formula carved into the chemistry building where the key ingredient for fluoride toothpaste was discovered.

Visit *Assembly Hall* to see the NCAA National Champion and Big Ten Champion banners that Hoosiers have won over the years. Nearby is Armstrong Stadium where the annual Little 500 Bicycle Race takes place very spring.

Bordered by state forests to the north and east, Bloomington is also home to *Monroe Lake*. With more than 12,500 acres of water, Monroe Lake is the state's largest manmade lake and a major recreational playground.

Opened to the public in 1965, the lake has *Fourwinds Resort and Marina* along with boat rentals, hiking trails, picnic areas, swimming beach, and campground. Rent a pontoon and watch a marvelous sunset over Monroe Lake.

state and a Civil War general. Near the Elm St. entrance to the cemetery is a monument that honors the memory of a former resident who isn't even buried here. John B. Crafton was on a trip to Europe in the early 1900s when, overwhelmed by homesickness for his family in Bloomington, he decided to return home early. The wealthy businessman canceled his reservation on a German liner and booked an earlier passage on another ship. His decision cost him his life. The year was 1912; the ship was the RMS *Titanic*.

Oliver Winery Started in Family Basement

The roots for the family-owned Oliver Winery go back to 1959 when William Oliver moved to Bloomington to join Indiana University's law faculty. In the 1960s, Oliver began making wine in the basement of the family home.

His enthusiasm for the craft soon led him to establish a vineyard northwest of Bloomington, in what would become the Indiana Uplands AVA. As his vines flourished and produced more grapes than he needed for his hobby, Oliver began plans to open a winery.

But he faced a major obstacle.

As a law expert, Oliver was well prepared to overcome that hurdle. In 1971, Oliver helped craft and was instrumental in passing the Indiana Small Winery Act, which allows for the creation of small commercial wineries. A year later, that is exactly what Oliver did—opened his own small commercial winery, Oliver Winery.

Oliver Winery has changed a lot since then. But the winemakers still have the same goal that William Oliver started with—to make the best possible wine and to bring people together through wine.

In 1983, William Oliver's son Bill Oliver assumed operating control of the winery. In 2006, Bill and his wife Kathleen decided to sell the company to its employees. With about 100 employees, Oliver Winery is the only 100 percent employed-owned winery in the United States. The Employee Stock Ownership Plan is open to all full and part-time staff who work at least 750 hours each year.

Together, Bill and Kathleen have transformed the company from a small hobbyist operation into a state-of-the-art winery that is the largest in Indiana and one of the fifty largest wineries in the United States.

The statistics are staggering. Oliver sold more than 435,000 cases of wine in 2019. That's roughly 5.2 million bottles of wine. Oliver wine is currently sold in twenty-nine states in retail stores, plus in thirty-three states where Oliver can ship online orders.

Oliver Winery has 54 acres of vines at *Creekbend Vineyard* about 3 miles west of the winery's tasting room. Although many folks don't expect to see rows of grape vines and grapes in the wooded hills of southern Indiana, the Hoosier State produces some fine grapes. Indiana is on the same latitude as Napa Valley and the Creekbend hilltop location has well-drained limestone soil that helps create healthy vines and grapes.

Since starting with its popular Camelot Mead, first bottled in the mid-1970s, Oliver Winery now makes more than forty wines from dry Cabernet Sauvignon and Pinot Grigio to dessert wines. In the last five years alone, Oliver wines have earned more than 272 medals in international wine competitions, including 86 gold.

The winery also draws an estimated 200,000 visitors a year. The tasting room reopened in 2019 after a major renovation. The new tasting room has custom-built wine racks, new fixtures, an updated tasting bar, and a wall of windows on the north side overlooking a pond and beautifully landscaped picnic area where live music is offered in warm weather.

Another addition is an enclosed patio with a retractable roof that can close when a sensor detects rain. The patio also is heated for use during winter months.

Rose Hill Cemetery at 1100 W. 4th St. extends westward from the corner of 4th and Elm Sts.; self-guided walking-tour maps are available at the cemetery office at 930 W. 4th St.; call (812) 349-3498 for hours.

Seven miles north of Bloomington on SR 37, **Oliver Winery,** Indiana's oldest and largest, offers free weekend tours, wine tasting for a nominal fee, and, on Saturday evenings in June and July, outdoor concerts (most of which are free) on the parklike grounds. If you're in the mood for lunch, you can have "a jug of wine, a loaf of bread," and your own "thou" beside you at a picnic table outside or at a table in the cozy tasting room inside. You can also stroll through the winery's lovely gardens. Cheeses, summer sausage, fruits, popcorn, maple syrup, and unique limestone gifts are also available. Open noon to 6 p.m. Monday through Thursday; 11 a.m. to 8 p.m. Friday and Saturday; and noon to 6 p.m. on Sunday. Write or call Oliver Winery, 8024 N. SR 37, Bloomington 47404; (812) 876-5800 or (800) 258-2783; oliverwinery.com.

Morgan-Monroe State Forest wanders over 23,916 acres, most of which occupy northeastern Monroe County. Nestled in a clearing in the midst of the woods is a rustic log cabin where a true get-away-from-it-all experience awaits you. **Draper Cabin** is described by the state as primitive, and the description is apt. There's no electricity, all water has to be carried in, heat is provided by a stone fireplace, you make your bed on the floor, and your toilet is an outdoor vault. The forest provides plenty of wood for the fireplace, but it's up to you to gather it and carry it in. Only dead material can be used, and no saws are allowed. You can cook in the fireplace or, if you bring your own grill, on a concrete slab outdoors. The cabin contains nary a stick of furniture, but two picnic tables are just outside the door. A few yards away a small stream sometimes trickles by and sometimes doesn't—it depends on the rainfall.

Draper Cabin is the only such cabin on any state-owned land, and you can rent it for $35 a night, plus tax and reservation fee. Available by advance reservation from April to mid-November and on a first-come, first-served basis the rest of the year. Contact Morgan-Monroe State Forest, 6220 Forest Rd., Martinsville 46151; (765) 792-4654 in.gov/dnr/forestry/4816.htm.

For more plush accommodations that get you out in the woods but doesn't neglect all the comforts of home, try **Cherry Lake Lodge** nestled deep in Morgan-Monroe State Forest. Guests will have comfy beds, hot and cold running water, indoor restroom and shower plus full kitchen facilities. The Lodge features two bedrooms, two bathrooms, and a pull-out sleeper in the great room. Linens are provided. A fireplace in the great room is a cozy spot as is a wide deck across the entire back of the house overlooking the woods. Reservations are $150 per night plus tax and reservation fee.

To reach the forest, go north from Bloomington on SR 37 to Forest Road, the main entrance road, which runs east off SR 37 into the forest just before you reach the Morgan-Monroe county line. If you go in the spring or fall, you probably won't be able to resist a hike through the woods. Brochures for the trails—which include two 10-mile loops, a 0.5-mile pathway through the **Scout Ridge State Nature Preserve,** and a 0.67-mile orienteering course called the Pathfinder Trail—are available at the office building. If you do your walking during hunting season, it's best to wear bright colors.

Orange County

Railroad buffs will be intrigued by the **Indiana Railway Museum,** located just north of **French Lick** at 8594 W. SR 56. Operated as a nonprofit corporation, the museum has its headquarters in the old Monon Railroad station, where several steam locomotives, a rare railway post office car, and a 1951 dining car are among the memorabilia on display; it's open free of charge from 8:30 a.m. to 4 p.m. Monday through Friday. Visitors can also buy a ticket and board the **French Lick Scenic Railway** for a 1.75-hour, 20-mile round-trip ride between French Lick and Cuzco, IN. A diesel locomotive pulls 1920s-era passenger cars away from the station and plunges into the wooded terrain of Hoosier National Forest, offering its passengers views of rugged Orange County backcountry where no roads penetrate. Along the way, the train passes through the 2,200-foot-long Burton Tunnel, one of Indiana's longest. Children are especially delighted by the Wild West train robberies staged on special weekends; other themed rides include the Easter Bunny Express, the Polar Express, and a haunted train ride known as the Legend of the Lost Train. For additional information, a schedule of train rides, and fares, contact the Indiana Railway Museum, PO Box 347, French Lick 47432; call (812) 936-2405 or (800) 748-7246; or visit frenchlickscenicrailway.org.

Approximately 1 mile north of French Lick on SR 56, visitors can see the magnificent **West Baden Springs Hotel.** The architectural masterpiece, once known as the "most unique hotel on Earth" and the "Carlsbad of America," was world famous in the early 1900s, but through the years it did not fare as well as French Lick's resort.

Begun in October 1901, construction on the West Baden Springs Hotel was completed eight and a half months later—an astonishing accomplishment in any day but truly extraordinary given the technology of the time. Its imaginative owner, Col. Lee Sinclair, had conjured up visions of a sumptuous hotel that established architects of the day said was impossible to build. Urged on by his daughter Lillian, Colonel Sinclair finally found an enterprising young architect who accepted the challenge not only to build the hotel but to do so for $414,000—with a $100-a-day penalty clause if construction took longer than the agreed-on 200 working days.

When finished, the dome above the immense central atrium, larger than the dome at St. Peter's Cathedral in Rome, was regarded as the "eighth wonder of the world." Two hundred feet in diameter, 130 feet above the floor, ribbed with twenty-four steel girders mounted on rollers to accommodate expansion and contraction, it remained the world's largest self-supporting dome until the Houston Astrodome was completed in 1965. The atrium floor was covered with 12 million Italian marble tiles, and the elaborate sunken gardens were planted with rare flowers from Europe and the Orient. Circling the atrium and its gardens were 708 guest rooms on six floors.

West Baden Springs Hotel thrived for thirty years, attracting an illustrious clientele that included Gen. John J. Pershing, J. M. Studebaker, Helen Keller, and Diamond Jim Brady, as well as the likes of Al Capone. In 1932, however, it became a casualty of the Great Depression.

Subsequently it served as winter headquarters for the old Hagenbeck-Wallace Circus, as a Jesuit school, and as the home of Northwood Institute, a college that trained its students for employment in the hotel restaurant field. During the Jesuits' tenancy, the face of the old hotel was altered to rid the building of some of its grander touches that the Jesuits felt were unseemly for their austere lifestyle. The Roman-style baths were wrecked and hauled away, the gardens were left untended, the lavish furniture was sold, the beautiful Moorish towers were removed from the roof, and the arabesque brickwork atop the building was straightened.

The hotel was allowed to deteriorate for years. In 1991, a 180-foot, six-story section of the once glorious hotel collapsed. The hotel was placed on the National Trust's list of eleven Most Endangered Historic Properties in the United States. Then a miracle happened. Indiana Landmarks, the largest non-profit preservation group in the nation, joined forces with Bloomington medical entrepreneurs Bill and Gayle Cook to save the hotel and the depressed area around it. The deal was finalized with a handshake by Bill Cook.

Today, a gorgeous formal Italianate-styled sunken garden features fountains and brick pathways, just as it did when the hotel was first built, and the Moorish towers have been replaced. The amazing atrium is once again a breathtaking wonder, and the entire six-story hotel has been restored to its Gilded Age grandeur, a grand old dame ready to welcome her guests.

The Cooks' investment not only saved West Baden Springs Hotel, but also restored French Lick Springs Hotel to its former glory. After about $600 million in renovations, "The Save of the Century" is once again flourishing.

French Lick's Pluto Water Claimed to Have Healing Powers

French Lick has long been a mecca for people seeking to improve their health.

More than 200 years ago, French traders were drawn to the area of French Lick because their livestock, attracted by the rich springs, flocked here to lick the mineral-rich waters and rocks. That's why the valley was called "The Lick."

In 1832, Dr. William Bowles bought some land and opened a swanky spa resort 10 years later. The hotel became an immediate success as people flocked from hundreds of miles to experience the touted healing powers of the mineral waters.

Dubbed Pluto Water because it came from the depths of the earth, the water was said to have twenty-two different minerals in it.

Bowles ran ads throughout the country boasting that the water cured fifty-five different ailments—ranging from arthritis and gout to impotence and exhaustion. Visitors would bathe in the water and they also would drink bottles of it.

A natural laxative, the water also was bottled for shipment around the world and carried the slogan "When Nature Won't, Pluto Will." Today, a French Lick Hotel display shows the old green bottles with their distinctive log of a red devil with horns, a tail, and a pitchfork.

A rare photograph in the hotel hall shows Franklin Delano Roosevelt with braces on his legs seated next to his wife at the 23rd Conference of Governors held in French Lick in 1931. After a bout with polio, Roosevelt relied on braces, crutches and wheelchairs—but he was seldom seen using them in public.

The **French Lick Springs Hotel** 1 mile to the south on SR 56 is nearly as luxurious as West Baden Springs. Whereas the latter is remarkable architecture and opulence, French Lick is gold leaf and glamour. Once visited by both celebrities and gangsters, it, too, had fallen into disrepair, but has also been fully restored with the help of Indiana Landmarks and Bill and Gayle Cook and their son Carl of Bloomington.

West Baden tours are offered daily at 2 and 4 p.m. on Friday and Saturday; 10 a.m. and 2 p.m. on Sunday. French Lick tours offered at noon Wednesday through Saturday. Tour tickets are available at Landmarks Emporium, Indiana Landmarks' shops in each hotel and the departure for the tours. For additional information and to make a reservation, call (812) 936-5870 or (866) 571-8687; indianalandmarks.org/tours.

Folks who want to try their luck can stop in the **French Lick Casino** located in French Lick Resort. Open 24 hours daily, the casino boasts the largest nonsmoking room in Indiana. The 51,000 square-foot, single level gaming facility has soaring 27-foot ceilings.

French Lick is also a golf paradise. Nowhere else in the world can a golfer play courses designed by Donald Ross, Pete Dye, and Tom Bendelow at one resort destination. The rolling hills of southern Indiana provide a beautiful and challenging golf course. The **Pete Dye Course at French Lick** hosted the 2015 Senior PGA Championship. No wonder, legendary designer Pete Dye carved the course into one of the highest points in Indiana. The **Donald Ross Course at French Lick** was originally constructed in 1917 and hosted the 1924 PGA Championship. The **Valley Links Course** is a nine-hole conversion of the original 18-hole Tom Bendelow Valley Links adjacent to the French Lick Springs Hotel.

Body Reflections, a beauty salon in French Lick, is home to the only museum of its kind in the world. Owner Tony Kendall has collected antiques related to hair styling for several years, and you can view them in his **Wild Hair Museum.**

Tony's collection includes vintage combs, hairbrushes, permanent-wave machines, razors, shears, and hair tonics. Relics heated by kerosene and gaslight share a shelf with more modern instruments heated by electricity. Tony's most prized possessions are a lock of hair that has been authenticated as belonging to Elvis Presley and a rare antique hair wreath. The wreath dates from Civil War times, when locks from generations of the same family were woven into an open-ended wreath of perfectly shaped flowers, with each flower representing an individual. Only a few survived because so many of them were burned during a plague scare in the early 1900s. People believed the hair could pass on the disease.

indianatrivia

Tomato juice was first served as a beverage at the French Lick Springs Hotel in 1917. The chef ran out of oranges, so he squeezed tomatoes instead.

Since Tony was featured in an A&E documentary about hair a few years back, he's become a very popular guy in the industry. He's had to expand a bit because people keep bringing him things for his collection. The aforementioned lock of the King's hair now occupies a place of honor in Tony's new Elvis room.

Tony's latest project, which he hopes will earn him a place in the *Guinness World Records,* is the construction of the world's largest hairball.

You can view Tony's collection free of charge at his salon at 448 S. Maple St. during his normal business hours of 9 a.m. to 6 p.m. Tuesday through Saturday; call (812) 936-4064 for additional information; bodyreflectionsfrenchlick. com.

Orleans has called itself the Dogwood Capital of Indiana since 1970, a few years after Mr. and Mrs. C. E. Wheeler started planting dogwood trees along SR 37, one of the town's main thoroughfares. It was a labor of love for the Wheelers, who believed that the dogwood's pink and white blooms had no equal for beauty. Today, the trees cover a 12-mile stretch between Mitchell on the north and Paoli on the south, and more trees are added each year in what is now a communitywide project. They're usually in full bloom in late April and early May.

Orange County is also the site of two of the Hoosier State's most unusual natural landmarks. On the southern edge of *Orangeville,* which lies about 7 miles southwest of Orleans via country roads, you can view the ***Orangeville Rise of the Lost River,*** designated both a State Nature Preserve and a National Natural Landmark. The country's longest underground river surfaces here as an artesian spring, flowing from a cave into a 220-foot-wide rock-walled pit at the base of a limestone bluff. The 3-acre preserve is well marked, and there's a pull-off for parking. For additional information, write or call the Department of Natural Resources, Division of Nature Preserves, 402 W. Washington St., Room W267, Indianapolis 46204; (317) 232-0209; in.gov/dnr/naturepreserve /4698.htm.

Not far from Paoli, on the edge of Hoosier National Forest, is an 88-acre tract of virgin woodland known as ***Pioneer Mothers Memorial Forest,*** whose magnificent trees range from 150 to 600 years old. Its crown jewel is the Walnut Cathedral, a moist cove that, according to the US Department of the Interior, contains the finest stand of black walnut trees in the entire country. From Paoli go south on SR 37 for about 1.25 miles to the Pioneer Mothers State Wayside on the east side of the road. From this picnic area, you can follow marked trails for a short distance into the memorial forest. Write or call the Forest Supervisor, Hoosier National Forest, 811 Constitution Ave., Bedford 47421; (812) 275-5987, (812) 275-5987, or (866) 302-4173; fs.usda.gov/hoosier.

Parke County

All of Parke County is a museum of *covered bridges.* Within its boundaries are more covered bridges than you'll find in any other county in the United States—more, in fact, than you'll find in most states. At last count, thirty-one of them were intact. What's more, they're all authentic, with the two oldest dating back to 1856 and the youngster of the bunch to 1920. All thirty-one were placed on the National Register of Historic Places in 1978.

So many bridges were built here because of the numerous zigzagging streams in the county. Most of the bridges still support traffic, and the folks in Parke County have mapped out four automobile routes that provide access to most of them. A free map outlining each route is available at the Parke County

Convention and Visitors Bureau, located at 401 E. Ohio St. in Rockville; hours vary; (765) 569-5226; coveredbridges.com.

The northwest route leads you to **West Union Bridge,** at 315 feet the longest in the county. The community of **Bridgeton,** with its many unusual shops, is a highlight of the southernmost route. Standing on the bank of Big Raccoon Creek next to the **Bridgeton Bridge** is the **Weise Mill.** It's been grinding meal since it was built in 1823, making it the oldest known gristmill west of the Allegheny Mountains that's still in service. Directly west of Rockville is the **Sim Smith Bridge,** which claims the distinction of being the county's only haunted bridge.

Parke County originally had more than fifty covered bridges, but several were lost to fire, flood, and natural deterioration before a preservation effort had begun. Each October since 1957, the county has celebrated its heritage with a ten-day **Covered Bridge Festival.** The nationally recognized event regularly lures some 500,000 visitors.

Another popular festival is the late-winter **Maple Fair,** which takes place when local sugar camps are producing maple syrup. For more information, write or call the Parke County Convention and Visitors Bureau (see contact information above).

If you head northeast from Rockville, you'll come to **Turkey Run State Park,** noted for its steep ravines, its sandstone formations, and the **Rocky Hollow–Falls Canyon State Nature Preserve,** which protects a lush primeval forest. The **Narrows Bridge,** one of the most photographed in the county, crosses Sugar Creek in the park. A tree-shaded inn in the park offers overnight accommodations in fifty-two rooms and twenty-one nearby cabins, and it has two swimming pools and four tennis courts; call (765) 597-2211 for additional information; in.gov/dnr/parklake/inns/turkeyrun/. Contact Turkey Run State Park, 8121 E. Park Rd., PO Box 37, Marshall 47859; (765) 597-2635; in.gov/dnr /parklake/2964.htm.

Although many Hoosiers have never heard of **Mordecai "Three Fingers" Brown,** he has never been forgotten by his hometown of **Nyesville** and by diehard baseball fans. Brown, who was born in 1876, earned his nickname at age seven when his right hand was mangled in a corn-grinding machine. Undaunted, he started throwing baseballs at a barn wall and developed a unique curve ball that made him one of the greatest pitchers ever to play the game.

During his fourteen years in the major leagues, Mordecai won 239 games and had a lifetime 2.06 earned-run average that remains to this day the third best in baseball history. Additionally, he had a lifetime batting average of .248, remarkable for a pitcher. His greatest fame came during his 1905–1916 tenure with the Chicago Cubs. While in Chicago he won twenty or more games six years in a row. He won twenty-nine games in 1908 and that same year became the first pitcher ever to record four consecutive shutouts. As the team's star pitcher, Mordecai helped the Cubs earn four National League pennants and two World Series championships.

When the arrival of the year 2000 prompted the compilation of lists of the greatest athletes of the twentieth century, *USA Today* listed Mordecai as one of the five greatest from Indiana, and *Sports Illustrated* listed him in the state's top ten. The great Ty Cobb once called Mordecai's curve ball "the most devastating pitch I have ever faced." When asked how he could achieve so much with only three fingers, Mordecai replied, "All I know is I had all the fingers I needed." In 1949, one year after his death, Mordecai Brown became the first Indiana native to be inducted into the Baseball Hall of Fame in Cooperstown, New York.

Today his memory is honored with a monument in a cornfield near Nyesville, where his boyhood home once stood. Engravings on the 3-foot-high, black-and-gray-granite marker depict the image of Mordecai launching his famous curve ball and relate the remarkable achievements of a man who turned adversity into achievement. To see the **Mordecai Brown monument,** go east from Billie Creek Village on US 36 a short distance to CR 160 East (also known as the Nyesville-Judson Road); turn north and proceed to Nyesville. The monument can be seen near Nyesville, about 100 yards off the road at 1309 Nyesville Rd. Ask locally for exact directions.

Perry County (Central Time Zone)

Besides its bountiful natural beauty, this Ohio River county is worth visiting for its array of unusual monuments.

If **Tell City** has a landmark, it is the life-size statue of William Tell and his son that serves as the centerpiece for the fountain in front of city hall. The statue is a reflection of the town's Swiss heritage and a tribute to the legendary Swiss hero from whom Tell City took its name. Town residents were delighted when, in 1974, plans were announced for the construction of the fountain that would honor the town's namesake, but they never dreamed it would cause such a fuss.

After the statue had been formed by Evansville sculptor Don Ingle, it was sent to a New York foundry to be cast in bronze. Ingle and his wife then personally picked up the 500-pound statue in New York, placed it in a rented U-Haul van, and headed home for the formal dedication. Imagine their horror when, after spending the night in an Ohio motel, they discovered that the van—statue and all—had been stolen as they slept. Everyone got into the act, with local police and the FBI cooperating in a frantic search and news media throughout the country warning everyone to be on the lookout for the kidnapped William Tell. The nationwide furor was such that the thief eventually abandoned his ill-gotten gain on a side street in Cleveland, and the statue was escorted the rest of the way home without further ado. You can see William Tell today in his place of honor atop the fountain—one arm holding his crossbow, the other arm around his son's shoulder, and not an apple in sight.

Poised above SR 66 near *Troy,* a towering 19-foot-tall statue of Christ overlooks the Ohio River, arms extended in an eternal blessing of all who gaze on it. Herbert Jogerst, a German artist, sculpted the statue when he was a prisoner of war in Indiana during World War II. It stands on a bluff once owned by Robert Fulton, of steamboat fame, and is now part of a summer camp for physically challenged children. Illuminated at night, the all-white *Christ of the Ohio* is always visible to travelers on land or water.

At St. Augustine's Church in *Leopold* stands the *Shrine of Our Lady of Consolation,* whose strange history dates back to the Civil War. Three young Union Army soldiers from Perry County, members of the church, were confined in the infamous prison at Andersonville, GA. They vowed to one another that if they lived through the horror of that experience they would donate a shrine to their church as a token of their gratitude. Miraculously they all survived, and one of them personally made a trip to Belgium to oversee the making of an exact reproduction of a shrine he remembered seeing in a small village church there.

Some historians claim that, unable to obtain the reproduction he desired, the young man stole the original and transported it back to Indiana, sparking an international incident between the governments of the two countries. It happened, however, that Leopold had been named for the Leopold who was then king of Belgium. The Belgian leader was so pleased to learn of his namesake that he allowed the shrine to remain there. It can be seen today, a statue of Mary and the infant Jesus, each wearing a white gown, a blue robe, and a crown of jewels. The church is located at 18020 Lafayette St. Call (812) 843-5143 for information.

One of the Hoosier State's finest historical landmarks, the huge, castle-like *Cannelton Cotton Mill,* was a beehive of activity from 1849 to 1965. Once the busiest industry in Indiana, it contained the most modern textile machinery, rivaling the better-known mills of New England. Some 400 laborers operating 372 looms spun raw cotton into thread and cloth; a good worker in the old days could sometimes earn as much as $4.50 a day. Union Army uniforms were made here during the Civil War.

Often honored for its architecture and described as one of the most outstanding engineering feats of its time in the Midwest, the mammoth stone structure is 60 feet wide by 280 feet long and has 5-foot-thick interior walls. Two copper-roofed towers, each more than 100 feet tall, serve as landmarks for Ohio River traffic. One of the towers held water that could be used to flood each of the five floors in case of fire, a constant threat in a cotton mill. The second tower, besides serving as a fire escape, was designed to reduce the risk of fire; it contained five trapdoors that were opened twice each working day so that air could be drawn down through a chimney to remove accumulated lint.

Despite its magnificence and its status as a National Historic Landmark, the mill remained a gaunt gray ghost until 2001. That was when government grants provided the wherewithal to renovate the mill and convert it into an innovative apartment complex. The first tenants moved into the complex in January 2002, and the townsfolk celebrated the mill's rebirth at a special festival in June 2002. For information about the mill, located on the southwest corner of 4th and Washington Streets at 310 Washington St. in *Cannelton,* write or call the Perry County Convention and Visitors Bureau, 333 7th St., Tell City 47586; (812) 547-7933 or (888) 343-6262; pickperry.com.

Rising from a soybean field not far east of Cannelton is a grim reminder of one of Indiana's worst air tragedies. The *Air Crash Memorial Monument,* 9 feet tall and 12 feet wide, recalls a March day in 1960 when a Northwest Airlines flight from Minneapolis to Miami plummeted to the ground at this spot. According to a witness, the plane's wings simply broke off in midair. The plane

Gone, but Not Forgotten

On August 21, 1865, the steamboat USS *Argosy III* was transporting a group of mustered-out Civil War veterans up the Ohio River to Cincinnati. A sudden storm hurled the boat against some rocks near the Perry County town of Magnet (then known as Rono) and caused its boiler to explode. Ten Union soldiers, on their way home after surviving years of brutal warfare, either drowned or were scalded to death. The survivors and local farmers pulled the dead from the waters and buried them in a mass grave.

The history of that accident and the mass burial site did not come to light until 1962. To commemorate the dead, the federal government supplied ten white stone markers that were anchored in a concrete base, and the Indiana Civil War Centennial Commission supplied a *Civil War Memorial Grave* marker. The names of the victims are carved into nine of the stones; the 10th bears the poignant message Unknown US Soldier. One day before the centennial of the riverboat tragedy, a gathering of Perry County citizens and interested visitors officially dedicated the site.

There are no road signs to direct you there, but you can reach it by taking US 66 to the turnoff road for Magnet. Go east through Magnet and continue for about 0.5 mile to the cemetery, nestled in a grove of maples, poplars, laurels, and cottonwood on the right.

fell 18,000 feet straight down, literally burying itself in the ground. The impact killed all sixty-three people on board and created a crater 20 feet deep and 30 feet wide. It took two weeks to complete the recovery operation; debris and body parts were scattered over 5 miles in every direction. Even today, small pieces of debris occasionally surface after a heavy rain. Investigators later blamed the crash on structural faults in the engine, which caused a flutter in the wings that caused them to snap off.

The Cannelton Kiwanis Club raised funds to erect the monument seen today at the crash site. Topped by a "torch of life," the granite memorial is inscribed with the names of all of the victims.

To reach the monument, which stands on a 1-acre dedicated site, head east from Cannelton on SR 66 to SR 166 and turn right. Follow 166 southeast about 1.5 miles to Millstone Road. Turn left onto Millstone Road and proceed approximately 1 mile to the monument on the left side of the road.

Another monument, a tall obelisk in Tell City's **Greenwood Cemetery,** memorializes the same tragedy. Here, an 1,800-square-foot plot was set aside in which to bury 55 of the crash victims, of whom only 17 could be identified. The obelisk, inscribed with the names of the dead, was placed here by Northwest Airlines.

Visit **Eagle's Bluff Park** on E. SR 66 near Cannelton for a fascinating view of Ohio River traffic passing through the **Cannelton Locks,** located 3 miles upstream from Cannelton. Twenty-five million gallons of water are transferred when the locks operate. You'll find a lockside walkway and an observation tower from which you can see not only the locks but the roiling water at the base of Cannelton Dam; open daily free of charge. For information about the park, contact the Perry County Parks and Recreation Department, 125 S. 8th St., Room 24, Cannelton 47520; (812) 547-3453.; perrycounty.in.gov/departments /parks-and-recreation. For information about the Cannelton Locks and Dam, contact the US Army Corps of Engineers, 5821 E. SR 66, Cannelton 47520-9725; (812) 547-2962 or (877) 444-6777; lrl.usace.army.mil/Missions/Civil-Works/ Navigation/Locks-and-Dams/Cannelton-Locks-and-Dam/

While in Tell City, tour the **Tell City Pretzel Company,** which may be the only company in the United States and one of the few in the world that still produces pretzels the original way—by hand-twisting them. A Swiss baker brought the recipe with him from Europe when he settled here more than 100 years ago. Although the recipe is still a secret, passed down from owner to owner, visitors are welcome to watch the twisters at work each Monday through Friday; open from 8 a.m. to 5 p.m. The 12,000 pretzels produced daily are sold on the premises and by mail order. Tell City Pretzels is located at 1315 Washington St., Tell City; (812) 548-4499 or (877) 334-4499; tellcitypretzel.com.

Posey County (Central Time Zone)

In 1814 a group of German Lutheran separatists migrated westward from Pennsylvania to the verdant valley of the Wabash River. There they purchased some 30,000 acres of land along the riverbank and carved from the dense woodlands the personification of a dream—a tiny communal settlement they named Harmony. An industrious people, the Harmonists established a variety of successful industries that included the manufacture of fine silks and whiskey distilling, and their products were much in demand throughout the eastern United States. They developed prefabricated houses, dug tunnels beneath them, and used the cool air therein to air-condition their dwellings. Oranges were grown year-round in their greenhouses. Eventually they found themselves with enough leisure time to start bickering among themselves, and in 1825 their leader, Father George Rapp, sold the entire town to Robert Owen, a wealthy industrialist from Scotland.

Owen envisioned a utopia of a different sort, a commune that focused on innovative education and intellectual pursuits. His *New Harmony* lured scientists, social reformers, writers, and artists whose ideas and creations made a lasting impact on our country's history. America's first free public school system, kindergarten, day care center, free library, trade school, women's club, and civic dramatic club came to fruition here. One of Owen's sons, David Dale Owen, became an eminent geologist and was commissioned to make the first survey of new government lands in the West. After David Dale was appointed US Geologist in 1839, he ran the US Geological Survey from New Harmony for seventeen years. Another of Owen's sons, Richard, entered Congress, became an early crusader for the rights of women, and drafted the legislation that established the Smithsonian Institution. Yet another son became president of Indiana's Purdue University.

Although many of the concepts developed at Owen's New Harmony have survived, the commune foundered quickly in 1827. One reason for this was that its inhabitants did not possess the husbandry skills needed to feed its populace. While lofty ideas and ideals were being discussed inside, the hogs were invading the vegetables outside.

New Harmony was never deserted, however. Its reputation as an intellectual center gradually faded, but many residents stayed on, putting down roots that have kept the community alive to this day.

In the 1940s the late Jane Owen, wife of a direct descendant of Robert Owen, visited here and became so enamored of the settlement she initiated a restoration project. Today New Harmony is a state historical site, and people come from all over the country to take a 12-point tour that traces the history of the settlement from its original log cabins to some striking structures added in recent years.

Enclosed within the brick walls of the Harmonist cemetery at the west end of Granary Street are more than 200 unmarked graves—symbolic of continued equality in death—and several Native American burial mounds. The Labyrinth, a fascinating maze of paths and hedges on the south edge of town, represents the twists and turns and choices that confront each of us in our passage through life.

Completed in 1979, the stark white ***Atheneum*** that rises from a meadow near the riverbank has garnered many honors for its architectural design. The visitor center within periodically shows a film entitled *The New Harmony*

The Thousand-Year Storm

Tornadoes, nature's most destructive storms, occur more frequently in the United States than in any other country on earth. Seventy-five percent of the world's tornadoes take place in the United States, and the vast majority of those strike our country's midsection. As residents of a tornado-prone heartland, Hoosiers are well acquainted with these violent whirlwinds (Indiana experiences an average of twenty-three tornadoes each year). Few people today, however, remember that Indiana was one of three states devastated by the single most destructive tornado in recorded history.

The weather forecast for much of the Midwest on March 18, 1925, called for "rains and strong shifting winds." It was a common forecast for a spring day in this part of the world. Midwesterners went about their business as usual but kept a wary eye on the sky, aware at all times how violent a spring storm could suddenly become.

No one, however, expected the unprecedented fury of the tornado that dropped from the skies that day. The Tri-State Tornado, as it is known in the record books, is the one tornado that stands apart from all others—before and since. The tornado was born at 1:01 p.m. in the Missouri Ozarks. From there it raced northeastward across the Mississippi, through Illinois, and into Indiana, hugging the ground with a vengeance for 3.5 hours. It did not lift, skip, or, until the last few miles of its life, veer from its straightforward path. When it finally dissipated, it had traveled 219 miles at forward speeds of more than 70 miles per hour. Its winds at times were in excess of 300 miles per hour. Its width varied from 0.5 mile to more than 1 mile wide. (By way of comparison, the average tornado lasts a few minutes, travels 5 miles at a forward speed of 30 miles per hour, produces winds of 150 miles per hour or less, and averages 220 yards in width.)

When the storm crossed the Wabash River and entered Indiana at about 4 p.m., it headed straight for Griffin, a small village located approximately 3 miles from the river in northwestern Posey County. It took less than 3 minutes for the twister to obliterate the entire town. Not a single structure was left standing. Stunned survivors could only guess where they had once lived.

Still the twister raced on, turning slightly northward toward Owensville and Princeton. Although narrowing in width, it increased its forward speed to nearly 75 miles per hour—faster than its top speed in either Missouri or Illinois. It created havoc in Owensville and swept away half of Princeton before finally exhausting itself at 4:30 p.m., about 3 miles southwest of Petersburg.

As survivors came together in the aftermath of the storm, tales of bizarre phenomena surfaced. The river mud that had been sucked up into the tornado by the time it reached Griffin left people there with mud so thoroughly embedded in their skin that they were unrecognizable. A baby, completely covered with mud, was dug from a ditch after its cries were heard; no one in the area had a baby, and its rescuers never learned if its parents had been found. At the site of one house, only a carton of eggs and a remnant of the floor on which it was sitting were found intact. A cow was found standing and chewing her cud, seemingly unperturbed, although the barn around her had been lifted up and carried away. An office in Princeton was razed to the ground, but a bundle of paychecks that had been stored in an office cabinet was found undamaged 55 miles away.

Property damage wrought by the storm was estimated at $16.5 million in 1925 dollars (equal to more than $159 million today). The storm had completely annihilated four towns and 15,000 homes, severely damaged six more towns, and injured 2,027 people. Most significant of all, there were 695 confirmed deaths, still a record for a single tornado in this country.

On average, 800 to 1,000 tornadoes occur in the United States each year. Some 1,800 tornadoes were reported in 2004. But to this day, the 1925 Tri-State Tornado remains the deadliest tornado in US history, a rare storm that some weather historians say comes along once in a thousand years.

In April 2004, ten survivors of that storm were among the onlookers as a black memorial marker was unveiled in the town of Griffin. The Indiana Historical Bureau marker on the southeast corner of Main and First Streets relates the horror of that day, and a brass plaque attached to a rock alongside the marker contains the names of Griffin residents who lost their lives.

Experience and exhibits a scale model of the original town. Open 9:30 a.m. to 5 p.m. daily; closed major holidays. Located at 401 N. Arthur St.; (812) 682-4474 or (800) 231-2168; usi.edu/hnh/atheneum.php.

Serving as the altar for the ***Roofless Church,*** a paved courtyard that's open to the sky, is a unique dome that's shaped like an inverted rosebud but casts the shadow of a full-blown rose. Its design was inspired by writer George Sand, who remarked that the sky was the only roof vast enough to embrace all of worshiping humanity. When Paul Tillich, the world-renowned philosopher and theologian, visited here in 1963, he was so impressed by the Roofless Church that he said it alone justified our century. When Tillich died not long afterward, his ashes were buried in ***Tillich Park*** opposite the church.

One of the most beautiful sights at New Harmony, however, is a seasonal event orchestrated by nature. The first golden raintree in the nation was planted at New Harmony, and today there is scarcely a lawn or street anywhere in town that does not boast at least one of these lovely trees. An ornamental tree that originated in Asia, the golden raintree is unusually beautiful throughout the year but is most glorious around the third week in June when it bursts into full bloom, then sheds its petals in a virtual shower of brilliant gold. There's no place in the United States where this tree grows in greater quantity.

New Harmony is easily explored on foot. Historic New Harmony, Inc., has its headquarters at 506 1/2 Main St. and offers general information as well as guided tours for nominal fees; office hours vary. Write or call the organization at PO Box 579, New Harmony 47631; (812) 682-4488 or (800) 231-2168; usi .edu/hnh.

By driving south from New Harmony on SR 69 for about 24 miles, almost to the Ohio River, you are suddenly confronted with a scene that might have been transported here from the Deep South. **Hovey Lake** resembles a south- ern swamp, particularly in the slough areas to the east of the lake. Its waters are studded with huge bald cypress trees—one noteworthy old patriarch has lived to about 260 years of age. Along the lakeshore are southern red oak, wild pecans, mistletoe, holly, and swamp privet.

Birders spot great blue herons, American egrets, double-breasted cormo- rants, and pileated woodpeckers. Osprey and blue heron have been known to nest here, and white ibis, bald eagles, hawks, and owls frequent the area. In the autumn, usually beginning in the first week in October, some 500,000 ducks and geese arrive for the winter.

Hovey Lake, formed about 500 years ago, is an oxbow lake that occupies an old channel of the nearby Ohio River. It's now part of a 6,900-acre state fish and wildlife area, but even if you don't like to fish, you can rent a rowboat, glide among the majestic trees that rise from the surface of the water, and enjoy the serenity and seclusion of this lovely place. When seen through the mists of early morning, Hovey Lake takes on a dreamlike aura.

Close to the launching ramp, you'll find an oak-shaded picnic area and forty-eight primitive campsites. Write or call Hovey Lake State Fish and Wildlife Area, 15010 SR 69 South, Mt. Vernon 47620; (812) 838-2927; in.gov/dnr/fishwild /3092.htm.

To see one of Indiana's most intriguing nature preserves, go west from the entrance to Hovey Lake Fish and Wildlife Area for about 1.25 miles to the first intersection and turn north. You're now on the gravel portion of CR 300 West. Go north for about 1 mile to a parking lot on the left. From here, a trail and boardwalk traverse the 598-acre **Twin Swamps State Nature Preserve,** home to a cypress swamp and an abundance of rare plants, animals, and birds. Part of the trail may be wet and muddy, especially in the spring and summer, so it's a good idea to wear waterproof footwear. You can pick up a brochure that describes the preserve in a wooden box on a post just before you enter the swamp; open daily free of charge. For additional information, contact the Indiana Department of Natural Resources, Division of Nature Preserves, 402 W. Washington St., Room W267, Indianapolis 46204; (317) 232-4052; in.gov/dnr/naturepreserve/4698.htm.

The Nature Conservancy has called the Hovey Lake and Twin Swamps pristine environment one of the "last great places."

Putnam County

In the valley of Big Walnut Creek lies one of the most beautiful and unusual natural areas in Indiana. The clear waters of the creek calmly meander southward through steep ravines studded with limestone outcroppings. A great blue heron rookery that has been continuously occupied for more than 60 years shares the forest with the great horned owl and more than 120 other species of birds. What is thought to be the largest sugar maple in the world, as well as the two largest sassafras trees, and the second biggest hemlock in Indiana, thrive within the preserve's confines.

Located about 1.5 miles northeast of Bainbridge, the **Big Walnut State Nature Preserve** lies primarily along that part of the creek between Pine Bluff Covered Bridge and Rolling Stone Covered Bridge. It's open daily, free of charge, during daylight hours. For additional information and exact directions, write or call the Indiana Department of Natural Resources, Division of Nature Preserves, 402 W. Washington St., Room W267, Indianapolis 46204; (317) 232-4052; in.gov/dnr/naturepreserve/4698.htm.

It took an act of Congress to get it there, but one of only two buzz bombs in the country is displayed on the courthouse lawn in **Greencastle** (the other is in storage at the Smithsonian Institution in Washington, DC). Perched atop a giant limestone *V,* the German-built bomb is one of the first guided missiles. It was among some captured military ordnance brought to the United States at the end of World War II, and a local Veterans of Foreign Wars post was given permission by Congress to bring the bomb to Indiana for use as part of a memorial. The buzz bomb monument can be seen at the corner of Washington and Jackson Streets. For additional

indianatrivia

Eli Lilly, who later founded the world-renowned pharmaceutical company, opened his first drugstore in Greencastle in early 1861.

information, contact the Putnam County Convention & Visitors Bureau at 12 W. Washington St., Greencastle, 46135; (765) 653-8743 or (800) 829-4639 or visit goputnam.com.

Spencer County (Central Time Zone)

Poised majestically atop a hill, the *St. Meinrad Archabbey* emerges unexpectedly from the trees and hills of northeastern Spencer County. Your eyes are first drawn to the soaring twin spires of the Abbey Church, then to the entire complex of beautiful buildings that house a theological school, a college, a monastery, and such income-producing enterprises as a publishing company, a winery, and a meat-packing plant.

When the abbey was founded by immigrant missionaries from Switzerland in 1854, the monks themselves transported the sandstone from a quarry 1 mile distant, hand-chipped it into the desired shape, and erected buildings patterned after the European medieval style so vivid in their memories. Newer, more modern buildings appear among the old ones these days, but all interiors remain starkly simple in keeping with the order's dedication to a spiritual rather than materialistic lifestyle.

Visitors who roam the well-maintained grounds find themselves in the company of priests and brothers in simple black gowns—teachers, lay employees, and students who are training for the priesthood. Although silence is part of the Benedictine life, it is expected only from 9 p.m. through breakfast the following day and at all times in the halls of the monastery. Otherwise, the monks and brothers are fun-loving, hospitable people who enjoy conversing with visitors. Overnight accommodations are available by reservation.

You're welcome to join the monks for a worship service; Mass is in English. Brochures for self-guided tours can be picked up at the Guest House Office; hours vary. Free guided tours are available by advance appointment at 1:30 p.m. Saturday; write or call St. Meinrad Archabbey, 200 Hill Dr., St. Meinrad 47577; (812) 357-6611 or (800) 581-6905; saintmeinrad.org. The abbey is located on SR 62, just south of I-64, near the Perry-Spencer county line; follow the signs.

Two notable residents have made their homes in this county, and it would be tough to decide who is more famous—unless you are six years old or younger.

The US Postal Service receives several million pieces of mail each Christmas addressed to Santa Claus, and it's all forwarded to Santa Claus's true domicile—a small town in southern Indiana. A few million more letters and packages are sent to the local postmaster with the request that they be stamped

Santa Claus Comes to Town

A long time ago, a group of people lived in a small, southern Indiana community known as Santa Fe. When the Christmas season rolled around, the townspeople were so excited that for the first time they would have their own post office to mail their greetings and gifts.

Unfortunately, a big official envelope arrived notifying residents that Indiana already had a "Santa Fe." The town couldn't get a post office until it had a new name. The people thought and thought, but every name they came up with seemed already to be taken. So the town that was formed mostly by German settlers in the late 1840s became known by the sad moniker of the "Nameless Town."

Determined to finally get their name and post office, the citizens of Nameless Town decided to discuss the matter at the town's 1852 Christmas Eve celebration. Gathered around the potbellied, wood-burning stove in the little log church, folks suggested this name and that. They even mentioned naming the town Wyttenbach after the popular circuit-riding preacher, the Reverend Christian Wyttenbach, who had just preached the holiday service. Although he was honored, the reverend respectfully declined. He didn't even live there.

Suddenly, a cold December gust blew open the door of the church. In the distance could be heard the faint sound of sleigh bells ringing through the quiet winter night. It was quite puzzling since there was no one around for miles. Everyone was in the tiny church.

But the children were not puzzled. The voice of a small child excitedly rang out, "It's Santa Claus, it's Santa Claus." The congregation had its answer. Nameless Town became Santa Claus.

And the name of Santa Claus, Indiana—along with its distinctive postmark—has become known around the world. On May 21, 1856, the US Post Office Department approved a post office for the newly renamed town of Santa Claus, Indiana. The tiny Hoosier town is the only place in America named after the Jolly Ol' Elf, and every year—well, practically, every day—they go crazy for Christmas.

with the **Santa Claus,** IN, postmark before being sent on to their final destinations. Pretty heady stuff for a town with a population of about 2,400, give or take a few elves.

Although the town has borne its unusual name since 1852, it became world famous only after Robert Ripley featured it in his *Believe It or Not* column in 1929. Such a hullabaloo followed that the annual Town Christmas Party had to be rescheduled for early October, when there was time to deal with such things. Today, the **Santa Claus Post Office** probably gets more visitors than any other post office in the country. Folks can't believe the stacks of mail they see there each year just before Christmas, sent there in batches from all over the world to be hand-stamped with a postmark that changes each year but always features an image of Santa. Of course, they also receive letters addressed to the man himself, and volunteers from the community make it their mission to see that each one is personally answered.

The town is all about fun all year long. In fact, in July 2011 the readers of *USA Today* chose Santa Claus as one of the top six most-fun towns in the country. The town was further honored in December 2011 when *Forbes* magazine named it one of world's top ten Christmas destinations. Virtually everything in the community is Christmas themed. Visitors will find a Santa Claus Museum, Santa's Candy Castle, a giant Santa Claus statue, and Santa's Stables, which offer a family friendly horseback-riding experience (sorry, no reindeer). The names of just about everything contribute to the aura of fantasy—Silver Bell Terrace, Donner Lane, Sled Run, Lake Rudolph, Lake Holly, Lake Noel, the Snowflake Drive-in, and the Christmas Lake Village housing development. Town shops carry out the Christmas theme in their architecture, and Santa Claus Land opened in 1946 as the first theme park in the nation.

Santa Claus Land has since been renamed **Holiday World,** but it still has all the attractions that endeared it to countless children—and adults—in the past. It also boasts 3 of the world's top wooden roller coasters and **Splashin' Safari,** a water park that TripAdvisor has named the number-one water park in the world. In keeping with its policy of adding a new ride each year, the park introduced a new water ride called Cheetah Chase in 2020. The coaster invites riders to experience a water-powered flat launch before racing against their families toward the finish line. The ride features the first-ever head-to-head dueling zone on a water coaster. Additionally, visitors have repeatedly named Holiday World tops in friendliness and cleanliness

The one-price admission to both parks, extremely reasonable by today's standards, includes all rides, all shows and attractions, an unlimited amount of free soft drinks, free sunscreen, free inner tubes in the water park, free parking, and reasonable food prices. One-day admission starts at $34.99. In general, Holiday World and Splashin' Safari are open from early May to October; operating hours and days vary from year to year; it's best to check the schedule in advance. Write Holiday World, PO Box 179, Santa Claus 47579; call (812) 937-4401 or (877) 463-2645; or visit holidayworld.com. The privately owned **Lake Rudolph Campground and RV Resort** adjacent to Holiday World offers RVs or cabins to rent as well as RV and camping sites; (888) 929-7010 or lakerudolph.com. Santa Claus, the village, is located at the junction of SRs 162 and 245 in the north central part of the county.

Spencer County's second famous resident is immortalized in the pages of history books. When people think of Abraham Lincoln, they usually think of the state of Illinois, but it was in Indiana that young Abe went to school, worked the land, and grew to manhood. Abe's father, Thomas Lincoln, brought his small family here in 1816 and homesteaded 160 acres along the banks of Little Pigeon Creek. Indiana was a wilderness then, a forest of giant oaks, maples, and hickories where open views of even 200 yards were rare. Lincoln himself described it thus, in a poem he wrote many years after leaving the state.

When first my father settled here
'Twas then the frontier line.
The panther's scream filled the night with fear,
And bears preyed on the swine.

In 1818, when Abe was nine and his sister Sarah was eleven, their beloved mother died, and little more than a year later a lonely Thomas married Sara Bush Johnston. A widow with three children, she raised Abe and Sarah as

Abraham Lincoln's Years in Indiana

The young boy kneels before a grave, telling his baby brother goodbye. It's December 1816, and the family is leaving Knob Creek, Kentucky, for the Indiana frontier.

But first, seven-year-old Abraham Lincoln wants to visit his brother Thomas' final resting spot. The baby had lived only long enough to receive his father's name.

Although it's early winter, Thomas and Nancy Hanks Lincoln are leaving their Kentucky home. Tired of trouble over property rights, the Lincolns have decided life would be better in Indiana, where people can buy land directly from the government. Besides, Thomas Lincoln does not believe in slavery, and Indiana has no slavery.

The family had no way of knowing that their son would grow up to become the sixteenth president of the United States. Living in Indiana from a youngster of seven to a young man of twenty-one, Abraham Lincoln later said that he gained many of his values and skills as a Hoosier. The oft-quoted man said, "Here I grew up," when recalling his life in the Indiana wilderness from 1816 to 1830.

Abe worked with his father—splitting rails, plowing and planting, building a cabin, and drawing water from a spring. The log cabin was only 18 feet square with a packed dirt floor and a stone fireplace used for both cooking and heating. Abe described the place as "the very spot where grew the bread that formed my bones."

Although he was still a child, Abe was large for his age and had enough strength to swing an ax. For as long as he lived in Indiana, he was seldom without his ax. He later called it "that most useful instrument."

In the fall of 1818, tragedy struck the family. Nancy Hanks Lincoln went to tend some neighbors who were ill. As "milk sickness" struck the Little Pigeon Creek settlement,

Abraham's mother herself became a victim. Although they didn't know it back then, milk sickness was caused by the white snakeroot plant. The illness was most common in dry years when cows wandered from poor pastures into the woods in search of food. The illness developed when a person ate the butter or drank the milk of an animal that had eaten the plant. Kind of like arsenic, the white snakeroot plant has pretty, white flowers in late summer, but it is toxic.

Recovery was slow and might never be complete. But more often an attack was fatal. So it was for Nancy Hanks Lincoln. On October 5, 1818, she died. Thomas and Abraham hammered together a rough wooden coffin and the family buried wife and mother on a wooded knoll south of the cabin. Abraham was only nine; his sister Sarah was eleven.

In November 1819, Thomas journeyed back to Kentucky in search of a new wife. He found her in Sarah Bush Johnston, a widow with three children.

On December 2, 1819, they were married in Elizabethtown, Kentucky. On January 20, 1828, Abe's sister died in childbirth at age twenty. Her child, a boy, was stillborn. Sarah Lincoln Grigsby was buried with her baby in the churchyard behind the Little Pigeon Creek Baptist Church. Her husband, Aaron Grigsby, who outlived her by only three years, was later buried beside her. Their graves are now located within the boundary of Lincoln State Park.

The two most important women in young Abe's life were now gone. The following year, the Lincolns decided to quit Indiana for the fertile prairies of Illinois. In fourteen years, Thomas Lincoln had wrung only a modest living from his land. The family also feared a new outbreak of the terrible scourge of milk sickness.

Again, Abraham Lincoln is bidding farewell at another grave—that of his mother. Abraham Lincoln, product of the Kentucky hills and Indiana forests, is now on his way to his place in history.

though they were her own, lavishing love and affection on them. She recognized the intimations of future greatness in young Abe and encouraged him to study, as his biological mother had before her, and Abe, on his part, loved her as few children love even their natural parents. When an adult Abe said, "All that I am, or hope to be, I owe to my angel Mother," he was speaking of his stepmother.

Lincoln left Indiana when he was twenty-one and moved to Illinois with his family, but his tenure in Spencer County is honored in a series of memorials. The **Lincoln Boyhood National Memorial** is next door to Lincoln State Park on SR 162, just south of Lincoln City. Abe's biological mother, Nancy Hanks Lincoln, is buried at the memorial, and her grave and the reconstructed Lincoln cabin can be visited in this 200-acre park. A living-history farm that covers 80 acres of the Lincolns' original homestead is worked as Abe and his father once worked it and provides a fascinating, accurate insight into a way of life that shaped one of our nation's greatest men.

At the handsome visitor center, you can view exhibits related to Lincoln's fourteen years in Indiana and see a 27-minute film about his life. You can also learn much about the human side of Lincoln, little-known facts that breathe life into the saintly image. Young Abe, for instance, loved to wrestle and was recognized as one of the area's best tusslers. His great physical strength earned him the nickname "young Hercules of Pigeon Creek," and he could hoist more weight and drive an ax deeper than any other man around. In 1828, his horizons widened greatly when he accompanied the son of the richest man in the community on a flatboat journey down the Ohio and Mississippi Rivers to New Orleans. And one can only speculate how the course of history might have differed had Abe grown up in Kentucky, where slavery was legal. The national memorial is open 8 a.m. to 5 p.m. daily early May to late October and 8 a.m. to 4:30 p.m. the rest of the year; closed major winter holidays; there's a nominal admission fee. Costumed interpreters work the farm from mid-April to late September. Write the Lincoln Boyhood National Memorial, National Park Service, 3027 E. South St., PO Box 1816, Lincoln City 47552; call (812) 937-4541; or visit nps.gov/libo.

The adjacent **Lincoln State Park,** which covers nearly 1,800 acres, includes the grave of Lincoln's sister, who died in childbirth; the site of the Little Pigeon River Primitive Baptist Church, where the Lincoln family worshiped; and the site of the first school attended by Abe, who was eleven years old at the time. You'll find many opportunities here for outdoor recreation, as well as campsites and housekeeping cabins.

A public plaza honoring the 200th birthday of President Abraham Lincoln (February 12, 1809) and his years as a boy in Indiana opened at the park in 2009. A large circular plaza is punctuated with limestone pedestals and interpretive signs signifying key milestones in Lincoln's formative Indiana years between ages seven and twenty-one. A central half circle reminds visitors of young Abraham's growth from boyhood to manhood; in the near future, it will contain a twice-life-size bronze bust of Lincoln, accompanied by some of his quotes.

Another park venue, the **Lincoln Amphitheatre,** is an outdoor theater that offers different productions from late April to late September. A roof protects against inclement weather, so that the show can go on. For a schedule and prices, contact the amphitheater at 15032 N. CR 300 East, PO Box 7-21, Lincoln City 47552; (812) 937-92329. The box office is open from 9 a.m. to 5 p.m. Monday through Friday; the park admission fee is waived for people who are coming just to see a theater production.

Lincoln State Park is open daily year-round during daylight hours; a nominal vehicle admission fee is charged. Write or call Lincoln State Park, SR 162, Box 216, Lincoln City 47552; (812) 937-4710; in.gov/dnr/parklake/2979.htm.

If you visit here in April through October, you may want to include a visit to the nearby *Colonel William Jones State Historic Site,* where you'll see the restored 1830s home of a merchant, farmer, and Civil War soldier who was a friend and former employer of Lincoln's. He was also a politician who first exposed Lincoln to Whig politics; the Whig Party evolved into the Republican Party in 1854, the party to which Lincoln belonged when he was elected president in 1860. The Jones home is now listed on both the Indiana Register of Historic Sites and Structures and the National Register of Historic Places. Situated on 100 acres of forest, the site also offers a self-guided nature trail, a picnic area, and a restored log barn. It's located at 620 E. CR 1575 North in *Gentryville.* Grounds can be seen daily free of charge; guided weekend tours of the home are available by advance reservation. The home is open mid-March through mid-December, Wednesday through Saturday from 9 a.m. to 5 p.m.; Sunday from 1 p.m. to 5 p.m. Additional information is available at Lincoln State Park or by writing Jones House State Historic Site, 620 E. CR 1575 N., Gentryville 47537; call (812) 937-1979; abrahamlincolnonline.org/lincoln/sites/jones.htm.

On the banks of the Ohio River just west of Troy, the *Lincoln Ferry Landing State Wayside Park* on SR 66 preserves another historical segment of Abe's life. Here, as an employee of a local farmer, sixteen-year-old Abe operated a ferry across the mouth of Anderson Creek, a tributary of the Ohio now called Anderson River. To increase his income, Abe built himself a scow to carry passengers to Ohio River steamboats in midstream. His first experience with the legal profession came when he was hauled into a Kentucky court for ferrying passengers on the Ohio without a license (the Ohio River was considered part of Kentucky). Lincoln pleaded his own case, stating that he didn't believe the law applied to a ferryman who went only halfway across the river. Agreeing with him, the judge dismissed the case. Abe's fascination with the law began with that encounter.

Sullivan County

The town of *Dugger* was built because of coal, laid out in 1879 in conjunction with the construction of the adjacent Dugger Coal Mine. To celebrate their heritage, the townsfolk established the *Dugger Coal Museum* in 1980. Visitors to the small but informative museum will see working mining equipment and learn how it has evolved through the years. Such artifacts as battered and scarred miners' hats bear mute testimony to the hardships endured by men who work at what has been described by many as the most dangerous job on earth. The history of the region has been further documented in the hundreds of photos, newspaper clippings, and scrapbooks on display. Each September the town hosts a weeklong *Dugger Coal Festival.* The museum is located next to the post office at 8178 E. Main St. Hours vary according to the availability of volunteers. If the museum should be closed when you arrive, you may call one of the phone numbers posted on the door, and a volunteer will be happy to come and let you in. For additional information, write Cunningham Memorial Library, Indiana State University, 510 N. 6½ St., Terre Haute 47809; (812) 237-2580; library.indstate.edu.

You can read the unusual story of Jane Todd Crawford on her tombstone in *Graysville*'s *Johnson Cemetery* (sometimes called Hopewell Cemetery). Ms. Crawford was a forty-six-year-old resident of Greensburg, KY, in 1809 and already the mother of four when she was told by doctors that her large stomach growth was likely twins. Because she was in so much pain, doctors tried to induce labor, with no results, and finally diagnosed the growth as a huge ovarian tumor. Her only hope was an experimental operation, and the only doctor who might perform it was Dr. Ephraim McDowell of Danville, KY, some 60 miles from where she lived. So, in the dead of winter and in increasing pain, she set out on horseback to ride the rough trails of the day.

When she reached the doctor's office, he told her that as far as he knew no one had ever performed an ovariectomy. He agreed to try but advised her it would be dangerous and very painful (anesthesia had not yet been invented, and there was no medicine to treat possible infection). With his patient's permission, Dr. McDowell made a 9-inch incision and 25 minutes later removed a 22-pound cystic ovarian tumor. It's reported that his patient sang hymns throughout the surgery, which was performed on Christmas Day. Five days later the remarkable Ms. Crawford was up and about. She returned home to Greensburg, again on horseback. Subsequently, she and her family moved to Madison, IN, where Jane's husband, Thomas, later died accidentally in a fall. She then moved to Graysville, IN, to live with her son, and it was there that she died in 1842 at the age of seventy-eight. She was the first patient known to have had a successful abdominal operation, and Dr. McDowell's surgery made him world famous.

To reach Johnson Cemetery, go north from Graysville for about 1 mile on SR 63. A state historical marker at the entrance to the cemetery on the west side of the road tells Jane's story and describes her as a Pioneer Heroine of Abdominal Surgery. Her burial site is marked by a granite monument dedicated in 1940 by the American Hospital Association and by her original, barely legible 1842 tombstone. The Sullivan County Historical Museum can provide additional information; located at 10 S. Court St. in the town of Sullivan; (812) 268-6253.

Vanderburgh County (Central Time Zone)

If architecture is your cup of tea, you'll want to tour two aesthetic treats in **Evansville**. The *John Augustus Reitz Home* at 112 Chestnut St. was erected in 1872 when Evansville was the hardwood capital of the country and Reitz was the "pioneer lumber king." Encircled by a black wrought-iron fence, the French Imperial house boasts three stories, seventeen rooms, ten fireplaces, and a display of Victorian-era opulence in the parquet floors, gilded bronze chandeliers, stained-glass windows, pier mirrors, gold-leaf cornices, and rare carved woods. Some of the first-floor ceilings are canvas, hand-painted in oil to match the original rugs. All heating units were turned on their sides and placed under the floor so that the radiators wouldn't show. The fireplaces were apparently for ornamentation only—they were never used. In the basement is a huge clothes dryer where clothes were hung on movable racks and dried by a gas heater beneath them.

The Reitz home sits in a seventeen-block historic district amid other massive homes built by wealthy owners who spent a considerable part of their fortunes trying to outdo the next fellow, but the home of the pioneer lumber king is the most impressive showplace of them all. Now a museum, it's open to the public from 11 a.m. to 2:30 p.m. Tuesday through Saturday; 1 to 2:30 p.m. Sunday. Admission: adults $7.50; students $2.50; children (age twelve and under) $1.50. Special tours can be arranged by calling (812) 426-1871, reitzhome.com.

The **Old Courthouse** that dominates the Evansville cityscape, built between 1888 and 1891, is one of the grandest in the country. During its construction special excursion trains brought visitors from Louisville, St. Louis, and many other midwestern towns to admire what was then regarded as one of the most elegant buildings ever erected in the Midwest.

Its Indiana limestone face is encrusted with an unbelievable number of sculptures and stone carvings, some of heroic proportions, each intricately detailed—fourteen statues, national emblems, ornamental friezes, cherubs, innumerable garlands of flora indigenous to the area, and Indiana's state seal. Inside are marble floors and wainscots, oak woodwork, brass handrails, silver-plated hardware, domes, and an awesome rotunda.

Abandoned by the county government in 1969, the Old Courthouse now contains boutiques, art galleries, import shops, clothing stores, and a community repertory company. You'll find the

indianatrivia

The first freestanding Sears, Roebuck and Co. retail store opened in Evansville in 1925.

magnificent old building at the corner of 4th and Vine. Guided tours are available by appointment. For additional information, write or call the Evansville Convention and Visitors Bureau, 401 SE Riverside Dr., Evansville 47713; (800) 433-3025; visitevansville.com.

Willard Library Haunted by 'The Grey Lady'

On a cold, snowy night, the janitor at the Willard Library in Evansville was making his usual rounds. It was his chore to shovel coal into the furnace at 3 a.m.

As he entered the dark basement, the janitor nearly bumped into a shadowy figure. Focusing his flashlight, the janitor froze at the ghostly sight of a veiled lady dressed in glowing grey. Even her shoes were grey.

That was in 1937. It was recorded as the first known sighting of "The Grey Lady." After that, the janitor quit.

Since then, countless employees and patrons and even police have reported seeing the apparition. So popular has she become that ghost tours are offered around Halloween each year and a ghost cam of various rooms in the library invites people to look for her at any time of the year.

No one is afraid of her. But many people have had strange things happen to them at the library. The list is long:

Footsteps when no one is around. The strong smell of heavy perfume from a mysterious source. An empty elevator that goes up and down, with floor buttons lighting and doors opening. Bathroom faucets turned on forcefully by unseen hands. Motion sensor devices set off when the library is closed and vacant. Unseen hands touching a visitor's hair or earrings.

Books that fall off shelves. A chair that is repeatedly pulled out after it is pushed in. A file box jumping off a desk and spilling its contents in a fan shape. A photograph of a woman standing in a library window, which is blocked and inaccessible. A feeling of cold when there should be none.

During a visit to the library, lecturers from the University of Southern Indiana say they saw the ghost peering into water. Policemen responding to a security alarm at the library spotted two ghosts in an upstairs window of the library.

And the experiences have happened to people of all ages. Back in the 1960s, some small children were raising quite a ruckus at a library party, running and skipping on the hallway stairs. Suddenly, a little 3-year-old ran to his mother, afraid of a woman who was reprimanding them. The little boy said she was a ghost lady shaking her finger at him. The party ended rather abruptly.

Countless speculation and opinions exist about whose ghost the famed Grey Lady actually is. Some believe the ghost traveled from a nearby cemetery. The Discovery Channel, ghost hunters, and physics have visited Willard Library trying to determine who the spectral image might be. But the Grey Lady remains a mystery.

Funded by Evansville philanthropist Willard Carpenter, **Willard Library** is Indiana's oldest public library. Listed on the National Register of Historic Places, the Victorian Gothic structure was opened in 1885. Willard Library was the dream of a man who received very little formal education but was said to be very intelligent and successful.

One of twelve children in a Vermont farming family, Carpenter left home at the age of eighteen with $7 in his pocket. Known as the "born king of real estate speculators," Carpenter became one of the most powerful and influential men in Evansville and served as a city councilman for thirty years.

Willard Library is a real beauty. With a wide stone stairway leading into the vestibule with its unique patterned tile flooring, the library features heavy oak finished woodwork and corniced ceilings. With plate glass and ornamental stained glass windows, the library has lovely furnishings and beautifully carved wood staircases. A popular community landmark, Willard Library is known for its programs, extensive collection, and huge wealth of genealogical records, including photographs, newspapers, and city directories dating back to the 1840s.

The library is open 9 a.m. to 8 p.m. Monday and Tuesday; 9 a.m. to 5:30 p.m. Wednesday through Friday; 9 a.m. to 5 p.m. Saturday; and 1 to 5 p.m. Sunday. Located at 21 1st Ave.; (812) 425-4309; willard.lib.in.us.

At **Wesselman Park**, you'll find 210 acres of primeval woodland where trees reach heights of more than 100 feet. A virgin forest is extremely rare, but this one is particularly unusual because it lies entirely within the limits of a city and is of such high quality (most stands of woodland in or near cities have been adversely affected by pollution). A melting pot of northern and southern botanical species, Wesselman Woods is dominated by sweet gum trees. Spring here is bright with the blossoms of dogwood and redbud trees and with the wildflowers that are at their feet; autumn is a blaze of color. At the edge of the woods is a nature center where one-way glass provides a unique view of wildlife activity and a microphone brings sound and song indoors.

The woods, designated both a State Nature Preserve and a National Natural Landmark, make up approximately half of Wesselman Park; the remaining 200 acres offer typical recreational facilities, including a swimming pool. Along the park's northern boundary is a remnant stretch of the old Wabash and Erie Canal, the longest ever built in this country. Only two boats ever traveled its entire 468-mile length from Evansville to Toledo, Ohio.

The park lies on the east side of Evansville at 551 N. Boeke Rd. Admission is free. The grounds are open daily year-round, from early morning until sunset. Wesselman Woods Nature Preserve and its nature center are open 9 a.m. to 5 p.m. Tuesday through Saturday and noon to 5 p.m. Sunday; hours sometimes vary. Call (812) 479-0771; wesselmanwoods.org.

The last remaining building of the former Lincoln Gardens, the second federal housing project created under the administration of Franklin D. Roosevelt's New Deal in 1938, now houses the *Evansville African American Museum.* One section showcases life in the 1938 era; the remaining sections of the building have been renovated as a modern history museum that depicts the history and traditions of African American families through visual art forms and historical documents. Admission: adults $5; children (under twelve years old) $3. Open 10 a.m. to 5 p.m. Tuesday through Sunday; hours extended to 7 p.m. on Friday; also open by appointment. Located at 529 S. Garvin St.; (812) 423-5188; evvafricanamericanmuseum.wordpress.com.

One of Evansville's most unique museums floats on the Ohio River. The last fully operational World War II Landing Ship Tank (LST) in existence is open for public tours. An amphibious vessel designed to land battle-ready tanks, troops, and supplies directly onto enemy shores, it's about 50 feet wide and as long as a football field. Winston Churchill called the LST the ship that won World War II. The LST 325, as this ship is known, is most famous for making 40 round-trips between England and France, hauling troops and supplies to and the wounded from the D-Day invasion of Normandy on June 6, 1944. Its permanent home is a dock at Marina Pointe in Evansville, but it takes a cruise to other ports along the Ohio River once or twice a year, so be sure it's dockside before you visit. The *LST 325 Ship Memorial* is located at 610 NW Riverside Dr. During the informative tours conducted by the ship's crew members, you'll learn about Evansville's role in producing LSTs during World War II. Hours vary so check the website. Admission: adults $15; children (ages 6–17) $7.50. For additional information, call (812) 435-8678; lstmemorial.org.

Mound-builder Indians, too, found this part of the country to their liking. Sometime around AD 1300, they built a village on the banks of the Ohio River southeast of Evansville and stayed there for about 200 years before moving on. The 11 mounds they abandoned in this spot constitute the largest and best-preserved group in the state. One, the central mound, covers more than 4 acres in area and measures 44 feet in height, making it one of the largest such structures in the eastern United States.

After years of archaeological excavations here, the 430-acre site was opened to the public as *Angel Mounds State Historic Site.* Visitors can view a life-size replica of an ancient Mississippian Indian village, a simulated excavation site, and many artifacts from the digs in a state-of-the-art interpretive center, then walk the trails that lead among the mounds and reconstructed buildings of the Indian village. The site is located at 8215 Pollack Ave., 7 miles southeast of downtown Evansville. Admission: adults $8; senior citizens $7; children (ages 3 to 17) $5. The site is open 10 a.m. to 5 p.m. Wednesday through Sunday; closed major holidays; (812) 853-3956; indianamuseum.org/hi storic-sites/angel-mounds/.

Vermillion County

Journalist Ernie Pyle wrote about World War II as experienced by the common foot soldier. His newspaper columns were read by millions, and his writings were compiled in several books. When his life was ended by a Japanese sniper in 1945, he was mourned by millions and eulogized by the president of the United States. Today veterans of that war are among the visitors who come to Indiana each year to pay homage to the beloved correspondent at the **Ernie Pyle World War II Museum** in **Dana.**

A focal point of the site is the house in which Ernie was born in 1900, moved here in 1975 from its original location about 2 miles away. It is adjoined by an interpretive center that occupies two World War II military Quonset huts. They are filled to overflowing with memorabilia from every part of Pyle's life, from the cradle he slept in as a baby to his high school report cards to the tattered wool jacket he wore when he had tea with Eleanor Roosevelt. Exhibits include recreated scenes from the war that Pyle wrote about so eloquently—Omaha Beach after D-Day, a Marine campsite in Okinawa that features a restored 1944 Willy's Jeep, and a soldier saying his last goodbye to his fallen captain, Henry T. Waskow. Pyle won a Pulitzer prize in 1944 for a column he wrote about Captain Waskow's death; a mannequin of the journalist sitting at his typewriter can be prompted by the touch of a button to read that famous column.

A 1945 movie, *The Story of G I Joe,* told Ernie Pyle's story. Pyle was played by Burgess Meredith, and Robert Mitchum, in the role that made him a star, played Captain Waskow. Years later, Pyle was also an inspiration for Charles Kuralt. Kuralt wrote that "Ernie Pyle was there first. He showed everybody else the way."

A sense of what Ernie Pyle meant to the soldiers of World War II can be gleaned from the fact that he is the only civilian who was allowed a burial plot in the National Memorial Cemetery of the Pacific in Honolulu, Hawaii. More than 33,000 veterans are buried there, but to this day more people request directions to Pyle's gravesite than to any other.

The homestead and interpretive center are located at 120 W. Briarwood Ave. in Dana. Open 10 a.m. to 4 p.m. Saturday and 1 to 4 p.m. Sunday, through Veterans Day on November 11. Hours may vary. Admission: adults $5; senior citizens $4; children (ages 4 to 12) $3. For additional information, contact the Friends of Ernie Pyle at 120 W. Briarwood Ave., Dana 47847; (765) 665-3633; erniepyle.org.

Vigo County

Bibliophiles and intellectuals will find the **Cunningham Memorial Library** on the campus of Indiana State University (ISU) in Terre Haute of special interest. It houses what is said to be the world's largest collection of old and rare dictionaries—more than 12,500 volumes dating back to 1475 that represent the entire history of Western lexicography. Among them are more than 200 editions and issues of Samuel Johnson's *A Dictionary of the English Language.* Known as the **Cordell Collection,** it grew from an initial donation of 453 dictionaries by the late Warren Cordell, an ISU alumnus and longtime executive with Nielsen's television-rating firm. The collection, housed in the library's Rare Books and Special Collections section on the third floor, is open free of charge throughout the year; hours vary. The library is located at 510 N. 61/2 St.; (812) 237-2580; library.indstate.edu.

Baking powder and open-wheel racing may seem an unlikely pairing, but they both figure prominently in the history of the Hulman family of Terre Haute. That's why, when you visit the **Clabber Girl Museum,** you'll see a race car that was driven in the 1925 Indianapolis 500 alongside such items as

The Bottle Known 'Round the World

Until 1915, Coca-Cola was sold in flat-sided bottles. That was the year the Coca-Cola Company began bottling its product in the curvy bottle now recognized around the world.

It all started with the soft drink company's desire to market a product unique in taste in a container unique in shape. A nationwide campaign was launched for a design that would let customers know instantly what they were holding, even in the dark.

The company that came up with the winning design was the Root Glass Company of Terre Haute, whose answer to Coke's quest was a bottle shaped like an encyclopedia drawing of a cocoa bean pod.

In 1950 a bottle of Coke became the first consumer product to be featured on the cover of *Time* magazine, elevating it to national icon status. In 1994 the state of Indiana placed a marker alongside US 41 in Terre Haute that officially recognizes the historic event. The marker reads in part: BIRTHPLACE OF THE COCA-COLA BOTTLE, THE WORLD-FAMOUS TRADEMARK CREATED IN 1915 ON THIS SITE AT ROOT GLASS COMPANY.

In 1994, the Coca-Cola Company returned to Terre Haute to test market a new container for its soft drink—a 20-ounce plastic bottle contoured like its original glass bottle. In 1997 the company once again came to Terre Haute to market another new container—a 12-ounce can with curves. A spokesperson for the company said it chose Terre Haute because it was the place in which Coke's curves were born.

antique appliances and household items, vintage toys, a hansom cab, and an old-fashioned coal generator.

Hulman & Company has been producing the Clabber Girl Baking Powder that has become its signature product since 1879. That product and others the company created brought a great deal of wealth to the family, and so it was that in 1945, Tony Hulman, the late grandson of the company's founder, was asked to buy and restore the Indianapolis Motor Speedway. The fabled race, which was first run in 1911, had been discontinued during World War II, and the track had fallen into disrepair. Tony spent millions on improvements, and the first post-war race was held on May 30, 1946. It was his voice that for many years spoke those now-famous words over the loudspeaker, "Gentlemen, start your engines!" (That was prior to female participation, of course.)

Today, Tony is recognized as the man who saved the Indianapolis Motor Speedway and made the Indianapolis 500 popular. He was also the creator of some clever advertising that first popularized Clabber Girl Baking Powder in the 1930s. You can learn all about the family, the company, and the history of baking at the free museum, which shares space with the *Clabber Girl Bake Shop* in the historic 1892 Hulman and Company building at 900 Wabash Ave. in Terre Haute. The museum is free and open Monday through Friday 8 a.m. to 5 p.m.; Sunday 8 a.m. to 2 p.m. The bake shop offers cooking demonstrations and guided tours for groups by advance reservation and also serves breakfast and lunch; (812) 478-7189; clabbergirl.com.

A sobering experience awaits you at the *C.A.N.D.L.E.S. Holocaust Museum* at 1532 S. 3rd St. in Terre Haute. The name of the museum stands for Children of Auschwitz Nazi Deadly Lab Experiments Survivors. Founder and owner Eva Mozes Kor and her twin sister, Miriam, were ten years old in the spring of 1944 when they, their mother, father, and two older sisters were taken to the infamous Auschwitz concentration camp. There the twins were separated from the rest of their family and never saw them again. Because Eva and Miriam were twins, they were of special interest to Dr. Josef Mengele, well known today for his experiments on twins. Unlike many others, they both survived and were liberated by a unit of the Soviet Army in January 1945, staying close until Miriam's death in 1993.

Eva married Michael Kor, another death camp survivor, and moved to Terre Haute, where she first opened her small museum in 1996. Eight years later, an arsonist burned it to the ground, but the whole community pitched in to build another museum on the same spot. The new brick-and-limestone building features narrow vertical windows that resemble candles; two sets of eleven windows on the north side represent the 11 million who died in the Holocaust and 6 more above the entrance memorialize the 6 million who were

Pay as You Go

When restrooms were installed at the Terre Haute railroad station in 1910, they became an attraction for curious tourists and townspeople. Indoor restrooms were a novelty at the time. So many people came to see them that passengers on incoming trains, for whom the restrooms were intended, couldn't get in to use them.

The stationmaster came up with an ingenious solution. He installed nickel-operated locks on the toilets to discourage their use by non-passengers. When a train arrived, he would temporarily remove the locks because toilet privileges were included in the price of a train ticket.

Thus, Terre Haute gained the unique distinction of having the first pay toilets in the country.

Jews. Some of the artifacts displayed within were salvaged from the fire, and new artifacts are being displayed as they are collected. The primary purpose of the museum and its special programs is to educate the public about the effects of hatred and prejudice.

Eva Kor died in 2019 at Krakow, Poland, just miles from the Auschwitz concentration camp. Eva was on a museum educational trip doing what she did best—educating others by telling them her story. She was eighty-five years old.

The museum is open from 1 to 4 p.m. Tuesday through Saturday. Admission is $5 per person; (812) 234-7881; candlesholocaustmuseum.org.

Warrick County (Central Time Zone)

First settled in 1803, **Newburgh** perches picturesquely on the banks of the Ohio River. Footpaths lead along the riverbank, with views that include the Newburgh Locks and Dam. River traffic passing through these locks carries more tonnage than passes through the Panama Canal. Sit on a bench at the foot of Water Street and watch a picture-perfect sunset. The town contains some lovely restored homes, and a 4-square-block section in the downtown area is on the National Register of Historic Places. For additional information, write or call Historic Newburgh, Inc., 333 State St., Newburgh 47630; (812) 853-2815 or (800) 636-9489. Historic Newburgh's office is generally open 10 a.m. to 4 p.m. Monday through Friday; historicnewburgh.org.

Places to Stay in Southwest Indiana

BLOOMINGTON

The Beaumont House
9030 W. SR 48
(812) 876-3900
thebeaumonthouse.com

Fourwinds Lakeside Inn & Marina
9301 S. Fairfax Rd.
(812) 824-2628
fourwindslakeside.com

Graduate Bloomington
210 E. Kirkwood Ave.
(812) 994-0500
graduatehotels.com

The Grant Street Inn
310 N. Grant St.
(812) 334-2353 or
(800) 328-4350
grantstreetinn.com

Indiana Memorial Union Biddle Hotel at Indiana University
900 E. 7th St.
(812) 856-6381 or
(800) 209-8145
imu.edu/hotel/index.html

Showers Inn Bed & Breakfast
430 N. Washington St.
(812) 334-9000
showersinn.com

The Walnut Street Inn
130 N. Walnut St.
(812) 345-8378
thewalnutstreetinn.com

The Wampler House
4905 S. Rogers St.
(812) 929-7542
(877) 407-0969
wamplerhouse.com

BRISTOW

Mary Rose Herb Farm Yurt Bed and Breakfast
23112 Cattail Rd.
(812) 357-2699
maryroseherbfarm.com

DERBY

Ohio River Cabins
13445 N. SR 66
(812) 836-2289
ohiorivercabins.aiwaycent.com

EVANSVILLE

Cool Breeze Estate Bed and Breakfast
1240 SE 2nd St.
(812) 422-9635
coolbreezebb.net

Le Merigot Hotel
615 NW Riverside Dr.
(812) 433-4700
tropevansville.com

Tropicana Evansville
421 NW Riverside Dr.
(812) 433-4000
tropevansville.com

FRENCH LICK

Big Splash Adventure
8505 SR 56
(812) 936-3866
bigsplashadventure.com

French Lick Springs Resort
8670 W. SR 56
(812) 936-9300 or
(888) 936-9360
frenchlick.com

Lane's Motel
8483 W. SR 56
(812) 936-9919
lanemotelfrenchlick.com

Patoka Lake Village Log Cabin Rentals
7900 W. CR 1025 South
(812) 936-9854 or
(888) 324-5350
plvlogcabins.com

GREENCASTLE

The Inn at DePauw
2 W. Seminary Sq.
(765) 653-2761
innatdepauw.com

Namaste Lofts
15 W. Franklin St.
(765) 721-7692
greencastleaccommodations.com

9 East on Poplar
9 E. Poplar St.
(765) 653-7896
greencastleaccommodations.com

JASPER

Winfield West Bed & Breakfast
325 W. 6th St.
(812) 556-0111
winfieldwestbb.com

MARSHALL

Granny's Farm Bed and Breakfast
4329 E. SR 47
(765) 597-2248
grannys-farm.com

Turkey Run Inn at Turkey Run State Park
8102 E. Park Rd.
(765) 597-2211 or
(877) 500-6151
turkeyrunstatepark.com

MITCHELL

Spring Mill Inn
Spring Mill State Park
3333 SR 60 East
(812) 849-4081 or
(877) 977-7464
In.gov/dnr/parklake/inns/
springmill/

MONTGOMERY

Gasthof Village Inn
6747 E. Gasthof Village Rd.
(812) 486-2600
gasthofamishvillage.com
Nashville

**1875 Homestead Bed
and Breakfast**
3766 E. SR 46
(812) 988-0853
1875homestead.com

**Abe Martin Lodge and
Cabins at Brown County
State Park**
1405 E. SR 46
(812) 988-4418 or
(877) 265-6343
in.gov/dnr/parklake/inns/
abe/

The Allison House Inn
90 S. Jefferson St.
(812) 365-0690
theallisonhouseinn.com

Artists Colony Inn
105 S. Van Buren St.
(812) 988-0600 or
(800) 737-0255
artistscolonyinn.com

Cornerstone Inn
54 E. Franklin St.
(812) 988-0300
cornerstoneinn.com

**Iris Garden Downtown
Cottages & Suites**
79 N. Van Buren St.
(812) 988-2422
irisgardenlodging.com

Lil Black Bear Inn
8072 SR 46
(812) 988-2233
lilblackbearinn.com

**Oak Haven Bed &
Breakfast**
2668 Owl Creek Rd.
(812) 679-7477
oakhaven.net

Olde Magnolia House
213 N. Jefferson St.
(614) 638-8849
oldemagnoliahouseinn.com

Rawhide Ranch USA
1292 SR 135 South
(812) 988-0085 or
(888) 947-2624
rawhideranchusa.com

Robinwood Inn
914 Highland Ave.
(812) 988-7094
robinwoodinn.com

The Seasons Lodge
560 SR 46 East
(812) 988-2284 or
(800) 365-7327
seasonslodge.com

Story Inn
6404 S. SR 135
(812) 988-2273 or
(800) 881-1183
storyinn.com

NEW HARMONY

**Cooks on Brewery Bed
& Breakfast**
815 Brewery St.
(812) 682-3646
cooksonbrewery.com

**Ludwig Epple Guest
House**
520 Granary St.
(812) 270-4360
newharmonyguesthouse
.com

New Harmony Inn
504 North St.
(812) 682-4431 or
(800) 782-8605
newharmonyinn.com

NEWBURGH

**Lockmaster Cottages at
Lock & Dam #47**
Old Lock & Dam Park
SR 66 East
(812) 853-3578
newburgh-in.com/copy-of-l
ock-and-dam-rental

PAOLI

Big Locust Farm B&B
3295 W. CR 25 South
(812) 723-4856
biglocustfarm.com

**Lost River Inn Bed and
Breakfast**
3593 N. CR 200 West
(812) 865-4496
s458597967.onlinehome.us

ROCKVILLE

Corner House B&B
3984 N. CR 200 W.
(812) 660-0331
cornerhousebb.com

**Bubble Gum Bed and
Breakfast**
517 W. Ohio St.
(765) 569-6630
bubblegumandb.com

Old Jail Inn
127 S. Jefferson St.
(765) 592-6737
oldjailinnparkecounty.com

SOURCES FOR ADDITIONAL INFORMATION ABOUT SOUTHWEST INDIANA

Clinton/Vermillion County Chamber of Commerce

Old National Bank
407 S. Main St.
Clinton 47842
(765) 832-3844
vermillion-chamber.org

Crawford County Tourism Center
6225 E. Industrial Ln.,
Suite A
Leavenworth 47137
(812) 739-2246 or (888)
755-2282
crawfordcountyindiana.co(

Daviess County Visitors Bureau
1 Train Depot St,
Washington 47501
(812) 254-5262 or (800)
449-5262
daviesscounty.net

Evansville/Vanderburgh County Convention and Visitors Bureau
401 SE Riverside Dr.
Evansville 47713
(812) 421-2200 or (800)
433-3025
visitevansville.com

Gibson County Visitors & Tourism Bureau
702 W. Broadway St.
Princeton 47670
(812) 385-0999 or
(888) 390-5825
gibsoncountyin.org

Greene County Economic Development Corporation
4513 W. SR 54
Bloomfield 47424
(812) 659-2109
insidegreencounty.com

Historic Newburgh, Inc.
(Warrick County)
333 State St.
Newburgh 47630
(812) 853-2815 or (800)
636-9489
historicnewburgh.org

Lawrence County Visitors Center
533 W. Main St.
Mitchell 47446
(812) 849-1090 or (800)
798-0769
limestonecountry.com

Martin County Chamber of Commerce/Tourism Commission
210 N. Line St.
Loogootee 47553
(812) 295-4093

Monroe County Convention and Visitors Bureau
2855 N. Walnut St.
Bloomington 47404
(812) 334-8900 or (800)
800-0037
visitbloomington.com

Mount Vernon/Posey County Chamber of Commerce
915 E. 4th St.
Mount Vernon 47620-0633
(812) 838-3639

Nashville/Brown County Convention and Visitors Bureau
211 S. Van Buren St.
Nashville 47448
(812) 988-7303 or (800)
753-3255
browncounty.com

Orange County Convention and Visitor Bureau
8102 W. SR 56
West Baden 47469
(812) 936-3418 or (866)
309-9139
visitfrenchlickwestbaden
.com

Parke County Convention and Visitors Bureau
401 E. Ohio St.
PO Box 165
Rockville 47872
(765) 569-5226
coveredbridges.com

Perry County Convention and Visitors Bureau
333 7th St.
Tell City 47586
(812) 547-7033 or (000)
343-6262
pickperry.com

Putnam County Convention and Visitor Bureau
12 W. Washington St.
Greencastle 46135
(765) 653-8743 or (800)
829-4639
goputnam.com

Seymour/Jackson County Visitor Center
100 N. Broadway St.
Seymour 47274
(812) 524-1914 or (888) 524-1914
jacksoncountyin.com

Spencer County Visitors Bureau
39 N. Kringle Place
Santa Claus 47579
(812) 937-4199 or (888) 444-9252
santaclausind.org

Terre Haute/Vigo County Convention and Visitors Bureau
5353 E. Margaret Dr.
Terre Haute 47803
(812) 234-5555 or (800) 366-3043
terrehaute.com

Vincennes/Knox County Convention and Visitors Bureau
779 S. 6th St.
Vincennes 47591
(812) 886-0400 or (800) 886-6443
visitvincennes.org

SPENCER

Canyon Inn
McCormick's Creek State Park
451 McCormick Creek Park Rd.
(812) 829-4881 or (877) 922-6966
in.gov/dnr/parklake/inns/canyon/

TASWELL (PATOKA LAKE)

White Oak Cabins
2140 N. Morgan Rd.
(812) 338-3120 or (877) 338-3120
patokalake.com

TERRE HAUTE

SMWC Goodwin Guest House
3301 St. Marys Rd.
(812) 535-5131
smwc.edu

UNIONVILLE

Red Rabbit Inn
9200 E. SR 45
(812) 330-1216
redrabbit.com

VINCENNES

Vincennes Bed and Breakfast
727 Buntin St.
(812) 887-1628
vincennesbedandbreakfast.com

WEST BADEN SPRINGS

West Baden Springs Hotel
8538 W. Baden Ave.
(812) 936-9300 or (888) 936-9360
frenchlick.com/hotels/westbaden#

Places to Eat in Southwest Indiana

BLOOMINGTON

Anatolia Restaurant
405 E. 4th St.
(812) 334-2991
restaurantanatolia.com
Turkish

Anyetsang's Little Tibet Restaurant
415 E. 4th St.
(812) 331-0122
anyetsangs.com
Tibetan

Bear's Place
1316 E. 3rd St.
(812) 339-3460
bearsplacebar.com
American

Big Woods
116 N. Grant St.
(812) 335-1821
bigwoodsrestaurants.com
Pub fare

Bub's Burgers & Ice Cream
480 N. Morton St
(812) 331-2827
bubsburgers.com
Burgers

Cardinal Spirits
922 S. Morton St.
(812) 202-6789
cardinalspirits.com
New American bites

Crazy Horse
214 W. Kirkwood Ave.
(812) 336-8877
crazyhorseindiana.com
American

DeAngelo's Italian Creole Restaurant
2620 E. 3rd St.
(812) 961-0008
deangelosbloomington.com
Italian, Creole

FARMbloomington
108 E. Kirkwood Ave.
(812) 323-0002
farm bloomington.com
Farm-inspired cuisine

Feta Kitchen & Café
600 E. Hillside Dr.
(812) 336-3382
fetakitchen.com
Health food

The Irish Lion
212 W. Kirkwood Ave.
(812) 336-9076
irishlion.com
Irish

Juannita's Restaurant
620 W. Kirkwood Ave.
(812) 339-2340
Mexican

The Laughing Planet Cafe
322 E. Kirkwood Ave.
(812) 323-2233
thelaughingplanet.com
Mexican

Lennie's Restaurant
514 E. Kirkwood
(812) 323-2112
lenniesbloomington.com
Italian/American

Longfei Chinese Restaurant
113 S. Grant St.
(812) 955-1666
longfeichinesein.com
Chinese

Malibu Grill
106 N. Walnut St.
(812) 332-4334
malibugrill.com
Steaks/seafood

Mother Bear's
1428 E. 3rd St.
(812) 332-4495
motherbearspizza.com
Pizza/Italian

Nick's English Hut
423 E. Kirkwood Ave.
(812) 332-4040
nicksenglishhut.com
American

Red
1402 N. Walnut St.
(812) 650-3807
redbloomington.com
Sichuan

Runcible Spoon
412 E. 6th St.
(812) 334-3997
runciblespoonrestaurant
.com
American/regional/
continental

SmokeWorks
121 N. College Ave.
(812) 287-8190
thesmokeworks.com
Barbecue

Southern Stone
405 W. Patterson Dr.
(812) 333-1043
southernstonebloomingto
n.com
Southern

Trojan Horse
100 E. Kirkwood Ave.
(812) 332-1101
thetrojanhorse.com
Greek/American

Truffles
1131 S. College Mall Rd.
(812) 330-1111
trufflesblown.com
New American

Uptown Brewing Co.
350 W. 11th St.
(812) 364-2337
uplandbeer.com
Pub grub

EVANSVILLE

Acropolis Restaurant
501 N. Green River Rd.
(812) 475-9320
acropolisevv.com
Greek

Arazu on Main
415 Main St.
(812) 401-1768
visitarazu.com
Mediterranean

Canton Inn Restaurant
947 N. Park Dr.
(812) 428-6611
cantoninnevansville.com
Chinese

Cavanaugh's
421 NW Riverside Dr.
(812) 433-4000
tropevansville.com
Steak/Seafood

DiLegge's
607 N. Main St.
(812) 428-3004
dilegges.com
Italian

Hacienda Restaurant
990 S. Green River Rd.
(812) 474-1635
haciendafiesta.com
Mexican

Iwataya Japanese Restaurant
8401 N. Kentucky Ave.
(812) 868-0830
iwatayaevansville.com
Japanese

Lincoln Garden
2001 Lincoln Ave.
(812) 471-8881
lincolngardeninc.com
Chinese

Ma T 888 China Bistro
5636 Vogel Rd.
(812) 475-2888
mat888chinabistro.com
Chinese

Old Mill Restaurant
5031 New Harmony Rd.
(812) 963-6000
oldmillevansville.com
American

Pangea Kitchen
111 S. River Rd.
(812) 401-2404
tastepangea.com
Italian/Global soul food

Turoni's Pizzery & Brewery
408 N. Main St.
(812) 424-9871
turonis.com
Pizza

Wolf's Bar-B-Que
6600 N. 1st Ave.
(812) 424-8891
wolfsbarbq.com
Regional American

FERDINAND

Fleig's Cafe
905 Main St.
(812) 367-1310
American

FRENCH LICK

1875: The Steakhouse
8670 SR 56
(812) 936-8001
frenchlick.com
Steak

German Café
452 S. Maple St.
(812) 936-1111
german-café.business.site
German

Hagen's Club House Restaurant
1917 Country Club Dr.
(812) 936-5550
frenchlick.com
Steak/Seafood

'Ohana Hawaiian Grill & Bar
8695 W. Jack Carnes Way
(812) 936-1788
ohanasgrill.com
Steaks/Seafood

Power Plant Bar & Grill
8670 SR 56
(888) 936-9360
frenchlick.com
American

33 Brick Street
480 S. Maple St.
(812) 936-3370
33brickstreet.com
American

GREENCASTLE

Almost Home
17 W. Franklin St.
(765) 653-5788
amosthomerestaurant.com
American

Bridges Craft Pizza & Wine Bar
19 N. Indiana St.
(765) 653-0021
bridgeswinebar.com
American

The Fluttering Duck
2 W. Seminary St.
(765) 658-1006
innatdepauw.com
Comfort food

Grateful Pie
308 E. Berry St.
(765) 301-9700
mygratefulpie.com
Pizza

Myers' Market
302 E. Washington St.
(765) 653-1335
myersmarketllc.com
Sandwiches

No 1 Chinese Restaurant
1360 Indianapolis Rd.
(765) 653-0828
no1chinese.netify.app
Chinese

The Putnam Inn
400 N. Jackson St.
(765) 653-8777
putnaminn.com
Comfort food

HAUBSTADT

Carriage Inn
103 E. Gibson St.
(812) 768-6131
carriageinnhaubstadt.com
American

Haub Steakhouse
101 E. Haub St.
(812) 768-6462 or
(800) 654-1158
haubsteakhouse.com
American

Log Inn
12491 CR 200 East
(812) 867-3216
theloginn.net

Nisbet Inn
6701 Nisbet Rd.
(812) 963-9305
nisbet-inn.com
American

JASPER

Azul Tequila Mexican Restaurant
101 Place Rd.
(812) 482-7550
azultequilaindiana.com
Mexican

El Maguey Grill
3570 N. Newton St.
(812) 481-1799
elmagueygrilljasper.com
Mexican

The Mill House Restaurant
1340 Mill St.
(812) 482-4345
themillhouserestaurant.com
American

Schnitzelbank Restaurant
393 3rd Ave.
(812) 482-2640 or
(888) 336-8233
schnitzelbank.com
Traditional German

Snaps
1115 Main St.
(812) 848-7627
snapsinjasper.com
American

LEAVENWORTH

The Overlook Restaurant
1153 W. SR 62
(812) 739-4264
theoverlook.com
American
Lincoln City

Hoosier Land Pizza & Wings
3804 SR 162
(812) 937-2799
Pizza

LINTON

Goosepond Pizza
1983 SR 54 East
(812) 847-3030
goosepondpizza.com
Comfort food

The Grill
60 NE A St.
(812) 847-9010
American

Sportsmans Pub
54 N. Main St.
(812) 847-8759
Comfort food

MONTGOMERY

Gasthof Amish Village Restaurant
6659 E. Gasthof Village Rd.
(812) 486-4900
gasthofamishvillage.com
Amish buffet

NASHVILLE

The Artists Colony Restaurant
Franklin and Van Buren
Street
PO Box 1099
(812) 988-0600 or
(800) 737-0255
artistscolonyinn.com
American

Bird's Nest Café
36 Franklin St.
(812) 720-7040
birdsnest.cate
Comfort food

Brozinni's Pizza
140 W. Main St.
(812) 988-8800
brozinnis.com
Pizza

Casa Del Sol
101 E. Washington St.
(812) 988-4535
casadelsolnashville.com
Mexican

Gyros Food
177 S. Van Buren St.
(812) 318-0840
gyrofoodnashville.com
Greek/American

Harvest Dining Room
51 SR 46
(812) 988-2291
browncountyinn.com
American

Hobnob Corner
17 W. Main St.
(812) 988-4114
Hobnobcornerrestaurant
.com
American

Little Gem Restaurant at Abe Martin Lodge
Brown County State Park
1405 SR 46 East
(812) 988-4418 or
(877) 265-6343
in.gov/dnr/parklake/inns/
abe/dining.html
Home cooking

Nashville House
15 S. Van Buren St.
(812) 988-4554
nashvillehousebc.com
Home cooking

The Original
60 Molly's Ln.
(812) 988-6000
bigwoodsrestaurants.com
Comfort food

The Seasons Lodge
560 SR 46 East
(812) 988-2284 or
(800) 365-7327
seasonslodge.com
American/home cooking

Story Inn
6404 S. SR 135
(812) 988-2273 or
(800) 881-1183
storyinn.com
American innovative

Trolly's
11 E. Gould St.
(812) 988-4273
trolly.business.site
Barbecue

NEW HARMONY

MaryScott's Kitchen
518 Main St.
(812) 270-5030
maryscottskitchen.com
American

Red Geranium
504 North St.
(812) 682-4431 or
(800) 782-8605
newharmonyinn.com
American

Sara's Harmonie Way Too
500 Church St.
(812) 682-3611
sarasharmonieway.com
Café food

Yellow Tavern
521 Church St.
(812) 682-3303
theyellowtavern.com
Pizza/Sandwiches

NEWBURGH

Archie & Clydes
8309 Bell Oaks Dr.
(812) 490-7778
archieandclydes.com
Pizza

Café Arazu
17 W. Jennings St.
(812) 842-2200
visitarazu.com
Middle Eastern

Jalisco Mexican Restaurant
4044 Professional Ln.
(812) 490-2814
jalisconewburgh.com
Mexican

Knob Hill Tavern
1016 SR 662
(812) 853-9550
knobhilltavern.com
Italian

Nellie's Restaurant
8566 Ruffian Ln.
(812) 629-2142
nelliesnewburgh.com
Comfort food

Ninki Sushi
4222 Bell Rd.
(812) 518-3055
ninkisushi.com
Japanese

ROCKPORT

Angelo's Pizza
824 Sycamore St.
(812) 649-9134
angelosrockport.com
Pizza

Los Panchos Mexican Grill
715 N. 5th St.
(812) 649-4137
lospanchosmexican.com
Mexican

The Rustic Golf Course & Country Club
1375 S. Old SR 45
(812) 649-9258
therusticcountryclub.com
American

ROCKVILLE

Thirty Six Saloon
108 E. Ohio St.
(765) 569-9441
thirtysixsaloon.com
American

SOLSBERRY

Yoho General Store
10043 E. Tulip Rd.
(812) 825-7834
yohogeneralstore.com
Comfort food

SPENCER

Chambers Restaurant
72 W. Market St.
(812) 829-3022
American

Civilian Brewing Corps Brewpub
14 N. Washington St.
(812) 652-5072
civilianbrewingcorps.com
Pub food

Jit's Thai Bistro
6 E. Market St.
(812) 714-8276
jitsthaibistrospencer.com
Thai

Pizza Pantry
357 W. Morgan St.
(812) 829-4115
pizzapantryspencer.com
Pizza

TELL CITY

Fiesta Grande Mexican Restaurant
27 US 66
(812) 547-7110
fiestagrandecantina.net
Mexican

Tokyo Express
619 SR 66
(812) 772-2588
tokyoexpresstellcity.com
Japanese

TERRE HAUTE

J Ford's Black Angus
129 S. 7th St.
(812) 235-5549
Jfordsblackangus.com
Steak/American

M. Moggers Restaurant & Pub
908 Poplar St.
(812) 234-9202
moggers-restaurant
American

Magdy's Restaurant
2026 S. 3rd St.
(812) 238-5500
magdystorrehaute.com
American

Piloni's Italian Restaurant
1733 Lafayette Ave.
(812) 466-4744
pilonis.com
Italian

Saratoga Restaurant
431 Wabash Ave.
(812) 234-1161
thesaratogarestaurant.com

Stables Steakhouse
939 Poplar St.
(812) 232-6677
stablessteakhouse
Steak/Seafood

Umi Grill
2002 S. 3rd St.
(812) 232-7874
umigrillsushibar.com
Japanese

VINCENNES

Bill Bobe's Pizzeria
1651 N. 6th St.
(812) 882-2992
billbobespizzeria.com
Pizza

The Café Moonlight
512 Main St.
(812) 225-0228
thecafemoonlight.com
American

El Corral Mexican Restaurant & Bar
630 Kimmel Rd.
(812) 895-9422
elcorralmex.com
Mexican

Gilbert's Restaurant & Pub
1350 Willow St.
(812) 316-0800
gilbertspub.getbento.com
Steak house

Pea-Fections
323 Main St.
(812) 886-5146
pea-fections.com
Comfort food

Procopio's Pizza & Pasta
127 N. 2nd St.
(812) 882-0914
procopiosrestaurant.com
Pizza/Pasta

WEST BADEN

The Cowboys Grille
6000 W. CR 250 North
(812) 936-9199
crazyhorser.com
Steak

El Compadre Mexican Restaurant
8345 W. SR 56
(812) 936-0340
elcompadremexicanindiana.com
Mexican

Sinclair's Restaurant
8538 W. Baden Ave.
(812) 936-5579
frenchlick.com
American

Index